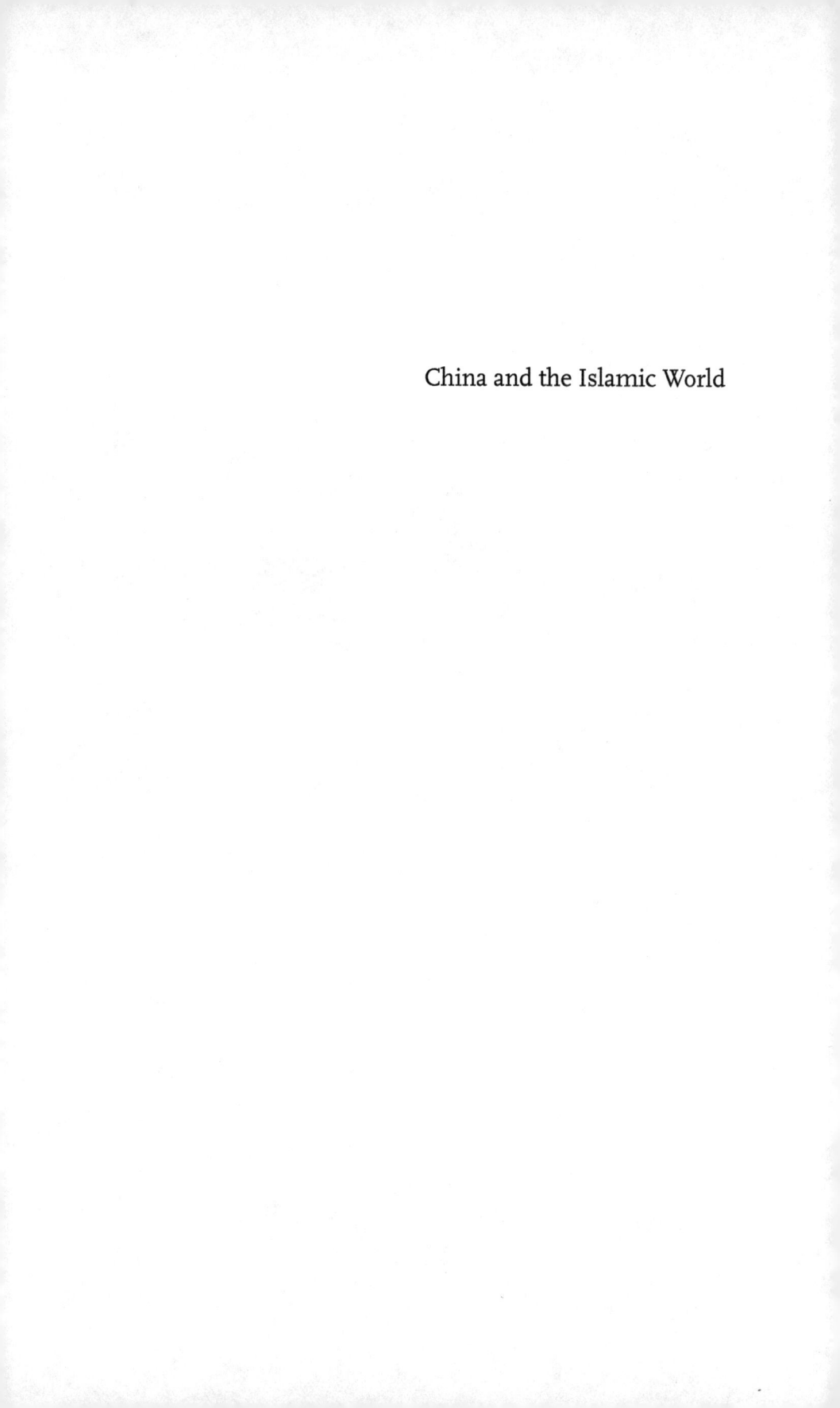

China and the Islamic World

China and the Islamic World
How the New Silk Road Is Transforming Global Politics

ROBERT R. BIANCHI

OXFORD
UNIVERSITY PRESS

OXFORD
UNIVERSITY PRESS

Oxford University Press is a department of the University of Oxford. It furthers
the University's objective of excellence in research, scholarship, and education
by publishing worldwide. Oxford is a registered trade mark of Oxford University
Press in the UK and certain other countries.

Published in the United States of America by Oxford University Press
198 Madison Avenue, New York, NY 10016, United States of America.

© Oxford University Press 2019

All rights reserved. No part of this publication may be reproduced, stored in
a retrieval system, or transmitted, in any form or by any means, without the
prior permission in writing of Oxford University Press, or as expressly permitted
by law, by license, or under terms agreed with the appropriate reproduction
rights organization. Inquiries concerning reproduction outside the scope of the
above should be sent to the Rights Department, Oxford University Press, at the
address above.

You must not circulate this work in any other form
and you must impose this same condition on any acquirer.

Library of Congress Cataloging-in-Publication Data
Names: Bianchi, Robert, 1945- author.
Title: China and the Islamic world : how the new Silk Road is
transforming global politics / Robert R. Bianchi.
Description: New York, NY : Oxford University Press, 2019. |
Includes bibliographical references and index.
Identifiers: LCCN 2018040398 (print) | LCCN 2018055643 (ebook) |
ISBN 9780190915292 (updf) | ISBN 9780190915308 (epub) |
ISBN 9780190915285 (hardback) | ISBN 9780190915315 (online content)
Subjects: LCSH: Middle East—Foreign relations—China. | China—Foreign
relations—Middle East. | Islamic countries—Foreign relations—China. |
China—Foreign relations—Islamic countries. | Middle East—Foreign economic
relations—China. | China—Foreign economic relations—Middle East. |
Islamic countries—Foreign economic relations—China. | China—Foreign
economic relations—Islamic countries. | World politics—21st century. |
BISAC: RELIGION / Religion, Politics & State. | RELIGION / Islam / General.
Classification: LCC DS63.2.C5 (ebook) |
LCC DS63.2.C5 B53 2019 (print) | DDC 327.51017/67—dc23
LC record available at https://lccn.loc.gov/2018040398

9 8 7 6 5 4 3 2 1

Printed by Sheridan Books, Inc., United States of America

For 美丽丽, Mei Li Li
who led me to China

CONTENTS

List of Figures ix
List of Tables xi
Quotations xiii
Preface xvii

Introduction 1

CHAPTER 1 What Is New about the New Silk Road? 5

CHAPTER 2 Megaregions and Coevolution in World Politics 18

CHAPTER 3 Pakistan: Deep Democracy and Shallow Strategy 29

CHAPTER 4 Turkey: A Competing Partner 49

CHAPTER 5 Indonesia: Inherent Weakness and Increasing Leverage 63

CHAPTER 6 Iran: The Great Divider 80

CHAPTER 7 Nigeria: A Shaky Bridge 97

CHAPTER 8 Egypt: Weighing the Tolls 113

CHAPTER 9 Islam and the Opening of the Chinese Mind 127

CHAPTER 10 Learning Abroad, Evading at Home 139

CHAPTER 11 The Bitter and the Sweet 150

Notes 159
Selected Bibliography 215
Index 277

LIST OF FIGURES

3.1 The Western Route through Balochistan and Khyber Pakhtunkhwa 31
3.2 The Punjabi Route as the New Main Artery 32
3.3 The Evolution of China-Pakistan Exchanges 35
3.4 The Triple Branches Network and Early Harvest Projects 36
3.5 Pakistan Links Maritime and Overland Sections of the New Silk Road 42
3.6 Xinjiang's Triple Junctions and the Straits of Malacca 43
3.7 Pakistan's Trade with China, 1995–2015 45
3.8 Cumulative Chinese Investment in Pakistan, 2005–2016 45
4.1 Results of the Turkish Constitutional Referendum April 16, 2017 by Region and Province (Percent Voting "Yes") 57
4.2 Provincial Distribution of Votes in the Turkish Constitutional Referendum, 2017 58
4.3 Turkey's Trade with China, 1995–2015 60
4.4 Cumulative Chinese Investment in Turkey, 2005–2016 60
5.1 Results of the Jakarta Gubernatorial Elections by District (*Kecamatan*), Round 1 February 15, 2017, and Round 2 April 19, 2017 68
5.2 Votes for Jakarta Governor by District (*Kecamatan*), Rounds 1 and 2 70
5.3 Cumulative Chinese Investment in Indonesia, 2005–2016 77
5.4 Indonesia's Trade with China, 1995–2015 78

6.1 Iran's Trade with China, 1995–2015 89
6.2 Cumulative Chinese Investment in Iran, 2005–2016 90
6.3 Major Rail Connections across Iran 91
6.4 Linguistic and Religious Diversity in Iran 92
6.5 Geographic Distribution of Votes for Hassan Rouhani and Opponents in Presidential Elections of 2013 and 2017 94
7.1 Nigeria's Total Exports, 1990–2015 105
7.2 Nigeria's Trade with China, 1995–2015 105
7.3 Cumulative Chinese Investment in Nigeria, 2005–2016 106
7.4 Nigerian Presidential Votes by State, 2011 and 2015 108
7.5 Nigerian Railway Routes 110
8.1 Egypt's Trade with China, 1995–2015 123
8.2 Cumulative Chinese Investment in Egypt, 2005–2016 124

LIST OF TABLES

3.1 Early Steps toward Disclosing CPEC Finances and Local Benefits 37
3.2 Further Disclosures of CPEC Project Details 39
3.3 China's Largest Investments in Pakistan, 2005–2016, Projects Worth $1 Billion or More 46
4.1 China's Largest Investments in Turkey, 2005–2016, Projects Worth $1 Billion or More 61
5.1 Results of the Jakarta Gubernatorial Elections by District (*Kabupaten*), Round 1 February 15, 2017, and Round 2 April 19, 2017 67
5.2 Results of the Jakarta Gubernatorial Elections by District (*Kecamatan*), Round 1 February 15, 2017, and Round 2 April 19, 2017 71
5.3 China's Largest Investments in Indonesia, 2005–2016, Projects Worth $1 Billion or More 78
6.1 China's Largest Investments in Iran, 2005–2016, Projects Worth $1 Billion or More 90
6.2 Vote for Hassan Rouhani in Iran's Presidential Elections of 2013 and 2017 by Province 93
7.1 China's Largest Investments in Nigeria, 2005–2016, Projects Worth $1 Billion or More 106
7.2 Nigerian Statewide Vote for President, 2011 and 2015 109
8.1 China's Largest Investments in Egypt, 2005–2016, Projects Worth $1 Billion or More 124

10.1 Hong Kong Legislative Council Election Results by Geographic and Functional Constituencies, September 4, 2016 142

10.2 Functional Constituencies Represented in the Hong Kong Legislative Council, 30 Seats 144

QUOTATIONS

"We are heirs to two Silk Roads: not the ancient and the modern, but the invented and the reinvented."
—TAMARA CHIN, "The Invention of the Silk Road, 1877,"
Critical Inquiry, Autumn 2013, p. 194.

"Marco Polo describes a bridge, stone by stone.
'But which is the stone that supports the bridge?' Kublai Khan asks.
'The bridge is not supported by one stone or another,' Marco answers,
'but by the line of the arch that they form.'
Kublai Khan remains silent, reflecting. Then he adds: 'Why do you speak to me of the stones? It is only the arch that matters to me.'
Polo answers: 'Without stones there is no arch.'"
—ITALO CALVINO, *Invisible Cities*, translated by William Weaver,
London: Vintage Books, [1972] 1997, Chapter 5, p. 74.

" . . . [W]anting to understand Southeast Asia without integrating a good deal of southern China into our thinking is like wanting to give an account of the Mediterranean world after removing Turkey, the Levant, Palestine, and Egypt."
—DENYS LOMBARD, "Another 'Mediterranean' in Southeast Asia,"
translated by Nola Cooke, *The Asia-Pacific Journal*,
March 1, 2007 (original in 1998).

"Conventional views of how the modern world has been forged do not prepare us to identify patterns of diversity that have existed in the past and present within world regions, patterns that are not simply miniature versions of global variations . . . Large world regions form an alternative to the local and global that strike so many Anglo-American analysts as crucial."

—ROY BIN WONG, "East Asia as a World Region in the 21st Century," *Nihon Kezai Shimbun*, August 13, 2004.

"Just as Latin Christianity and Turkish Islam shared a Mediterranean where Jews and northern Europeans also traded, so was China's northwestern frontier inhabited by people of diverse cultures: Tibetan, Mongolian, Han Chinese, and Sino-Muslims. The two regions were also connected across vast expanses by the flow of merchants who travelled long distances."

—ROY BIN WONG, "Entre monde e nation: les régions braudéliennes en Asie," *Annales*, 2001, p. 19, translated by the author.

"From the beginnings of the Eurasian and African world-system, China played a crucial role. Every period of growth in the world-system followed China's phases of unification and its economic rises, with the Chinese momentum spreading like a wave from east to west, reaching the West with some delay . . . Conversely, each Chinese recession initiated a downward trend in the system and/or its restructuring."

—PHILIPPE BEAUJARD, "The Indian Ocean in Eurasian and African World-Systems before the Sixteenth Century," *Journal of World History*, December 2005, p. 424.

"[T]he entire Afro-Eurasian landmass has been linked by complex networks of exchange since at least the Bronze Age . . . Afro-Eurasia has a common history despite the ecological and cultural variety of its many different regions . . . [T]he Silk Roads played a fundamental role in creating and sustaining the unity of Afro-Eurasian history."

—DAVID CHRISTIAN, "Silk Roads or Steppe Roads? The Silk Roads in World History," *Journal of World History*, Spring 2000, pp. 1–2.

"[I]t may be a profound mistake to focus primarily . . . on the various component regions or 'civilizations' of Eurasia. Instead, to understand the history of each of these parts, it is necessary to see that there is, underlying them, a single Afro-Eurasian history, which is distinct from the history of other major world zones . . . For Afro-Eurasian societies shared many important things as a result of the exchanges that occurred along the Silk Roads."

—DAVID CHRISTIAN, "Silk Roads or Steppe Roads? The Silk Roads in World History," *Journal of World History*, January 2000, p. 18.

"The rise of modernity itself can best be seen as a product of the rich economic and technological synergy generated over several millennia between different parts of Eurasia, rather than as a product of the peculiarities of any particular regional culture or 'civilization.'"

—DAVID CHRISTIAN, "Silk Roads or Steppe Roads? The Silk Roads in World History," *Journal of World History*, January 2000, p. 21.

PREFACE

My travels in China really began in Mecca, but more by chance than design. When I made the Hajj in 1989, I had no inkling that the path would lead to Nanjing, Shanghai, Xinjiang, Yunnan, and Hong Kong. The first spark came with the sight of so many pilgrims from Southeast Asia—particularly Indonesia, Malaysia, and Singapore—who seemed so out of place in the Arabian desert.

The common thread between them was a flair for group organization. They had a confidence and direction that stood out amid the confusion of most Arab, African, and South Asian pilgrims who kept bumping into one another and pushing against the flow, creating bottlenecks that put everyone in danger. The Indonesians were instantly identifiable by the bright batik suits that signaled their hometowns and districts. Malaysians wore coordinated shirts and dresses with their national flag stitched on the back. Most of them had paid for the Hajj with installments years in advance as though mortgaging a second home they would only visit far in the future. But it was the Singaporeans, especially the tiny young women, who caught everyone's eye—always springing up by the dozen with arms locked so tightly they could slice through the thickest crowd and vanish before anyone figured out who they were.

Once I grasped East Asia's growing power in the Islamic world, it was natural to visit these countries when doing fieldwork for my study of Hajj and politics. That was when I first encountered the profound overlap and interpenetration of Islamic and Chinese civilizations that has intrigued me ever since. In 1996, while traveling through the neighborhoods of Singapore, the states of Malaysia, and the islands of Indonesia, I saw that every community was a hybrid, combining Muslim and Chinese elements in countless ways on every level.

My visit coincided with the simultaneous celebrations of Ramadan and the Chinese lunar New Year. Adherents of both traditions were eager to display their connections and rivalries with special intensity. All of the conventional boundaries and dichotomies blurred and faded together—only to re-emerge around the corner or down the road where they jostled for a different balance. Race, language, cuisine, dress, architecture, music, children's games, crafts, boat designs, farming patterns—all were so similar across religious communities it was hard to know what was Islamic and what was Chinese, what was indigenous and what was imported.

In Kuala Lumpur's side streets, political candidates gave stump speeches in four languages—Hokkien Chinese, Malay, English, and Mandarin. In Singapore shopping malls, the first performances of the Beijing Opera met with suspicion from older Chinese locals who were perplexed by both the language and the political implications. Meanwhile, Malay and Indian Singaporeans joined the delighted tourists in waves of applause. Downtown Jakarta was buzzing with gossip about the Suharto family's recent Hajj, including the Chinese Muslim timber baron, Bob Hasan, who tagged along and appeared everywhere in the official photos. Although Suharto was trying to send a message of personal piety and interracial brotherhood, it was clear that the effort had miscarried. The city's poor viewed the Hasan connection as simple cronyism and it stoked their resentment of Chinese privilege regardless of religion—resentment that soon erupted in the anti-Chinese riots that accompanied Suharto's overthrow.

These post-Hajj journeys to Southeast Asia convinced me that I had to start learning Chinese if I wanted to explore the multicultural worlds I was discovering. That decision eventually led me to Nanjing, where my wife and I lived and traveled for three years (2006–2009) while I was helping to create a graduate program in international law at the Johns Hopkins-Nanjing University Center for Chinese and American Studies. The following year, I visited Qatar University where I taught Islamic studies and international politics to young women from the Persian Gulf countries and Africa. Then, we moved to Singapore—my original gateway to East Asia—for three more years (2011–2014) to help launch a Middle East Research Institute at the National University of Singapore. Soon thereafter, we returned to China, hosted by the Shanghai International Studies University, for a Fulbright year of research and lecturing across mainland China, Hong Kong, and Taiwan (2015–2016).

It was during these busy years that I gained the materials, language skills, friendships, and experiences that made this book possible. A wide network of generous and distinguished scholars—Asian, Middle Eastern, Western, and Afro-Eurasian—guided me in tracing China's long encounters with Islam in many eras and disciplines. Conference organizers and editors in several countries have given me invaluable opportunities to develop, debate, and refine my thinking. I am deeply grateful to all of these colleagues for their encouragement and kindness.

Some of my informants and friends would prefer not to be mentioned by name, but there are many I can thank openly. In Nanjing, Hua Tao and Robert Daly were superb guides to Chinese history and diplomacy. Ma Shuang Shuang and a number of Nan Da graduate students patiently helped me improve my speaking and reading skills in Chinese. The Tang poems and tongue-twisters they taught me have become a permanent part of my dream life. In Doha, I enjoyed the hospitality of Amira Sonbol and Ahmad Ibrahim and the freewheeling debates that my students unleashed at every meeting.

Singapore exposed me to a rich collection of international experts in multiple disciplines. The Asia Research Institute was a constant source of stimulation thanks to Prasenjit Duara, Arun Bala, and Michael Feener who allowed me to join dozens of seminars and workshops blending Asian civilizations, comparative religion, and social science. I would also like to thank Chen Weitseng and Juliette Duara of the Law School; Wang Gungwu, Guo Liangping, and Qian Jiwei at the East Asian Institute; and Lilia Labidi and Ali Kadri from the Middle East Institute.

During my Fulbright research year in China, I was fortunate to be the guest of the Middle East Studies Institute of the Shanghai International Studies University where I met many of China's top scholars and diplomats specializing in Middle Eastern affairs. Several other universities and research centers invited me for lectures and conferences, including Nanjing Normal University, Fudan University, Tongji University, Sichuan University, The Ocean University of China, Ningxia University, the Shenzhen Municipal Government, the Shanghai Institute of American Studies, and the Hopkins China Forum. In every case, scholars were eager to share their writings and viewpoints, influencing my thinking on countless issues long after we parted company.

A number of scholars in Europe and the Middle East invited me to present the early findings of my research in international conferences and seminars. I am most grateful to the Sudairy Foundation in Al-Ghat, Saudi Arabia; the National Museum of Ethnology in Leiden, Netherlands; Goethe

University in Frankfurt, Germany; the French Cultural Center and CEDEJ in Cairo, Egypt; and the University of Nottingham in the United Kingdom.

In the United States, I owe a special debt to Marvin Weinbaum, Marvin Zonis, Engseng Ho, Robert Lee, David Blears, and Miriam Pollack who read and criticized much of the draft manuscript, and to Jefferson Gray who provided a steady flow of helpful information and commentary that broadened my vision in many ways. Most of all, I relied on the support and companionship of my wife, Vicki Mayfield, who shared nearly every step of these travels with keen cross-cultural instincts that magnified my fun and knowledge beyond measure.

Introduction

AMERICA'S ATTENTION IS RIVETED on China and Islam—and in both cases the dominant emotion is fear. Some of this is fear of the unknown, but much of it stems from the half-truths and distortions we have created in our minds and media, particularly about the China Threat and Islamic Terrorism. A powerful segment of American policymakers and scholars is urging the country to prepare for supposedly inevitable wars with Chinese and Muslim enemies or to admit that the battles have already begun despite denials on all sides. Predictions of conflict usually rest on faulty assumptions about China's relentless drive for international dominance, Islam's inherent belligerence, and history's verdict that major shifts in the balance of power trigger disastrous military responses.[1]

Exaggerating imagined threats from presumed adversaries creates its own dangers. If America's leaders focus on shoring up an old hegemony or fending off a new one, they might neglect the skills of statecraft and political learning that increasingly outweigh the value of military force in the contemporary world. They are likely to overlook important opportunities for diplomacy and cooperation in a multipolar community where many countries can contribute resources to overlapping alliances and shifting coalitions. In fact, China and the Islamic world stand out as two of the most influential actors in the emerging international order—powerful partners that every nation can respect and confident civilizations that no foe can expect to subdue. Moreover, Chinese and Muslim societies are moving closer together than ever before. The New Silk Road initiative reaches every corner of the Islamic world as it ties Asia, Africa, and the Indian Ocean into a hemispheric market with Europe and the Western Pacific.

Although China is taking the lead in promoting the rise of Afro-Eurasia, no country can dominate such a vast collection of megaregions or control their fiercely independent members. China has no choice but to compromise with a wide array of contentious partners pursuing their own ambitions and responding to domestic pressures that grow more organized and self-assured every day. Some critics of the New Silk Road describe it as a Chinese exercise in neocolonialism, but it seems more accurate to view the emerging webs of relations as a coevolution of multiple megaregions in the making. China's leverage is likely to vary widely from place to place and over time. In addition, Chinese society is increasingly susceptible to developments abroad—not just in neighboring countries, but everywhere Chinese businesses and migrants are present. In many matters—particularly ethnic and religious relations, environmental practices, and labor policies—outsiders are influencing attitudes in China at least as much as the Chinese are affecting people along the New Silk Road.

The international relations of Afro-Eurasia are not moving toward a new hierarchy or toward the globalization of an imaginary Chinese tribute system. Instead, we see a number of overlapping networks being shaped by competing governments and organized interest groups with no predetermined endpoint. In each country and region, the distribution of power and resources is under constant scrutiny and subject to endless bargaining. This fluidity and unpredictability is especially notable in most of the Islamic countries that China is courting, and the reverberations inevitably extend into Chinese society as well, shaping debates between elite factions and in public opinion.

In one country after another, China's leaders are learning to adapt to these changes with flexible statecraft—by showing more effective negotiating skills and by listening more attentively to popular viewpoints beyond privileged government and business circles. But their learning is highly uneven, and it virtually disappears in dealings with their own citizenry. As Chinese politicians become more willing to fashion networks and reciprocity on the New Silk Road, they seem increasingly determined to buttress hierarchy and dictate at home. The contradiction is becoming more evident to Chinese people of all backgrounds and that makes it much harder to sustain indefinitely.

The interplay and abiding tension between centralizing state hierarchies and decentralized social networks is a shared theme in Chinese and Islamic history. Ira Lapidus, the noted student of medieval Islam, argued that political hierarchy was a more common pattern in China compared to the extensive networking of nonstate actors that typified Muslim societies. But he stressed that both civilizations developed sophisticated blends of hierarchy and networking that were negotiated rather than imposed and that constantly adapted to shifting domestic circumstances and international challenges.[2] Joseph Fletcher, the Qing dynasty historian of Islamic Inner Asia, reached similar conclusions. In addition, Fletcher also highlighted the constant give and take between China and its Muslim neighbors, including many pacts and quasi-alliances that regularly strengthened or reduced the relative power of rulers in both civilizations.[3]

Taken together, the insights of Lapidus and Fletcher provide comparative and historical perspective for understanding the coevolution of Islamic and Chinese societies. The New Silk Road initiatives are writing a new chapter of that story, and no one can predict its trajectory or conclusion. Nonetheless, two matters seem clear already. The citizens of Muslim countries will reject any appearance of tutelage from China just as vigorously as they resisted earlier efforts of domination by the United States, Europe, Russia, and Japan. In addition, China's leaders will have to fashion a patchwork of loose and pragmatic arrangements with foreign partners in all directions. An expansive imperial or tributary system is beyond Beijing's capabilities. Indeed, part of China's appeal in the non-Western world is that many people see it not as a superpower, but as another developing country that remains highly vulnerable to external disruptions and domestic divisions. It is precisely because China seems so overextended economically and so limited militarily that weaker nations regard it as a pliant and manageable partner.

China and the United States suffer from a common shortsightedness. Intensely preoccupied with one another's intentions and maneuvers, they easily neglect their mutual need to share power with many other nations, particularly the rising societies of the Islamic world. The largest and most ambitious Muslim countries are well aware of their importance in world politics and determined to maximize their leverage regardless of which Great Powers compete for the leading role on an increasingly fragmented global stage. The more the New Silk Road succeeds in fostering an integrated Afro-Eurasian community, the more it will enhance the power of the critical societies that control the lands and seas connecting the Atlantic and Pacific shores.

These regions are the heartlands of the Islamic world—Southeast Asia, South Asia, Central Asia, the Caucasus, the Middle East, and every coast of Africa. China's bid for world leadership is strengthening Muslim nations' interconnections with one another, with the global economy, and with the rapidly changing transnational political order. The most successful Islamic countries will become indispensable partners in the emerging megaregions that span Afro-Eurasia—and that will make them, individually and collectively, more formidable bargainers in all efforts toward global governance.

For all of these reasons, the New Silk Road should encourage America to overcome its exaggerated fears of both China and Islam. No one will dominate the sprawling networks of a transcontinental and transoceanic community—not the United States or China or any coalition they try to assemble. On the other hand, everyone will be more vulnerable to disruptions in the extended channels of commerce and migration. Proxy wars and resource wars will become more costly; vassals and satellites will be harder to find and impossible to control. The coevolution of mutually dependent megaregions will require collective management that is more similar to governing a global commons than to pressing claims of sovereignty and exclusivity. Insuring open access to transportation corridors and natural resources will be more important than asserting unilateral control. Preserving common resources for future generations will require moderating demands to consume them and popular pressures will push ruling elites to share more of the profits not merely with one another, but with their citizens as well.

In these circumstances, the United States and its allies might conclude that they will be the greatest victims of efforts to stigmatize or attack either China or its new friends in the largest Muslim nations. The societies that today seem to be America's worst adversaries could instead prove to be its most effective partners in fashioning a safer and fairer world.

CHAPTER 1 | What Is New about the New Silk Road?

CHINA'S LEADERS ARE GAMBLING that they can transform the world without turning their own society upside down in the process. Even if they win the first part of the wager, they are certain to lose the second. Running away from the risks of political reform at home, they have embarked on an audacious project of hemispheric integration that is generating social conflict and political turmoil in every country they touch. The effects are already creating multiple backlashes in China itself where chain reaction grievances are undermining the monopoly of power that the party-state factions so dearly want to preserve.

Hemispheric Scope and Global Impacts

China's version of the New Silk Road is far more than a revival of the many historical routes we usually describe with that metaphor. It encompasses all of those crossroads as well as far-flung areas they never reached—not merely the Eurasian heartland and the Indian Ocean, but also the Arctic Circle, all of Africa, and even the Americas via both Pacific and Atlantic shores.[1]

China's New Silk Road reverberates far beyond its current projects in the key nations of the Islamic world. It generates immediate consequences that radiate both globally and within China itself. Overlapping and interconnected megaregions are taking shape across the Old World, the New World, and the seas that increasingly link them more than they separate them. The scope of these networks is not merely transcontinental and transoceanic, it is hemispheric and inter-hemispheric.[2]

Students of geopolitics are accustomed to Great Powers promoting rival visions of Eurasian integration. But the Chinese venture is far more than a replay of the Great Games.[3] It is old-style geopolitics combined with what Chinese writers commonly refer to as geoeconomics[4] and geo-religion[5]—a coordinated campaign of commercial and cultural outreach that magnifies political influence without relying primarily on military strength. This is a rich set of resources that packs greater potential to reshape world affairs than the phrase "soft power" would suggest.[6]

The constant interplay of economic, cultural, and military strength is a key element of Chinese statecraft. For example, China's dominance of maritime commerce creates the need for a blue water navy to protect its carriers and shipping lanes.[7] Every navy, in turn, requires ports and bases in distant lands to support its permanent patrols. Naval missions might begin with quasi-military goals such as antipiracy and humanitarian assistance, but they easily blossom into full-blown armadas that can carry expeditionary forces in all directions.[8] Beijing has made the military implications of the New Silk Road more explicit than ever by tying it to China's expanding space program. Countries that partner in Silk Road projects will receive priority access to China's Beidou telecommunications satellites, including their advanced navigation capabilities that rival and often surpass Western-dominated GPS networks.[9]

China's digital Silk Road in outer space parallels the e-commerce ventures of Alibaba and JD.com to build a world trade platform of online shopping and payment services. With a chain of new warehouses and banks along the emerging transport and communications lines, Chinese merchants also plan to promote yuan-denominated transactions in line with Beijing's efforts to globalize its currency.[10] All of these space-based and cyber activities dovetail with China's so-called parallel system of international institutions that many see as rivals to the Bretton-Woods and North Atlantic structures led by the United States. Washington and Brussels have had little success in discouraging the growth of the Asian Infrastructure Investment Bank, the BRICS New Development Bank, the Silk Road Fund, and the Shanghai Cooperation Organization. Even the World Bank and the Asian Development Bank have begun to seek joint ventures with these China-backed groups instead of treating them as hostile competitors.[11]

Islamic Foundations and Competing Ambitions

China's edition of the New Silk Road is also distinguished by its intimate connections with Muslim societies. Indeed, the association is so close that commentators in China and elsewhere often describe it as China's Islamic Silk Road.[12] Chinese engineers and bankers are busily laying the hardwired components of connectivity—the infrastructure, loans, and natural resources deals—that have dominated the attention of media and policymakers around the world. But China's rulers as well as the diplomats and scholars who advise them understand that they are building upon already existing networks of Muslim cultures and aspirations—a palimpsest of living Islamic history—that both enables and limits their every move.[13]

Chinese leaders have wisely chosen to focus their greatest efforts on a handful of Muslim countries that are indispensable to their success—particularly Indonesia, Pakistan, Iran, Turkey, and Nigeria. Beijing views these nations as invaluable partners because they all possess a potent combination of location, size, natural resources, human skills, military strength, and political influence that reaches far beyond their borders. In global politics, these are swing states that could become key allies in China's long-term effort to create a multipolar order in which American and European dominance yields to greater power-sharing with non-Western countries and with nonwhite peoples in dozens of former colonies.[14]

Chinese policymakers are also learning that these countries have their own ambitions for greatness and social justice that are incompatible with subordination to any foreign power. Nationalist sentiments limit appeals from all outsiders, no matter what their racial or ideological color, including fellow victims of imperialism, past and present. Those ambitions extend so deeply into the citizenries—rural and urban, female and male, illiterate and literate—that their governments face certain criticism when they engage in self-dealing with foreign investors, especially if the projects are grandiose and the details are hidden from public view.

Many of the Muslim countries along the New Silk Road are highly organized societies filled with vigilant and politically astute groups demanding ever greater shares of power and wealth. At every turn, Chinese who venture abroad are faced with countless political parties, interest groups, state legislatures, and local development initiatives. As China's leaders seek to wire the developing world, they are discovering that—politically if not electronically—much of it is already wired to the hilt.

The sheer variety of actors and volume of demands forces China's representatives to reach beyond the formal channels of national governments and ruling parties so that they can build support for their projects in the world's most diverse and expansive countries. No matter how eagerly Chinese officials cling to the catechism of nonintervention in local politics, they inevitably become mediators, pitchmen, confidants, and targets—both symbolic and physical.[15] More and more, they are enmeshed in daily interactions with rival interests who often see dealing with Beijing's representatives as preferable to butting heads with one another.

Greater Chinese involvement along the New Silk Road stimulates rising social demands and political assertiveness. This, in turn, pushes China's leaders toward more obtrusive and visible activity, trying to manage conflicts in societies they do not understand and cannot control. Under these conditions, mistakes are inevitable; untruths become transparent; reversals are bound to be routine. Meanwhile, multiple audiences are watching together—in the Islamic world, in the global media, and, most of all, in China itself. What happens on the New Silk Road does not stay there—sooner or later it comes home and stirs the pots in cities, towns, and villages from Kashgar to Hong Kong and everywhere in-between.[16]

Clamorous Democracies and Unruly Dictatorships

China is encountering particularly strong headwinds in Muslim countries with vibrant democratic traditions.[17] Where democracy predated the rise of Chinese influence, it is being tested and invigorated at the same time. Opposition parties, citizens' groups, and independent journalists constantly criticize the bargains their governments strike with Chinese partners. It is common for projects to be renegotiated or cancelled because of popular objections over alleged favoritism, environmental damage, labor violations, and civil rights abuses. In many cases, democratic institutions are still struggling to overcome long legacies of military rule and social inequality. Nonetheless, these societies are unlikely to succumb to a new wave of authoritarianism inspired by Chinese investments and ideologies. In fact, China's leaders are increasingly worried that political contagion will run in the opposite direction—from tumultuous democracies on the New Silk Road toward a more restive collection of young netizens and educated middle-classes in dozens of Chinese cities.[18]

Each country presents China with a formidable set of headaches—political, economic, and religious. In Pakistan, competing regions and ethnic groups demand greater transparency and equity for dozens of projects that China touts as the grand opening for the Silk Road as a whole.[19] Leaders in Islamabad and Beijing have no choice but to comply because of the enormous strategic and military stakes at risk—countering Indian ambitions in South Asia, fending off separatist threats to Xinjiang, and securing land routes for Middle East oil that still has to travel through the Straits of Malacca.[20]

Tensions with Turkey are more deeply rooted in persistent religious and ethnic quarrels over the fate of Uyghurs in Xinjiang. No matter how much Ankara and Beijing relish the prospect of wielding Eurasian power against Europe and the United States, they cannot escape the rounds of mutual recrimination that follow every outburst of rebellion and repression in Xinjiang.[21] Compared to the passions of Sino-Turkish clashes, the Pakistani haggling over routes and costs seems tame indeed.

With Indonesia, on the other hand, the Chinese are doubly vulnerable. Racial and religious prejudice against Indonesians of Chinese background threatens both government and private business deals.[22] At the same time, Jakarta is determined to project maritime power and to lead the creation of a broader Pacific community—ambitions that openly contradict China's desire for preeminence in East Asia.[23] Indonesian politicians can use the threat of Islamic militancy to great advantage, seeming to restrain it when Beijing is pliable and quietly encouraging it when China becomes overbearing.

Nigerian democracy is particularly vexing for Chinese efforts to promote the Silk Road as a pan-African venture. Beijing would like to turn Nigeria into a keystone of stronger South-South alliances that can wage a common struggle against Western control over the international system. But China's intrusive and disruptive presence has engendered popular resentment all across Africa. Instead of developing into a showcase of Sino-African collaboration, Nigeria seemed to confirm former colonies' fears that China would be just another domineering empire perpetuating dependency and subverting native industries.[24] Fearing a failure that could reverberate throughout Africa and beyond, China's leaders scrambled to show their commitment to Nigerian industrialization. Beijing quickly boosted investments in infrastructure and energy and, then, gave new pledges to relocate factories and technology to make Nigeria an export platform for Chinese manufacturing.[25] China's willingness to take on greater risks in such a troubled partnership stemmed from its conviction that Nigeria was important not only for building influence in all of Africa, but also for expanding its reach in Latin America where economic nationalists voiced similar accusations that Chinese policies were making independent development impossible.[26] Beijing reasoned that it had to turn around its African relations if it wanted to gain greater access to skeptical South American regions that Washington still treats as its backyard.

Dealing with Silk Road partners ruled by authoritarian regimes is also troublesome for China, especially when they appear increasingly unstable and alienated from their own populations. The recent uprisings in Iran provide a poignant example of a common dilemma. The mullahs and security forces can contain the blazes with Chinese-inspired controls over the internet and social media, but they cannot prevent future ignitions or rule out a wider conflagration.[27] On the other hand, reformers have little hope of winning meaningful freedoms or promoting a less adventurous foreign policy. There is no sign of an authoritarian silver bullet to quash unrest or of a revolutionary breakthrough that could propel the country in a new direction.[28] As Beijing expands the New Silk Road, it confronts similar problems in one country after another. Stronger linkages between domestic politics and transnational relations promote ongoing turmoil and crisis management across interdependent regions and cultures. This certainly represents an important surge in transcontinental connectivity, but hardly the kind that Chinese planners anticipated.

China's deep misgivings toward Egypt flow naturally from a heightened awareness of these dangers. For Egyptians, the Arab Spring of 2011 replaced a hated dictator with an even more ruthless tyrant, creating the widespread expectation that another revolt was just a matter of time.[29] In contrast to Iran, Egypt has few assets to recommend it as a Silk Road partner. It is a country in perpetual debt with declining diplomatic influence—especially as China develops multiple shipping routes to bypass the costly Suez Canal. In Egypt, Chinese leaders see all of the critical factors pointing in a negative direction. Geopolitically, it is increasingly unstable and marginalized. Economically, it seems like a bottomless money pit that no single donor could hope to rescue. And, religiously, it has crushed all hopes for a liberal Islamic future, allowing extremist and terrorist movements to fill the vacuum. The more Cairo presses Beijing for closer ties and larger investments, the more the Chinese back away—convinced that the country is ruled by a frightened and greedy clique intent on wringing as much profit as possible from foreigners and Egyptians alike.[30]

Taken together, the evidence from these key countries suggests that China's leaders will find no peaceful havens or extended eras of goodwill—not along the New Silk Road or in their own society. China's actions provoke various types of popular mobilization and protest that, in turn, influence attitudes and actions inside China as well. In this sense, the unrest and stalemate in many Silk Road countries resonate with China's own predicament—recalling the turmoil of its recent past and foreshadowing its likely future.

Reverberations across Chinese Society

Blowback from the New Silk Road—particularly its key Muslim links—takes many forms and travels multiple routes. Chinese security forces continue their preoccupation with the threats of terrorism and religious extremism radiating from Xinjiang.[31] However, the most serious consequences are aggravated grievances of the Han Chinese. This is particularly important for the younger, more educated middle classes in the booming and choking cities—not just the first-tier conurbations of the east, but the 30 to 40 metro-regions that span the entire country.[32]

The greatest blind spots in the party-state vision are not the remote and exotic lands of Islam, but the most talented and disheartened people living right under their noses. China's rulers are well aware of their growing vulnerabilities due to widespread discontent over pollution, food safety, and a host of obstacles to social mobility such as rising costs of education, housing, and healthcare.[33] But the leadership cannot accurately assess the relative dangers of applying too much coercion or too little, of fostering creativity too broadly or too narrowly. Precisely because of the authoritarianism they embody, they are bound to make miscalculations about social risks followed by halfhearted efforts at damage control.[34]

Projecting greater power around the world will not protect China's rulers from their own people. It will merely intensify China's domestic problems by linking them to mounting grievances in many other countries. Holding up the roof domestically for another decade—or even another generation—will only make it fall with greater force when the weight proves too much to bear.

China's statecraft is struggling with a split personality—daring and imaginative in foreign relations, but timid and paralyzed in domestic governance. Each day the contradiction between overreach abroad and underperformance at home becomes more glaring and more incompatible with the balance and moderation that are so celebrated in traditional Chinese culture and philosophy.[35]

Ironically, this predicament also generates some unexpected benefits because it encourages sharper debate and deeper self-reflection among the multiple voices competing for attention not only in factious policymaking circles, but also in Chinese society at large. As China becomes a global power, disagreements over the nation's destiny are inevitable. As Chinese citizens become more educated and politically alert, they feel a patriotic duty to keep their leaders accountable and their nation on the best course.[36] This is hardly an ideal environment for the censors, dogmatists, and political officers who try to police and filter public discussion. In fact, they seem to be fighting a hopeless battle in what is quickly becoming a regulator's nightmare.[37]

The party-state elite is ever mindful of the supposed lessons from the collapse of the Soviet Union. They are determined to avoid a Chinese perestroika that would recreate the time of troubles that Gorbachev and Yeltsin unleashed in their day. But the embattled leadership cannot agree on a way forward. Power-sharing seems both unacceptable and unavoidable. Even though they can't carry it out, they can't stop talking about it and, more importantly, they can't stop their globalized citizens and netizens from debating it in countless forums, both legal and illegal.[38]

Debates in China often link foreign policy and domestic issues in a seamless manner. Discussion often moves laterally instead of in a straight line. Word association and analogy pervade the subtext just as punning infuses popular conversation. Many observations about distant lands could easily be applied to China itself where explicit criticism would cross the bounds of permissible commentary.[39]

For example, nearly everything about Pakistan or Turkey is potentially also—or really—about Xinjiang. Questions concerning Indonesia or Malaysia carry dark undertones of vulnerable Chinese minorities struggling to lead normal lives in volatile Muslim societies.[40] No treatment of China's troubles over censorship in Nigeria or labor strife in Kenya can avoid the obvious connections to how Guangdong authorities mete out punishment to Chinese and Africans alike.[41] When Chinese negotiators draw Iran, Saudi Arabia, and other oil exporters into long-term contracts and market-sharing deals, every parent and health-minded person in China knows they are also locking in another decade of foul air and respiratory disease for millions of people across the nation.[42]

When Chinese citizens learn that their government is gaining ground abroad with new diplomatic and commercial ventures such as the New Silk Road, they often react with mixed feelings. Although they are pleased that China is acquiring more friends and influence around the world, they naturally want to know more about the implications for their families and neighborhoods.[43]

They are particularly ambivalent if they think that China's gains involve accommodating foreigners' demands for better working conditions and stricter environmental control or for cooperation with civic associations and media investigations. On these issues and others, Chinese representatives are learning they have to bend to local conditions by responding to grievances from many organized sectors, including government opponents. Mutual concessions are natural in diplomatic relations, especially with democratic countries. But Chinese who struggle with very similar issues wonder why their leaders appear more flexible and responsive in bargaining with foreigners than with their own people.[44]

Straining Religious and Ethnic Relations

Drawing closer to so many Muslim countries is forcing China to rethink its relations with Islam as a powerful world religion and as a living part of Chinese society. Throughout China, policymakers and common citizens are debating their historic and current ties to the Islamic world. Are Chinese and Muslims neighbors or distant relatives, former rivals or natural allies? When their civilizations overlap, do they clash or enrich one another? Is it possible to say that China has incorporated aspects of Islamic civilization or even that China itself is becoming part of the Muslim world?[45]

By showcasing the romance of the Silk Road as the signature trope for their global outreach, Chinese leaders are trying to identify with widespread yearnings for harmony and cross-fertilization between all civilizations. But many Chinese audiences are drawing very different conclusions about the implications for ethnic and religious relations in their own communities. In 2016, for example, a seemingly trivial act such as opening a new halal restaurant in downtown Shanghai spiraled into a national row when competitors tried to shut it down because it supposedly violated binding territorial covenants between Muslim merchants.[46] When local authorities attempted to mediate the dispute, they were swamped by accusations of favoring some Muslims over others, granting Muslims privileges that were denied to the Han majority, and giving official backing to Islamic standards in a secular and avowedly atheistic country. The fallout was so severe that the central government quickly scrapped its proposed law to adopt nationwide standards for halal establishments and products.[47] A measure that party leaders portrayed as advancing food safety for everyone was suddenly regarded as an insult to law-abiding members of the ethnic majority who lacked political connections and favored status.

Similar misunderstandings abound when Chinese leaders and scholars try to explain their views to Muslims in China and beyond. Some of the most sensitive problems surround the ideas of Chinese Islam that have become fashionable in government and university circles.[48] Examining relations between China and Islam is inherently controversial because of the fraught history of interactions and the shifting political contexts that have shaped them. Discussing Islam in China raises equally difficult problems of generalizing across ethnic, regional, and social groups with varied ties to non-Muslim majorities and governments.[49] But these debates are tame compared to the heat generated by suggestions that Islam's experiences in China have turned it into something different from its origins and from its evolutions everywhere else.

Chinese Islam is a classic example of a well-intended misnomer that defeats its proponents' goals. For educated and cosmopolitan Chinese people, nothing could be more flattering than to be acculturated into Chinese civilization. But most of the time this process is portrayed as a one-way exchange between superiors and inferiors rather than a matter of mutual learning and coevolution.[50] Worse still, both Chinese and Western scholars frequently describe Muslims' adaptations to Chinese society as examples of assimilation, syncretism, and synthesis.[51] Even when non-Muslims regard these developments as positive and mutually beneficial, Muslims in China and beyond usually dislike the implication that Islam has become diluted, distorted, or absorbed by other cultures and faiths.[52]

Of course, notions of Chinese Islam are directed at non-Muslim audiences in China as much as anyone else. The aim is to promote social harmony by stressing the sameness of the other, particularly Muslims who speak Chinese and live among non-Muslim neighbors. But here again the message frequently backfires. Many Han citizens complain about reverse discrimination in favor of Muslims, about the Arabization of Islam in China, and even about the possible Islamification of China in general.[53] Faced with widespread fears of terrorism and Islamic radicalism, the government usually changes course by adopting a harder line against the public practice of religion, especially by young Uyghur men.

Heavy-handed efforts to reassure nervous Han communities merely confirm the suspicions of many Muslims that the idea of Chinese Islam is part of a wider policy of dividing Muslims into multiple factions and playing them against one another. All of China's major religions express similar complaints about the government's divide-and-rule tactics toward churches, temples, and charities. Party-state leaders want to discourage collective action by imposing different controls on each religion, but they unwittingly generate interfaith cooperation in demanding greater freedom of religion for everyone.[54]

Accentuating Regional Divergences in China

Inside China there are several crossroads along the New Silk Road where people see direct links between opportunities in the Islamic world and local conflicts. These concerns play out in multiple ways depending upon the local mix of ethnic groups and economic ambitions. In provinces where Muslims are a sizeable minority, Silk Road initiatives can quickly aggravate longstanding communal tensions. In overwhelmingly Han regions, the ripple effects are more subtle but potentially more upsetting because they stir economic and political conflicts among the regime's core supporters.

In Ningxia, for example, Han officials and scholars view indigenous Muslim culture as a magnet for Arab tourists and investors. They are pleased that Beijing supports their initiatives to showcase Hui customs and businesses that cater to Muslim markets overseas. But they are also frustrated when central party leaders repeatedly reject pilot projects to encourage Islamic banking and to enlist Muslim preachers as mediators in dispute resolution.[55]

Yunnan leaders are forging commercial and cultural ties with Iran and Bangladesh to the west and with Malaysia and Indonesia to the south. But they worry that security forces are stirring up needless resentments by pressuring the local Hui community to shun fellow Muslims coming from Xinjiang. Hui people in Yunnan are pleased to hear Beijing's apologies for abuses during the Cultural Revolution, but they are concerned that police are repeating similar injustices with forced deportations of Uyghurs who want to work and resettle in more peaceful provinces.[56]

Meanwhile, in Xinjiang, Han leaders tout their role as a double gateway to Central Asia and Europe as well as to South Asia and the Middle East. Nonetheless, many influential Han in business and university circles fear that attacks on routine religious practice are self-defeating because they alienate Chinese-speaking Hui as well as apolitical Uyghurs who have no sympathy for terrorism or separatism.[57]

Provinces with smaller concentrations of Muslims also feel the contradictions between opportunities in the Islamic world and tensions in their own communities. Many Han-dominated regions are feeling deeper strains with the central government and sharper competition with one another. The New Silk Road is paving the way for more overt inter-Han conflict over divergent economic interests and political aspirations. As regional rivalries sharpen, they reveal long-standing cultural and ethnic cleavages among the—supposedly homogeneous—majority nationality.

Shenzhen and Yiwu are the eastern hubs of maritime and rail networks for all branches of the New Silk Road. For many years, both cities have attracted thousands of Muslim traders from the Middle East, South Asia, and Africa. Increasingly, however, these visitors are turning into permanent residents with Chinese spouses and multiracial children. As their communities become larger and more conspicuous, they highlight the growing dissatisfaction with ethnic and religious policies that seem discriminatory and outdated.[58]

In Qingdao attention is focused on the future opening of Arctic shipping lanes. But that, in turn, depends on peaceful maritime relations elsewhere, particularly in the South China Sea where Beijing and Washington are sparring more openly than ever. Many of Qingdao's leaders are well-versed in maritime law and realize that China has no territorial claims to Arctic waters. They would prefer to see China's diplomats working with Indonesia and Malaysia to calm southern seas so that the Arctic Council will have no reason to shut the door on Chinese vessels heading to Rotterdam and Hamburg.[59]

Among the cities of China's western interior, Chengdu is one of the greatest beneficiaries of the Silk Road's overland and maritime connections. As a low-cost manufacturing and exporting center, it will increasingly compete with all of the traditional east coast powerhouses. Chengdu's new economic prominence foreshadows an equally important political role in the future. If China should experience a power struggle between evenly matched forces in the north and south, then the fast-growing west could be decisive in breaking the deadlock. Regional clashes are a salient aspect of interparty feuding, and they would become even stronger if more open elections were permitted.[60]

Nanjing is a thriving center of green technology and clean energy research with consulting projects in many Muslim countries. Local leaders believe their future-oriented economy is indispensible in overcoming China's reputation as the world's worst polluter where the state keeps propping up zombie industries. Nanjing officials and scientists want to leverage their role in foreign trade to gain greater powers of self-governance. Universities and think tanks are promoting a number of reforms such as "deliberative democracy" (协商民主) that combine administrative reorganization with popular elections. These are modest steps compared to the calls for political opening that circulated before Xi Jinping came to power. But, these days, they stand out against the drive toward greater centralization and party supervision.[61]

The more one thinks about the New Silk Road, the more it looks like folly—certain to generate so many headaches for China's rulers that it hardly seems worth the effort. Why would a dreary club of party bosses and state bureaucrats embrace so much unpredictability? Perhaps they are persuaded that they know enough about history and human nature to take calculated risks that no other country can imagine now or in coming decades.

Their starting point is not the well-known checklist of China's current weaknesses, but the steady flow of wealth and power that seems destined to strengthen China's hand in the near future. Their statecraft is grounded in a vision of current history in which developing countries across the non-Western world are converging toward more integrated transcontinental megaregions. In their view, China is best positioned to shape and lead these megaregions as they coevolve to form the backbone of a more inclusive international system.[62]

CHAPTER 2 | Megaregions and Coevolution in World Politics

CHINA IS IMAGINING THE New Silk Road and building it at the same time. In the last decade or so, Chinese writers have gradually migrated from gloomy metaphors of global fragmentation and conflict toward more hopeful visions of integration and prosperity. Integrationist views come in two main forms. A more romantic version imagines the ancient Silk Road springing back to life as if rising from a long sleep. A more workmanlike approach sees China constructing a new system over many decades, region by region and link by link.

The interplay between fantasy and craftsmanship was already on display during the opening ceremony of the 2008 Beijing Olympics. One of the showstoppers was a tribute to the legendary Seven Voyages of Admiral Zheng He, the fifteenth-century Muslim commander who took China's armadas across the Indian Ocean to Arabia and Africa. On the stadium floor, dozens of treasure ships suddenly appeared, sailing in majestic formation across the field. Each ship was an illusion—created by hosts of blue-clad sailors holding up long painted oars in perfect sequence to form a galleon, gliding over an imaginary ocean the actors themselves embodied.[1]

In China and beyond, the possibility of creating hemispheric markets is capturing the attention of policymakers and scholars alike. As Europe splinters and the United States turns inward, China declares itself the leader of a more inclusive globalization that can lift all nations and classes. Government agencies and the think tanks that advise them are weighing the geopolitical implications of multiple megaregions for a future that promises to be filled with fluid alliances and unstable balances of power.[2] Social scientists and world historians are portraying trans-regional networking as a welcome example of growing exchanges between civilizations in an era when nothing less than universal human action can cope with environmental threats to planetary survival. More and more scholars are viewing intercontinental connections through interdisciplinary lenses, borrowing perspectives of natural sciences that liken societies to evolving ecosystems and complex adaptive systems.[3]

Comparing social systems to the natural world inevitably spawns debates between those who stress direction from above or emergence from below. Supporters of megaregional development tend to espouse a blend of improvisation and planning, but they disagree on whether integration requires more central coordination or more freedom for intrinsic forces of self-organization and autonomy.[4] The Chinese are avid consumers and original contributors to all of these debates. Particularly in dealing with the Islamic core of the Silk Road, they are rediscovering the importance of reciprocity—realizing that if China wants to influence other societies, it must adapt to their needs and expect to be influenced by them as well.[5]

In its initial stages, critical responses to the New Silk Road have been particularly strong in the leading countries of the Islamic world—Pakistan, Turkey, Indonesia, Iran, and Nigeria. These reactions limit Beijing's options in international politics and push China's leaders to rethink their relations with Muslims in their own country. As Chinese writers absorb these criticisms, they increasingly describe the New Silk Road as an effort to create many megaregions at once—a tangle of overlapping networks spread out over disparate cultures and environments. This is vastly different from seeing the Silk Road as heralding a new era of Sino-centrism and supercontinental empire. When Chinese observers grasp the complexity and contradictions of the venture, they come to understand it as unleashing myriad exchanges that can transform China as well as its potential partners. Emerging power relations are more likely to resemble a mosaic of interdependent ecosystems than a chain of command with China at the apex.

Historical Momentum and Political Fallacies

Chinese political writings commonly insist that wise leadership begins by accurately assessing the flow of history—by reading the river currents that can carry us safely and smoothly to a distant shore if we let them guide us instead of rowing furiously toward a predetermined destination. World affairs have an innate momentum that can strengthen leaders who appreciate its power and destroy those who ignore it. But this belief in destiny is tempered by the certainty of constant change. The greatest lesson is that all lessons are tied to temporary circumstances that no human power can hold in place indefinitely.[6]

Statecraft demands more than intuition—it requires effective action based on sound analysis. But analysis always relies on imperfect information and partial perspectives, so successful leaders must listen to divergent views and correct course regularly. Miscalculation is more likely when we rely on metaphors to simplify complex realities. Metaphors are the useful half-truths we tell ourselves to highlight a few facets of a problem even though they often obscure the rest.[7] Chinese writers tend to use the same metaphors that shape discussions of world affairs in most other cultures—buffer zones, security dilemmas, balance of terror, soft power, and other familiar tropes. Small wonder, then, that China's debates bundle the same splits and fallacies that pervade scholarly and popular opinion elsewhere.[8]

Four metaphors are particularly influential in Chinese discussions about global politics, including relations with the Muslim world. These views can be described as Global Fracture, Great Games, New Mediterraneans, and Silk Road Romanticism. Each metaphor carries a different combination of insights and fallacies while favoring distinct—and often contradictory—interests. Commentators rely on all four views, but their relative importance has shifted over time. Understanding the assumptions of these intentional untruths is one way to gain an overview of China's contentious conversations about the meaning and consequences of the New Silk Road.

Global Fracture and Great Games are narratives of political division whereas New Mediterraneans and Silk Road Romanticism envision an era of transnational interdependence. Global Fracture and Silk Road Romanticism are the polarized metaphors of writers who believe that fragmentation or integration are irresistible trends that overshadow human action. Both views downplay the role of statecraft in shaping the future.[9] Writers who believe that wise leadership can guide world affairs are more likely to think in terms of Great Games and New Mediterraneans. Great Games is the favored metaphor of those who believe that diplomacy can keep power struggles within safe ranges. New Mediterraneans stresses the role of statecraft for more optimistic reasons—it can make certain megaregions the leading members of an interconnected global society.

During the governments of Hu Jintao and Wen Jiabao (2003–2013), there was great concern that China's rise might provoke a world war whether most politicians and generals wanted it or not. Debunking fears of a China threat required reassuring the world of Beijing's peaceful intentions, especially its determination to avoid the long string of conflagrations that Western nations had unleashed during their futile quests for global hegemony.[10] But reassurance seemed unlikely when the decline of America and Europe were generating shock waves around a multipolar world—tremors that resembled the seismic activity of tectonic plates colliding below the surface. Images of continental drift always seemed to belie the confident insistence that China could change history by managing a peaceful rise.[11] After all, continental drift is a theory for explaining earthquakes—natural events of immense destruction that cannot be predicted, much less prevented, by human beings.

As international gaps of wealth and power seemed to narrow in China's favor, Chinese writers began to sense a more positive potential of integrative forces that their country could lead and perhaps control. History seemed more friendly and more malleable. A crumbling global order might not trigger unavoidable suffering, but rather pave the way for reintegration around an emerging power with the foresight to lead the effort. By the time Xi Jinping came to power in 2013, there was a growing appetite for China to step forward and help the world pull itself back together. However, this new self-confidence has not produced a consensus about the type of statecraft that could make the most of China's new opportunities. There is constant debate over the relative importance of assertiveness and accommodation—competing more openly with the United States for world leadership versus providing more valuable public goods to benefit the international community in general.[12]

The voices of assertion frequently invoke the conflict-laden metaphor of Great Games whereas proponents of accommodation embrace Silk Road Romanticism with its promise of civilizational exchange and harmony. Both views suffer from crippling blind spots that opponents are quick to expose and exploit.[13] In their boldness, the Great Gamers discount the risks of escalation, betting that rival nations will expand their spheres of influence with enough self-control to avoid confrontation or to contain it if their calculations go awry.[14] This expects too much of diplomats who rely on shifting intentions and of generals who feel the need to plan for the worst long before it appears on the horizon.

In contrast, Silk Road Romanticism rests on a dreamy-eyed faith that statecraft merely needs to lend a helping hand to spontaneous forces of integration and brotherhood. In this view, the partisans of Pan-Asianism and South-South solidarity are finally on the march after centuries of Western suppression. Their collective will is so powerful and so just as to be virtually self-executing. To succeed, leaders simply need to go with the flow and let history run its course.[15]

In the context of these debates, Chinese writers are beginning to assess the Islamic world and its megaregions with more sober and open-ended views. Global Fracture seems less perilous and inhibiting to a rising power than it was a decade ago. A more confident China is ready to stand up and pitch in to reform global governance in ways that would have been inconceivable in the days of Deng Xiaoping.[16] Nonetheless, Chinese leaders realize they do not have the resources and skills necessary to dive wholeheartedly into the constant confrontations of Great Games. Nor are they willing to place blind faith in their own rhetoric about the promise of a Silk Road utopia.

Instead, Chinese writers are trying to imagine an up-to-date statecraft that can accomplish goals their teachers have valued for countless generations—exploiting historical opportunity for the common benefit. This demands a balanced view of imperfect human talents and competing social trends that neither exaggerates nor minimizes their respective powers. In seeking such a perspective, China's leaders and scholars have turned greater attention to the emergence of new megaregions, particularly when they are centered on strategically located countries in the Islamic world.[17]

The New Mediterraneans of Eurasia and Africa

The preeminent metaphor for students of megaregions is the portrait of the Mediterranean Basin as the world's most enduring crossroads of multicultural exchange and political conflict. In modern times, the leading depiction of the Mediterranean world was developed by the French historian, Fernand Braudel, and his followers in the interdisciplinary Annales School. Braudel's Mediterranean was a diverse and self-sustaining fusion of natural and human forces that evolved over centuries despite the constant rise and fall of transient political units such as city states, empires, and nations.[18]

This model soon became the archetype of ecological systems in which nature, civilization, and individuals made starkly unequal contributions to the unfolding of history over vast territories and many centuries. Eventually, scholars exported the metaphor to more and more places beyond southern Europe and northern Africa, including non-Western cultures and former colonial lands with divergent values and experiences.[19] Every depiction of a New Mediterranean ignited debates and reformulations of Braudel's assumptions that natural conditions were the most important historical forces in contrast to the supposedly lesser influence of social institutions, and especially to the marginal role he often attributed to individual actors.

In China and abroad, many students of Chinese history have popularized the notion that Mediterranean-like regions have long overlapped with China's shifting territories and that China is instrumental in shaping several new Mediterraneans that are arising throughout Asia and Africa in our time. These ideas appeared years before Xi Jinping cast his version of the New Silk Road as China's signature foreign policy initiative, and they have gained even wider currency during his time in office.[20] Indeed, the meeting of the Mediterranean metaphor and the One Belt, One Road policy seems unusually well timed—the trope's proponents are searching for ways to give it new meaning, and China's leadership needs a grand vision that inspires foreign and domestic audiences while leaving themselves wide freedom of maneuver and interpretation.

Xi's version of the New Silk Road is sparking debate about megaregions in all directions, stimulating creative thinking that Braudel and his followers would never have imagined. China's dreams of rewiring the world come just in time to fuel the lively conversations about how Mediterraneans emerge, how they imitate and reshape one another, and how they transform their environments, globally and locally. The soaring ambitions of Chinese statecraft drive Beijing to both encourage and exploit these conversations—inviting wider dialogues between science and policy and between multiple faiths and civilizations.[21] This convergence of interests creates valuable learning opportunities for China's leaders even if the lessons make them uncomfortable about their modest abilities to steer developments either internally or around the world.

In many ways, China's efforts contradict basic assumptions about megaregions that Braudel advanced and that other scholars have strengthened in describing Mediterranean-like systems elsewhere. The New Silk Road seeks to connect several geographic and cultural clusters at once instead of regarding them as separate or self-sufficient networks. China's approach is highly obtrusive—building upon well-established ties and identities in some cases, but trying to remold or even create them when political expediency requires.[22]

Plugging into so many volatile societies at once exposes China to endless cross-pressures and boomerangs. Wherever China's influence grows, people can quickly see what the Chinese are doing everywhere else and respond accordingly. All of the envisioned megaregions are emerging, interacting, and competing at the same time, paving the way for chain reactions that no government can anticipate or contain. Sooner or later, what happens along the New Silk Road reverberates in China, too. The good that China fosters beyond its borders can enrich its own people immeasurably. Likewise, any damage it causes—even unintentionally—is also bound to be felt back home.

Students of megaregions who want to adapt Braudel's insights to these new circumstances can draw upon related disciplines, particularly theories of complex adaptive systems that social scientists are increasingly borrowing from the natural sciences. The concepts of emergence and coevolution highlight inherent tensions in the growth and interaction of megaregions—between the need for self-organization and autonomy on the one hand versus coordination and control on the other. In addition, the ideas of agency and feedback suggest that pressures for reciprocal influence can spread rapidly and help to reverse power relations along the way.[23]

None of this is good news for the guardians of China's party-state establishment, most of whom trained as engineers and technocrats, accustomed to building things and running teams instead of listening to people and earning their trust. Braudelian historians and natural scientists teach that megaregions become viable ecologies due to countless generations of adaptation and constant self-transformation.[24] But the would-be Mediterraneans of China's New Silk Road are hot house transplants by comparison—fragile upstarts in man-made environments that are susceptible to contagion from all directions.

Moreover, when complex systems survive, their adaptations begin to resemble learning and self-correction—an inner logic or intelligence, if not a fully independent consciousness. Every social system is an assembly of individual wills prone to change their minds and directions according to perceived interests and identities. Megaregions are products of human choice rather than genetic code or remote control.[25]

The Achilles heel of China's New Silk Road are the problems of agency and volition—who counts and who speaks for whom? Chinese statecraft is frozen in the view that sovereignty belongs to nation-states instead of individuals.[26] China wants to lead the fight for greater democracy in global governance by promoting wider representation and power-sharing. But this sort of democracy is reserved for governments and the privileged few who control them.

The New Silk Road is supposed to be a bold experiment in political reform that fosters inclusiveness and participation. However, China's leaders only want to open the door halfway—to the often self-appointed representatives of nation-states, but not to the people themselves and, above all, not to the people of China.

For current practitioners of Chinese statecraft, the most important lesson of the Silk Road ventures is that the doors of inclusion are opening wider than they prefer and faster than they imagined. This is a lesson that reverberates in every land that China touches, forcing Chinese representatives to listen more attentively and respond more generously to grievances they would rather not hear. Eventually, China's rulers will have to show the same deference to their own citizens—not just the ethnic and religious minorities in the borderlands, but also the urban middle classes that comprise more and more of the Han majority.

China's statecraft might be able to launch hemispheric campaigns of integration that spur the rise of many megaregions simultaneously. But who will direct and profit from these efforts once they take on a life of their own? How will the lands of the Islamic world interact with transcontinental communities in such competing ventures as Afro-Eurasia, the Indian Ocean Basin, the Pacific Community, and the Americas with multiple centers and overlapping goals? If powerful Muslim countries choose to form and lead megaregions as well, what transformations can we expect in geopolitics, digital capitalism, religious modernization, collective security, gender relations, and generational power?

These are just a few of the day-after questions China's leaders are asking themselves. Building the New Silk Road is a colossal undertaking that no other nation could dream of tackling. The plans bespeak a hubris that naturally puzzles and worries us all. Yet no matter how much of the Silk Road China's current rulers manage to build, eventually they will have to hand it over to the billions of people who are paying for it with depleted natural resources and soaring debt. Those handovers might begin sooner than planners expect—along the Silk Road and in China as well.

Mosaics of Coevolution on the New Silk Road

China is encouraging regional connectivity at many levels simultaneously—subnational, transnational, and intercontinental. At each level, developments have their own dynamic, stimulating both greater conflict and greater integration while aggravating tensions between centralizing governments and local communities. Conflicts can be destabilizing and destructive, but they can also promote integration in the long run if they deepen participation and transparency.[27] A more contentious society can also be a stronger polity if power-sharing gives ordinary people a stake in the system as a whole, whether that system is a well-defined nation-state, an emerging multinational consortium, or a future vision of global community.

Every level of regionalism becomes more open to influences from all other levels. Self-contained societies gradually give way to reciprocal flows between overlapping networks. Smaller regions can become nested within larger ones, creating a web-like universe of constant exchange and mutual adaptation. Growing complexity and susceptibility to disruption increase the need for coordination, which depends on an exchange of top-down and bottom-up communication. Balancing the interplay of planning and self-organization is a pervasive problem for members in every region and its neighbors.[28]

Environmental scientists who study natural and human ecology commonly describe their work in these terms—as exploring complex adaptive systems that evolve together as their interactions increase over time. They use the concept of coevolution to examine the far-reaching impacts that humans have on one another and their environments. They stress the importance of relationships—sometimes in diverse networks over wide territories—as the driving force in long-term adaptations and environmental changes.[29] In contrast to older assumptions that evolution is a barely visible process occurring over many epochs, students of coevolution argue that changes in behavior frequently trigger cascading responses—sudden and accelerated adaptations with potentially profound environmental effects.[30]

Ecologists commonly speak of the geographic mosaic of coevolution to describe divergent adaptations across neighboring regions or subregional zones. In different regions, the same group often changes both appearance and behavior—even to the point of becoming a separate type altogether.[31] A major disruption, such as the extinction of a group or the introduction of new migrants, can create ripples through the wider ecosystem and upset its balance. Disruptions become more likely—and potentially more harmful—as regions become increasingly interconnected and more exposed to influences beyond their control.

All of these insights are useful in trying to understand the New Silk Road initiatives, particularly efforts to develop connectivity between emerging megaregions—new Mediterraneans—across a more integrated Afro-Eurasian hemisphere and beyond. If the venture is viewed as a grand blue print handed down from the party-state in Beijing, then it seems like a highly choreographed power play with geopolitical implications that could shape the destiny of generations to come. In fact, this may be true even if only a fraction of the projects comes to fruition, particularly in the southern Pacific where China is trying to impose its own version of the Monroe Doctrine by asserting an exclusive sphere of influence.[32]

On the other hand, if the New Silk Road is seen as a poorly understood experiment in megaregional development—the social equivalent of upending the geographic mosaic of coevolution across a fragile hemispheric ecology—then we would have a very different set of expectations. Instead of predicting the steady spread of China's sphere of influence—the emergence of a modern Kingdom of Heaven (Tian Xia) rooted in a hierarchy of Chinese Mediterraneans—we would expect a chain reaction of unintended consequences, creating greater uncertainty and new opportunities for political realignment.

China's boundaries have expanded and contracted many times. Its current borders include many non-Han communities that were often detached from the central zones commonly known as China proper. In addition, Chinese culture and settlements spread to many other lands that are now independent nations dominated by non-Chinese majorities. Many of these areas, in China and abroad, can be described as more or less Chinese—as overlapping circles with hybrid cultures rather than separate worlds.

When China selects a local partner to develop a multinational region, it often finds a coauthor or an explicit rival instead of a passive agent. Turkey has its own ambitions for the Black Sea and Caspian Basin just as Iran seeks wider influence in the Persian Gulf and Middle East. Indonesia is determined to assert sovereignty over internal waters it was formerly powerless to defend, and Nigeria sees its future as a leader of south-south coalitions across Africa and the Atlantic. Negotiating with these aspiring powers is even harder when Beijing becomes entangled in quarrels between their subnational regions. Chinese officials claim to remain aloof from domestic politics, but they inevitably find themselves in the crossfire between Punjabis and Pakhtuns, Yoruba and Igbo, Javanese and Sumatrans, Turks and Kurds. Building connectivity across nations can then expand to include brokering compromises within them. To create a megaregion, Beijing must also juggle microregions that are competing for China's aid in their quests for both national and transnational power.

Critics of American foreign policy often point to Washington's failures in nation-building—misguided expectations that the United States could refashion distant and vastly different societies to conform to its values and interests.[33] Imagine how quickly the chances of failure would multiply if one raises the stakes to region-building, continent-merging, and hemisphere-linking. These are precisely the purposes of the New Silk Road and some of the reasons it cannot be understood as a mere reprise of earlier namesakes. An even more important distinction stems from the heightened political consciousness and ambitions of the people whose lands and resources control the well-being of the world economy. A sizeable portion of those people are Muslim citizens with national identities and global connections—the palimpsest of Islamic civilization—that are just as powerful as China's or anyone else's.

Initial evidence on the progress of Silk Road ventures in the Islamic world strongly supports expectations of disruption and unintended consequences instead of the prevailing concerns over China's new spheres of influence and creeping hegemony. Beijing's projects to integrate national and regional markets quickly backfire when they appear to favor some ethnic groups or provinces over others. Equally important, the Chinese themselves already understand these trends and are trying to adapt accordingly. That willingness to admit error and to self-correct suggests a healthy capacity for political learning—the hallmark of statecraft in all civilizations and traditions.

Nonetheless, Chinese leaders are still unwilling to apply at home the flexibility and adaptiveness they are learning to show abroad. The profound split between farsightedness in foreign relations and blindness toward fellow citizens in China is the most striking flaw in the party-state establishment and those who support it. If uncorrected, the flaw is certain to undermine China's rulers—and perhaps undo them—because Chinese society is an integral member of the transcontinental communities they want to promote.

Indeed, of all the New Silk Road societies, China itself may be the most vulnerable to external disruptions and internal divisions. China's leaders understand this predicament quite well—and that helps explain the curious blend of swagger and paranoia that pervades their policies and personas.

CHAPTER 3 | Pakistan

Deep Democracy and Shallow Strategy

FOR CHINA, PAKISTAN IS an old friend it is just getting to know. Prior experience played a big role in China's decision to make Pakistan the opening showcase for the New Silk Road. But the friendship always rested on mutual interests more than shared sentiments, and most of the time it was an arm's length arrangement between officials bolstered by a parallel network of army connections. Neither side expected too much of the other, and they had no plans to complicate matters by peering too deeply through their neighbor's windows.[1]

The desire to strengthen relations followed years of frustration with the United States and India accompanied by mounting evidence that these common foes were joining forces against them. Beijing eventually decided to forge a virtual counter-alliance with Islamabad capped with a fabulous package of investments in energy and infrastructure that no other country could provide. Pakistanis widely agreed that the help was desperately needed and long overdue—a $50 billion connectivity campaign, known as the China-Pakistan Economic Corridor (CPEC), targeting bottlenecks that have crippled the country for decades.[2] Yet even before the projects were launched, they faced protests and threats of mass opposition from multiple directions.

The Chinese were stunned. They knew that Nawaz Sharif's government was in serious trouble—at times, practically under siege.[3] But they felt confident of China's overwhelming popularity in Pakistan and did not anticipate stirring up so much anger through well-intentioned efforts to benefit the country and its people. Chinese who were not experts in Pakistan affairs had to go through a crash course in ethnic and regional relations that were every bit as complex as the situation in their homeland.

For Chinese observers, the most surprising discovery was that Pakistan—long known for its deep state of military and intelligence services—has also developed a deep society filled with assertive and well-organized interests. To their consternation, Chinese visitors learned that Pakistan's democracy is sprouting stronger roots with wider reach than they had ever realized.

China's officials are still recovering from the shock. The rebound is pushing them beyond their comfort zone toward give and take with Pakistani groups they poorly understand. Such encounters are exposing Chinese to heightened scrutiny for which they have little patience.

To their credit, the Chinese are trying to adapt to the rough and tumble of a mostly friendly society filled with opinionated people who are accustomed to speaking their minds. The lessons the Chinese are learning—and failing to learn—will follow them far beyond Pakistan. Indeed, similar stories are playing out in many other Muslim countries where democracy, however fragile, is nonetheless highly valued and practiced with growing fervor.

Triggering a Cascade of Regional and Ethnic Protests

The crux of the problem was uncertainty over the main route that would cross the length of Pakistan, linking Kashgar in southern Xinjiang with the port city of Gwadar on the Arabian Sea.[4] This central artery would bring new life to every community it touched. It would combine railroads, highways, and pipelines with fiber optic connectivity. In the best of scenarios, there would be scores of new energy projects driven by natural gas and coal as well as solar and wind power. Dams would generate electricity for the entire country and perhaps even for export. The route's branches would be filled with manufacturing zones drawing local and foreign investment to make Pakistan an industrial and military power second to none.[5]

At first, it seemed priority status would go to the western regions of Khyber Paktunkhwa (K-P)—previously known as the Northwest Frontier Province—and Balochistan (Figure 3.1). This was the shortest route that could concentrate economic stimulus where it was needed most—in the backward and restive borderlands of ethnic minorities, particularly the Pakhtuns and Balochis. But, as the official launch date grew nearer, everything seemed to be up in the air, with rival provinces and parties accusing one another of plotting to snatch the prize for themselves alone.

Suddenly, the planned route changed direction. Instead of heading due north from Gwadar, it followed the coast eastward toward Karachi before veering upward to Punjab (Figure 3.2). This meant showering benefits on

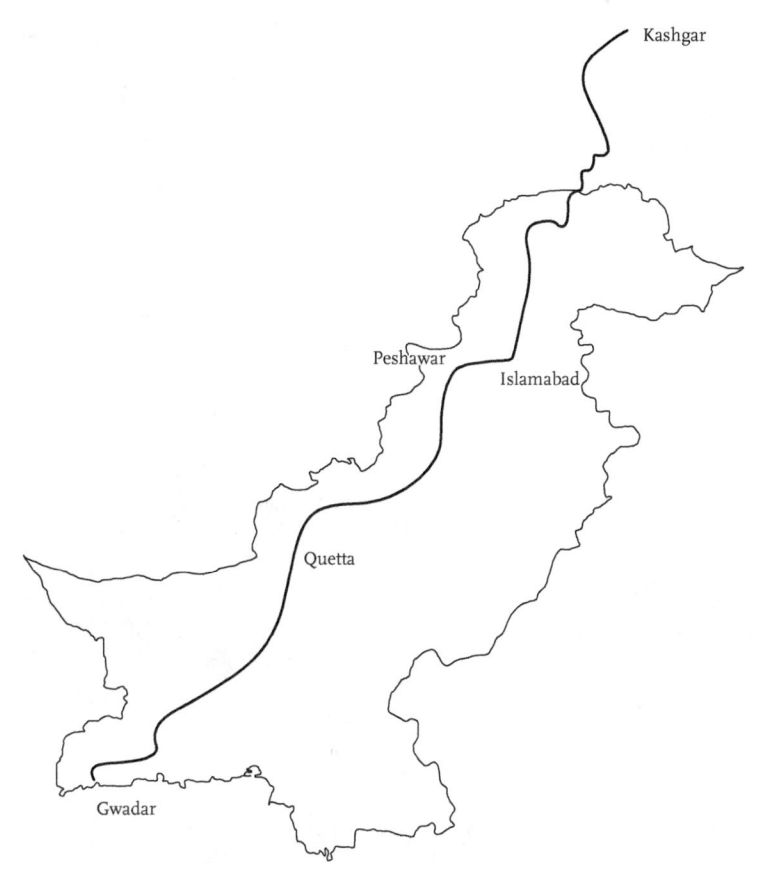

FIGURE 3.1. The Western Route through Balochistan and Khyber Pakhtunkhwa. Author's illustration.

Pakistan's most prosperous province, which already enjoyed the lion's share of infrastructure and the strongest political clout. Adding insult to injury, at least half the country believed that Punjabi business groups were pulling strings through the Sharif brothers who ran the governments in Islamabad and Lahore at the same time.[6]

As suspicions hardened, Chinese spokesmen tied themselves in knots with a string of contradictions that make them look like bumbling co-conspirators. "No," they said, the plan had not changed and the original route was still in place. "Yes," they admitted, the route had shifted, but only at the suggestion of Pakistani officials who were concerned about persistent security problems all along the western borders. "Who told you that?" they wondered when Islamabad claimed the Chinese themselves had demanded a new and safer route because they doubted Pakistan could protect workers and assets from terrorist attacks.[7]

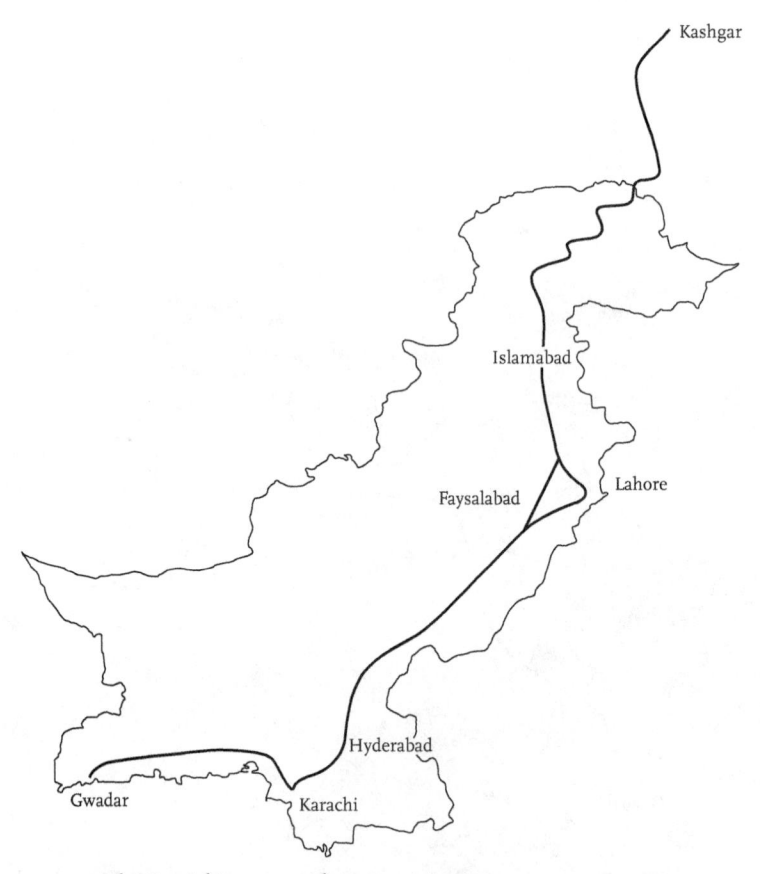

FIGURE 3.2. The Punjabi route as the new main artery.
Author's illustration.

The crowning touch came from a Chinese academic who was an expert in South Asia and a leading consultant to the project planners. The new economic corridor, he declared, was a development plan and not a social welfare program. It was perfectly natural and rational to invest in the most advanced areas because they would make the best use of the opportunities. Efficiency and productivity were the proper priorities—not social justice and redistribution.[8]

These pronouncements came not from a Chicago boy critic of the China-Pakistan partnership, but from an insider who seemed to spill the beans that both governments were desperate to hide. Pakistan's media went to town, filling in the details of a story the public had heard a thousand times before: The deal was done—cooked up behind closed doors by a handful of self-dealing politicians and foreigners who were lying to the rest of the world all along.

32 | China and the Islamic World

Such gaffes quickly galvanized opposition to both governments throughout Pakistan. Politicians gathered in All-Party Conferences demanding explanations from ministers leading the negotiations with China.[9] Attendees taunted Nawaz Sharif, dubbing him the Prime Minister of Punjab instead of Pakistan. They ganged up on the Minister of Planning and Development, Ahsan Iqbal, demanding fuller disclosure of project finances and discussions with Chinese officials. Many began renaming the project the China-Punjab Economic Corridor. Provincial legislatures in K-P and Balochistan passed resolutions denouncing the route shift and threatening to withdraw security protection for federal projects in their districts.[10] Community groups and anticorruption activists marched and sued to force full disclosure of all project details, including precise locations and financial provisions.[11]

The tone of these protests was unusually sharp even for observers accustomed to Pakistan's high decibel politics. Opponents vowed to stop at nothing to restore the original western route. Long-standing threats to break up the country took on new credibility.[12] Civil disobedience is hardly new to public life in Pakistan, but this time it was coming from more directions than usual. One of the most outspoken opponents was Sikander Hayat Khan Sherpao, K-P's young Minister of Irrigation and Social Welfare from the powerful landholding family of Charsadda, just northeast of Peshawar. Along with his father Aftab, leader of the opposition Qaumi Watan Party, he pledged mass action against the central government unless it compensated the northwest border districts for their long-suffering in battles against terrorism. They vowed that the CPEC would not proceed unless the route through their province received top priority.[13]

Supporters of the corridor started speculating that China might abandon the whole enterprise out of exasperation with Pakistani divisions. Many compared the current bickering to the spats that scuttled the Kalabagh Dam project in 2008. The proposed giant dam over the Indus River was billed as the remedy for Pakistan's chronic power shortages and catastrophic floods. But Pakhtun landlords and politicians were determined to veto the effort because they saw it as a Punjabi ploy to divert Indus waters for their growing urban and industrial centers.[14] Ever since then, references to Kalabagh had become a familiar shorthand for Pakistan's inability to think and act as a unified society instead of a collection of feudal enclaves. Commentators who dredged up these memories intended to shame their leaders into compromise, but the impact on public opinion was frequently demoralizing.

Meanwhile, the army was already overstretched by armed conflicts in three corners at once. The border with Afghanistan needed constant attention and permanent manpower. The Zarb-e-Azb ("sharp and cutting strike") campaign, launched in 2014, took on the Pakistani Taliban (PTT).[15] Balochi politicians accused the army of waging a dirty war of assassinations and disappearances that targeted the slightest dissent, particularly from journalists and university students.[16] Human rights groups in Europe and the United States were confirming the charges with testimonials from Balochi refugees and exiles.[17] Karachi was ablaze yet again. Army rangers used deadly force against Muhajir militias battling to protect their stranglehold on city business from a looming invasion by China-connected politicians in Islamabad.[18]

Chinese leaders had no choice but to reverse course. The entire Silk Road venture seemed to hang in the balance. Pakistan was supposed to be a launching pad, but now it looked more like an early grave. Beijing and Islamabad never stopped blaming India and the United States for trying to sabotage their plans, but they knew very well they had become their own worst enemies.[19]

Gradually, China dropped the pretense that it abstained from domestic politics. They pressured Sharif's government to negotiate a new deal with its opponents or lose the promised investments altogether.[20] As Pakistanis in and out of government learned of the shift, they looked to Beijing for information, advice, and inevitably for explicit support of their competing proposals. In a country where patron-client exchange is second nature, people had no difficulty recognizing the power behind the throne and no qualms about lining up to win its favor (Figure 3.3).

In a matter of months, alternate routes emerged and itemized price lists were revealed. What began as a trickle of unattributed leaks crystallized into public bargaining positions and, eventually, a new nationwide blueprint backed by widespread consensus emerged.[21] China's hand remained in the background, but was easily visible to anyone who paid attention. In effect, Chinese sponsors waited in one room while Pakistanis in nearby meetings thrashed out a workable division of the pie. But this time the recipe had a major new ingredient—explicit undertakings from Pakistan's army, which committed a new division to safeguard the projects and assumed sweeping powers to run the districts that hosted them.[22]

Triple Routes and Early Harvests

The makeover that emerged from these negotiations was a less than miraculous piece of logrolling. It included three routes instead of one—crossing separate regions and converging at northern and southern terminals.[23] The western segment was restored and assigned top priority. The rival eastern

Engineering and finance

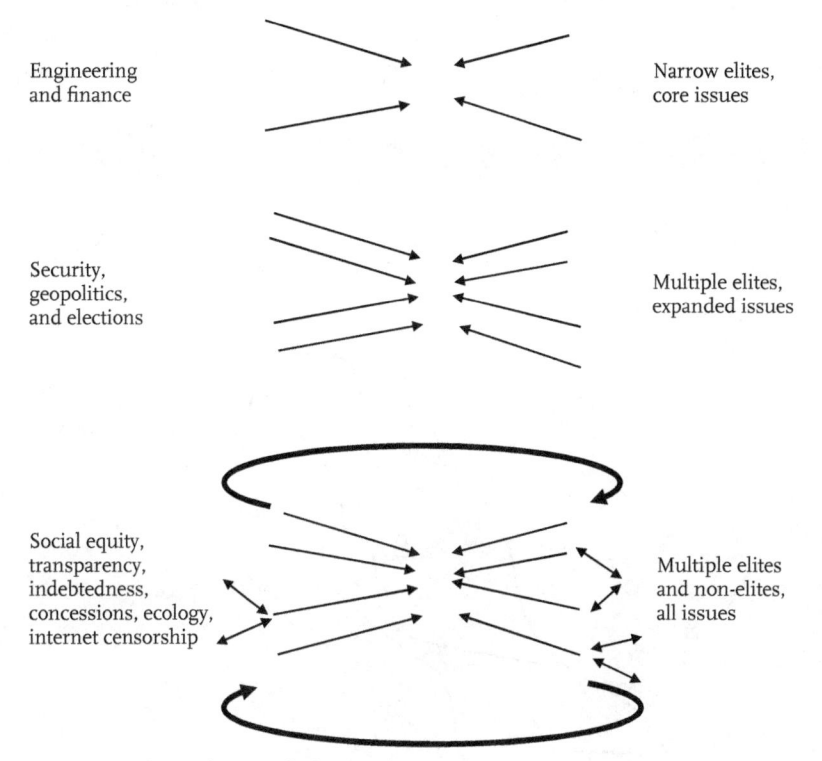

Narrow elites, core issues

Security, geopolitics, and elections

Multiple elites, expanded issues

Social equity, transparency, indebtedness, concessions, ecology, internet censorship

Multiple elites and non-elites, all issues

FIGURE 3.3. The evolution of China-Pakistan exchanges. Author's illustration.

route was approved but downgraded to second place. In addition, a new central section arose, zigzagging along the Indus valley districts and touching the other two routes at selected junctures (Figure 3.4).

The triple route formula aimed at reconciling regional and ethnic splits in a single stroke. In theory, more privileged Punjabis would defer to neglected Pakhtuns and Balochis. A special place at the table was created for Sindhis and Saraikis (those from the southern areas of the Punjab often identified with religious hard-liners), but not for the Muhajirs whose status had tumbled from being respected as Pakistan's founding fathers to being stigmatized as its most unruly urban ghetto dwellers.[24] In this manner, efforts to redress ethnic inequalities ironically served to aggravate smoldering grievances against a perceived hierarchy. Instead of leveling the playing field for all groups, the negotiators merely tilted it toward another state of imbalance that would satisfy none of them.

As the interregional horse-trading advanced, it encouraged Pakistani and Chinese officials to make some gestures of greater transparency—or,

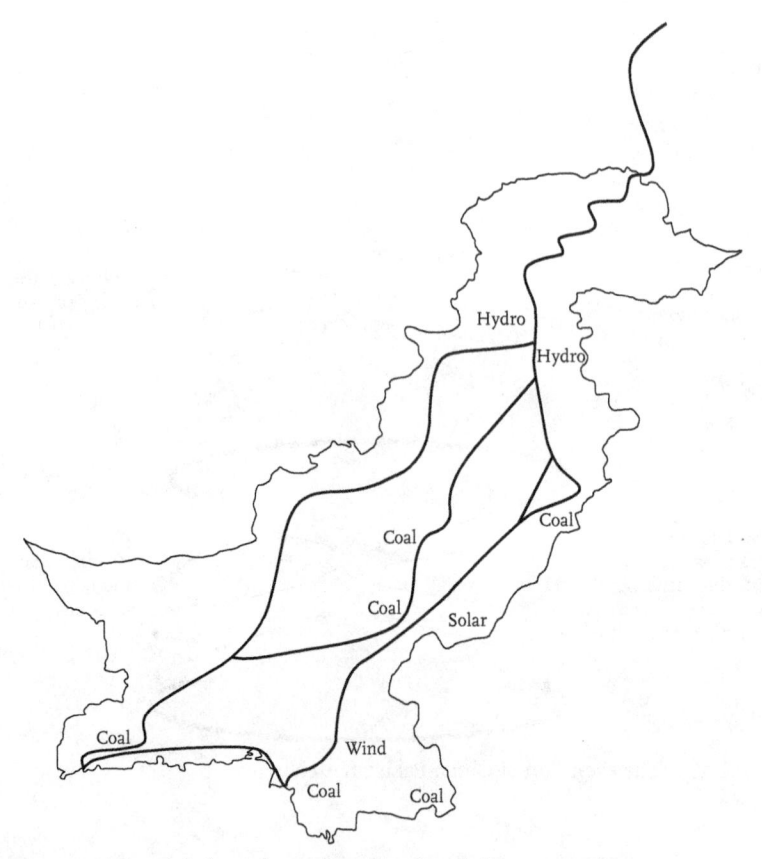

FIGURE 3.4. The triple branches network and early harvest projects.
Author's illustration.

at least, translucence. They published increasingly detailed lists of projects by type, location, and priority. Attention focused on a flock of so-called early harvest investments—mainly in energy and power generation—that were fast-tracked to come on line in time for the next round of national elections.[25] This was widely viewed as a concession to help the Sharif brothers answer Punjabi complaints that they had given away too much for the sake of regional harmony. With something tangible to show for their development efforts, the ruling party was hoping to boost its prospects in coming polls.[26]

Even after Pakistan's Supreme Court ousted Nawaz from the prime ministership over the Panama Papers scandal, his brother, Shehbaz, burnished his own reputation by claiming the credit for shepherding early harvest projects as governor of Punjab.[27] When it seemed that Shehbaz might try to become prime minister, some ruling party leaders argued it was more important that he stay put and guard the Punjabi vote bank. Everyone would be

TABLE 3.1 Early steps toward disclosing CPEC finances and local benefits Estimated Construction Costs

SECTOR	COST $ BILLION
Energy	33.79
Roads	5.90
Rail	3.69
Lahore mass transit	1.60
Gwadar port	.66
Fiber optics	.04
Total	**45.64**

Wall Street Journal, April 21, 2015.

better served, they reasoned, if Shehbaz cut ribbons at opening ceremonies for the Chinese-built metro in Lahore instead of stepping into the firing line of national politics in Islamabad.[28]

The early harvest projects aimed at consolidating the ruling party's support in Punjab, but they merely divided Punjabi voters by favoring the most developed areas over the least developed. The perceived regional discrimination created huge openings for Imran Khan's insurgent party, the Pakistan Tehreek-e-Insaf (PTI), in the very province that was supposed to be the Sharif family's fortress. During the July 2018 elections, Imran-backed candidates ran neck and neck with Nawaz's allies in Punjab as a whole, scoring its greatest victories in the most disadvantaged western and southern districts that had seen little benefit from Chinese investments.[29]

In the lead up to the 2018 elections, Pakistani voters also showed a lively interest in the fine points of financial understandings with China (Table 3.1 and Table 3.2). Professionals and common citizens alike pored over each announcement about grant-loan ratios, interest rates, debt forgiveness provisions, and sovereign guarantees. Pakistanis had decades of experience in struggling to measure—let alone pay—the chronic indebtedness their leaders incurred during endless rounds of structural adjustment demanded by the International Monetary Fund and punitive sanctions imposed by the U.S. Congress.[30] Chinese officials made a point of disclosing interest charges project by project and lender by lender, repeatedly distinguishing market and concessionary rates whenever they offered terms that were unrivaled by Pakistan's traditional friends and donors.[31]

However, transparency abruptly halted when inquiries broached the topic of concessions. Many of the biggest projects went to power and transportation providers with mixed boards of Chinese and Pakistani directors.[32] In

TABLE 3.2 Further disclosures of CPEC project details

LOCATION/PROJECT	COST	START DATE	FINISH DATE
Gwadar			
International airport	230 million	6/2015	2017
Fresh water treatment	130 million	4/2015	6/2017
Export zone infrastructure	33 million	12/2016	6/2018
East Bay Expressway 18.9 km	135 million	6/2015	2017
China-Pak Friendship Hospital	100 million	6/2015	12/2017
Pak-China Technical and Vocational Institution	10 million	1/2016	12/2017
Land acquisition for free zone 2,282 acres	65 million		
Dredging of berthing areas and channels	28 million	10/2016	12/2017
Breakwater construction	122.6 million	10/2016	12/2017
Coal-fired power plant 2 x 150 MW	360 million	4/2015	6/2017
Karachi			
Port Qasim coal-based power project 1320 MW	1.8 billion	3/2015	2017
Wind project	130 million	3/2015	3/2016
Hyderabad			
Wind project 50 MW	130 million	3/2015	3/2016
Wind project 100 MW	260 million	2015	2016
Nawabshah-Gwadar			
Liquid natural gas pipeline and terminal		3/2015	

Tharpakar
Coal mining 3.8 MT	900 million	3/2015	2017
Coal mining 6.5 MT	1.3 billion	3/2015	2017
Coal-fired power 660 MW	900 million	3/2015	2017
Coal-fired power 1320 MW	1.9 billion	3/2015	2017

Rahim Yar Khan
Coal-based project 1320 MW	1.9 billion	3/2015	2017

Bahalwalpur
Solar power park	1.33 billion	3/2015	3/2016

Multan-Sukkur
Highway 387 km	2.6 billion	6/2015	12/2017

Muzaffargarh
Coal-fired power	1.9 billion		

Sahiwal
Coal-fired power	1.6 billion	3/2015	2017

Lahore
Metro 27.1 km	1.62 billion		

Islamabad
Karot hydropower project	1.5 billion	3/2015	2020

Abbottabad
Suki Kinari hydropower project	1.8 billion	4/2015	2020

Thakot-Havelian
Karakoram Highway phase 2 120 km	920 million	6/2015	

Express Tribune, May 17, 2015.

some cases, the public learned the ownership shares of corporate partners, especially when Pakistanis held controlling interests. But the important information on concessions never saw the light of day.

Concessions are typically an accountant's playground and a consumer's trap. The overriding goal is to create a monopoly with a guaranteed stream of revenue that earns as much profit as possible and for as long as one can.[33] China and Pakistan agreed to many contracts allowing Chinese firms to build facilities, operate them for a profit over a specified period—usually several years or decades—and, then, to hand them over to Pakistani owners.

The holder of the concession is expected to recover its initial costs and to earn a profit on its investment and management services. In principle, that profit should reflect the project's level of risk and returns in related industries and markets. That's an equation with a lot of unknown quantities. Calculating those numbers is the job of contentious teams of accountants and lawyers who negotiate in private with little outside involvement except for technical input from consulting engineers.

Such a system creates infinite opportunities for abuse and self-dealing—activities not unknown to government and business leaders in China as well as Pakistan. The public is still in the dark concerning most of the key concessionary terms. Some of the hottest issues are the precise guarantees that Pakistan's treasury must provide over the lifetime of the concessions and beyond.[34] This includes potentially backbreaking sums for reserve funds, security warranties, minimum purchase requirements, and service charges. Pakistanis who are yet to be born will be obligated to pay these debts whether the enterprises survive or fail.

The Silk Road negotiations highlighted equally serious pitfalls in Pakistan's constitution—both written and unwritten. China's willingness to follow through on its investments hinged on pledges from the Pakistani army that it would safeguard the people and assets at risk. This would require deploying enough military force to subdue lands and populations that had been in open revolt for decades, particularly in Balochistan and near the coastal city of Gwadar.[35]

In practice, army commanders who accepted such a mission would become martial law governors under a state of emergency. Federal and provincial politicians would have to agree on how much power to delegate and when to renew the authorizations.[36] They would be embroiled in endless debates about oversight, judicial review, and human rights while facing constant criticism from media and citizens' groups in Pakistan and internationally.

Chinese negotiators had already pushed Pakistanis to settle on routes that would satisfy their regional and ethnic ambitions. Now China was demanding a new defense force to protect those routes—imposing added pressures on Pakistan's already strained civil-military relations. Such pressures could undermine the legitimacy of both civilian and military institutions with futile quarrels over separating antiterrorism from politics, particularly when army preferences contradict those of elected governments and sovereign voters.

Proponents of the Silk Road have long touted it as a game changer for Pakistan, meaning that it would usher in a new era of prosperity and international influence.[37] In fact, the consequences are proving to be more far-reaching than they anticipated. The games that are being challenged most are the long-standing tussles between ethnic blocs and the seesaw power-sharing of civilian and military elites. Building the inaugural branch of the New Silk Road is reigniting Pakistan's long-running debates over its entire system of social relations and constitutional government—and much of the impetus radiates from Beijing.[38]

Pakistan as a Silk Road Junction and an Indian Front Line

In Pakistan and elsewhere, China's increasingly visible hand is promoting tendencies that are both democratic and antidemocratic. Does that mean that China's leaders have already come halfway toward supporting democracy in friendly countries where they have vital security interests? Perhaps so, even if that is not their intent.

China needs a successful Pakistan for its own security rather than as a political statement about the benefits of a so-called Beijing Consensus.[39] As China's leaders learn more about Pakistani society, they might conclude that it has crossed a threshold where it is more governable as a messy democracy than as an unruly dictatorship. Such a pragmatic judgment could open the door for a more sensitive statecraft, willing to nudge friends toward goals they have already chosen rather than professing indifference or peddling a patented recipe of one's own.

For China, Pakistan's position in the New Silk Road is exceptional in many ways. Pakistan is the crossroads where otherwise separate overland and maritime networks intersect. By land and sea, Pakistan offers access to Xinjiang, Tibet, and Central Asia, to Iran and the Persian Gulf, and via the Indian Ocean to the Mediterranean and the Pacific (Figure 3.5 and Figure 3.6).

Pakistan has useful links in many directions, but it has only modest influence beyond its borders. The understanding of strategic depth in Islamabad is little more than maintaining an influential hand in Afghanistan and keeping India out.[40] Pakistan possesses a formidable nuclear deterrent,

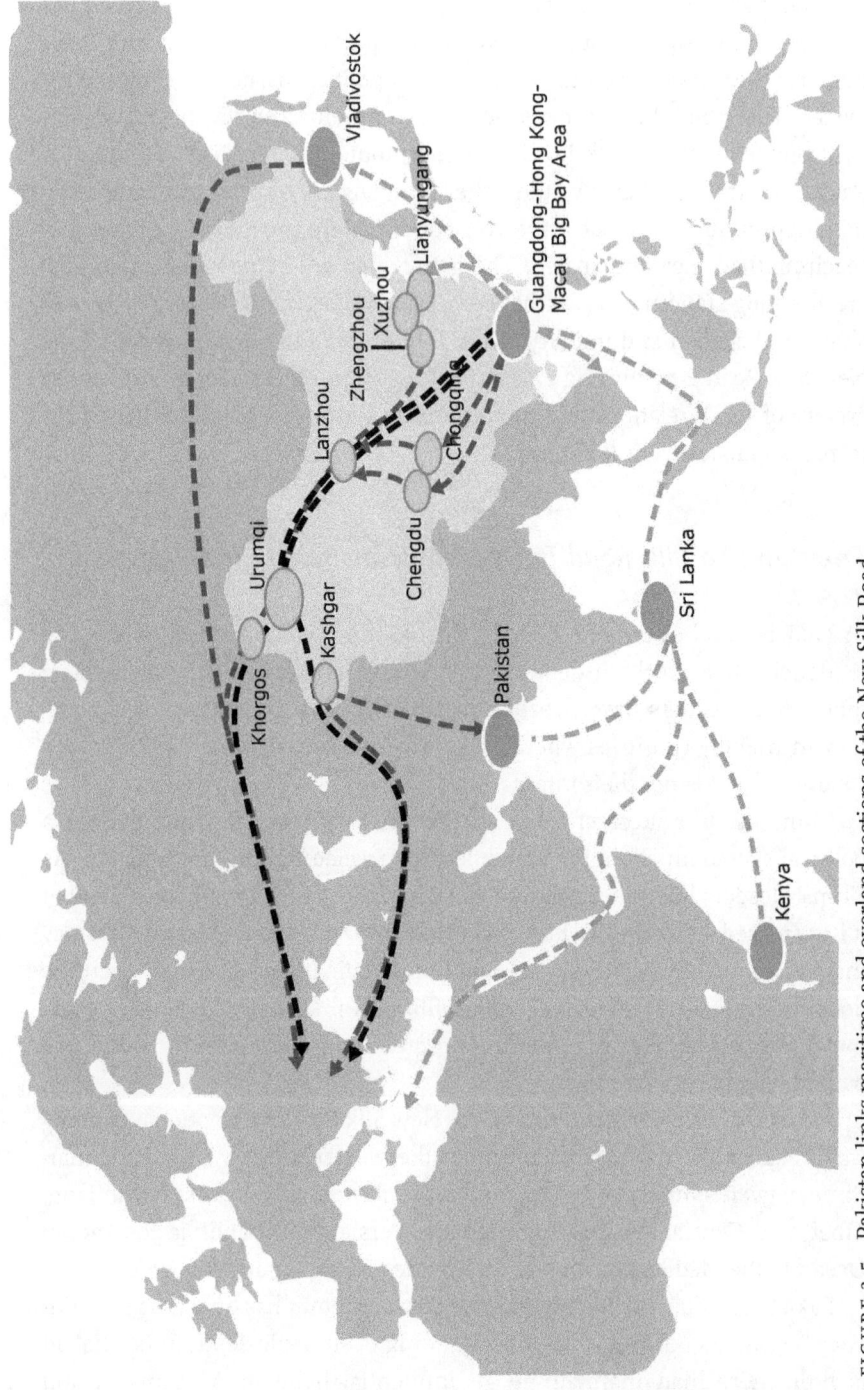

FIGURE 3.5. Pakistan links maritime and overland sections of the New Silk Road. *Hong Kong Trade Development Council*, August 6, 2015.

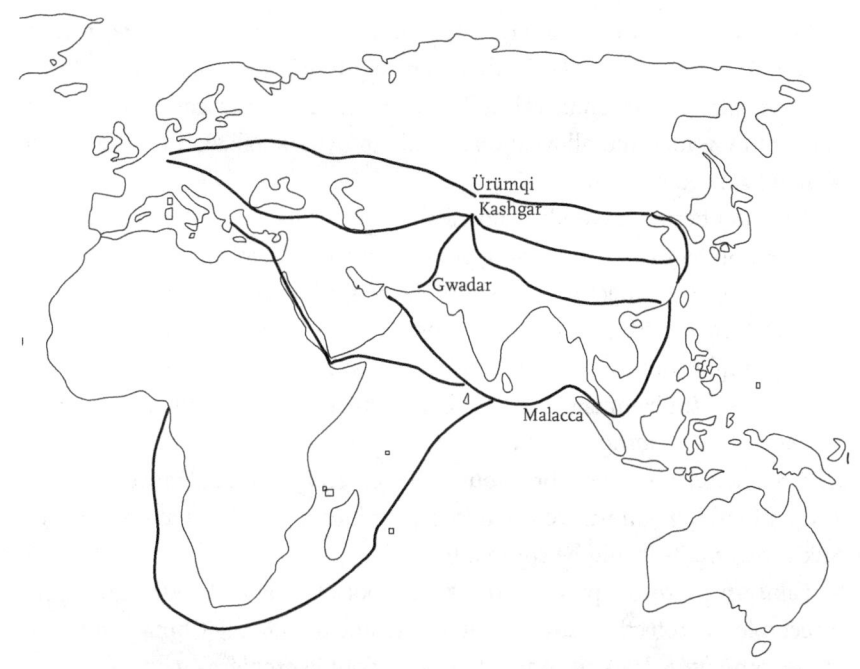

FIGURE 3.6. Xinjiang's triple junctions and the Straits of Malacca.
Author's illustration.

but its diplomatic and commercial influence lack the reaching power of China's more ambitious partners in Turkey, Indonesia, Iran, and Nigeria. Unlike Pakistan, those countries envision becoming epicenters of their own megaregions—not merely nodes and switches in multiple networks beholden to Beijing.

Pakistani leaders are far more concerned with holding the country together than projecting power beyond Afghanistan. Their sight is firmly fixed on India, and that is precisely where China would like it to remain. Together, China and Pakistan force India to split its forces in far-flung hot spots along its northern borders in Kashmir, Aksai Chin, and Arunachal Pradesh.[41] If Sino-Indian relations deteriorate in the future, China could view Gwadar and Karachi as multipurpose bases for thwarting New Delhi's dreams of becoming the dominant sea power between the Pacific and Atlantic Oceans.[42]

Iran could also connect the continental and maritime branches of the New Silk Road and provide easier access to Europe and Russia. But from China's perspective, Iran's foreign ambitions have created too many enemies among the very Middle Eastern countries that Beijing wants to cultivate as future partners. Ironically, Chinese doubts about Iran have grown since the nuclear agreement that Barack Obama championed.

Even with American-Iranian relations on constant edge, there is hope in Washington and New Delhi that Iran might offset the deepening China-Pakistan partnership. India is building a port in Chabahar Iran that can compete with Gwadar and allow Indian trade to bypass Pakistan on the way to Afghanistan, Russia, and Europe.[43]

The duel between Gwadar and Chabahar reflects an increasingly explicit competition between overlapping projects to build megaregions across Afro-Eurasia and to connect them to rival centers of power. China seeks to foil New Delhi's maritime ambitions, and there is constant speculation that Beijing might want to expand Gwadar to host its navy in the Indian Ocean. In response, India enlists Iranian help in breaking out of this perceived encirclement by opening its own sea and land links to Europe and the Middle East.[44] Encirclement and breakout, alliance and counter-alliance, flanking and outflanking—these are the underlying forces driving much of the New Silk Road and its would-be competitors.

Pakistan shares disputed borders with both China and India, giving it a direct role in protecting Chinese territories and distracting China's adversary at the same time. Iran, in contrast, poses a double problem—consolidating a separate sphere of influence that frightens its influential neighbors and trying to cut side deals with India that aim to slow the Silk Road's momentum.[45] In this context, China predictably maintains cooler ties with Iran—whose transnational options are growing—while wading deeper into neighboring Pakistan, which stays riveted on the common foe to the south.[46]

Strategic Investments in Power and Water

Chinese investment in Pakistan is unusual in several ways. Beijing often increases direct investment to help offset growing trade imbalances with countries that buy far more from China than they export. In Pakistan, however, Chinese investment is surging ahead of trade instead of trailing it (Figure 3.7 and Figure 3.8). Sino-Pakistani trade is still quite modest compared to Indonesia and Nigeria, for example, but Chinese investments have risen steadily in all three countries. Pakistan's most serious trade dispute with China involves domestic steel producers who complain that Chinese competitors are dumping their excess production with the connivance of both governments.[47] This has been an embarrassing accusation for the Sharif family—especially given their own large holdings in Pakistan's steel industry—but it does not sour otherwise good relations between the countries.

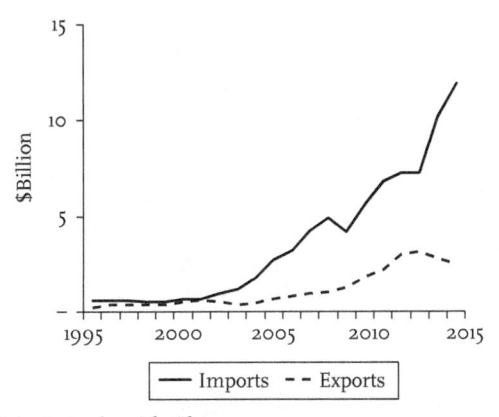

FIGURE 3.7 Pakistan's trade with China, 1995–2015.
Author's calculations of data from MIT Media Lab, "Observatory of Economic Complexity," atlas.media.mit.edu, 2017.

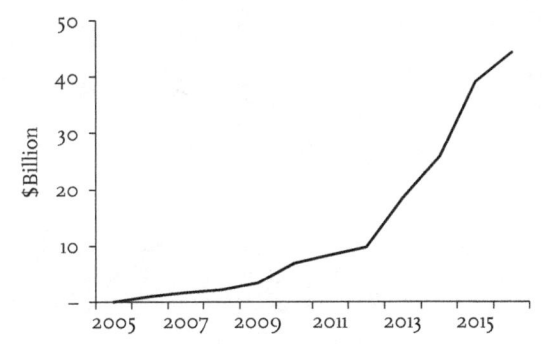

FIGURE 3.8. Cumulative Chinese investment in Pakistan, 2005–2016.
Author's calculations of data from MIT Media Lab, "Observatory of Economic Complexity," atlas.media.mit.edu, 2017.

Another striking feature of China's investments in Pakistan is that capital outlays are tightly bundled in very large projects targeting energy production, particularly dams and hydroelectric plants (Table 3.3). Since 2010, nearly two-thirds of China's biggest investments have gone to the energy sector, and about one-third of them have exceeded $2 billion dollars.

The largest amount went for expansion of the nuclear power facility in Karachi—a project that China embraced soon after the United States agreed to partner with India's nuclear industry.[48] Smaller sums have been spread out among coal plants, solar farms, and wind turbines in Punjab and Sindh.[49] Some of the most celebrated and controversial ventures are led by the famous Three Gorges Corporation that built the super dam on the Yangtze River.

TABLE 3.3 China's largest investments in Pakistan, 2005–2016, projects worth $1 billion or more

YEAR	CHINESE ENTITY	$MILLIONS	PARTY	SECTOR	SUBSECTOR
2010	Sinomach and Gezhouba	$2,690		Energy	Hydro
2013	China National Nuclear	$6,500		Energy	
2013	Three Gorges	$1,650		Energy	Hydro
2014	Sinomach	$1,990		Energy	Coal
2014	Power Construction Corp	$1,300	Oracle	Energy	Coal
2014	Sinomach	$1,130	Sindh Eng	Energy	Coal
2015	State Construction Engineering	$2,890		Transport	Autos
2015	Huaneng, Shandong RuYi	$1,810		Energy	Coal
2015	Zhuhai Port, State Const Eng	$1,620		Transport	Shipping
2015	China Railway, Norinco	$1,460		Transport	Rail
2015	China Railway Construction	$1,460	Z Khan Bros	Transport	Autos
2015	ZTE	$1,440		Energy	Alternative
2015	Power Construction Corp	$1,070	Al Mirqab Cap	Energy	Coal
2015	China Comm Construction	$1,040		Transport	Autos
2016	Three Gorges	$2,400		Energy	Hydro
2016	State Power Investment	$1,770	Abraaj	Energy	
	Total	**$44,400**			
	$1–2 B	$17,740			
	$2 B+	$14,480			
	Energy	$29,470			
	Transport	$11,500			

Author's calculations of data from American Enterprise Institute, "China Global Investment Tracker," *aei.org*, 2017.

Two dam complexes have generated particularly bitter exchanges with Indian observers who accuse Beijing and Islamabad of teaming up to dominate Himalayan water resources. The Karot hydropower project on the Jhelum River in northern Punjab challenges India's claim that it can divert headwaters located in the Indian-administered section of Kashmir.[50] Even more contentious is the Diamer-Bhasha Dam on the upper Indus River in Gilgit-Baltistan, which India continues to regard as disputed territory.[51] The World Bank and the Asian Development Bank long opposed the project, citing a combination of political and environmental reservations. China pledged about $12 billion to begin its construction and a total of $50 billion for a wider network of five dams in various parts of K-P known as the North Indus River Cascade.[52] If these dams are completed, their cost alone would equal the entire sum originally earmarked for all CPEC projects.[53]

China's experiences in Pakistan resonate in many other countries as well. All along the New Silk Road, prospects of economic development and social change are stirring political rivalries with remarkable speed and intensity. Chinese planners and their local partners are constantly confronted with organized protests and insistent demands for greater inclusiveness and transparency. Time and again, they are stunned by the rapid spread of information, the increasing ease of collective action, and the staying power of determined constituencies. Trying to adapt to these pressures creates a near permanent state of crisis management where information is never adequate and consensus seems beyond reach. In Pakistan and elsewhere, these conflicts quickly attract the scrutiny of multiple audiences—throughout the Silk Road partner nation, among its neighbors and regional rivals, and, before long, in China itself where policymakers and ordinary citizens are debating the implications for domestic politics and social relations.

While grappling with these Silk Road conflicts, China's leaders might be seeing uncomfortable glimpses of their own society's future. The common themes are the speed and unpredictability of popular challenges to authority, particularly among groups that are often regarded as disorganized and disempowered. China's efforts to promote the transnational integration of new megaregions is also stoking demands for power-sharing among rival regions within the major nations along the New Silk Road. These national societies are reshaping themselves in ways that will influence the larger megaregions that Chinese initiatives are trying to construct across Afro-Eurasia. The coevolution of nations and megaregions in the making will create new incentives for fluid international alliances that China and other great powers cannot anticipate or control. The constant need for adjustment through bargaining and rebalancing that Chinese leaders face in Pakistan is becoming a familiar pattern—one they are likely to encounter repeatedly all along the Silk Road, including the evolving regions and strata of the new China.

CHAPTER 4 | Turkey
A Competing Partner

THERE IS A STRIKING mismatch between the way the world looks at Turkey and the view Turks have of themselves. Looking from afar, outsiders usually see Anatolia with a sliver of Europe attached to one corner. But when Turks survey the world, they recognize their ancestors' handiwork everywhere. They see an unbroken history of imperial, martial, and nomadic peoples who shaped Europe's balance of power system, ruled the Middle East and North Africa, and coauthored civilizations in Central Asia, India, and China.¹

No one needs to explain the Silk Road or Eurasia to Turks today whatever their age or education. In China, young people are still getting used to the terms. They often smile when hearing the catchphrases their government uses to promote such ventures, particularly One Belt, One Road (一带一路), which looks and sounds like it belongs on a big character propaganda poster. In Turkey, the same expressions can make audiences wide-eyed and filled with adventure.²

People in Turkey are convinced their destiny leads far beyond their borders. Even when paths in one direction seem blocked, they are confident that new prospects will open up somewhere else. Turkey's admiration for Europe does not preclude turning toward the Pacific if fortune beckons, especially when nationalist and ethnic sentiments magnify the attraction. For millions of Turks, the long roads eastward do not pass through foreign territory—they connect to people who are their flesh and blood on the way to the homelands of all Turks and Mongols, including vast territories they often shared with Chinese neighbors.³

In many ways, the Silk Road vocation is more attuned to Turkey's self-image than to China's. If objective measures of national power were decisive, then China's citizens should be more swept up by the prospect of projecting worldwide influence than Turkey's. Yet we see just the opposite. China has the world's largest population, the biggest cash reserves, and an arsenal of nuclear weapons. But its people are quite comfortable with the knowledge of their cultural superiority and satisfied to manage for themselves. Meanwhile, Turkey—a splintered society fighting for its life in a region ablaze—is filled with dreams of distant horizons.

This anomaly helps to explain why even as Turkey and China draw closer their relations are jolted by repeated flare-ups of anger and recrimination. In Silk Road matters—as in most others—China is looking for partners, not rivals. But, in the case of Turkey, it has found both.

Fluid Frontiers and Nationalist Mythologies

Memories of the long history of Sino-Turkish conflict and mutual borrowing are engrained in the self-images of these modern nations. Chinese built the Great Wall to parry incursions by nomadic ancestors of the Turks and Mongols.[4] For centuries, both sides struggled over sparse lands shared by pastoral and settled peoples that neither could safely hold. Across the Ordos plateau—the arid transition zone just below the northern loop of the Yellow River—the legions of khans and emperors destroyed one another in ever greater and more futile campaigns.[5] Even today, Chinese express sorrow but little surprise when they learn that *ordu* is the Turkish word for army.

Year by year, as China absorbs its borderlands physically and socially, it also incorporates them more deeply into its history and psyche. Implacable dichotomies of civilized and barbarian are giving way to blurred notions of familiar strangers and cousins with mixed blood. Chinese are becoming accustomed to a more favorable view of the borderlands and their diverse peoples in fashioning the cosmopolitan civilization they share today.[6]

Chinese historians more frequently acknowledge the importance of non-Han leaders who aided embattled emperors against common enemies and internal rebellions. Well-known marriages between rival realms are often recast as political alliances instead of as acts of submission or hostage taking.[7] Paying tribute—once considered the hallmark of subordination to Chinese supremacy—has been reinterpreted as mutually negotiated exchanges, including officially forbidden commerce and thinly disguised protection money to pay off supposed vassals. In this portrayal, the tribute system was carefully designed by Chinese and barbarians alike to carry mixed messages for different audiences, a diplomatic sleight of hand that court-appointed chroniclers intentionally misrepresented in order to exaggerate imperial power.[8]

Chinese historians increasingly regard the Yuan reign as a Chinese dynasty instead of a Mongol occupation. Kublai Khan and his cohorts brought thousands of Muslims to China from Central Asia, including many Turkic groups, who served as junior partners in governing indigenous Han society. Generations of their descendants intermarried with the Han to form the Hui Muslim minority that speaks Chinese as its native language and lives very much like its Han relatives and neighbors.[9]

For today's China, the Mongols symbolize manifest destiny—a natural projection of transcontinental power for the biggest and richest nation not just in Asia, but in the entire hemisphere. Similarly, celebrating the legendary Muslim admiral, Zheng He, recalls the voyages of his Ming-era armadas to India, the Persian Gulf, and Africa.[10] The current cult of Zheng He foreshadows China's rebirth as a maritime nation with a blue water navy at the same time it highlights the unbroken bond that patriotic, Chinese Islam nurtures with Muslims the world over. Sino-Islamic Silk Roads by land and sea—a new vision for the Old World, reclaiming its historic place as the center of civilization after a long detour through Western hegemony.

Meanwhile, in Turkey, Asian history is recast so that Turks and Chinese can share heroic encounters that were traditionally seen as tales of everlasting enmity. For example, Timur—also known as Tamerlane—is lauded as a scion of Genghis who marched his armies across the Middle East and taught humility to the Ottoman upstart, Beyazit, by imprisoning him in his own Anatolian headquarters.[11] A Turkish diplomat once explained the lesson in contemporary geopolitical terms. In his view, Beyazit was so busy conquering European territories surrounding Constantinople that he discounted looming dangers in the east. Timur's long march was a stunning reminder of the ever-present might of Inner Asia that no Turkish ruler could ignore, then or now.[12]

Popular culture in Turkey and China carries a common fascination for the wolf as a symbol of innate courage and communal solidarity that every nation needs to survive. But in each society the wolf totem resonates with different meanings—inspiring pride and boldness among Turks as opposed to envy and self-doubt for more introspective Chinese. Many Turkish nationalists see themselves as gray wolves who have the right stuff to lead and win against all odds.[13] In China, nationalists—including ethnocentric and hard-line types—often exhort Han Chinese to put aside sheepish instincts and to cultivate the bravery they attribute to pastoral cultures of the frontier.[14]

Sparring over Central Asia

As a less sheepish China moves westward, it encounters many breeds of wolves whose tracks lead from Kashgar and Tashkent all the way to Ankara. Once again, Turkish and Chinese leaders are busily crafting multilayered bargains—privately and in public—they want to interpret differently for their citizens and for audiences around the world.[15]

Turkey and China are giving one another more and more headaches as they strengthen their connections. Turkey is far too strong and willful to enter into tributary-like exchanges resembling the current flow of Sino-Pakistani relations. Turkish politicians—thoroughly adept at scrambling their own economic plans and constitutional arrangements—would reject even a fraction of the tutelage that Beijing is practicing in Islamabad. This makes life especially difficult for Chinese and Turkish diplomats whose considerable skills are stretched by embarrassing public flare-ups over Xinjiang that threaten both side's long-term goals of hemispheric integration.

Things might have turned out much worse if Turkish politicians had insisted on filling the supposed vacuum in Central Asia after the Soviet Union's collapse. During the 1990s, Turgut Özal (1989–1993) and Süleyman Demirel (1993–2000) held the presidency while nationalist and religious parties took turns joining and breaking coalition governments. Both presidents encouraged right-wing parties, eager to spread Turkey's influence eastward through appeals to Turkic and Islamic solidarity.[16] Their campaigns were crippled by a double miscalculation—overestimating the receptivity of Central Asian audiences and underestimating China's determination to push back.

Deeply suspicious of Ankara's pan-Turkist and pan-Islamic rhetoric, Beijing believed it was facing a direct challenge to its domestic security in Xinjiang and beyond. Finding exuberant Turkish leaders deaf to its protests, China decided to show it could create trouble on Turkey's doorstep from several directions at once.

In quick succession, many of Turkey's oldest enemies suddenly became China's friends. Beijing offered loans for port expansions in Greece and weapons for the Greek-dominated government of Cyprus. China gave diplomatic cover for Kurdish groups that Turkey wanted the United Nations to label as terrorists, and it supported Serbia in its battles against Bosnian Muslims and NATO.[17] China was located at the other end of Asia, but was lighting fires that menaced Turkey on all corners.

Turkish leaders, already disappointed with the tepid welcome they were receiving in the former Soviet republics, gradually scaled back their Central Asian expectations. Instead of pushing a broad transnational agenda all the way to China's borders, they settled for more modest goals closer to home around the Caspian Sea and Caucasia. Kazakhstan, Turkmenistan, and Azerbaijan occupied most of Ankara's attention, leaving the rest of Central Asia firmly under Russian and Chinese influence.[18]

China and Turkey had a common interest in new Caspian energy resources that offered some relief from dependence on the Persian Gulf and Russia. Turkey wanted to host gas and oil pipelines to European markets, and China financed the eastward routes through Central Asia to Xinjiang and the Pacific coast. Together, they opened the way for a transcontinental energy network crossing the Russian-controlled north-south routes that had monopolized Caspian trade flows for decades.[19]

China's Turks, Turkey's Kin

By the time the Justice and Development Party came to power in 2000, Turkey had turned the corner from competing with China to seeking its economic and diplomatic help. Under Ahmet Davutoğlu, the academic strategist who eventually rose to foreign minister and prime minister, Turkey tried to project influence in so many directions that Central Asia seemed like an afterthought. Intent on placing Turkey at the center of great power bargaining, Davutoğlu saw Chinese friendship as a potential counter to Western and Russian habits of dismissing Turkish views.[20]

Davutoğlu's approach had strong backing from Abdullah Gül, who spent years pitching commercial and investment deals to Beijing as prime minister and, after 2007, as president. By June 2009, the turnaround seemed complete. Turkish diplomats were routinely affirming the One China policy, and Gül made a historic state visit to China, including a special stopover in Ürümqi where he proclaimed Xinjiang a "bridge of friendship" between Turkey and China.[21]

A week later Ürümqi exploded. The interracial riots and bloodshed sent shockwaves from Beijing to Ankara—quickly followed by an equally unanticipated jolt from Turkey's prime minister, Recep Tayyip Erdoğan, who accused the Chinese of genocide and vowed to censure them in the United Nations.[22] Just when all seemed lost, Davutoğlu and Gül teamed up once again, determined to rescue the package of agreements that had taken so many years to put together.

To nearly universal amazement, they succeeded. Within a matter of months, Erdoğan cooled off, the Chinese stuck by their contracts, and the diplomats were back at the table looking over new deals. By September 2010—a mere 14 months after the Ürümqi riots—Chinese and Turkish military jets were flying together over Konya.[23] It was the first appearance of China's air force in a foreign country and a seemingly inconceivable breach of NATO norms. The exercise was supposed to include the United States and Israel, but Turkey's running arguments with both countries upended the schedule and China stepped in as a last-minute substitute.[24]

As Erdoğan saw the growing benefits of Chinese friendship, he began to speak openly about joining the Shanghai Cooperation Organization, the China-led treaty group that is often billed as a budding Asian counterpart to NATO. At first, he claimed he was only joking—just teasing Putin who loved to scold him for caving into the Americans and getting nothing in return.[25] But the more Erdoğan pondered the idea, the more he liked it. By 2016, when Pakistan, India, and Iran were in line for membership, Turkey seemed like a natural nominee, particularly after the European Union again suspended deliberations on Ankara's long-stalled application.[26]

The resilience of Sino-Turkish cooperation stems, in large part, from mutual concessions they made over festering disputes in Xinjiang before and after the Ürümqi crisis. Turkey expelled Uyghur nationalist leaders it had harbored for many years, forcing their groups to relocate in Europe and the United States. China, in turn, agreed to regular meetings with Turkish politicians in Ankara, including opposition parties that championed pan-Turkic and Uyghur causes.[27]

For China, this was an exceptional concession that could only be justified by exceptional interests. It amounted to a tacit agreement to discuss questions of domestic security and minorities policy with foreigners. This was not a move the Chinese advertised, and they had no intention of replicating it elsewhere.

Neither side gained much of substance from the closed-door meetings. The Turkish nationalists would hold press conferences to boast about giving the Chinese another dressing-down, and the government would deny it had sold out the Uyghurs for foreign cash. Afterward, Chinese spokesmen would try to correct the record of who said what, but they were always embarrassed to admit there was a meeting in the first place.[28]

Meanwhile, Xinjiang kept reeling from bloody clashes between angry Uyghurs and heavily armed security forces. The violence spread beyond Xinjiang to Kunming in southern Yunnan province and to the eastern cities. Beijing responded with even stronger repression and hated restrictions on routine religious practice, prompting more and more people to flee the province and the country.[29]

By 2015, thousands of Uyghurs were flowing into Thailand and Malaysia, seeking asylum or safe passage to Turkey. China insisted they be repatriated to stand trial for terrorism.[30] Turkey declared them victims of religious and racial persecution who required protection under international humanitarian law. Beijing accused Ankara of handing out Turkish passports to fugitive criminals. Ankara claimed they were entitled to Turkish citizenship even though most had never set foot outside of China.[31]

Trapped in the middle, Thai and Malaysian authorities cut the baby in half—dispatching large groups to China and Turkey after hasty determinations of their citizenship and refugee status.[32] Throughout this melodrama, more and more Uyghur fighters were turning up in Syria and Iraq. Beijing claimed that many of them eventually made their way back to Xinjiang, fueling wider insurrection and refugee flows.[33]

Chinese and Turkish leaders tacitly admitted that, because of their fumbling responses to Uyghur unrest, both countries were jeopardizing their own safety. They could join in a common vocation to remake Eurasia, but they could not stop undercutting one another at home, deliberately in some cases and indirectly in others.

Erdoğan's Shrinking Base

Xinjiang is just one of many contradictions running through China's relations with Turkey. In the long run, the most serious tensions arise from economic and geopolitical issues—the same type of interests that have brought Beijing and Ankara together in recent decades.

For Turkey, the biggest irritant is the huge trade deficit in China's favor.[34] Both sides know the gap can only narrow if China agrees to vastly expand Turkish manufacturing and its exports of finished goods. Turkey wants to become a preeminent export platform for international firms seeking easy access to markets in Europe, Africa, and the Middle East. China is scouting several candidates for exactly such a role.[35]

China is a unique investor in many ways but, in the end, it calculates risk just like anyone else. Beijing has the funds and know-how Turkey needs and the means to deliver with unbeatable terms. China also has sound reason to take a measured gamble when long-term prospects and political side benefits merit. After all, that is what the New Silk Road is all about.

Nonetheless, the Turkish wildcard looks risker than ever. Erdoğan is shaking the rafters at home, and his dance with Putin and Trump has everyone off balance, China included.[36] Erdoğan is trying to concentrate greater powers in his own hands at the same time that his popular support is contracting to a narrower portion of the electorate. His margin of victory in the 2017 constitutional referendum is much too weak to support the sweeping grants of authority in question. The ruling party's constituency has shrunk not just numerically, but socially and geographically as well (Figure 4.1 and Figure 4.2). Erdoğan's core of support is confined to the interior provinces of Central Anatolia and the Black Sea, particularly the more rural districts. In Central Anatolia, his referendum succeeded in every province except industrialized Ankara and Eskişehir. Along the Black Sea, it prevailed everywhere except in the labor stronghold of Zonguldak and the ethnically mixed eastern province of Artvin.

In contrast, Erdoğan's bid was firmly rejected across the most developed and urbanized districts of western Turkey—the Marmara, the Aegean, and Mediterranean regions. A handful of inland provinces narrowly supported the measure, but the coastal areas uniformly opposed it. In eastern Turkey, voting mirrored the local divisions between Kurdish and Turkish settlements. The higher the proportion of Kurdish residents, the greater the margin of defeat for the referendum. The nine provinces of southeastern Turkey solidly voted no. Thus, the richest and poorest regions—ethnically diverse border areas with strong ties to neighboring countries—joined in resisting the ruling party's thinning base in the predominantly Turkish-speaking towns and villages of Anatolia's heartland.

Turkey's growing divisions make Beijing pause and think hard about committing Pakistan-style resources to a distant and pro-Western country. From China's perspective, there is no compelling case for raising relations with Turkey to such a favored level. Many of Turkey's apparent attractions can also be seen as reasons to stay away or simply preserve the status quo.

Turkish manufacturers are already quite experienced and well connected. They have powerful trade associations that can drive hard bargains to guard markets and supply chains they have built over several generations. Their political clout allows them to be just as tenacious as the Chinese themselves in limiting access to the national economy.[37]

Turkey's workforce is educated and filled with veterans of European industry. But it is densely unionized in parallel labor movements with alliances to rival political parties. Turkish unions are weaker now than in their heydays

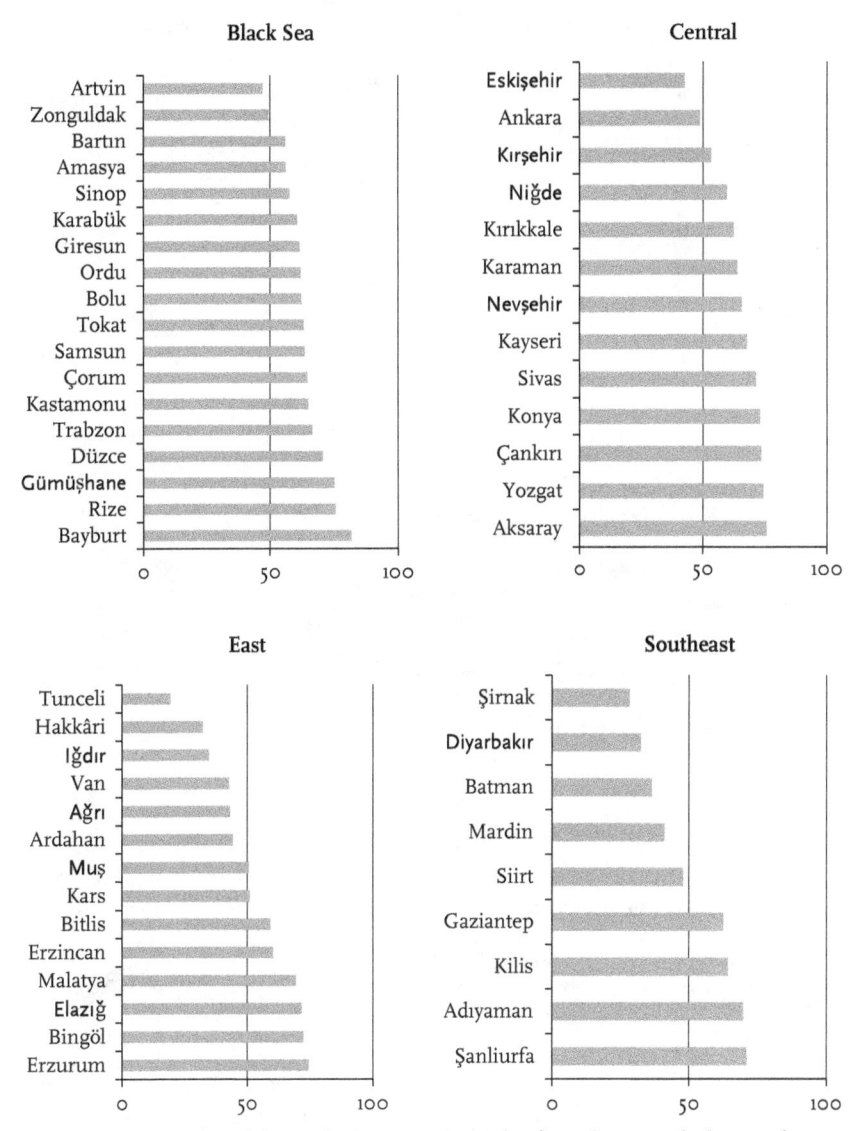

FIGURE 4.1. Results of the Turkish constitutional referendum April 16, 2017, by region and province (percent voting "yes").
Author's calculations of data from "Türkiye'nin Kararı" (Turkey's Decision), *CNN Türk*, April 19, 2017, http://www.cnnturk.com/referandum-2017.

30 years ago, but the core of foreign-employed workers is as militant and nationalist as ever.[38]

The Turkish market is dominated by young consumers with an eye for fashion and gadgets that matches their counterparts in China. Youthful Turks—particularly university students—are also highly suspicious of

TURKEY: A COMPETING PARTNER | 57

Mediterranean

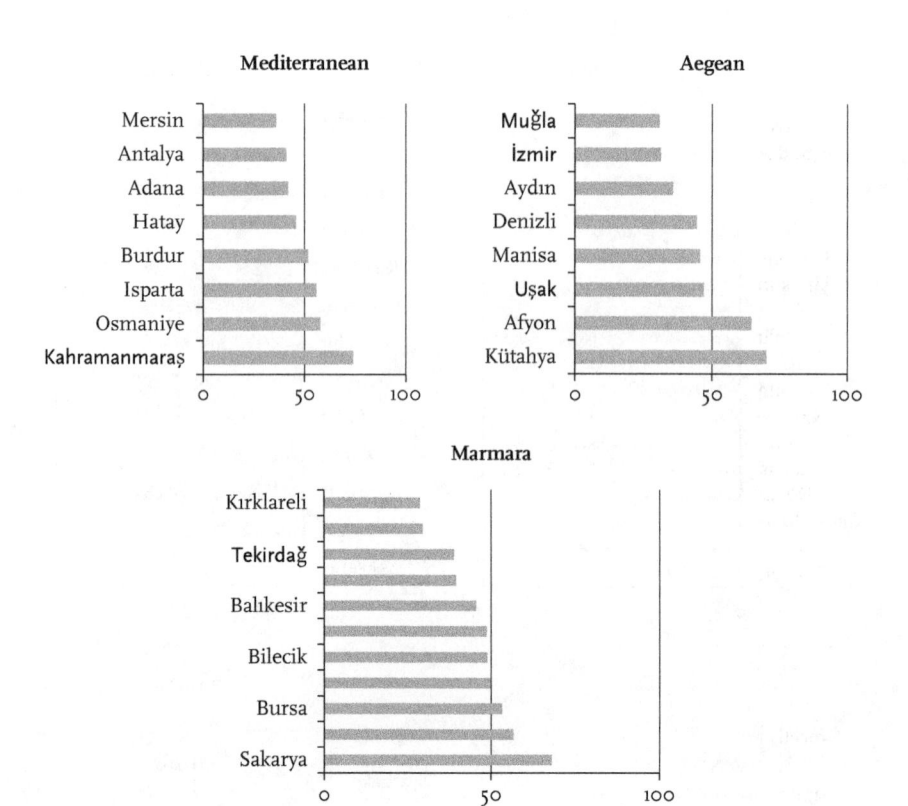

- Mersin
- Antalya
- Adana
- Hatay
- Burdur
- Isparta
- Osmaniye
- Kahramanmaraş

Aegean

- Muğla
- İzmir
- Aydın
- Denizli
- Manisa
- Uşak
- Afyon
- Kütahya

Marmara

- Kırklareli
- Tekirdağ
- Balıkesir
- Bilecik
- Bursa
- Sakarya

FIGURE 4.1. Continued

FIGURE 4.2. Provincial distribution of votes in the Turkish constitutional referendum, 2017.
Y indicates 50 percent or more voting "yes", N indicates 50 percent or more voting "no"
Author's calculations of data from "Türkiye'nin Kararı" (Turkey's Decision), *CNN Türk*, April 19, 2017.

foreigners who want to profit from their country and influence its policies. Again, the similarities to China are uncanny—every political faction is filled with former student leaders who cut their teeth in demonstrations with anti-imperialist themes.[39]

Turkey's diplomats are as skilled and polished as any team China can field. They pride themselves on being able to think on several levels at once—imperial, European, Third World, and Eurasian. The top ranks are filled with economics and international relations specialists who move freely between government service, journalism, and university life.[40] Viewing themselves more as intellectuals than bureaucrats, they are more than ready to lock horns with the most overbearing negotiators Beijing wants to dispatch.

Then, there is the Turkish military to consider. Guardians of NATO's advanced weaponry who are split between old Kemalists and new Islamists, Turkey's officer corps would always remain an enigma to Beijing. Erdoğan's politically motivated purges of the armed forces might curb endemic cliques and conspiracies—or drive them further underground, creating greater dangers in the long run.[41]

As China weighs the case for Turkish membership in the Shanghai Cooperation Organization, it must ask the same questions that have paralyzed the European Union. Is Turkey so big, so strong, and so unpredictable that full membership would turn the club upside down instead of bolstering it?[42] If so, then perhaps the best course would be to grant Turkey some kind of special status that lets it operate as everyone's quasi-ally—a free radical that is useful for creating megaregions everywhere, but not particularly reliable in guaranteeing security for any of them.

Chinese Investments and Turkey's Eurasianists

For more than a decade, Turkey has had a widening imbalance of trade with China. In 2015, Turkey's total trade deficit was about $34 billion, and with China alone it reached nearly $22 billion (Figure 4.3). Repeated requests for China to invest more in Turkish infrastructure and manufacturing have yielded only modest success. Cumulative Chinese investments totaled just under $13 billion, and about half of that went to coal power plants (Figure 4.4 and Table 4.1).

Turkish governments have rolled out several grand projects with transnational political implications only to see them flounder in bickering over permits and financing. China agreed to finance part of a nuclear power facility in European Turkey, but there is no firm timeline for construction.[43]

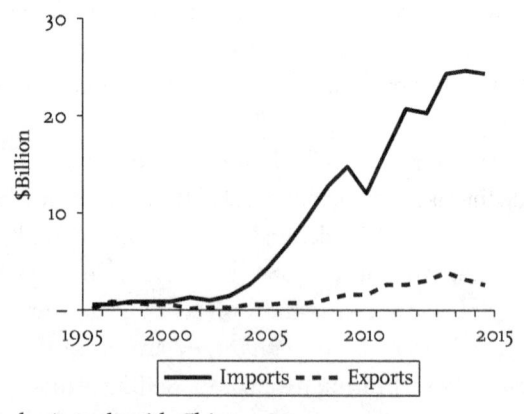

FIGURE 4.3. Turkey's trade with China, 1995–2015.
Author's calculations of data from MIT Media Lab, "Observatory of Economic Complexity," *atlas.media.mit.edu*, 2017.

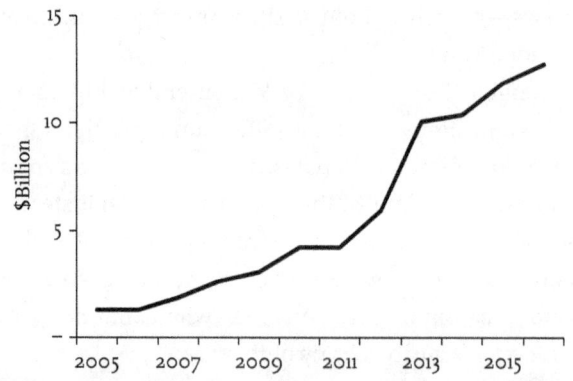

FIGURE 4.4. Cumulative Chinese investment in Turkey, 2005–2016.
Author's calculations of data from American Enterprise Institute, "China Global Investment Tracker," *aei.org*, 2017.

Similar delays hamper the Trans-Caspian energy corridor for carrying Turkmen gas across Azerbaijan and into Europe.[44] A planned purchase of Chinese missile defense systems was abruptly cancelled when angry NATO officials intervened.[45]

In the meantime, China and Turkey have struck many small deals hoping to create at least the appearance of momentum and growing cooperation. Turkey is giving Chinese investors special treatment in telecommunications, real estate, and banking, hoping to pave the way for bigger outlays in infrastructure and industry.[46] China is the prospective leader in most of the grand transport projects linking Europe and Central Asia. Chinese shippers have purchased the Kumport container hub west of Istanbul.[47] The Bank of China

TABLE 4.1 China's largest investments in Turkey, 2005–2016, projects worth $1 billion or more

YEAR	CHINESE ENTITY	$MILLS	PARTY	SECTOR	SUBSECTOR
2005	China Railway, Genertec	$1,270	Cengiz, IC Ictas	Transport	Rail
2013	Harbin Electric	$2,400	Hattat Holding	Energy	Coal
2013	China Natl Chemical Eng	$1,100	Ciner Holding	Chemicals	
	Total	**$12,750**			
	$1–2 B	$2,370			
	$2 B+	$2,400			
	Coal	$5,280			

Author's calculations of data from American Enterprise Institute, "China Global Investment Tracker," *aei.org*, 2017.

is helping to finance the $10 billion Kanal Istanbul waterway as an alternative to the overcrowded Bosporus Straits for connecting the Black Sea and the Sea of Marmara.[48] Chinese firms also want to extend the high-speed rail line currently linking Ankara and Istanbul so that it spans the entire country from Edirne to Kars.[49]

The political backdrop for Sino-Turkish collaboration is constantly shifting and often precarious. Erdoğan is not the first Turkish leader to clash with Washington, Moscow, Beijing, Brussels, and Berlin, but he stands out for taking on all of the great powers in rapid succession. Since the failed coup of 2015 and the deepening American alliance with Kurdish forces in Syria and Iraq, there has been wide speculation about the influence of a so-called Eurasianist faction in Erdoğan's inner circle.[50] Responding to Turkey's alienation from Europe and the United States, these voices are pressing for open alignment with Russia and China both economically and politically. These Eurasian advocates cover the spectrum from far left to far right, expressing familiar anti-Western views that have come and gone many times. Few of them are rooted in the ruling party's core constituency of business leaders and pious voters in Central Anatolia. They are unlikely candidates for a stable coalition of foreign policymakers in any government, particularly under such an independent leader as President Erdoğan.

China's predicament in Turkey arises from the need to deal with a fragmenting nation that is shared by three disjointed societies—each pulling in a different direction internationally and culturally. The ruling party's base in Central Anatolia and the Black Sea stresses Islamic and Turkic connections. The more Europeanized coasts and Western regions look instead toward the Mediterranean and the Atlantic. The Kurds of the southeast are in open revolt, wavering between demands for federalism and for a separate nation that would include lands in neighboring Middle Eastern states.

Even as Erdoğan tries to monopolize power, his party's coalition is splintering around him. The Black Sea is a patchwork of feuding towns along the coast—more tied to one another than to the isolated villages of their mountain hinterlands. Central Anatolia is divided among at least a dozen fast-growing cities flush with export earnings and a shrinking rural population that survives on repatriated savings from foreign workers. Overall, Turkey is more integrated than ever with global markets, but less coherent as a national community. It engages more freely with all the great powers, yet finds no stable alliances with any of them.

CHAPTER 5 | Indonesia

Inherent Weakness and Increasing Leverage

INDONESIA IS A COUNTRY on the rise, pulling itself together as an archipelago nation and gaining an important voice in Asia and the world. Its progress meets many external cross-pressures, forcing its leaders to tack toward one side and then another instead of forging ahead in a straight line. The maneuvering aims to reduce head-on resistance from outsiders, but it also puts added stress on cracks within—fissures of race, class, and religion that have shaken Indonesia many times in the recent past.

More than any other country, China has been the greatest stimulant to Indonesia's ascent and the worst irritant to its internal divisions. For centuries, Indonesia has occupied many crossroads at once.[1] Today, these junctures are more crucial than ever as we appreciate their role in sustaining global commerce and, potentially, in tilting the world toward war or peace. Westerners have wide experience in helping to shape Indonesian society and its relations with other countries. But the Chinese have been there longer, their roots are deeper, and their current influence is more powerful than any would-be rival's.[2]

Of course, Indonesians understand that in dealings with China—as with all nations—power and dependence run both ways. In this relationship, reciprocity is especially salient precisely because Indonesian nationalists believe that China already threatened their newly won independence in the days of Sukarno. Deterring similar adventures seems all the more urgent as both countries gain strength and self-confidence.

This places China in an awkward position where the appearance of dominance can repel rather than attract. Chinese bluster might earn grudging respect from great powers and waves of fear from small neighbors. But, in

Indonesia, the instinctive reaction is to push back, and the first target is usually the most vulnerable—the ethnic minority with ancestral roots and extensive business ties to the Chinese mainland.[3]

The overlap of Islamic and Chinese civilizations pervades daily life throughout Southeast Asia. Each country has evolved a distinctive blend of cultures and set of mutual adaptations that respond to shifting political conditions, domestic and international.[4] In Indonesia, Chinese diplomacy makes special efforts to stress its Islam-friendly nature. Two messages are particularly important in this regard—Chinese Muslims were among the earliest founders of Islam in Indonesia, and contemporary China is a multiracial society where Muslim minorities enjoy wide freedom of religion.[5]

These are sensible and at least partly credible attempts to spread goodwill where it is sorely needed. However, such campaigns also draw the Indonesian public's attention to China's running conflicts with many of its own Muslims. Indonesian politicians are quick to bend these problems to their own competing purposes, depending on the particular mix of nationalist and religious sentiments each wants to evoke. Inevitably, they make comparisons between China's conduct toward minority Muslims and Indonesia's treatment of minority Chinese.[6]

Most of the time, Indonesian politicians invite Chinese authorities to follow Indonesia's supposedly enlightened example of protecting all citizens. But not always. There are frequent suggestions—some might regard them as threats—that bad behavior in China could trigger similar misdeeds in Indonesia. By implying that both countries are responsible for one another's extended families, they also invite the more dangerous attitude that both minorities can be regarded as hostages subject to reprisal if passions get out of hand.

Neither country benefits from playing with that sort of fire, and the distant peoples they claim to care about are the most likely to be burned. For Indonesian hardliners—nationalists and Islamists alike—there is a constant need to draw red lines that Chinese dare not cross. In their view, pluralism and tolerance should go only so far. Prominence in culture and business is one thing, but state power is a special sphere where native sons and daughters—pribumi—must remain firmly in charge.

Indonesia's dilemma is that greater prosperity and openness are erasing these red lines, but political reactionaries still gain momentum—and a measure of power—by trying to enforce them. This predicament creates endless tensions in Indonesia's relations with China and with its own traditions of Islamic modernism. For Indonesia's 200 million Muslims, coming to terms with China's rise also sharpens basic debates about religion and power—over affirming or changing the universalist views of Islam and humanity that their founding fathers embraced before and after independence.

Indigenous Chinese culture is flourishing in Indonesia. In the final days of Suharto's rule, his supporters unleashed a wave of racist attacks against Indonesians of Chinese descent, trying to scapegoat them during mass protests against corruption and economic meltdown. Soon after Suharto was gone, his discriminatory bans on Chinese culture vanished as well.

There was a steady revival of Chinese print media, schools, temples, and churches. Celebrations of the Lunar New Year and local festivals became more public and elaborate, inviting Muslim neighbors to join the crowds. Beijing donors sponsored a new mosque in Surabaya named for Admiral Zheng He (known locally as Laksamana Cheng Ho) whose crewmen were said to have founded East Java's most famous Chinese Muslim community. Indonesia eagerly promoted tourism from mainland China, offering special group packages for the holidays. Today, Indonesia is a leader in two of the world's most lucrative travel markets—Muslim pilgrimage to Saudi Arabia and Chinese tourism from all parts of Asia.[7]

Indonesian businesses with personal links to China played a more prominent role in brokering trade and investment throughout Southeast Asia. One of the most outspoken economic reformers in the governments of Susilo Bambang Yudhoyono was Mari Elka Pangestu, a woman of Chinese ancestry. She drew frequent criticism from local manufacturers and Muslim politicians who sought stronger protections for domestic industry. Nonetheless, she held her own in cabinet posts for 10 turbulent years (2004–2014) while parliamentary democracy was coming back to life.[8]

Anti-Chinese Sentiment in the Jakarta Elections

Pangestu's clashes with indigenous businesses and their political allies foreshadowed growing difficulties for Chinese Indonesians, particularly those identified with foreign interests and invested with government authority. Her battles were mild compared to the onslaught against Basuki Tjahaja Purnama, who in 2014 became the first person of Chinese descent to serve as governor of Jakarta.

In 2016, Basuki—popularly known as Ahok—faced trial for blasphemy because, during a heated election campaign, he lightheartedly suggested that the Qur'an offered no objection to Muslims voting for leaders from other faiths, including Protestant Christians like himself. The affair polarized

Muslim politicians, scattering them across the full spectrum from compassion to bigotry.

The Nahdlatul Ulama (NU), Indonesia's biggest religious organization, opposed the trial and sent youth groups to protect churches from attack over the Christmas season.[9] This shield was helpful for the towns that fell within their East Java stronghold, but Jakarta was a larger universe where every faction converged and tried to mobilize a show of force. The extremist Islamic Defenders Front (Front Pembela Islam) led many mass demonstrations demanding conviction and stronger limits on free speech.[10] On November 4, 2016, they drove a 100,000-person march through the northern and western neighborhoods of Jakarta that vandalized scores of Chinese-owned shops and homes. Many of these Chinese families had also been targeted during the race riots of 1998.[11]

Leaders of the Muhammadiya, the mass movement with the largest urban following, tried to straddle the fence, but they contradicted one another constantly.[12] Some, like former chairman Din Syamsuddin, tried to deflect discussion to economic injustices that Muslims suffered at the hands of multinational corporations and their local agents. At the same time, however, he supported hard-line declarations against Ahok from the Indonesia Ulama Council (Majelis Ulama Indonesia).[13] One of the most respected Muhammadiya elders, Ahmad Syafi'i Maarif, remained silent for months before finally declaring that Ahok had committed no offense against Muslims, but by then few were listening to calls for calm.[14]

Indonesia's president, Joko Widodo, waffled repeatedly. He defended Ahok, who had been his running mate in his 2012 campaign for governor of Jakarta. Nevertheless, Widodo attended the anti-Ahok demonstrations, sharing the stage with extremist leaders and urging the crowds to contain their anger.[15] Widodo was covering his flank against challenges from former president Yudhoyono whose son, Agus Harimurtri, was now trying to unseat Ahok as Jakarta's governor. The Yudhoyonos denied any connection to the religious radicals, but Widodo was certain he needed to tread carefully among multiple threats that could turn against him next.[16]

Ahok lost the election by a wide margin—not to Agus, but to a fellow member of Widodo's own coalition who appealed to middle class Muslims in Jakarta's newer residential districts. Anies Baswedan had advised Widodo during his presidential campaign and then served as his Minister of Education of Culture. He was a leader of a new Islamic party, the Justice and Prosperity Party (Partai Keadilan dan Sejahtera, PKS), which tried to position itself near the middle of the seven parties that explicitly vied for Muslim votes. Anies's strategy was to market himself as a pro-Muslim spokesman

TABLE 5.1 Results of the Jakarta gubernatorial elections by regency (*kabupaten*), round 1 February 15, 2017, and round 2 April 19, 2017

REGENCY	ROUND 1 BASUKI	ROUND 1 ANIES	ROUND 1 AGUS	ROUND 2 ANIES	ROUND 2 BASUKI
Total Jakarta	44.47	39.20	16.34	57.95	42.05
South Jakarta	39.42	46.71	13.87	62.13	37.87
Thousand Islands	38.76	33.98	27.26	62.00	38.00
East Jakarta	38.81	41.76	19.42	61.84	38.16
Central Jakarta	42.99	39.14	17.87	57.72	42.28
West Jakarta	52.31	33.61	14.07	52.83	47.17
North Jakarta	53.66	31.02	15.32	52.74	47.26

Author's calculations of data from Komisi Pemilihan Umum, *Pilkada Provinsi DKI Jakarta*, pilkada2017.kpu.go.id, April 25, 2017.

who could finesse long-simmering controversies over how Indonesians should deal with Islamic law. He tried to carve out a special niche between older groups who adhered to Indonesia's pluralist doctrine of Pancasila and more radical factions who were calling for the sharia to become part of the nation's constitution.[17]

Anies argued that Muslim leaders should focus on mass religious education (*dakwah*) in order to create a more Islamic society. In theory, as Indonesian Muslims became more observant and knowledgeable, they would naturally introduce Islamic principles into their legislation.[18] In this way, Anies sought to win the support of hard-line voters without endorsing their demands for an Islamic state. In the post-Suharto era of decentralized government, this approach left ample room for Muslim politicians to adapt their messages to local campaigns where party loyalties were weak and public opinion was constantly shifting.[19]

Anies's maneuvers earned him a crushing victory over Ahok in the second round of the governor's race (Table 5.1).[20] Anies won big majorities in the newer residential neighborhoods of South and East Jakarta, but in the runoff election he also inherited virtually all of Agus's first-round supporters, including the militant marchers who accused Ahok of blasphemy (Figure 5.1).[21] In the first round, Ahok and Anies ran neck and neck across South and East Jakarta, but in the runoff election Anies swept all of these districts by a wide margin.

In contrast, Ahok's second-round performance hardly changed at all—his vote clustered in the poorer, flood-prone districts of North and West Jakarta where many Chinese-owned businesses had been looted during previous

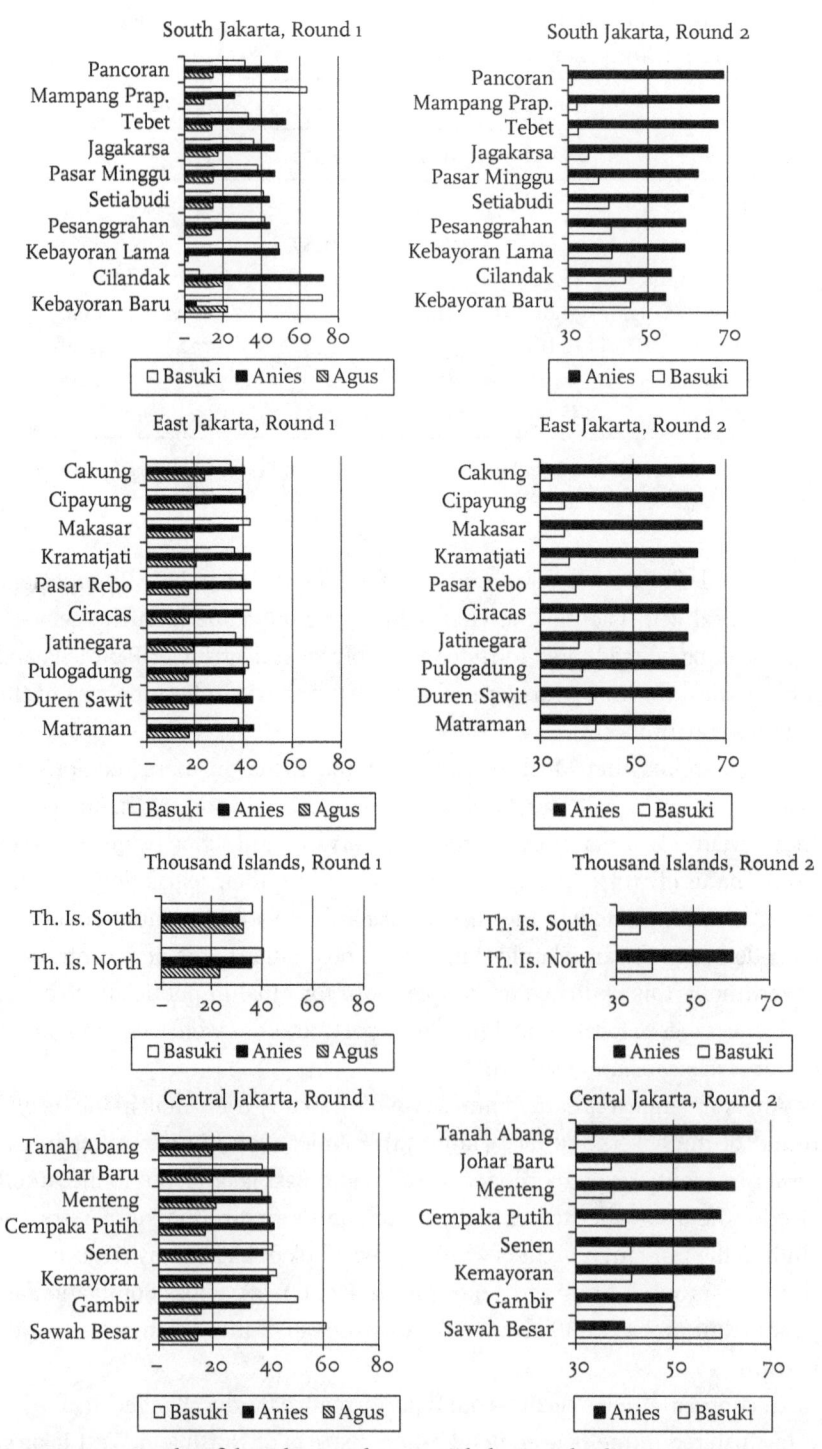

FIGURE 5.1. Results of the Jakarta gubernatorial elections by district (*Kecamatan*), round 1 February 15, 2017, and round 2 April 19, 2017.

Author's calculations of data from Komisi Pemilihan Umum, *Pilkada Provinsi DKI Jakarta*, pilkada2017.kpu.go.id, April 25, 2017.

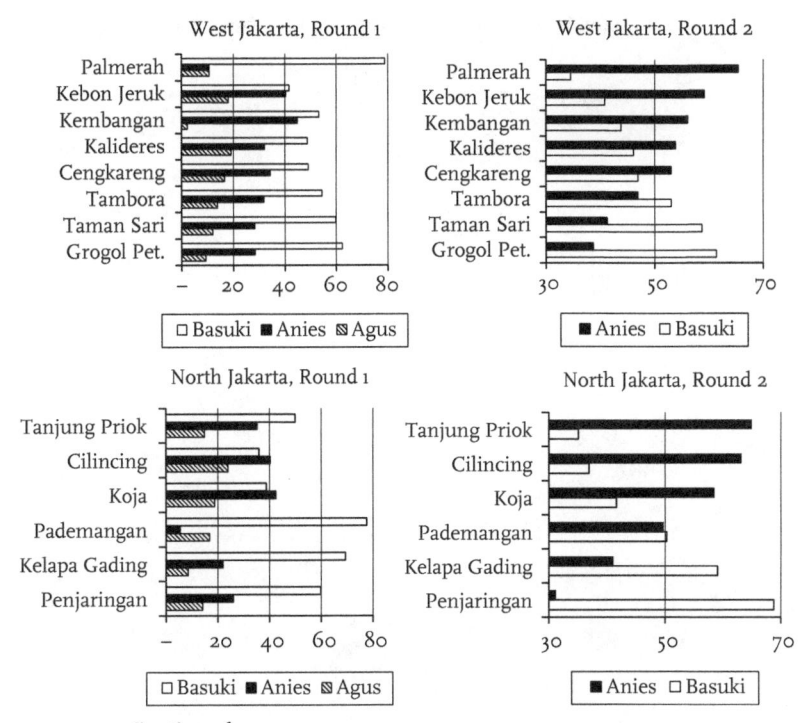

FIGURE 5.1. Continued

weeks of Islamist demonstrations (Figure 5.2 and Table 5.2).[22] Ahok's victories shrank to a nucleus of seven contiguous districts between the old waterfront in Penjaringan and the commercial centers around Gambir. His only other success came in the Chinese-dominated enclave of Kelapa Gading in the northeast where he won close to 70 percent of the vote.

Reshaping the Pacific Community

The Jakarta election clashes showed that all of Indonesia's weakest points were overstressed at once. Quarrels over religion, race, class, and party were so deeply intertwined it seemed impossible to treat one without tackling them all. Perhaps these were inevitable growing pains of development and democracy. But Indonesia's external environment looked equally perilous. Diplomacy and defense policy were becoming much bigger problems than when Widodo took office amid expectations that Indonesia would turn inward to sort out its economic and political troubles. In foreign affairs, China's growing influence on Indonesia was clearer and more direct than in domestic matters.

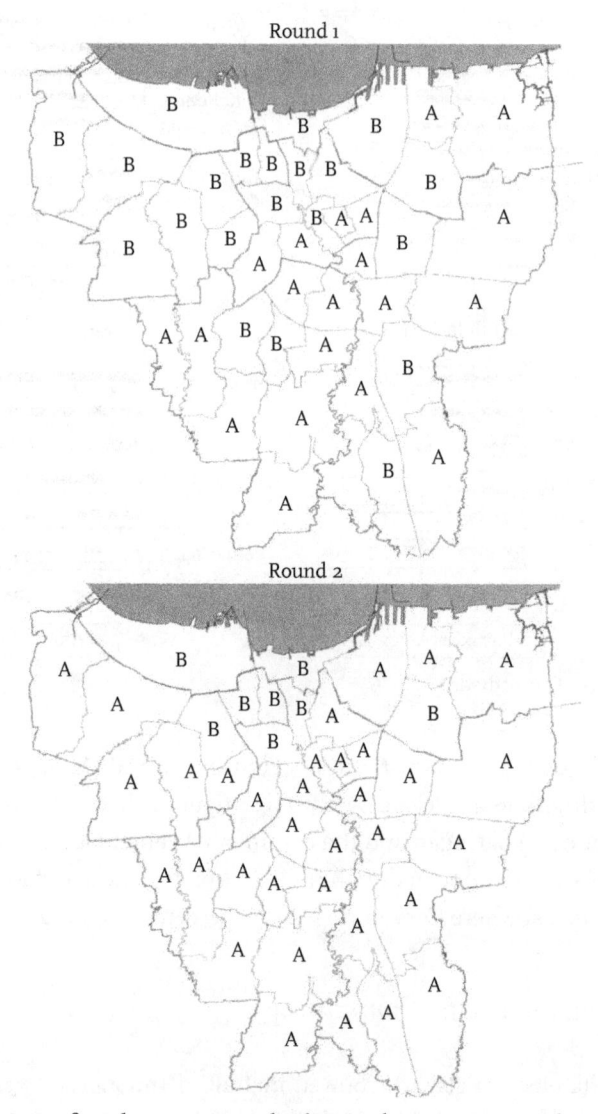

"A" indicates Anies victory, "B" indicates Basuki victory

Round 1

Round 2

FIGURE 5.2. Votes for Jakarta governor by district *(kecamatan)*, rounds 1 and 2. Author's calculations of data from Komisi Pemilihan Umum, *Pilkada Provinsi DKI Jakarta,* pilkada2017.kpu.go.id, April 25, 2017.

Widodo's dealings with China seemed as erratic as his response to racial and religious tensions at home. He soon surprised observers who assumed he had little interest in continuing Yudhoyono's high-flying diplomacy. Widodo quickly dismissed Marty Natalegawa, who had represented Indonesia with great flair at the United Nations and then as Foreign Minister. Natalegawa

TABLE 5.2 Results of the Jakarta gubernatorial elections by district (*kecamatan*), round 1 February 15, 2017, and round 2 April 19, 2017

	ROUND 1			ROUND 2	
DISTRICT	BASUKI	ANIES	AGUS	ANIES	BASUKI
South Jakarta					
Pancoran	31.50	53.55	14.95	69.06	30.94
Mampang Prapatan	63.65	26.24	10.12	67.84	32.16
Tebet	33.14	52.65	14.20	67.53	32.47
Jagakarsa	36.07	46.50	17.43	64.94	35.06
Pasar Minggu	38.10	46.93	14.98	62.48	37.52
Setiabudi	41.07	44.17	14.77	59.91	40.09
Pesanggrahan	41.61	44.40	13.99	59.27	40.73
Kebayoran Lama	48.82	49.38	1.80	59.05	40.95
Cilandak	7.77	72.18	20.05	55.71	44.29
Kebayoran Baru	71.68	6.09	22.23	54.41	45.59
Thousand Islands					
South	36.26	31.05	32.69	63.90	36.10
North	40.53	36.07	23.40	60.66	39.34
East Jakarta					
Cakung	35.08	40.65	24.27	64.73	35.27
Kramatjati	36.44	42.92	20.64	64.71	35.29
Jatinegara	36.80	43.74	19.46	63.75	36.25
Matraman	38.01	44.25	17.73	62.35	37.65
Cipayung	39.61	40.80	19.59	61.79	38.21
Duren Sawit	38.85	43.79	17.36	61.65	38.35
Pasar Rebo	39.65	42.93	17.41	60.88	39.12
Ciracas	42.81	39.53	17.66	58.73	41.27
Pulogadung	42.06	40.60	17.35	58.44	41.56
Makasar	42.78	37.96	19.26	58.02	41.98
Central Jakarta					
Tanah Abang	33.68	46.77	19.55	66.33	33.67
Johar Baru	37.92	42.32	19.76	62.77	37.23
Menteng	37.80	41.11	21.09	62.73	37.27
Cempaka Putih	40.60	42.14	17.27	59.73	40.27
Senen	41.64	38.15	20.21	58.75	41.25
Kemayoran	42.96	40.77	16.27	58.53	41.47
Gambir	50.84	33.46	15.70	49.81	50.19
Sawah Besar	60.99	24.60	14.41	39.99	60.01
West Jakarta					
Palmerah	78.87	10.56	10.56	65.36	34.64

(*continued*)

TABLE 5.2 Continued

DISTRICT	ROUND 1 BASUKI	ANIES	AGUS	ROUND 2 ANIES	BASUKI
Kebon Jeruk	41.68	40.29	18.02	59.18	40.82
Kembangan	53.14	44.72	2.14	56.20	43.80
Kalideres	48.66	32.16	19.17	53.88	46.12
Cengkareng	49.10	34.33	16.57	53.09	46.91
Tambora	54.37	31.84	13.79	46.86	53.14
Taman Sari	59.74	28.39	11.88	41.26	58.74
Grogol Petamburan	62.20	28.53	9.26	38.72	61.28
North Jakarta					
Cilincing	35.91	40.25	23.84	64.87	35.13
Koja	38.74	42.47	18.78	63.07	36.93
Tanjung Priok	49.82	35.36	14.82	51.57	48.43
Pademangan	77.63	5.50	16.87	49.71	50.29
Penjaringan	59.80	26.07	14.13	41.02	58.98
Kelapa Gading	69.42	21.98	8.61	31.26	68.74

Author's calculations of data from Komisi Pemilihan Umum, *Pilkada Provinsi DKI Jakarta*, pilkada2017.kpu.go.id, April 25, 2017.

was often compared to Turkey's Ahmed Davutoğlu as a master statesman—the press routinely dubbed them diplomatic whiz kids, the junior Kissingers of their time.[23]

Before long, Widodo pressed for a military buildup more ambitious than that of the retired general who preceded him in office.[24] He declared that Indonesia would become a world-class naval power befitting a nation whose vast territorial waters were as inviolable as its far-flung islands. With uncharacteristic candor, he warned other countries—particularly Australia, but also China—that Indonesia would no longer tolerate breaches of its sovereignty by foreign vessels.[25]

With Beijing dialing up territorial claims in the South China Sea, there was no avoiding an open spat with Indonesia as well. The main flashpoint was the Natuna Islands between Singapore and Kalimantan (Borneo) where both countries had overlapping fishing interests.[26]

Widodo demanded Beijing hand over fishing boats that the Chinese coast guard had rescued from Indonesian forces trying to apprehend them near the Natunas. Indonesia's maritime affairs minister, Susi Pudjiastuti, stepped up seizures of foreign fishing vessels, blowing up two-dozen Vietnamese and Malaysian boats with international media filming the spectacle.[27] For good measure, Widodo held a cabinet meeting aboard an Indonesian warship while sailing through the disputed waters.[28]

At the same time Widodo was brandishing naval power he had yet to build, he also was asking Beijing—and several of China's adversaries—to finance Indonesia's maritime ambitions. That was on top of the billions of dollars China was already providing in low-interest loans, giant infrastructure projects, special trade deals, and subsidies for small enterprises.[29] Widodo showed far more nerve than anyone expected from a former Central Java furniture manufacturer and mayor of Solo (Surakarta) with no military or international experience.

Widodo benefitted from the miscalculations of China and the United States alike. The Chinese were stoking nationalist fervor at home by making exaggerated maritime claims they were too weak to enforce. The Americans were so riveted on deterring China that they alienated countries in the wider region where most people wanted neither dependence nor war.[30]

Widodo understood that Beijing and Washington were giving Indonesia wider room for maneuver even as they tried to pull it in opposite directions. The more they pressured Pacific nations to choose sides, the more attractive Widodo's independence appeared to nationalist audiences in Indonesia and neighboring countries. Compared to the flip-flops of the Philippines and the belligerence of Vietnam, Indonesia's zigzags looked like sober and measured responses to repeated probing from stronger powers with selfish and overblown agendas. At a time when everyone else seemed frightened and reckless, Indonesians held fast and behaved like adults.[31]

This is precisely the kind of situation that allows Indonesia to stand apart from other ASEAN partners. Indonesia can only progress with massive economic assistance from wealthier nations. China is the major—but not the sole—source of that aid. However, China can only secure its Pacific-Indian Ocean lifelines with Indonesia's friendship. Chinese diplomats can raise their voices to counterparts from Singapore and the Philippines, but Beijing acknowledges that Indonesia is in a class of its own. To win Indonesia's goodwill, China—and its rivals—must actively support Jakarta's determination to become a preeminent regional power and an independent broker on the international stage.[32]

In this context, Widodo has no hesitation asking Beijing to strengthen his navy so that it can better chase Chinese fishing boats trespassing Indonesian waters. After all, Indonesia is not an official party to the wider South China Sea disputes. It is willing to settle its quarrels with China in bilateral talks instead of invoking international tribunals or third-party mediation.[33] Isn't that precisely what Beijing asks of the other ASEAN member states—smaller and weaker countries that are closer to China's borders and more vulnerable to its pressures?

Indonesia's diplomacy has attracted greater attention in Australia where more of the public sees their future as part of Asia instead of as English-speaking outsiders. Pacific commerce is vital to the powerful mining and ranching exporters as well as urban constituencies in the universities, technology industries, and tourism sectors. Australia's foreign policy debates reflect these shifts with mounting demands for more balanced approaches to Chinese and Western interests—attitudes quite similar to Indonesia's.[34]

Prime Minister Tony Abbott and his chief diplomat, Julie Bishop, pledged to steer a new course with "more Jakarta, less Geneva."[35] Foreign policy adviser Hugh White authored a bestseller urging Australia to make "the China choice" instead of clinging to a waning Pax Americana.[36] With Kevin Rudd, Australians had a Mandarin-speaking head of government who often seemed more considerate toward fellow diplomats in Beijing than toward his own cabinet members.[37]

These leaders have popularized the argument that if the United States and Europe make more room at the table for China, then Australia will gain a better seat as well. If Asia is the future and China the new gateway, then perhaps Indonesia is a pathfinder with instincts Australians can also develop.

Frequently, these debates compare Australia to India, which tries to advance its Pacific ambitions by moving closer to China's foes in Vietnam and Japan. Many commentators in Australia—and in India itself—have concluded that New Delhi is misjudging the prevailing mood in ASEAN.[38] Joining the Pacific club is becoming easier for China's friends, but much harder for would-be adversaries. In this context, Indian leaders seem to be foolishly embracing the sort of overtly pro-American course that Indonesia rejected long ago. The supposed lesson for Australia is to steer closer to Jakarta's example than New Delhi's.

Clashing views of Australia's interests spiked further as soon as Donald Trump took office, promising an American naval buildup to counter China's Pacific expansion. Australians are more divided than ever on where to draw the line in supporting U.S. military actions they cannot anticipate, much less control.[39] Old loyalties pull toward solidarity with Washington. However, more and more people reject the prospect of cold wars or hot ones that would turn Southeast Asian countries into satellites or battlefields.

For Pacific nations, Indonesia's approach to China is an attractive contrast to Turkey's penchant for confrontation and Pakistan's embrace of a quasi-alliance. Constant talk about China rebuilding an Asian hierarchy of tributary relations encourages ASEAN states to insist on a different way—reciprocity that is freely negotiated instead of tacitly imposed.[40] In their view, the wider Asia-Pacific community is still taking shape, and many configurations of great powers can be included. But any new megaregion will be an outgrowth of the various ASEAN-Plus formulas that have been circulating for many years—not a hub-and-spoke system with a single control center. All of the outside candidates are expected to fit in with local norms. In the parlance of international relations, this means they should become socialized and enmeshed in existing institutions and processes—agreeing to learn instead of expecting to dictate.[41]

Reaffirming ASEAN also puts renewed emphasis on Indonesia's habits of regional leadership—even though many ambitious Indonesians think they have already outgrown that role. For several years, Jakarta's foreign policy analysts have been urging their leaders to adopt a post-ASEAN approach that can lift Indonesia's global status through such forums as the G-20 and United Nations Security Council.[42] Indonesian diplomats seem increasingly confident they can stretch in both directions at once—beyond Southeast Asia to create a Pacific megaregion, and beyond the Pacific to promote a more inclusive global order.

This double mission is very similar to the vocation China has chosen for itself. Beijing is not accustomed to sharing the stage with what it regards as lesser powers, but Indonesia could become an exception. In addition to its influence over vital shipping routes, Indonesia possesses abundant assets that China needs for its own development, including natural gas, coal, forest products, minerals, and fisheries.[43]

Eventually, Beijing might view Indonesia as a welcome southern counterweight to northeast Asia's mutually hostile giants—Japan, Russia, and the two Koreas—which the United States is eager to influence for its own purposes. Indonesia could also play a gatekeeping role toward Australia and India, which are trying to link their fates more closely to an emerging Pacific community. If Beijing believes it can coordinate with Jakarta on such issues, China would have a strong incentive to nurture Indonesia's rise instead of fearing it.[44]

From this perspective, China faces Indonesia in much the same way that the United States has viewed China in recent decades. China can assist Indonesia's ascent to regional and global prominence, expecting both countries to benefit in the long run. Or it can dwell on possible threats to its dominance and turn a prospective partner into a tenacious adversary.

Politicized Investments and Investments in Politics

China's investments in Indonesia are growing rapidly and, while their economic contribution is already substantial, their political impact is even more immediate and far-reaching. New signs of Chinese wealth and power are triggering a backlash of nationalist and religious passions that threaten business and political elites in Jakarta and Beijing. Ahok's defeat suggested that Jokowi might be the next target when he ran for a second term in 2019. When Widodo visited China for the New Silk Road Summit in May 2017, he tried to grapple with the mounting tensions between the two governments and within his own society. He asked the Chinese to sign off on a joint plan to spread new infrastructure and industry across the outer islands—the remote and less developed regions that constantly complain of Java's dominance in national affairs, an irritant that seems even more serious in the post-Suharto era of mass democracy and Islamic factionalism.[45]

Widodo's pact with Beijing was touted as a plan for harmonizing Indonesian and Chinese aspirations for Pacific integration, but it could also be seen as a down payment on his re-election strategy. Both sides understood that Jokowi had to position himself as an independent representative and arbiter of Indonesian interests and not as a friend of transnational Chinese finance. Standing up to China's maritime claims was an important step in that direction, but his opponents were still criticizing his close ties to Ahok and the Chinese business community inside Indonesia.

In the months before the New Silk Road Summit, the spread of anti-Chinese sentiment was obvious on many fronts. Ahok's enemies tried to blame him for the alleged flood of illegal workers from China who were stealing Indonesian jobs. They used social media to incite street demonstrations with inflated estimates of Chinese immigration.[46] The Indonesian Laborers Union Confederation started publishing its own lists of undocumented foreigners, complaining that government monitoring was corrupt.[47] College students in Sulawesi launched vigilante campaigns to stop company buses and inspect the identities of workers on Chinese-related projects.[48] The specter of vigilantism triggers deep insecurities throughout Indonesian society, where organized bloodshed can erupt suddenly with or without official knowledge.[49]

In this climate, even Widodo's successes could work against him. When his government finally closed the deal on a high-speed rail link between Jakarta and Bandung, accusations of favoritism to Chinese interests gained greater credibility. Japanese firms led the early competition for the contract,

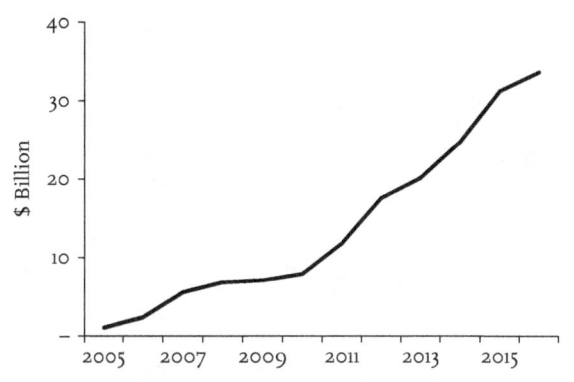

FIGURE 5.3. Cumulative Chinese investment in Indonesia, 2005–2016.
Author's calculations of data from American Enterprise Institute, "China Global Investment Tracker," aei.org, 2017.

boasting advantages in technology and safety that China could not match. Beijing countered with financing terms and price reductions that turned the tables.[50] Then, government agencies contradicted one another after repeated reviews and audits, stoking rumors that political pressure from China and its friends was overshadowing the technical and economic factors. When the Japanese learned of their defeat, they were incredulous—insisting that Widodo and Beijing had colluded against them. Officials in Jakarta tried to assure Tokyo that Indonesia's investment pie was big enough to offer them many future opportunities, but the incident damaged Widodo's reputation at home and abroad.[51]

The true scale of Chinese investment in Indonesia is hotly disputed. Because much of it is channeled through Hong Kong and Singapore, there is a tendency to underestimate mainland activity. On the other hand, some lists include lifetime project costs instead of actual expenditures, leading to inflated totals.[52] Most accounts put China's Indonesian investments in third place behind Singapore and Japan, but ahead of the United States, which is trending downward (Figure 5.3).[53] Jakarta still enjoys considerable leverage with Beijing because Indonesia's market is one of the world's biggest and it attracts many foreign suitors. Nonetheless, China's market share and political influence have quickly risen to the top ranks.

One reason that Indonesia seeks greater Chinese investment is the recent shift in trade relations, primarily because of a sharp drop in coal exports (Figure 5.4). Coal sales are Indonesia's leading revenue earner from China, and coal-fired power plants are the chief recipients of inbound Chinese investments (Table 5.3). As China plans to reduce its dependence on hydrocarbons, Indonesia needs to diversify its exports, and that requires

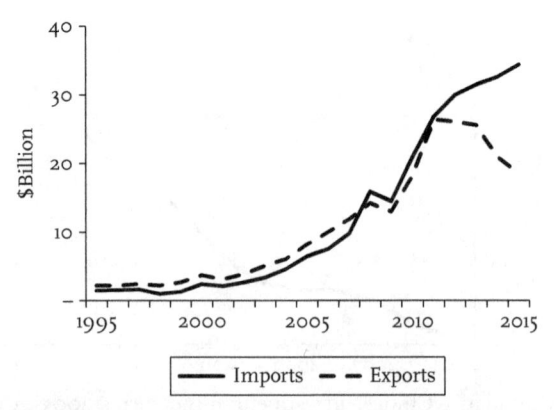

FIGURE 5.4. Indonesia's trade with China, 1995–2015.
Author's calculations of data from MIT Media Lab, "Observatory of Economic Complexity," atlas.media.mit.edu, 2017.

TABLE 5.3 China's largest investments in Indonesia, 2005–2016, projects worth $1 billion or more

YEAR	CHINESE ENTITY	$MILLIONS	PARTY	SECTOR	SUBSECTOR
2007	Dongfang Elec, China Power	$2,010	PLN	Energy	Coal
2012	China Nickel	$1,260	PT Jhonlinto	Metals	Steel
2014	CIC	$1,360	Bumi Minerals	Energy	Coal
2015	China Railway Constr	$1,710	PT Kayan Hidro	Energy	Hydro
2015	Shenhua	$1,320	PLN	Energy	Coal
2015	Sinomach	$1,160	PT Bantaeng Sigma	Energy	Coal
2016	Harbin Electric	$1,470	Malaysia's YTL	Energy	Coal
	Total	**$33,620**			
	$1–2 B	$10,290			
	$2 B+	$2,010			
	Coal	$15,880			

Author's calculations of data from American Enterprise Institute, "China Global Investment Tracker," aei.org, 2017.

financing for stronger transport and manufacturing capacity.[54] As the foreign demand for coal declines, Indonesia is encouraging domestic consumption by building more coal-powered generators, including many with Chinese backing and ownership.[55] Widodo's coal policies might alleviate some new economic strains, but they are aggravating twin political problems—from environmental groups demanding greener energy and from nationalist critics of foreign-controlled industries.

Chinese leaders and Widodo are pursuing a mutual interest in trying to blunt the power of Indonesia's religious and nationalist militants. Addressing the frustrations of outer island communities in Sumatra, Kalimantan, and Sulawesi can serve a number of common goals for Beijing and Jakarta. Improving their ports and industrial zones strengthens the maritime trade that binds the two nation's economies. Funding showcase investments through state-to-state channels bypasses the Indonesian Chinese intermediaries that Muslim businesses blame for corruption and favoritism. Assisting a diverse set of religious and ethnic minorities helps Widodo broaden his base beyond Central Java and the capital where Islamic opponents have gained the greatest momentum.

Cultivating these kinds of shared interests might help to alleviate some of the inevitable tensions that China and Indonesia will create with rival aspirations to project power in the Pacific and Indian Oceans. Just as Widodo needs Beijing's cooperation to consolidate his domestic control, China will have to make him a partner in securing the maritime heart of a wider Asian community.

CHAPTER 6 | Iran
The Great Divider

QUARRELS OVER IRAN SPLIT China's foreign policy community more than any other issue in the Middle East and Islamic world. The reason is clear—Iran remains a revolutionary society, and revolution is the last thing Chinese leaders want to see at home or in countries where they have growing investments.[1] Chinese are merely accidental revolutionaries whose good intentions often come back to bite them. But the Iranians are professionals, determined to shake up the status quo at every turn.

China pays a high price for its special relationship with Iran—constant tensions with valued partners throughout the Middle East and, particularly, with the United States.[2] Managing those tensions takes its toll and the frustrations frequently spill out in public. When Chinese writers caution that the Middle East is the graveyard of empires, they usually have Iran in mind, worrying that Tehran's recklessness might drag Beijing into just the sort of quagmires that have sapped America's strength and reputation.[3]

Many of China's leading diplomats, consultants, and business persons become visibly uncomfortable when they hear colleagues zealously defending Iranian policies, especially the nuclear research programs. Frequently, pro-Iranian speakers seem to believe they are winning the argument, without sensing that they are losing the audience. Sometimes these exchanges turn heated or veer toward communist sloganeering. That is when people nervously check their watches, counting the seconds in embarrassed silence until someone changes the subject. Nothing turns off well-heeled Chinese faster than echoes of Maoist rhetoric recalling the bad old days.

Even pro-Iranian Chinese who support Tehran in public make a point of cautioning them privately. The usual advice is to ease up on military might and stop frightening their neighbors.[4] Many Chinese would prefer to see Iran acting more like Turkey or Indonesia—relying on inherent advantages of geography and diplomatic savvy instead of threats of force.[5]

Chinese experts on Iran tend to be a breed apart from their colleagues specializing in other Middle Eastern countries. China's diplomatic corps is heavily populated with Arabic-speakers who have followed one another in regular rotations through the same dozen or so capitals. The contingent of Persian speakers is still relatively small. Persian is not a favored language for Chinese, who often find it difficult to learn and annoyingly indirect.[6]

China's ambassadors to Tehran have been some of Beijing's most experienced and skilled diplomats in the Middle East, but they have come from varied backgrounds and pursued their missions in different ways.[7] Hua Liming (1991–1995) set the standard for all of his successors. Fluent in Persian and an avid student of classical Persian poetry, Hua presided over the breakthrough in Sino-Iranian energy cooperation when Western companies were retreating. Long after Iran became one of China's top energy providers, Hua persisted in urging Beijing and Tehran to normalize relations with the rest of the world, particularly with the United States. He argued that Beijing's leverage in Iran was a unique opportunity to prove that China was a mature and responsible power that could help stabilize the international order.[8] Eventually, his position prevailed, but more hard-line views always had strong support in the military, the party, and the foreign service.[9]

After Hua, Beijing's embassy in Iran was headed by two different types of ambassadors—all of whom had previously served in Arabic-speaking countries. The most senior pair, Wang Shijie (1995–1999) and Sun Bigan (1999–2002), later acted as regional envoys who shuttled to all Middle Eastern capitals on troubleshooting missions. They tended to view Iran in the larger context of relations with the Arab world, Turkey, and Israel where American interests were still deeply entrenched and where China had to tread carefully to avoid unwanted provocations.[10] In contrast, after the American occupation of Iraq in 2003, China's ambassadors in Tehran focused on strengthening military ties between Iran and its allies in Lebanon and Syria. Liu Zhentang (2002–2007) and Xie Xiaoyan (2007–2010) were keen to resist American designs to control the so-called Greater Middle East. Liu had been ambassador to Lebanon before going to Tehran, and Xie later became China's special envoy for the Syrian peace negotiations.[11] By providing political and military backing for Iran's partners in the Arab world, they helped to position Tehran as the major beneficiary of American setbacks after the fall of Saddam Hussein.[12] The shifting projects of these ambassadors both reflected and amplified ongoing debates over Iran at the highest levels of Chinese politics.

Chinese who live in Iran have little incentive to travel beyond the big cities or mingle with ordinary people. Believing they have helped Iran through difficult times, Chinese are often dismayed to find that their country is unpopular with so many different groups. Iran's press is filled with complaints about cheap Chinese imports hurting small workshops and traditional crafts.[13] There are repeated accusations that Chinese companies gouge Iran's consumers on imports of refined petroleum and that they drag their feet on pledges to develop new oil and gas fields.[14]

The Islamic regime's supporters and opponents level angry charges at China from different directions. Religious groups insist that China prints Qur'ans with obvious errors that defame Islam.[15] Urban protestors show off tear gas canisters and truncheons used against them by security forces, claiming they were made in China. Bazaar merchants call for higher duties on Chinese consumer goods that threaten their sales and local suppliers.

All of these problems help to explain the impatience the Chinese showed whenever Iranian leaders resisted their efforts to limit nuclear research in return for softer sanctions. When Israel seemed intent on taking military action against Iran, many of China's Middle East experts sounded the alarm. Some even suggested giving Tehran an ultimatum—halt the brinksmanship or face the consequences on your own.[16] Even when China surreptitiously helped Iran develop centrifuges and enrich nuclear materials, it also increased pressures to negotiate a freeze with European and American diplomats.[17]

Writing a New Story Line

Once the nuclear deal went into force, it became obvious that China and Iran would move further apart. Tehran would have multiple options to do business with European and Asian partners, forcing China to offer more competitive terms. China would be under pressure to help in monitoring Iran's compliance, opening the door to constant haggling for years to come. In both countries, there was considerable relief that looser ties would allow China and Iran to pursue divergent interests with mutual tolerance. Perhaps a more arm's length relationship would promote greater objectivity so that future ties could rest on firmer ground.[18]

Iran's participation in the New Silk Road forces China to rethink more precisely where its long-term interests overlap and conflict with Tehran's.[19] As a natural junction between the overland and maritime branches of the

Silk Road, Iran is a logical match or rival for Pakistan. But Iran has greater ambitions than serving as a crossroads that benefits stronger countries. Iranian leaders hope to form a megaregion of their own centered on Tehran, not Beijing.[20]

Iran can pose a credible challenge to China's leadership because Tehran envisions a megaregion that blends geography with psychology—a potent combination that the infrastructure-minded Chinese do not adequately understand or appreciate. Iran relies upon a form of transnational connectivity that China cannot replicate. Iran's partisans share a largely latent and subjective set of ties between communities of the weak and powerless who have found their voice in quick succession across the Persian Gulf and Fertile Crescent.[21]

Chinese students of Iran tend to speak of Shi'ites as though they were Leninists with turbans, holding fast to rigid dogmas enforced through a clear chain of command. In fact, Iran's overseas power is rooted in multiple networks reflecting diverse customs and local alliances. Their supporters form social movements that thrive on theological pluralism and factional competition that Iranian patrons not only tolerate, but encourage.[22]

The élan of pro-Iranian groups springs from a common sense of oppression by ruling institutions rather than from uniformity of faith.[23] Their ranks include nonconformist Shi'ites beyond Iran's control as well as Sunnis and others with no clear sectarian identity at all. They are creating communities of sentiment that transcend borders more effectively than any bullet train or pipeline Beijing can promise. As long as Tehran serves as the chief inspiration for these movements, it will remain a thorn in the side of China's leaders and all of their would-be partners in the Persian Gulf and beyond.

Beijing and Tehran often seemed to pursue irreconcilable goals. One wanted to reassure nervous customers and investors that stability is around the corner. The other wanted to shake the system to its foundations. Both the geography and psychology of Iran's regionalism were profoundly troublesome to China.

Beijing would like to see an Iran at peace, operating as a universal intersection between neighboring regions, north and south as well as east and west. But a continuously embattled Iran is more likely to become a chronic bottleneck just as dangerous as the Malacca Straits where China is already vulnerable.[24] As for the psychology of historical grievance and transnational revolution, that is exactly what China's leaders rejected after Mao and want no part of today.

Chinese experts grappled with these problems for years before reaching a more balanced view of Iran's larger role in the Middle East. Pro-Iranian militias could be portrayed as revolutionaries or terrorists depending on one's ideology. But from a different perspective, they also looked like independent social movements with strong roots in local communities across the region.[25] As Chinese writers took these competing views more seriously, they realized that Iran might play a more constructive role than they had assumed—helping to stabilize emerging political orders instead of merely overthrowing the old ones.

Redefining the Objectives

When Xi Jinping made his much-awaited visit to Iran and Saudi Arabia in January 2016, everyone wondered if he would try to reconcile the dueling neighbors that China badly wanted to settle down. Could China recast its relations with Iran after the nuclear deal gave both sides more breathing room? If Tehran felt less isolated would it be more willing to advance Silk Road integration instead of stirring Middle Eastern turmoil?[26]

Xi had already delayed the trip because of nasty spats over the proxy war in Yemen and uproars over mass fatalities during the Hajj. There was talk of yet another delay when the Saudis executed a prominent Shi'ite cleric just days before Xi's arrival.[27]

Instead of addressing the immediate political quarrels that irked both sides, Xi focused on common economic interests he expected to carry greater weight in the years ahead.[28] In particular, he told Tehran and Riyadh that when they think about future oil revenues, they should stress stable flows and guaranteed shares more than absolute dollar amounts.

Xi sensed that leaders in both countries feared being undermined by falling oil prices if world demand slackened, especially because of slower growth in China. His remedy was a combination of fixed market shares and long-term purchase agreements between China and the biggest energy exporters.[29] The Chinese hoped that such a formula might provide a welcome cushion to unpopular authoritarian regimes that relied on windfall earnings to mollify their citizens.

China could not guarantee prices or import levels, but it could pledge not to take advantage of politically vulnerable elites by playing them off against one another in hard times. Energy markets would always expand and contract, but Beijing would use its leverage to help suppliers weather the swings with as little political turbulence as possible. Chinese representatives were pressing similar arguments in discussions with Russia and with long-time suppliers in Africa and Latin America as well.[30]

About one year later, Xi delivered an even more sweeping message of reassurance to the World Economic Forum at Davos. The very week that Donald Trump was sworn in as president, Xi proclaimed China's intention to lead the way toward a reformed global capitalism that would be more stable and inclusive than ever. Explicitly warning against the looming dangers of protectionism in Western societies, he cast China as the champion of free trade, environmentalism, and global governance.[31] The stewardship he had offered the Iranians and Saudis for energy markets now extended to the global economy as a whole.

Xi's keynote was a tightly worded address sprinkled with Chinese proverbs exhorting patience and perspective. The course of history was irresistible—toward integration and openness, not fragmentation and isolation. Protectionism was like shutting oneself in a dark room. It could shelter us from rain and wind, but it also kept out light and air. When civilizations interact they do not clash, they enrich one another.[32]

In conclusion, Xi introduced the New Silk Road as China's vision of global capitalism for everyone. China had always contributed to human progress, and now it offered a new network for delivering finance, know-how, trade, and regulation with equity and efficiency. World history, technocratic uplift, and folksy comfort—on schedule and to the point for financial notables who felt their world was crumbling.[33]

Meanwhile, China was encouraging Iran and Russia to join in forming the nucleus of Eurasian integration. Iran would help rebuild a peaceful Middle East beginning in Iraq and Syria, hopefully with Turkey's assent. As Russia and China drew closer, they would support Iran in connecting Caspian trade with maritime routes to Asia. Beijing, Moscow, and Tehran—megaregional partners driving prosperity across continents and oceans.[34]

By carving out special roles for Russia and Iran, the Chinese were shrewdly making the New Silk Road a shared venture that others could own as well. Many in Moscow warmed to the prospect, believing Russia could coax a stumbling Europe to look eastward. Greater Eurasia is the term some Russian experts use to highlight the Atlantic side of the equation—the prize they intend to attract through connections that Iran and China supposedly cannot match.[35]

For Iran, the prospective role of political broker amounted to a sharp turnaround. The revolution would lay the ground for a new establishment—the great divider would become a sensible manager. It was a message that seemed well-attuned to Iran's need to stress its rationality and responsibility in upholding the nuclear agreements despite American wavering and threats of renewed sanctions. Donald Trump was making the Iranians seem sober by comparison—a feat that had evaded Chinese diplomacy for years.[36] At last, it seemed that China might turn the corner with Iran, gaining a steady hand instead of a troublemaking client.

The budding partnership of Iran, Russia, and China formed the backdrop for a string of frantic moves that Trump's team instigated even before taking office. Flattering Putin, flirting with Taiwan, and putting the Ayatollahs on notice—sudden feints and headlines that added up to nothing like a big picture. If the new administration hoped to turn Moscow, Tehran, and Beijing against one another, they failed. Indeed, Trump's shenanigans probably strengthened arguments for coordinating common action in Eurasia while the West was in such disarray.[37]

For Iran, the nuclear deal paved the way for reintegration to a world economy that was moving quickly in its direction. China and Russia wanted to encourage the trend and harness its benefits for their own ventures. Europeans were attracted, but waiting to see if Iran was worth the risk.[38] Only a hostile America could reverse the momentum by slapping on new sanctions. For precisely that reason, Iran and its friends are determined to save the nuclear agreements. The more Washington tries to undercut the deal, the more valuable Iran appears to Beijing and Moscow, and the more reliable it looks to potential investors. Trump was trying to push Iran into a corner, but he was isolating himself.[39]

Iran and Russia believed that Trump was trying to drive them apart by playing on their shared need for oil revenue. Removing sanctions from Moscow and putting them back on Tehran seemed like an obvious ploy to stoke rivalry in a weakening oil market. This was exactly the opposite of China's efforts to reassure nervous oil exporters with long-term purchase contracts and stable market shares.[40]

From this perspective, Trump's flurry of seemingly random tweets and threats could foreshadow something like a strategy—an anti-Silk Road campaign targeting Iran, Russia, and China at the same time.[41] If such a plan succeeded, Iran would again become a source of division and instability with far-reaching effects. But this time it would be against Tehran's wishes, not because of them.

Juggling the Neighbors: Saudi Arabia, the Gulf States, and Israel

A post-sanctions Iran with Silk Road commitments disturbs neighboring countries that China needs to cultivate. Saudi Arabia tops the list for many reasons, particularly oil, trade, and diplomacy. Washington encouraged the Saudis to sell more oil to China, hoping that would make Beijing more willing to help rein in Tehran's nuclear program. Nowadays, China is the biggest customer for both countries and has to manage their relative shares carefully.[42]

Pilgrimage is another area where all three countries share common interests and vulnerabilities. Saudi Arabia is rapidly expanding religious tourism into a year-long flow of commerce that stretches from Senegal to the Philippines. Jeddah and Dubai are central gateways for the constant movement of people and goods back and forth between Africa and the Pacific.[43] It is along these routes that the New Silk Road most clearly intersects long-standing Islamic corridors that are flourishing once again. Both networks depend on Iranian-Saudi cooperation in managing the Hajj and the Holy Cities of Mecca and Medina. China has growing reasons for wanting the pilgrimage to flourish. China's Muslims are making the Hajj in greater numbers—over 14,000 annually.[44] In addition, Chinese companies built the rail links that carry pilgrims around the holy sites in Mecca.[45]

Beijing understands that Iranians and Saudis hold most of the cards in diplomatic efforts to resolve conflicts in Arabia and the Fertile Crescent. China's mediation in Middle East disputes is still a hotly debated topic among Chinese writers, but the prevailing view treats direct involvement as unavoidable. Even when commentators urge Beijing to let the Americans and Russians take the lead in Middle East discussions, they usually want a strong supporting role for China.[46]

Chinese mediation is increasingly welcome among the smaller states of the Gulf Cooperation Council (GCC) who traditionally rely on outside help to balance their powerful neighbors. Kuwaiti diplomats brokered the early bargains that brought Riyadh and Beijing together in package deals covering oil sales, visas for Chinese businesses, and joint investments.[47] Oman routinely separates itself from other GCC partners when it thinks their criticisms of Tehran are excessive. Commercial groups in Qatar and the Emirates often sympathize with Oman's cautious approach.[48] The growth of Chinese businesses in GCC countries is reinforcing those sentiments. Beijing is more willing to mediate Iranian-Saudi economic conflicts, but Riyadh still has great difficulty adjusting to a situation where it is more dependent on China commercially and less certain of American military guarantees.

Fearing that Iran and China were partnering at their expense, Saudi leaders provoked a confrontation with Qatar in 2017 that worsened divisions in the Gulf Cooperation Council.[49] The Saudis wanted to stigmatize Qatar because of its independent foreign policy, including friendship with Iran, but as the crisis unfolded it was Riyadh that became more isolated. Qatar enjoyed support within the GCC and beyond that cushioned it from Saudi and Emirati attacks. Kuwait and Oman were eager to broker a compromise solution, Turkey and Iran increased shipments of vital goods to break the boycott, and American military leaders reaffirmed their commitment to preserve the key air base on the outskirts of Doha.[50] Qatari port officials soon reported an upsurge in traffic as India, China, and Australia arranged direct maritime routes that bypassed the usual connection through Dubai.[51]

Meanwhile, bilateral ties between Qatar and China continued to strengthen. Qatar supplied China's second-largest share of natural gas via underwater fields that it shared with Iran. Doha's sovereign wealth fund invested widely in real estate and joint ventures in Hong Kong and the mainland. Chinese firms led the Qatari construction boom, and Doha banks were the first Persian Gulf institutions to offer yuan-denominated transactions.[52] In contrast, the GCC's long-anticipated free-trade agreement with China was frozen indefinitely because final approval required unanimous support. By trying to ostracize Qatar, the Saudis had unwittingly strengthened its veto power over the economic future of the entire region.[53]

Chinese diplomats were in no hurry to mediate the conflict because they expected cooler heads to prevail as the Saudis and their allies realized the economic damage they were inflicting upon themselves. Beijing also understood that Pakistan and India were viewing Saudi attacks on Iran as threatening their interests. Pakistan feared that Saudi support of Balochi rebels in eastern Iran would spill over to the troubled areas around Gwadar and Quetta.[54] New Delhi suspected that Riyadh wanted to undermine the Indian-backed port at Chabahar in order to fend off Iranian competition for energy markets in South Asia and the Far East.[55] Given this combination of economic and strategic interests, Chinese leaders preferred to keep their distance and let neighboring countries pressure the Saudis and Emiratis to de-escalate the conflict. Suspecting that hawks in the Trump administration were spoiling for a fight with Tehran and Beijing, China's diplomats urged Iran to avoid overreacting.[56]

In contrast to China's deepening involvement in the Persian Gulf, there is much less enthusiasm for negotiating Israeli-Palestinian issues. Beijing's chief interest in Israel is importing advanced technology with possible military applications. Previous efforts in this direction provoked Washington's wrath against both Israel and China. Now, Beijing wants to tread more carefully in cultivating both Israel and the United States, and that is easier if China stays away from Palestinian questions. Nonetheless, Beijing is advertising its willingness to play an over-the-horizon role by hosting Israeli and Palestinian leaders in China. In May 2013, Prime Minister Benjamin Netanyahu and Palestinian Authority President Mahmoud Abbas visited Beijing in quick succession—not meeting directly, but choreographed to leave no doubt they both had important friends beyond Washington and Moscow.[57]

Economic Integration Laced with Political Competition

After difficult years of trade and investment with sanctions-ridden Iran, China's efforts have helped to reshape the country's social and political landscape in ways we are just beginning to appreciate. Chinese trade with Iran has been modest, but well balanced and usually in Tehran's favor (Figure 6.1). Investments have been far below China's huge transfers to Pakistan, Indonesia, and Nigeria, but they have been more evenly distributed across Iran's economic sectors and geographic regions (Figure 6.2 and Table 6.1). In addition, under the governments of Hassan Rouhani, who was elected president in 2013 and re-elected in 2017, the benefits of Sino-Iranian economic cooperation have also strengthened both reformist and conservative factions of the polarized political establishment.[58]

About half of China's investments in Iran have targeted oil and gas projects, but the rest have gone to transportation, industry, telecommunications, and housing. Geographically, the activity has concentrated along two axes—a northern corridor between Tehran and Mashhad and a western route connecting Azerbaijan with provinces along the Persian Gulf and Indian Ocean (Figure 6.3). The northern line plans to link Xinjiang with Turkey and

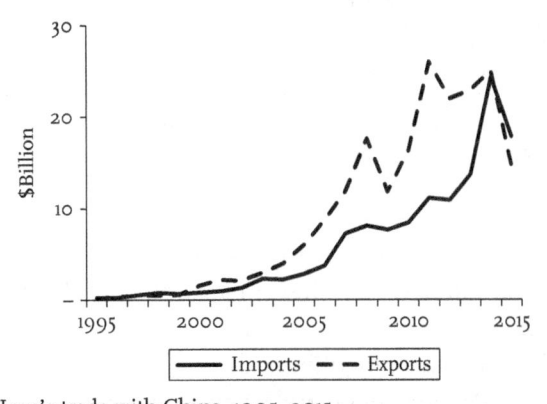

FIGURE 6.1. Iran's trade with China, 1995–2015.
Author's calculations of data from MIT Media Lab, "Observatory of Economic Complexity," atlas.media.mit.edu, 2017.

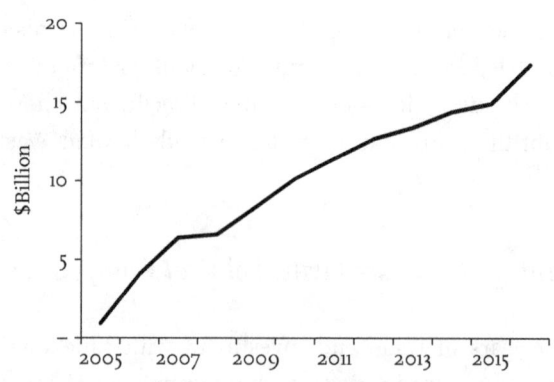

FIGURE 6.2. Cumulative Chinese investment in Iran, 2005–2016. Author's calculations of data from American Enterprise Institute, "China Global Investment Tracker," aei.org, 2017.

TABLE 6.1 China's largest investments in Iran, 2005–2016, projects worth $1 billion or more

YEAR	CHINESE ENTITY	$MILLIONS	PARTY	SECTOR	SUBSECTOR
2006	Sinopec	$2,840	North West Shelf	Energy	Oil
2007	Sinopec	$2,010	Natl Iranian Oil	Energy	Oil
2009	CNPC	$1,760	Natl Iranian Oil	Energy	Oil
2010	Sinohydro	$1,500	Zanjan Water	Energy	Hydro
2012	Norinco	$1,250	Tehran Rail	Transport	Rail
2016	Genertec, Beijing SU Power	$1,100		Transport	Rail
	Total	$17,410			
	$1-2 B	$5,610			
	$2 B+	$4,850			
	Oil	$6,610			
	Metals	$3,460			
	Rail	$3,310			

Author's calculations of data from American Enterprise Institute, "China Global Investment Tracker," aei.org, 2017.

the Mediterranean while the western route will tie India and Southeast Asia to Russia and Eastern Europe.[59] The combined effect could make Iran a central junction of the New Silk Road—an intersection of the east-west overland traffic with the north-south maritime route.

These Iranian development corridors amount to parallel and competing projects of national integration. The northern zone is still far more advanced

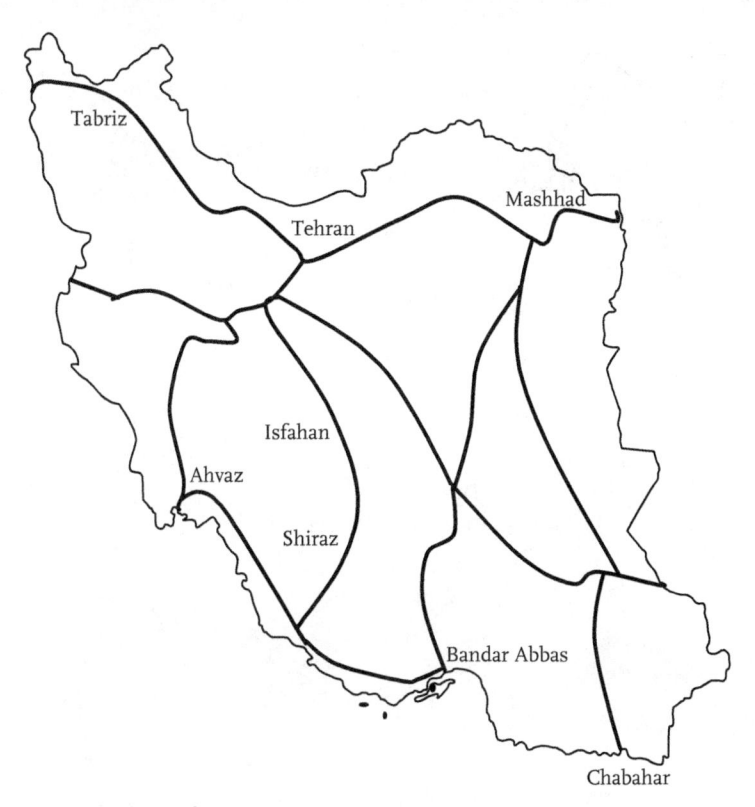

FIGURE 6.3. Major rail connections across Iran.
Author's illustration based on Railways of the Islamic Republic of Iran and *Global Construction Review*, December 14, 2015.

than the western districts, but Chinese assistance has promoted transregional connectivity in both areas. Demographically and culturally, these regions have always been divergent and poorly connected. The north encompasses the Persian-speaking heartland between the Caspian Sea and the central deserts. The west contains a diverse collection of Persian and non-Persian peoples, including several provinces with prominent linguistic and ethnic minorities that have close ties with kin in neighboring countries (Figure 6.4).

Historically, the inequalities of power between regions and cultures have been even greater than disparities in their economic conditions. Central governments have subordinated the outlying districts, discouraging their cultural distinctiveness and appropriating their natural resources. This combination of political, economic, and cultural tensions becomes more evident as Iran opens up to international exchange and more volatile as its leaders appeal for popular support through competitive elections. The strains have

FIGURE 6.4. Linguistic and ethnic diversity in Iran.
Author's illustration.

deepened considerably during the last two presidential contests between Hassan Rouhani and his more conservative opponents.

Regional Support for Rouhani and His Rivals

In 2013 and 2017, Rouhani and his opponents both enjoyed strong support in particular districts with divergent demographic profiles.[60] During Rouhani's 2017 campaign for re-election, each side experienced gains and losses in a few provinces, suggesting even greater consolidation of their rival regional bases (Table 6.2 and Figure 6.5). Anti-Rouhani vote was consistently strongest in the Persian-speaking north central region across an arc stretching south of Tehran into Seman and Khorasan in the east. In 2017, Rouhani's opponents extended their reach to two western provinces, Hamedan and Zanjan, that he had carried narrowly four years earlier.

In contrast, Rouhani's base was far more diverse and geographically extensive. In both elections, Rouhani did best in the northwest and along

92 | China and the Islamic World

TABLE 6.2 Vote for Hassan Rouhani in Iran's presidential elections of 2013 and 2017 by province

	ROUHANI 2017	ROUHANI 2013	GAIN (LOSS)
All Iran	57.14	52.43	4.71
Double Victories = 17			
Sistan and Baluchestan	73.02	73.30	(0.28)
Kurdistan	72.89	70.85	2.04
Gilan	69.03	58.62	10.41
Kermanshah	68.16	59.58	8.58
Azerbaijan, West	67.05	67.09	(0.04)
Alborz	66.83	51.28	15.55
Yazd	65.15	67.72	(2.57)
Azerbaijan, East	64.61	57.87	6.74
Mazandaran	62.22	59.82	2.41
Golestan	62.20	59.81	2.39
Fars	61.88	58.21	3.67
Ardabil	60.06	60.50	(0.45)
Bushehr	58.94	53.81	5.13
Ilam	57.98	56.40	1.57
Hormozgan	55.63	54.46	1.18
Qazvin	55.35	51.70	3.65
Kerman	52.22	59.33	(7.11)
New Victories = 6			
Tehran	69.45	48.51	20.93
Isfahan	55.98	45.80	10.18
Khuzestan	55.45	34.15	21.30
Lorestan	54.88	47.43	7.45
Chahar Mahaal and Bakhtiari	54.46	32.85	21.61
Kohgiluyeh and Boyer-Ahmad	50.66	39.12	11.54
New Defeats = 2			
Zanjan	45.81	50.29	(4.48)
Hamedan	45.35	50.68	(5.32)
Double Defeats = 6			
Markazi	48.96	45.94	3.01
Semnan	46.64	45.31	1.34
Khorasan, North	45.16	47.19	(2.02)
Khorasan, Razavi	42.51	43.99	(1.47)
Qom	37.28	38.70	(1.41)
Khorasan, South	34.26	44.51	(10.25)

Author's calculations of data from Ministry of Interior, *Natayej Tafsili Entekhabat Riyasat Jomhori* (*Detailed Results of the Presidential Elections*), Islamic Republic of Iran, 2013 and 2017.

R = Rouhani double victories, r = Rouhani gains 2017,
O = Opponents' double victories, o = opponents' gains 2017

FIGURE 6.5. Geographic distribution of votes for Hassan Rouhani and opponents in presidential elections of 2013 and 2017.
Author's calculations of data from Ministry of Interior, *Natayej Tafsili Entekhabat Riyasat Jomhori (Detailed Results of the Presidential Elections)*, Islamic Republic of Iran, 2013 and 2017.

the Caspian coastline. He ran well in the sparsely populated southeastern provinces bordering the Persian Gulf and Indian Ocean. In 2017, Rouhani also won six important provinces he had lost before. In Tehran, he gained nearly 70 percent of the vote and his supporters swept the city council. He also added an important cluster of new industrial districts, including Isfahan and its western neighbors near the Persian Gulf. Part of Rouhani's success stemmed from his government's ability to influence development plans, particularly big-ticket projects run by Chinese firms and the Islamic Revolutionary Guard Corps. Rouhani's ministers even cancelled some of China's largest oil and gas contracts in the west, complaining that Beijing was dragging its feet because of Washington's threats to sanction participating companies. Eventually, the government renegotiated the deal and reinstated the Chinese firms, but Rouhani's intervention paid off with southwestern voters.[61]

The electoral map of 2017 sent some alarming signals to Rouhani's opponents. For the first time, they faced an unbroken swath of pro-reform sentiment that virtually encircled their powerful strongholds in the north and northeast. The clerical and military establishment quickly pushed back with criticism and demonstrations designed to contain Rouhani's power during his second term.[62] Debate focused on the overriding split in Iran's public life—contradictory views over the ultimate source of political authority. Supporters of Ayatollah Ali Khamenei insisted that the Supreme Leader's legitimacy was rooted in divine inspiration whereas Rouhani argued that all rulers—including the highest clerics—could only govern with the consent of the people. Refuting charges that democracy was an anti-Islamic import, Rouhani claimed, "We are not following Western beliefs when we're holding elections and going after people's votes . . .We belong to a religion in which (Imam Ali) based his leadership on the people's will and the people's vote."[63] As Rouhani began his second term, the clash of opinions over legitimacy was more serious than ever because of Ayatollah Khamenei's advanced age and because one of his likely replacements was Ayatollah Ebrahim Raisi—the very man that Rouhani had just defeated in the national elections.[64] When mass protests broke out on the eve of the 2018 new year, they quickly spread through the northern and western provincial towns where Rouhani's electoral support was strongest.[65] This was a very different geographic pattern from the 2009 demonstrations against President Mahmoud Ahmadinejad's re-election that were concentrated in Tehran and other large cities. It suggested a gradual hardening of Iran's combined ethnic and ideological cleavages in more polarized regional blocks.

China's long experience with Iran is an important example of constant learning and adaptation. From modest beginnings, Chinese officials and scholars accumulated firsthand expertise that gave them new perspectives on Middle Eastern lands that Beijing had once treated as an Arabic-speaking preserve dominated by American power. China managed to endorse international sanctions on Iran while profiting from their loopholes. When support for sanctions became exhausted, the Chinese claimed a share of the credit for replacing them with an agreement to freeze Iran's nuclear program. Beijing encouraged the spread of Iranian influence across the Persian Gulf and Fertile Crescent while strengthening its own commercial ties with Israel and the states of the GCC. Inside Iran, China's leaders helped the mullahs crush mass protests after the fraudulent 2009 elections that kept President Mahmoud Ahmadinejad in power. But, since then, Chinese firms have also built much of the infrastructure and industry that empowers the reformist constituency of President Hassan Rouhani.

China managed to advance all of these seemingly irreconcilable goals entirely through commerce and diplomacy—without putting boots on the ground and without resorting to shock and awe. A similar learning curve is unfolding in China's relations with Africa, which we examine next.

CHAPTER 7 | Nigeria
A Shaky Bridge

IN NIGERIA, CHINA MAY have met its match. On paper, Nigeria is parliamentary and federal, but in person it is largely transactional. While law is the first word, it is seldom the last. Offices have rulebooks that are never opened and homes have money boxes that are always locked. People live by their wits and their friendships, with trust and reputation as the soundest currencies of all.

Such a fluid and open society has plenty of room for foreigners who are willing to adapt. Europeans, Lebanese, Indians, and Chinese have come over many generations and settled in overlapping social levels. Africa is filled with flourishing Chinese diasporas, and Nigeria's is one of the oldest and most vibrant on the continent. Its members come from both government and private backgrounds with a brisk traffic between them and with regular connections to the mainland, Hong Kong, and Taiwan.[1] Among China's many faces in Nigeria, the official Beijing presence is the most powerful, but it is also the most battered by controversy and political attacks. Having the deepest pockets and the most fragile reputation, China's government is the target of choice for politicians, journalists, and citizens determined to correct what they see as corruption and injustice.

Trains Can Be Fun if You Own Them

There is great irony in China's railway diplomacy across Africa. China itself was one of the earliest victims of imperialism by rail and debt.[2] The bitter labor of Chinese migrants laid the first lines spanning the Americas, both North and South. Today, the tables are turned as Chinese companies revamp and expand colonial-era systems—this time with Africans calling the shots instead of foreigners.[3]

In Nigeria, most citizens have never traveled by train. Highways are far more popular because roads are in better shape than rail lines and gasoline subsidies make it cheaper to drive. As a result, Nigeria has a huge number of traffic fatalities and, until recently, very little passenger service by train. Dilapidated railways are the most persistent and crippling bottlenecks blocking Nigeria's path to economic development. Most Nigerian governments neglected rail transport while scrambling to capture oil revenues for the benefit of their favored clients and regions. Several presidents launched short-lived renovations with a series of foreign contractors, including India, China, Romania, Brazil, and China once again. Each government scrapped the plans of its predecessors, opting for different routes and signing up a new set of firms and lenders to manage the projects.[4]

The practice of rotating the presidency between northern and southern coalitions encouraged frequent interruptions of construction. Routes from Abuja to Kaduna and Kano were started under northern leadership only to be postponed in favor of connections from Lagos to Port Harcourt and Calabar when southern politicians took over.[5] Logrolling became endemic. Funding a line through the western states was impossible without also approving another route for the eastern states. The federal government clung to its monopoly over railways long after privatizing other sectors such as air transport and telecommunications.[6] Thus, the ruling party in Abuja always kept the upper hand in juggling lucrative routes and contracts between rival ministries and states.

When the government of Olusegun Obasanjo restored Nigeria's democracy in 1999, it adopted a long-term plan to build an integrated national system that would connect every state within 25 years. Chinese firms won the lion's share of the business, offering soft loans in return for Nigerian pledges to sell oil at concessionary prices and to put up 15 percent of the project costs.[7] In effect, Nigeria mortgaged much of its future oil revenue and accepted increased indebtedness in order to pay for the new railway network. This was a price that Nigerian technocrats were willing to pay for necessary infrastructure they expected to return dividends for decades to come. They hoped the national railways would spur exports of agricultural and mining products. By linking new industrial zones to expanded ports, Nigeria would attract foreign investment and emerge as an export hub for manufactured goods throughout Africa and beyond.[8]

Debt Traps and Money Pits

The chief flaw in this plan is that Nigeria's debt is growing quickly while work on the railways is slower and more costly than expected. Meanwhile, oil revenues have fallen, the value of the national currency—the naira—has sunk, and the government is forced to borrow more just to cover current budget shortfalls.[9] China has responded by providing more financing, but on stricter terms that put Nigerians further in debt. Chinese banks are also tightening controls on disbursements for the railroads, releasing funds in tranches instead of lump sums and providing materials directly instead of relying on local sources.[10] In many cases, Chinese construction sites have had to hire special guards and build fences to protect imported materials from theft and sabotage—leading to still further cost overruns and delays.[11]

As Nigerians saw their debts skyrocketing, criticisms of China rose dramatically at all levels of government and in the mass media. One of the most devastating broadsides came from Lamido Sanusi, former governor of the Central Bank of Nigeria and emir of Kano.[12] In 2013, Sanusi accused China of enmeshing Nigeria in a new form of imperialism that was causing deindustrialization and underdevelopment. He noted that his father—Nigeria's ambassador to Beijing in the 1970s—was an admirer of Chairman Mao, but that China had become an altogether different country since then. "The days of the Non-Aligned Movement that united us after colonialism are gone. China is no longer a fellow under-developed economy—it is the world's second-biggest, capable of the same forms of exploitation as the west."[13]

Sanusi called on Nigerians to embrace economic nationalism as the only realistic way to benefit from China's power without being overwhelmed by it. "African love of China is founded on a vision of the country as a savior, a partner, a model . . . It is a critical precondition for development in Nigeria and the rest of Africa that we remove the rose-tinted glasses through which we view China . . . [W]e must see China for what it is: a competitor . . . We must not only produce locally goods in which we can build comparative advantage, but also actively fight off Chinese imports promoted by predatory policies."[14]

Urging a thorough renegotiation of Sino-Nigerian relations, Sanusi concluded, "A review of the exploitative elements in this marital contract is long overdue. Every romance begins with partners blind to each other's flaws before the scales fall away and we see the partner, warts and all. We may remain together—but at least there are no illusions."[15]

At the same time, Nigeria's political establishment came under blistering attack from labor unions, civic groups, and human rights organizations.[16] They argued that corruption in Nigeria was worse than in most other developing countries—not because the country was big and easy to penetrate, but because its leaders failed to promote economic growth. Pointing to the examples of South Korea and India, they claimed that politicians who routinely skimmed 15 percent from public contracts were tolerable if they, at least, approved sound projects in line with rational development strategies. They characterized Nigerian politicians as particularly pernicious because they stole indiscriminately with no intention of delivering on promises to cut red tape or issue licenses fairly.[17] Amid this outpouring of grievances, railway employees led a campaign to establish new regulatory bodies composed of citizens' groups and journalists to watch over legislators and civil servants, stressing the special need to monitor dealings with contractors from China.[18]

Chinese diplomats and businesses took these criticisms seriously because they realized that public opinion in Nigeria and many other African countries was becoming more hostile to a perceived pattern of Chinese misdeeds. Nigerians constantly complained that China was dumping shoddy goods and tainted products on low-income consumers, including phony drugs and spoiled foods.[19] A spate of electrical fires in Lagos office buildings was traced to defective equipment from China.[20] Hundreds of Nigerian detainees in Guangzhou prisons smuggled out widely read accounts of abuse after being convicted on false charges of drug trafficking.[21]

Chinese migrants had settled in every corner of Nigeria, and they were especially vulnerable to the popular backlash. Chinese shopkeepers were accused of illegally importing rice into Nigeria to take advantage of price spikes after a shortfall in domestic production. Some of the confiscated rice was identified as white plastic that had been mislabeled as food.[22] Deforestation was attributed to illegal logging by Chinese timber dealers.[23] Nigerian factories complained that they could not compete with Chinese imports because constant electricity outages forced them to use expensive diesel generators. Chinese traders could bring consumers' goods across the seas at lower cost than Nigerian manufacturers who had dominated their markets for generations.[24]

As accounts of Chinese exploitation mounted, many Nigerians seemed determined to retaliate in kind. There were frequent reports of Chinese businesses being scammed by Nigerian fraudsters, including a Yoruba practitioner of juju—witchcraft—who allegedly hypnotized his victims before ordering them to make wire transfers to his bank accounts.[25] Shanghai police seized three tons of pangolin scales smuggled from Nigeria that were intended for sale in China as traditional medicine even though the animals were protected in both countries and their active ingredient was nothing more than keratin.[26] As a diaspora community embedded in all levels of African society, Chinese families and businesses were constantly exposed to shifts in Nigerian sentiment—and those shifts could quickly reverberate in daily life in China too because African and mixed-race families were becoming more visible every year.[27]

Higher Risks for Wider Power: Nigeria as an Intercontinental Stepping Stone

Beijing responded to these threats by redoubling its stakes in Nigeria—making long-term commitments to direct investment and industrialization that promised to turn Nigeria into Africa's preeminent economic power. For decades, China had strengthened its position in Africa by taking on risks that other investors rejected. From that perspective, it seemed perfectly reasonable to consolidate those gains through a pan-African development plan with Nigeria as the centerpiece.[28]

Once again, railroads were a dominant theme, but this time the focus was transcontinental rather than national or regional. Pan-African connections were on the drawing boards for several routes between the Indian Ocean and the South Atlantic. At first, these projects aimed to integrate existing lines in East Africa before venturing into the more troubled interior of the Great Lakes and the Democratic Republic of the Congo.[29] Then, more ambitious plans combined high-speed trains, pipelines, and expressways across the center of Africa, reaching the Atlantic at Angola and the Gulf of Guinea just south of Nigeria.[30]

As continental integration appeared more feasible, discussions broadened even further to encompass a possible South Atlantic maritime zone. In this view, Africa's biggest economic powers—Nigeria, South Africa, and Angola—were natural trading partners and bridges to Brazil.[31] An industrialized Nigeria would not only spur pan-African integration, it would lead the way toward South-South development tying Africa with Latin America.[32]

China was beginning to see many overlaps between its interests in Africa and Latin America. In both continents, it was facing nationalist attacks for impeding industrialization by swapping commodities for infrastructure in lopsided deals that inflated debt and perpetuated dependency. In Africa and Latin America, government and business coalitions were demanding more Chinese investment in local manufacturing and faster transfers of advanced technologies.[33] In each case, long-time partners of Beijing were calling for a new deal that would give them a larger share of benefits and a better shot at replicating China's success as an exporter of finished goods with higher value added.

China and its partners are viewing the South Atlantic as a potential trade artery connecting Africa and Latin America instead of as an insurmountable barrier separating the Old and New Worlds. Projects that were dismissed as fantasy just a decade ago now seem merely questionable or overly optimistic. Transcontinental railroads across rain forests and mountain ranges, alternatives to the Panama Canal through Nicaragua and Columbia—all linking wider zones of manufacturing, farming, and mining in constant flows across Asia, Africa, and Latin America.[34] A prospering China would shed its old image as the world's sweatshop to become the angel investor of choice for emerging markets everywhere—offering them a way up the developmental ladder that Western countries had denied to poor people and aspiring middle classes for generations.

Managing Mistrust and Self-Importance

Chinese and Nigerian leaders have consistently dealt with each other as hardheaded realists ready to put aside past grievances and racial stereotypes in pursuit of common interests. Both countries are particularly adept at playing off wealthier and more powerful nations without alienating them altogether. Despite Lamido Sanusi's lament that Africans see China through rose-colored glasses, Nigerian politicians and businesses regard the Chinese as a useful lever for prying better terms from transactions with all foreigners. Since the Tiananmen massacre in 1989 and Sani Abacha's dictatorship in the 1990s, Abuja and Beijing have repeatedly cooperated to overcome isolation from Western governments over human rights abuses and corrupt business practices.[35]

Such cooperation required burying the hatchet over many past quarrels that would have haunted more ideological leaders elsewhere. Beijing supported Biafra's secession during the Nigerian civil war, but Abuja still encourages China's special ties with Igbo communities, including Mandarin classes for students in southeastern Nigeria and in Chinese universities.[36] Nigeria and China backed opposing sides during Angola's long and bitter civil war, yet today Beijing courts both countries as its top African oil suppliers.[37] When the Obama administration cut off military aid during the peak of fighting with Boko Haram, China filled the gap with enough arms and training to finish the job.[38] In 2016, as falling oil prices pushed Nigeria into its worst recession in 25 years, Chinese emergency aid freed Abuja from bowing to the International Monetary Fund's usual demands for structural reform in return for financial relief. Beijing's generosity could not have been more perfectly timed—coinciding with the rapid uptick in anti-Chinese publicity that threatened to strain relations beyond the breaking point.[39]

China has strong political incentives for treating Nigeria with special care. Beijing views Nigeria as a key swing state in Africa with greater potential influence than more predictable actors such as pro-Western Ethiopia and Zambia or anti-Western Zimbabwe. Nigeria endorses the One China policy, but began supporting Taiwan's participation in international trade meetings over Beijing's objections. Abuja agreed to downgrade its relations with Taipei, but only after Beijing reaffirmed support for a permanent Nigerian seat on the United Nations Security Council.[40] Nigerian diplomats reciprocated by endorsing Beijing's exaggerated territorial claims in the South China Sea—a dispute with no direct connection to Nigeria or any other African state.[41] After many years of privileging its partnership with South Africa, China shifted closer to Nigeria as it overtook Pretoria economically and Jacob Zuma's government sank into scandal and intraparty feuding. Nigeria also stands out as Africa's leading center for currency swaps using the Chinese yuan and promoting its wider acceptance in international trade—one of Beijing's highest priorities in reforming the global financial system.[42]

China's campaign of solicitude and reciprocity hopes to turn around a wider African policy that has suffered enormous criticism for indulging corruption and tyranny at the expense of the vast majority of the population.[43] Taking Nigeria seriously is a proper show of respect and a welcome sign that Chinese leaders are willing to learn from their mistakes. Is this the solution to Sanusi's call for a renegotiated marriage contract? Or is it another example of putting on rose-colored glasses that deceive both sides?

Nigerians can take great delight in mocking themselves, and their favorite target is their own vanity. Nigerian politicians have touted the inherent greatness of the country and its people for so long that citizens commonly deride predictions of manifest destiny as pure theatrics. Now that Nigerians are hearing their future glories foretold by Chinese oracles they are not sure what to think. Can the Chinese really deliver? Do they believe their own script? After years of skepticism about China, Nigerians are turning their skepticism on themselves.[44]

A splendid example of the problem appeared in a popular opinion piece of an online newsletter called YNaija.com in 2017. The essay was entitled "Reality Check: Nigeria's Sense of Entitlement Cannot Stand Empirical

Examination."[45] It recalled a friendly critique of Nigerian self-importance by a former American ambassador in the 1980s, contrasting his sober remarks with the inflated rhetoric of contemporary Sino-Nigerian dialogues. According to the author, "[O]ur delusion of our strategic importance to the world prevents us from posing the right questions such as what we should do to make ourselves more relevant to the world."[46] Nigerians, he argued, were obsessed with the idea that their country was too big and too powerful to fail, but in fact their size and oil could never support the swagger they affected or bring the respect they craved.

Chinese flatterers might be telling Nigerians what they wanted to hear today, but the candid American told them years ago what they needed to hear all along. For decades, diplomats and business leaders from China and Nigeria have prided themselves on their shrewdness, pragmatism, and unsentimental calculation of overlapping interests. Viewing one another as worthy adversaries encouraged trust and common action. But now that their friendship appeared to survive a long bout of quarrels, both sides felt they were entering unchartered territory where they had to take one another's measure more carefully than ever. In that context, the echo of an old American envoy gave an ironic sense of comfort to Nigerians and Chinese alike—whether as partners or competitors, they would still need to guard against a shared tendency to exaggerate their talents and potentials.

Foreign Cash and Local Conflict

China's deepening involvement in Nigeria occurred against a dangerous backdrop of economic and political dysfunction. With China's support, Nigerian leaders continued their long-standing habits of overdependence on oil exports, excessive borrowing, and aggravation of conflicts between rival regions and ethnic groups.[47] The breaking point came during the rule of Goodluck Jonathan (2010–2015)—an accidental president who rose and fell with economic tides he could not control and tribal jealousies he sought to exploit. Jonathan presided over tumultuous years of soaring imports and loans followed by deep recession and social unrest (Figure 7.1 and Figure 7.2). By the time of his failed re-election bid in 2015, both Chinese and Nigerian leaders had become alarmed by the waste of resources and began scrambling for a new course toward national integration and development.[48]

Disputes over railroad construction were a major preoccupation both during and after Jonathan's administration. Chinese investment soared

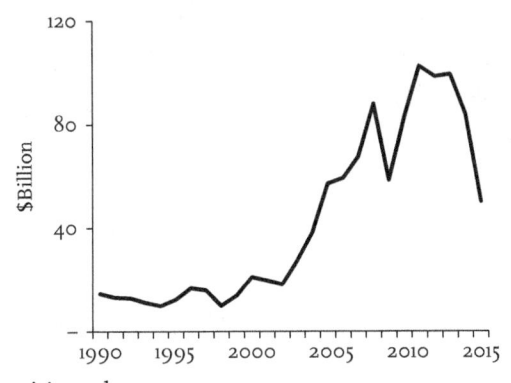

FIGURE 7.1. Nigeria's total exports, 1990–2015.
The World Bank and International Monetary Fund, *Balance of Payments Statistics Yearbook*, 2017.

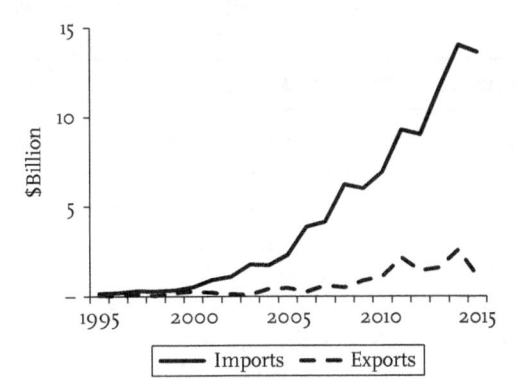

FIGURE 7.2 Nigeria's trade with China, 1995–2015.
Author's calculations of data from MIT Media Lab, "Observatory of Economic Complexity," atlas.media.mit.edu, 2017.

under Jonathan. More than half of it clustered in big rail projects, including some worth over $2 billion (Figure 7.3 and Table 7.1). A long backlog of stalled and half-finished projects reflected chronic discontinuities across presidential administrations and stalemates between competing states.[49] Because he was a southerner, it was unsurprising that Jonathan slighted the interests of the powerful northern states that were accustomed to leading the federal government and the military. But he focused so much attention on his homelands in the Niger Delta that he soon alienated pivotal neighbors, especially the Yoruba states of the southwest who often hold the balance in presidential politics.

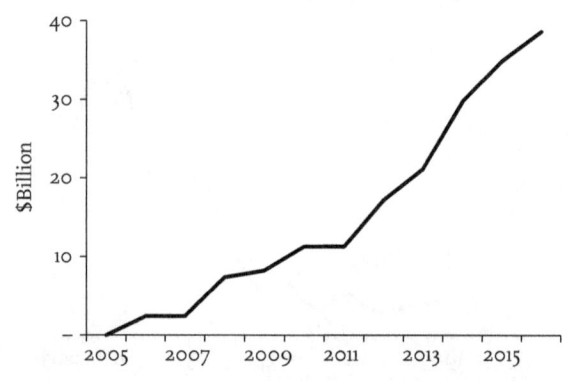

FIGURE 7.3. Cumulative Chinese investment in Nigeria, 2005–2016.
Author's calculations of data from American Enterprise Institute, "China Global Investment Tracker," *aei.org*, 2017.

TABLE 7.1 China's largest investments in Nigeria, 2005–2016, projects worth $1 billion or more

YEAR	CHINESE ENTITY	$MILLIONS	PARTY	SECTOR	SUBSECTOR
2006	CNOOC	$2,270	S Afr Pet	Energy	
2008	Shenzhen Energy	$2,400	First Bank	Energy	Gas
2008	Sinoma	$1,180	Dangote	Real est	Constr
2010	China Rail, Nanjing Govt, China Dev Bank, Guangdong Xinguang	$2,500		Other	Industry
2012	Sinopec	$2,500	Total	Energy	Oil
2012	China Railway Construction	$1,450		Transport	Rail
2013	Power Construction, Sinomach	$1,290		Energy	Hydro
2014	China Railway Construction	$6,810		Transport	Rail
2014	China Railway Construction	$1,210		Transport	Autos
2015	China Railway Construction	$3,510		Transport	Rail
2016	China Railway Construction	$1,850		Transport	Rail
2016	China Railway Construction	$1,690		Transport	Rail
	Total	**$38,650**			
	$1-2 B	$8,670			
	$2 B+	$19,990			
	Railways	$21,490			
	Oil, gas	$7,370			

Author's calculations of data from American Enterprise Institute, "China Global Investment Tracker," *aei.org*, 2017.

Yorubaland Shifts Alliances

Yoruba voters gave Jonathan solid support in his 2011 campaign against his northern opponent, Muhammadu Buhari, the retired general who had led one of Nigeria's military regimes in the 1980s. However, during the 2015 presidential rematch, the Yoruba states switched sides (Figure 7.4 and Table 7.2). Voting as a block, the southwest carried the day for Buhari, making Jonathan the only sitting president in Nigerian history who failed to win re-election.[50]

Two aspects of Jonathan's presidency were especially infuriating to Yoruba communities struggling to survive years of inflation and constant shortages. Jonathan's railroad policies put a new east-west route along the southern coast ahead of earlier projects to strengthen links between the southwest and the north. Jonathan tried to speed up construction of the line from Lagos to Port Harcourt and Calabar that would wind through most of the Niger Delta cities as well.[51] His government's agenda appeared to downgrade long-standing efforts to integrate the vast western states with refurbished lines from Lagos to Kaduna and Kano—routes that were vital to the centrally located Yoruba cities of Ibadan and Ilorin (Figure 7.5).

Yoruba opinion was even more outraged by Jonathan's drastic reductions in fuel subsidies that hit wage earners and merchants with greater costs when they could least afford them. The price hikes touched off mass protests that culminated in the Occupy Nigeria movement of 2012.[52] The Occupy demonstrations grew into a nationwide surge of civil disobedience, but its core was Lagos, and its strongest hinterland was the urban network of Yorubaland. The protests forced Jonathan to rescind most of the budget cuts, encouraging a renewed sense of Yoruba political consciousness that quickly undermined the ruling party's alliances in all of the southwestern states.[53]

As soon as Buhari took office, he moved to restore a sense of regional parity—not just between the north and south, but between the southern neighbors that Jonathan had pitted against one another. Buhari's government poured resources into Chinese-led railroad projects in every region at once. He kept Jonathan's promise to build the southern coastal line, but placed new emphasis on a host of big ticket projects his predecessor had neglected.[54] Buhari's ministers convened a regional forum in Ilorin for citizens' groups from the western states of Kwara, Niger, and Kogi where they highlighted the importance of rail links for developing agriculture and creating integrated export channels through the southern ports.[55] These were three of the key swing districts that had deserted Jonathan. In each

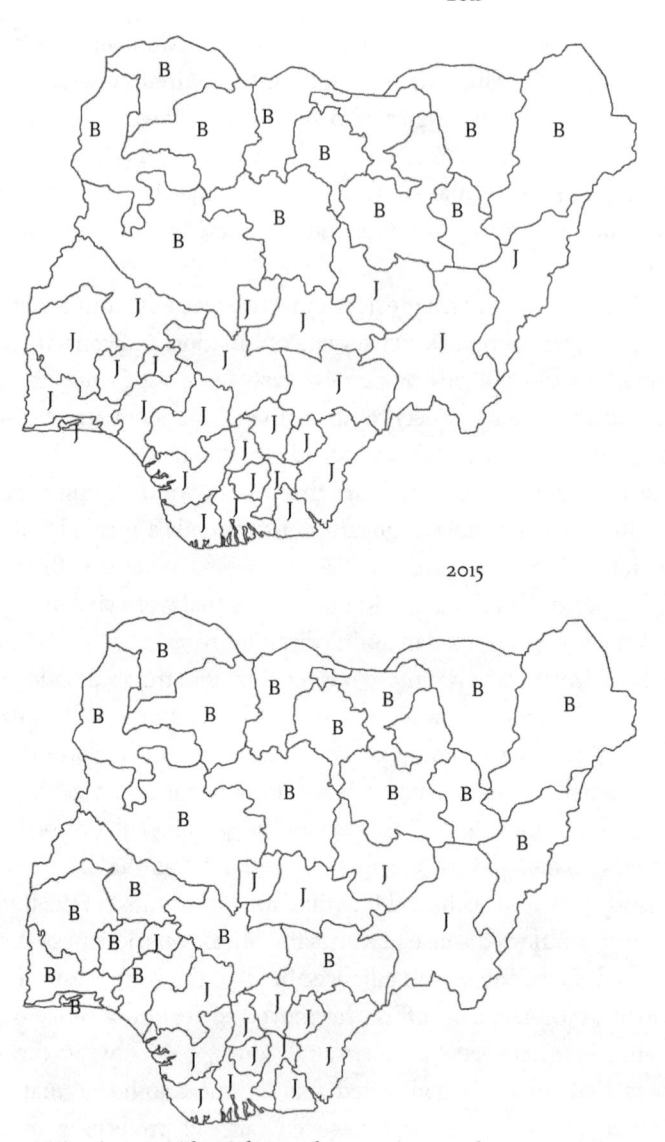

FIGURE 7.4. Nigerian presidential votes by state, 2011 and 2015.
Author's calculations of data from Independent National Electoral Commission.

case, Buhari's government was courting social activists instead of traditional politicians and offering them a leading role in the Nigeria of the future—an exporting power where a solid base of agriculture and manufacturing would replace the boom and bust cycles of oil dependency.

TABLE 7.2 Nigerian statewide vote for president, 2011 and 2015

REGION	STATE	JONATHAN 2011	BUHARI 2011	OTHER 2011	JONATHAN 2015	BUHARI 2015	OTHER 2015
Nigeria		58.48	31.76	9.76	44.99	53.99	1.02
South-West	Ekiti	51.56	1.03	47.42	58.69	40.02	1.30
	Lagos	65.90	9.77	24.34	43.80	54.89	1.31
	Ogun	56.86	3.25	39.89	39.00	57.82	3.18
	Ondo	79.57	2.44	17.99	44.80	53.45	1.75
	Osun	36.75	1.36	61.89	38.89	59.69	1.41
	Oyo	56.14	10.70	33.16	34.42	59.98	5.60
	S-West	**60.39**	**6.97**	**32.64**	**41.75**	**55.77**	**2.47**
South-East	Abia	98.96	0.31	0.72	94.18	3.43	2.39
	Anambra	98.96	0.36	0.68	95.96	2.60	1.44
	Ebonyi	95.57	0.20	4.23	88.94	5.36	5.69
	Enugu	98.54	0.46	1.00	96.48	2.47	1.05
	Imo	97.98	0.54	1.48	79.55	18.96	1.50
	S-East	**98.28**	**0.40**	**1.32**	**91.23**	**7.34**	**1.43**
South-South	Akwa Ibom	94.58	0.43	4.98	93.73	5.74	0.53
	Bayelsa	99.63	0.14	0.24	98.40	1.42	0.18
	C/River	97.67	0.55	1.78	92.09	6.30	1.62
	Delta	97.76	0.64	1.60	95.55	3.86	0.59
	Edo	87.28	2.86	9.86	57.32	41.66	1.02
	Rivers	98.04	0.71	1.25	94.99	4.42	0.58
	S-South	**96.34**	**0.79**	**2.87**	**91.22**	**8.10**	**0.68**
North-West	Jigawa	36.75	58.21	5.04	13.77	85.39	0.84
	Kaduna	46.31	51.92	1.77	29.93	69.72	0.35
	Kano	16.48	60.77	22.74	10.14	89.44	0.42
	Katsina	26.13	70.99	2.88	6.83	92.83	0.35
	Kebbi	39.95	54.26	5.78	14.91	83.88	1.20
	Sokoto	33.97	59.44	6.59	18.24	80.54	1.21
	Zamfara	25.35	66.25	8.40	19.03	80.44	0.52
	N-West	**31.44**	**59.75**	**8.80**	**15.75**	**83.65**	**0.60**
North-East	Adamawa	56.00	37.96	6.04	39.57	58.91	1.52
	Bauchi	16.05	81.69	2.27	8.44	91.30	0.26
	Borno	17.58	77.25	5.16	5.11	94.35	0.55
	Gombe	37.71	59.73	2.57	21.03	78.43	0.54
	Taraba	61.07	34.91	4.02	53.62	45.08	1.30
	Yobe	18.83	54.26	26.92	5.39	94.19	0.42
	N-East	**31.45**	**62.21**	**6.33**	**21.69**	**77.57**	**0.74**
North-Central	Benue	66.31	10.47	23.22	44.45	54.73	0.81
	FTC-Abuja	63.66	33.05	3.28	51.24	47.72	1.05
	Kogi	71.17	23.53	5.30	35.60	62.86	1.54
	Kwara	64.68	20.16	15.17	30.13	68.66	1.21
	Nasarawa	58.89	40.08	1.03	53.46	46.30	0.24
	Niger	30.93	64.60	4.47	18.34	80.83	0.83
	Plateau	72.98	25.27	1.75	55.95	43.68	0.37
	N-Cent	**60.65**	**31.33**	**8.02**	**41.25**	**57.97**	**0.78**

Author's calculations of data from Independent National Electoral Commission.

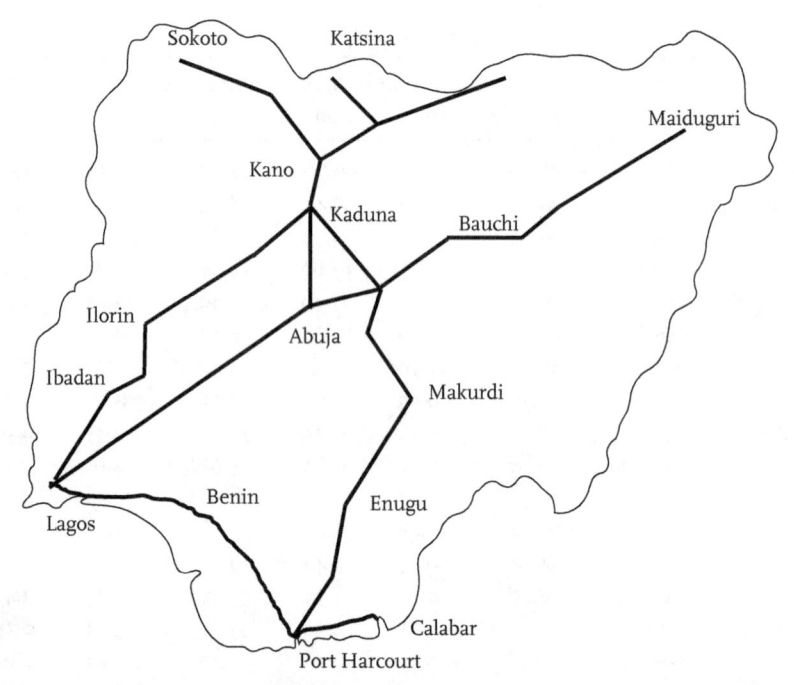

FIGURE 7.5. Nigerian railway routes
Author's illustration based on Nigerian Railway Corporation and China Railway Construction Corporation, May 9, 2014.

By 2017, Buhari's weakening health forced him to hand over power to his vice president, Yemi Osinbajo, who seemed likely to carry on the new government's western strategy of market integration and coalition building.[56] A prominent lawyer and pastor from Lagos, Osinbajo is married to a granddaughter of Obafemi Awolowo, one of independent Nigeria's founding fathers and an icon of Yoruba progressivism. Osinbajo's accession temporarily upset northerners' expectations that they would control the presidency for a full two terms, but unlike Jonathan—who rose to power under similar circumstances—most of the country regarded Osinbajo as a competent manager and a fair arbiter of regional differences.[57] When Buhari was well enough to return to office after treatment abroad, both men seemed to have gained in popularity.[58]

Nested Regions and Merging Continents

As China and Nigeria have deepened their commercial and political ties, the consequences have reverberated on several levels at the same time.

Exchanges between national governments were the tip of the iceberg, generating wider changes throughout Nigerian society and beyond. In order to gain access to Nigerian resources and markets, Chinese firms took risks that others rejected and offered incentives that no competitor could match. When critics doubted the benefits of these arrangements, Beijing tried to correct course and increased its investments instead of stonewalling or retreating. Those efforts were motivated, in large part, by Chinese estimates that Nigeria was likely to have a future importance—strategically, economically, and symbolically—beyond its borders.

China's leaders viewed Nigeria as a linchpin of their general strategy in Africa as a whole—a continent where they faced mounting criticism for encouraging neocolonialism, deindustrialization, and corruption. From their perspective, success in Nigeria was crucial for turning around an Africa-wide diplomacy that was in trouble and required serious adjustments. Building integrated railroads is a centerpiece of China's development plans not only for Nigeria, but for the rest of Africa as well. The ultimate goal is to construct a series of national networks and to connect them in a pan-African system stretching from the Indian Ocean to the Atlantic coast. African and Chinese planners describe these railroads as arteries for future exports of agricultural and industrial goods that will reduce and eventually end the continent's traditional dependency on extracting raw materials and importing consumer goods.

If China could demonstrate the ability to build infrastructure and industrial zones that promoted economic diversification, its appeal might extend well beyond Africa to other regions that had been disappointed with Western-led development efforts. From this perspective, Africa would be a natural component of the New Silk Road—just as important as the Eurasian routes. In addition, Africa might eventually serve as a trans-hemispheric bridge across the South Atlantic to Latin America. Indeed, Nigeria, South Africa, and Angola are already discussing joint projects to boost maritime trade between the southern continents. China has become a leading trading partner for several countries in South America that are also blaming it for their slow industrialization and prolonged dependency on exports of primary products. From Brazil to Peru, Chinese firms are mapping transcontinental railroads and, in Columbia and Nicaragua, they have pushed ahead with new canals to link Pacific and Atlantic shipping.

Meanwhile, within Nigeria subnational regions took on new life in a way that reshaped the political balance of power. Older divisions between north and south were overshadowed by a growing assertiveness in the western Yoruba states, which feared the central government was cheating them out of important Chinese investments. This was the same region that had tipped the balance against secessionist Biafra during the Nigerian civil war of the 1960s. Having played a decisive role in preserving Nigerian unity, the west emerged once again as the broker of national power struggles.

China's long involvement in Nigerian development has triggered the mental and political redrawing of regional maps in several directions at once. As a nation-state, Nigeria is evolving toward a more integrated market and society. As a multiethnic democracy, its western region is coalescing into a more powerful partner of the north and south. On an international scale, Nigeria is emerging as the Atlantic anchor of China's trans-African railroad system and as a possible hub for expanded maritime connections with South America.

Nigeria's future is certain to involve the coevolution of new megaregions, but it is likely to be a more complex and multilayered story than geopolitical commentators usually describe. Nigeria is emerging not just as a western branch of the New Silk Road, but as a hub nested in a web of interconnected regions—subnational, transcontinental, and inter-hemispheric—comprising a more integrated Afro-Eurasia that is tied to an increasingly interdependent world.

CHAPTER 8 | Egypt
Weighing the Tolls

FROM CHINA'S PERSPECTIVE, EGYPT is a land of rising costs and dangers that severely diminish the geographic and political benefits that seemed so irresistible to great powers in the past. Every Egyptian regime depends on foreign assistance for survival, but the more eagerly they look to China, the more tentative are Beijing's responses. Keeping Egypt afloat is in everyone's interests and China is willing to do its part while leaving the greatest burdens in American and European hands. Egypt is too distant and too volatile to inspire the efforts at long-term alliance building that China devotes to Pakistan and Iran or the open-ended investments it pledges in Indonesia and Nigeria. The result is a stark mismatch between Cairo's impatience to make deals with Chinese firms and Beijing's reluctance to wade in too deeply after the multiple shockwaves of the Arab Spring.

In the days of Gamal Abdel Nasser (1954–1970) and Anwar Sadat (1970–1981), Egypt's political clout attracted rival powers willing to accept its economic and social risks in return for military bases and diplomatic support.[1] But Egypt is no longer a center of Arab nationalism and nonaligned movements that can sway events in the Middle East and around the world. The Camp David Accords of 1978 effectively ended Egypt's ability to act as a swing state in regional politics. Instead, it became a pliable dependent of Western governments committed to bolstering a privileged military establishment in return for its pledge to keep the peace with Israel while subduing unrest at home.[2]

Since the fall of Hosni Mubarak's regime (1981–2011), China has helped Egyptian leaders create modest shows of independence from Washington. Mohamed Morsi (2012–2013) traveled to China before visiting the United

States, suggesting his intention to regain some of Cairo's long dormant diplomatic influence.[3] After Morsi's violent overthrow, Xi Jinping visited Egypt extending economic and political support to the army-backed regime of Abdel Fattah el-Sisi (2014–present). Xi's endorsement helped Sisi thwart Barack Obama's threat to punish the junta's human rights abuses by withholding American military aid.[4] Nevertheless, symbolic displays of Sino-Egyptian friendship have not lessened the underlying differences that keep the countries apart.

Sisi's rule is even more brutal and economically dysfunctional than Mubarak's.[5] It survives because frightened patrons in the West and the Gulf see no alternative and because Egyptians are still exhausted from years of turmoil and repression. All the problems that Sisi inherited are worse than before—uncontrolled police violence, runaway debt, and a demoralized citizenry seeing no end to poverty and unemployment. China's leaders were willing to help Sisi overcome the stigma of Egypt's counterpart to the Tiananmen massacre—the killings of hundreds of Muslim Brotherhood supporters following Morsi's overthrow in August 2013. For Beijing, it was a cost-free gesture that seemed to debunk Washington's human rights rhetoric when America quickly resumed military aid to Egypt.[6] But Chinese rulers pride themselves in judging the strengths and weakness of authoritarian regimes, and they doubt that the use of force in Egypt can have the long-lasting effects it has produced in China. Sisi may have won a temporary reprieve for military rule, but he has worsened most of the problems that ignited revolution in 2011 and they are likely to trigger similar explosions in the future.

In this context of skepticism and mistrust, tensions have accumulated between Chinese and Egyptian negotiators on several fronts, delaying or defeating their most important plans to deepen investment and economic alliances. Conflicts are particularly evident in three key issues where Egyptian and Chinese leaders have been unable to find common ground despite years of bargaining and well-publicized project launches—developing the Suez Canal Zone, building a new capital city on the outskirts of Cairo, and reviving the towns and villages of the Nile Valley.

The Suez Canal as a Wasting Asset

China's relations with Egypt are deeply colored by divergent attitudes toward the Suez Canal and its future importance in global transportation. For Egypt, the canal is a national treasure with projected revenues that should provide economic security for coming generations.[7] But for maritime shippers in China and many other nations, the canal is a costly tollgate with diminishing value and rising risks. Long-distance carriers have complained for years about Suez's high fees and chronic delays.[8] When choosing the most optimal routes, industry experts consider many factors besides mileage. Standing astride the shortest path does not eliminate competition when carriers need to adapt to shifting markets and costs.

More and more firms have been bypassing Suez and choosing alternative routes in spite of the added distance and time required. In many cases, the Panama Canal is a direct rival for Suez traffic, and sometimes the trans-African route around the Cape of Good Hope can be an attractive option.[9] For oil supertankers, added time at sea can be a hedge against volatile markets.[10] When oil prices fall, producers often prefer to keep part of their cargos afloat instead of paying for more expensive land storage. When the market rebounds, they can earn a higher return by delaying the sale and delivery.

Chinese engineers are preparing to create an overland rival to the Suez Canal route in nearby Israel—a Red Sea-Mediterranean rail and port link from Eilat to Ashdod that will lead directly to the China-run port of Piraeus in Greece. The so-called Red-Med high-speed rail would give China yet another alternative in channeling Indian Ocean commerce to Europe across volatile Middle Eastern territories.[11] Multiple routes might seem redundant on purely economic grounds, but they create flexibility that is useful to military planners in addition to strengthening diplomatic leverage with economic ties.

The strongest competition to the Suez Canal will appear in the coming decades as the Arctic passage opens to regular shipping. The savings in time and cost will be particularly important for China because its largest trade partners are in Europe. Using the Arctic route, Chinese shippers can reach ports in Rotterdam and Hamburg in 35 days instead of 50 days via Suez. The average costs are likely to drop 20 to 30 percent.[12] This means that China and Egypt have inherently diverging interests in the Canal's future—Egypt is becoming more dependent on Suez revenues to make ends meet whereas China feels less incentive to invest in an enterprise it expects to avoid whenever possible.

Sisi has spent over $8 billion to refurbish the canal, adding a new channel to allow two-way traffic and to accommodate modern supertankers.[13] The expansion was on the drawing boards well before Sisi took power, reflecting Egyptian planners' long-standing desire to fend off the growing competition for maritime traffic. But Egypt's post-revolutionary economic crisis has added a greater urgency because the government needs to boost Suez Canal revenues to offset the rapid plunge in tourism and workers' remittances. For decades, these were Egypt's two biggest sources of foreign exchange but, in recent years, both have been devastated by terrorist attacks against foreigners and by falling oil prices in the Gulf countries.[14] After terrorists shot down a Russian passenger plane over Sinai in 2015, Egypt lost its most lucrative flow of foreign visitors. Tourism officials tried to adjust by attracting more Chinese travelers, but their numbers are still quite small, and it would be years before they could close the gap left by fleeing Westerners.[15]

Sisi was worried that the canal's modernization would deepen Egyptian debt, leaving him more vulnerable to nationalist criticism and foreign pressure. After failed negotiations with China and several other prospective lenders, he decided to raise the money internally with contributions from the public. At first, the government planned to sell shares in the Canal Authority, allowing individual citizens to acquire direct ownership of the nation's most prized asset.[16] Before long, however, he changed his mind, preferring to keep exclusive control in state hands—and, thus, under continued military command. Instead, he gave the public an opportunity to buy long-term bonds at above-market interest rates and with guaranteed payouts either annually for small purchases or quarterly for larger amounts. The bonds sold out in eight days—faster than anyone had predicted.[17] Seeing a chance to earn a premium on idle savings, millions of citizens were willing to accept a bad bargain. They let their already indebted rulers assume even greater obligations as long as the potential victims of future devaluations and defaults were Egyptians instead of foreigners.

Regardless of its financing methods, the renovated canal did not yield a substantial increase in revenues, and Egypt's economic problems grew deeper than ever. With foreign reserves dwindling, Sisi's government faced the prospect of defaulting on foreign debt repayments and reluctantly sought assistance from the International Monetary Fund (IMF). Appealing to the IMF was a serious setback for Sisi because he had long objected to their pressures to undertake painful economic reforms. For years, the bulk of the government budget has been locked up in unproductive expenditures that Egypt's rulers regarded as politically untouchable—interest payments on foreign debt (30 percent), subsidies for energy and food (about 20 percent), and salaries of public employees (around 25 percent).[18] At first, Sisi managed to avoid dealing with the IMF by patching together special handouts from the Gulf states, but those funds dried up just when Egypt needed them most to make up for downturns in tourism, remittances, and canal fees.

By 2016, Sisi needed another source of foreign cash not to sidestep the IMF, but to become eligible for exactly the sort of stabilization program he had always denounced—emergency loans conditioned on unpopular cuts in energy subsidies and public-sector salaries. China was the only country willing to help Egypt raise the matching funds it needed to convince the IMF that default was avoidable.[19] The transaction enhanced Beijing's reputation in Egypt, but it also reinforced Chinese misgivings about Sisi's longevity and about betting on such an unpredictable society. In seeking to win over Chinese investors, Egyptians focused less on the supposed merits of the Suez Canal and more on the promise of the new Suez Canal Industrial Zone.

Egyptian planners tried to repackage the canal as the core of a vast industrial enclave that is supposed to pull foreign investment and excess population into exporting hubs between the peripheral cities of Port Said, Ismailia, and Suez.[20] A few Chinese firms have stepped forward to become the leading partners in developing the Suez economic corridor.[21] However, most of them are waiting to see if other foreigners tag along, and they show little enthusiasm for investing in Egypt's tumultuous cities or in the struggling farming regions along the Nile River. Thus, Chinese business activity in Egypt is gravitating toward a handful of outlying cities run mainly by bureaucrats and army officers and cut off from the major populations centers by miles of desert. By narrowing its presence to safe harbors and privileged enclaves, China risks treating Egypt more as a stepping stone than as a society and culture. If China wants Egypt to become a platform for re-export and transshipment, it needs to invest in human capital and social infrastructure for the entire country. Otherwise, Chinese enterprises will probably aggravate Egypt's inequalities and divisions, hastening the political upheavals they so desperately want to avoid.

Sisi's City in the Desert

Outside the Canal Zone, China's most publicized megaproject is the new capital city that Sisi's government is building in the desert outskirts west of Cairo. Faced with the steady deterioration of living conditions in the older urban neighborhoods, Egypt's rulers have chosen to carve out a new and more distant refuge for government workers and wealthy supporters of the military regime. In 2016, the $20 billion project was offered to two state-backed firms in China, but by February 2017 one of them pulled out of the deal, complaining of wide disagreements over pricing and permits.[22] The collapse of negotiations was a serious setback for both governments. China was trying to make a convincing display of its willingness to stand by Egypt when other countries retreated and Sisi was eager to claim credit for narrowing the huge imbalance in trade with China.

The most damaging fallout stemmed from Chinese suspicions that Egyptian officials and their contractor friends were grossly exaggerating land values and construction costs. Chinese firms were ready to bankroll a signature project of Sisi's regime that could bolster its prestige and shore up support among wavering middle-class voters. If successful, the new capital city might prime the pump for other badly needed investments from China and other countries. But the bad odor surrounding the New City business deals suggested that Egyptians could be their own worst enemies—overreaching to squeeze the most from the moment instead of showing they could restrain cronyism and cut red tape when the stakes demanded it. Sisi's planners managed to salvage the project by bringing in more local partners and by reaching out to private firms in China.[23] But the New City fiasco had a chilling effect on already tense commercial relations between Cairo and Beijing.

The sheer size of the failure and the acrimony it generated overshadowed diplomats' efforts to proceed with business as usual. Egyptian and Chinese negotiators retreated to more modest deals in telecommunications, satellite technology, and textiles as well as new currency swaps to promote yuan-denominated trade. None of these advances could support claims that Egypt was destined to become a linchpin of the New Silk Road or China's favored offshore production base for markets in Europe, Africa, and the Middle East. Many Egyptian commentators sensed that their leaders were squandering a fleeting opportunity and had no one but themselves to blame.[24]

As long-term commercial prospects wilted, the public rhetoric of Sino-Egyptian friendship seemed more hollow than ever. In both countries, diplomats and state-controlled media never tired of extolling their common resistance to Western domination and the parallel development of their ancient civilizations. Some of Sisi's defenders argued that China's authoritarian model had already replaced Western liberalism as the guiding vision for Egypt and the rest of the Arab world.[25] No doubt, they hoped to increase Egypt's attractiveness by appealing to Chinese pride and desire for global respect. However, these Egyptians put far too much stock in ideology instead of economic rationality. China's leaders have little interest in winning converts to their brand of one-party rule. They are far more concerned with free trade and efficient markets—practices that Egypt still avoids in fact even as it claims to embrace them in principle.

Rethinking Connectivity

The most striking aspect of Sino-Egyptian discussions about the New Silk Road is that leaders in both countries want to avoid dealing with the majority of the population and their immediate needs. Despite repeated stress on building connectivity and networks across continents and oceans, there is little attention to stimulating the branches and capillaries that could carry the Silk Road's benefits beyond its major nodes and into the deeper levels of society. The multiplier effects of combined projects are seen as spreading between the most active economic centers in neighboring countries—but not between those centers and their own hinterlands.[26]

Shallow networks that bypass most of the countryside and provincial towns cannot produce the sort of inclusive and egalitarian growth China claims to champion. On the contrary, compressing development around central arteries will widen gaps between urban privilege and rural deprivation, favoring the advantaged and politically connected over the marginalized majority. In more open democratic societies, excluded groups and regions can marshal political resources to demand a fairer share of development's benefits. They can use the courts, the media, and the party system to coordinate demands for transparency and access to decision-making. In many countries, organized citizens have forced national governments and their Chinese partners to revise and broaden Silk Road strategies several times. In just the last few years, we have seen numerous examples in Pakistan, Turkey, Nigeria, Indonesia, and even Iran where citizens still enjoy far less formal freedom.

Egypt, however, remains an exception. Ordinary citizens cannot correct the imbalances and injustices of policies shaped exclusively by authoritarian leaders and foreign governments. For two short years, Egyptians struggled to establish democracy and then watched it vanish as quickly as it had appeared. Sisi's rule is notable for its lack of structure and continuity apart from military domination.[27] Unlike his predecessors, he has no ruling party organization and no overarching program. The only permanent feature of Egypt's polity is the endless state of emergency, declared in the aftermath of the 2013 revolution and renewed to fight the subsequent rise of terrorism. This leaves the country in a state of suspended animation where people increasingly whisper about future social convulsions they fear but cannot openly discuss.

How could an Egyptian portion of the Silk Road be reconfigured to alleviate some of these fears instead of reinforcing them? The answer lies in directly confronting Egypt's most urgent social problems rather than avoiding them—moving beyond the illusory safety of the Canal Zone and the desert in order to rebuild the social and economic heart of the Nile Valley. If Egyptian citizens had the voice and freedom of their counterparts in Pakistan and Indonesia, what demands would they press upon the self-appointed architects of their Silk Road? Most likely, they would express the same concerns we hear elsewhere—make an explicit effort to bring the projects' benefits to the towns and villages where most of the people live instead of expecting them to wait indefinitely for the results to trickle down on their own.

Agriculture is the backbone of Egypt's society, but it has been decaying for decades. The key to Egyptian agriculture has always been a well-managed irrigation system, but that essential resource is threatened in several ways.[28] Water shortages and industrial pollution are sparking sharper conflicts between upstream and downstream neighbors. Poor drainage of cropland is causing salinized soils and rising water tables.[29] Rising sea levels along the Mediterranean coast are inundating farms and driving more people into overcrowded cities where they compete for survival with earlier migrants.[30] Crop yields have decreased in many regions and costly reclamation projects have failed to increase total farming area because every feddan (1.038 acres or 4,200 square meters) of new desert lands is offset by losses of cultivable fields from urbanization and maritime erosion.[31]

The most important measures of agrarian renovation are well known, but chronically underfunded. Replacing broken tiles in irrigation channels, covering open drains, and monitoring water consumption are long overdue projects that Egyptian and foreign experts have been urging for decades.[32] They require no controversial campaigns of land reform or peasant mobilization—only consistent financing and intelligent management that stays engaged with local governments and farmers' groups.

Connecting this basic infrastructure to regional and metropolitan markets is also familiar territory for Egyptian planners. After several waves of socialization and privatization, Egypt's farmers have adapted many effective approaches to collective marketing, finance, and transportation. Networking the villages and towns of the Nile Delta and Upper Egypt with one another and with the big cities is already quite advanced.[33] But all of the local channels require constant upgrading and even-handed treatment instead of erratic subsidies that rise or fall with the fortunes of rival allies in Cairo.

If networking strengthens the branches and tributaries of provincial life instead of concentrating on a handful of nodes and enclaves, then people of all classes and regions can see tangible improvements in daily life and look forward to better futures for their families. Eventually, Egyptians could eliminate some of the infectious diseases—carried by animals and water—that have nearly vanished in most countries but persist in the Nile Valley.[34] Dispersing more light industry and construction across the provinces would provide added income and seasonal employment for struggling families that want to remain in their villages and hometowns.[35] That kind of progress could ease pressures throughout society by stemming migration to the capital where the army and its supporters feel surrounded by urban villagers who threaten their privilege and safety.

Pinpointing the Neediest

Is it possible to identify specific localities where deepening connectivity would be especially helpful in raising living standards and moderating social discontent—where improving both social and physical infrastructure could promote political integration as well as stronger markets? Any attempt to answer that question needs to begin by understanding how Egyptians cast their votes in the revolutionary interlude between 2011 and 2012—the only times in recent history they have enjoyed relative freedom of choice between rival parties. In just two years, voters cast ballots in four nationwide polls— the constitutional referendum of March 2011, the parliamentary elections of November 2011–January 2012, the presidential elections of May–June 2012, and the constitutional referendum of December 2012.[36] These were tumultuous times when voter preferences reflected shifting alliances and coalitions. Nonetheless, several consistent patterns stand out that are likely to re-emerge if free elections resume in the future.

The strongest protest votes rallied around the Nur Party—an Islamist faction led by local imams who championed poor people in the most deprived villages and shantytowns. The Nur Party was usually portrayed as a more radical alternative to the Muslim Brotherhood's Freedom and Justice Party, but its constituency reflected social and economic divisions more than religious differences. Nur candidates won in several districts along the Mediterranean coast, where villagers were being displaced by rising sea levels, and in the migrants' slums of western Alexandria. In the Nile Delta, the Nur Party vote was particularly high in agricultural areas where canal water was polluted by industrial waste and where children were commonly infected by tainted milk from diseased animal herds. In Upper Egypt, Nur ran best in the most isolated and destitute districts of Qena and Sohag where they opposed local landlords who still supported the vestiges of Mubarak's old party.[37]

The Freedom and Justice Party (FJP) had a more prosperous social base. It was most popular among the provincial middle class, particularly in the towns where the Muslim Brotherhood was well represented in professional syndicates, business chambers, and farmers groups. The FJP's strongest bastions were the districts south of Cairo—Beni Suef, Fayum, Minya, and Asyut. In these areas, economic development had long been constrained by shortages of water, credit, and public services. Voters there viewed the Muslim Brotherhood as a potential corrective to decades of discrimination against Upper Egypt in favor of the Delta and the capital.[38] When Morsi's government was struggling to hold popular support in Cairo, his party bused thousands of demonstrators from these nearby provinces to Tahrir Square where they held mass rallies on behalf of the revolution. Their boisterous marches visibly unnerved the merchants in central Cairo, helping to tilt urban opinion against a government that many well-off Egyptians believed was too sympathetic to village and small-town interests.[39]

When Morsi tried to grab extraordinary executive powers, the army justified toppling him as a coup against the tyranny of the majority. But Sisi's coup was far more than a change in governments. It had the deeper effect of reversing the sudden rise of rural power that the revolution had unleashed. In this sense, Sisi has presided over a political and social restoration, bolstering the privileges of Cairo's wealthier residents and tying their fate more firmly to military rule. In March 2017, Egypt's courts finally acquitted Mubarak and released him after six years of imprisonment.[40] Mubarak and his party were gone, but Sisi had revived the failed policies—and many of the same discredited personalities—of his predecessor under a repressive regime that was more isolated and vulnerable than ever.

In Egypt, China encounters no pressures to expand the Silk Road's networks so that they reach into long disadvantaged regions and social strata. Egypt's rulers have, at least temporarily, suppressed the sort of popular demands that have encouraged a deeper and more ambitious version of connectivity in Pakistan, Indonesia, and Nigeria. There is little prospect that Chinese investments will reach the neediest Egyptians as long as their own leaders are determined to monopolize the benefits and confine them to special enclaves such as the Suez Industrial Zone and showcase projects such as the New Capital City. China sees no reason to become overextended in Egypt. The grievances that sparked the 2011 revolution could resurface with greater force at any time.[41] Meanwhile, Cairo's influence in Middle Eastern affairs has never been lower, and China is looking to neighboring countries to connect Mediterranean and Indian Ocean commerce—preferring the Persian Gulf monarchies as re-exporting centers and Djibouti as the western base for its growing navy.[42]

Under Sisi, Egypt seems more like a troubled backwater than the indispensible hub of tourism, transport, and diplomacy that its leaders are trying to market to investors and governments around the world. Like most foreigners, Chinese are less willing to pay for access and influence precisely when Egypt's rulers want to raise the costs of doing business in order to prop up a pampered army and a failing economy. This means that Egypt will play, at best, a secondary role in China's overseas expansion, and that Silk Road ventures will bypass the villagers and townsfolk who need them the most.

On the Nile, But off the Map

In less than a decade, Egypt's yearly trade deficit with China has skyrocketed from about $3 billion to nearly $10 billion (Figure 8.1). Meanwhile, Chinese investments trailed far behind. Cumulative investments reached $10 billion—the equivalent of a single year's trade gap—only in 2015, and about half of that was concentrated in big energy projects (Figure 8.2 and Table 8.1). Recent outlays for the Suez Industrial Zone bring China's investments in Egypt close to the total figures for Iran (over $17 billion) and ahead of Turkey (about $13 billion). Nonetheless, these amounts are far below the levels of Chinese commitments in Pakistan, Indonesia, and Nigeria, which range from $33 billion to $44 billion.[43]

Egypt's Minister of Investment, Dalia Khorshid, put the Chinese investment picture in perspective when she explained her restrained hopes for future cooperation with Beijing. She said that her government expected to elevate China's position in the rankings of foreign investors from twenty-third

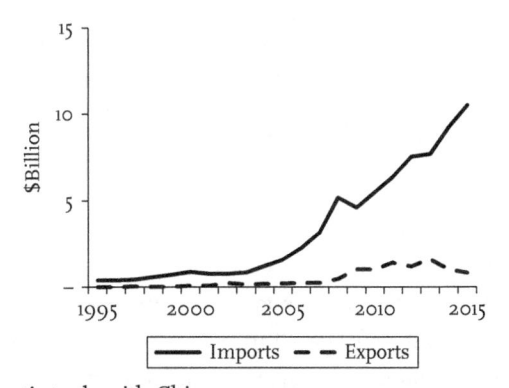

FIGURE 8.1. Egypt's trade with China, 1995–2015.
Author's calculations of data from MIT Media Lab, "Observatory of Economic Complexity," atlas.media.mit.edu, 2017.

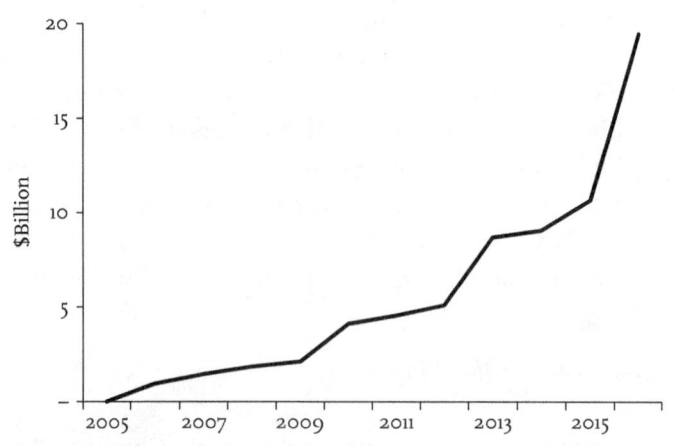

FIGURE 8.2. Cumulative Chinese investment in Egypt, 2005–2016.
Author's calculations of data from American Enterprise Institute, "China Global Investment Tracker," aei.org, 2017.

TABLE 8.1 China's largest investments in Egypt, 2005–2016, projects worth $1 billion or more

YEAR	CHINESE ENTITY	$MILLIONS	PARTY	SECTOR	SUBSECTOR
2013	Sinopec	$3,100	Apache	Energy	
2016	State Construction Eng	$2,700		Real estate	Construction
2016	State Power Investment	$2,640		Energy	Coal
2010	Rongsheng Holding, China NatlChem	$1,990		Energy	Oil
2016	China Railway, AVIC	$1,500		Transport	Rail
2016	Sinoma	$1,190		Real estate	Construction
	Total	$19,470			
	$1–2 B	$4,680			
	$2 B+	$8,440			
	Energy	$8,980			

Author's calculations of data from American Enterprise Institute, "China Global Investment Tracker," aei.org, 2017.

place to the top five or ten.[44] The economist Ahmed El-Sayed Al-Naggar, who is CEO of the Al-Ahram think tank, was more critical. He complained that Egypt was "off the map" of China's overseas investment strategy. Al-Naggar described China as "one of the least-supportive countries at a time when Egypt was desperately in need of direct investments to shore up its economy."[45]

Recent increases of Chinese investment have been quite modest compared to Egypt's urgent requirement. One of the Chinese firms that pulled out of the New City deal outside of Cairo has agreed to return with a much smaller role amid ongoing disputes over inflated land prices and local subcontractors' fees. More and more of Egypt's economists are questioning the value of the project, arguing that the money would be better spent on building small industries in the provincial towns instead of catering to upper-class Cairenes and state employees.[46] Some large Chinese companies are expanding ongoing operations, particularly in fiberglass plants and mobile phone distributorships.[47] Construction firms are building a new port at Ain Sukhna on the Red Sea, including four nearby theme parks designed to attract reluctant workers and their families to the desert region.[48]

But these small steps in foreign investment were overshadowed by greater preoccupations with lingering political threats. Sisi's government remained vulnerable to labor unrest, which flared up in Alexandria and the factory towns of the Nile Delta.[49] Disruptive unions were the last thing Chinese firms wanted to contend with in an already unruly country where special economic zones seemed to be the only safe havens. As Egypt's economic distress deepened, Beijing began to pressure Sisi to cooperate in dealing with China's own domestic troubles. At Beijing's request, Egyptian police arrested dozens of Chinese Uyghurs, including many religious students at al-Azhar University. Many were seized while trying to flee to Turkey and deported to China where they faced charges of terrorism and long prison terms. Those who managed to escape abroad learned that their family members were being rounded up and detained in Xinjiang until they agreed to return home and surrender to the local police.[50]

Egypt's rulers have painted themselves into a corner. They assure foreigners the country has returned to normal and reopened for business, but their actions belie their words. On Sisi's watch, what passes for business is more like the frantic grasping of brokers and cronies intent on stuffing their pockets before the next round of calamities and social upheaval. The chain of predation is well defined—the military first, followed by contractors and fixers, with a swarm of public workers scavenging at the bottom. When multinational firms test the waters, they soon discover higher tolls for the canal, steeper taxes in the industrial parks, and incredible price tags on desert property. Prospective partners realize they are being shaken down, but they suspect they may be buying a building that is about to catch fire before they have a chance to move in. Even if foreigners are willing to bear the added costs and risks, they are deterred by the local elite's profound lack of confidence in their own future.

In this environment, the space for commercial cooperation shrinks more and more. As the canal loses its global luster, the surrounding land is offered up for factories and terminals. When the middle class flees the city, a new capital is built as a desert refuge. Viable investments are confined to fortified enclaves and gated communities—intentionally bypassing the urban slums and village poor. The New Silk Road always runs the risk of concentrating greater resources on already privileged hubs instead of sprouting multiple branches that can bring new life to neglected communities. But, in Egypt, the problem is far more serious than usual. Under Sisi's regime, exclusion of the majority is not temporary or incidental—it is explicit state policy. Unlike citizens in many other countries, ordinary Egyptians have few opportunities to challenge or overturn elite bargains that leave them out in the cold. China's leaders are gradually learning to appreciate the value of popular protests that signal the need to rethink development projects around the world. Like prospective investors everywhere, the Chinese are beginning to show heightened caution in dealing with local partners—including Sisi's entourage—who are willfully indifferent to their own people.

CHAPTER 9 | Islam and the Opening of the Chinese Mind

ISLAM'S IMPACT ON CHINA is growing because its external and internal influences are more intertwined than ever. Islamic civilization permeates the New Silk Road, shaping all of China's efforts to create and integrate megaregions throughout Afro-Eurasia. At the same time, the continuous development of Islam inside China changes the way Chinese people define themselves as a nation and as members of the human family. Both processes are intimately connected. The deeper China enmeshes itself in the Islamic world, the more Chinese must ask themselves what it means to be Chinese. When Chineseness is understood more inclusively and universally, China gains greater confidence and effectiveness in relating to Muslims everywhere, regardless of nationality.

Daily life in China provides countless concrete examples of coevolution in Sino-Islamic relations. More and more citizens are involved in personal interactions with people from different religious and ethnic backgrounds. Anyone who lives in downtown Shanghai is surrounded by the Silk Road without having to look for it. Walking eastward from People's Square along Nanjing East Road, you pass popular Muslim restaurants, yogurt shops, bakeries, boutiques, and leather stores while meeting tour groups and street artists dressed in many distinctive styles of the interior and border provinces. Strolling westward along the side streets of busy arteries such as Guangdong Road and Yan'an Road, you find dozens of halal butchers and grocers displaying fresh meats and handing out samples of fruits and teas from distant fields in Qinghai, Ningxia, Gansu, Shaanxi, Xinjiang, and Yunnan.[1]

Han Chinese with a sense of curiosity have many opportunities to learn about Muslims in their midst and to ponder China's changing place in the world. City dwellers are well aware that geographic and social mobility are changing the face of their neighborhoods, but most are too preoccupied with routine life to reflect on the broader consequences. Intercultural exchange is rising because of greater migration and residential overlap.[2] Nonetheless, physical proximity does not guarantee learning or acceptance. Han attitudes toward Muslims are extraordinarily diverse and unpredictable. In chance encounters with Han acquaintances, I was frequently surprised by the range of reactions people showed to my own research and travel. Three examples stand out because they occurred in quick succession and covered the gambit from academic collaboration to genuine puzzlement to business offers.

During a visit to the mammoth Yangshan Deep Water Port—the world's largest cargo port and a capstone of the maritime Silk Road—a Chinese companion asked about my research interests. "Oh, how wonderful," she laughed, "You must meet my father—he's a leading scholar of Islamic civilization in China. I'll call him tonight and arrange a visit to his university in Yinchuan. He's one of the advisors for the World Muslim City in Ningxia." Our four-day visit was packed with examples of cultural mixing and religious resilience. Our hosts described works of Islamic-Confucian literature, customary laws that local Muslims still apply in private dispute resolution, and an assortment of hybrid languages that have flourished along the northern frontier. There was even a special museum dedicated to the universal themes of prehistoric rock paintings from around the world.[3]

After I returned to Shanghai a neighbor asked what I'd seen in Ningxia. When I mentioned visiting a famous mosque, her younger friend couldn't contain her surprise. "There are *mosques* in China? You mean places where Muslims *pray*?" "Of course," the neighbor responded, "We have millions of Muslims who practice their religion everywhere. They're some of our most important minority nationalities." Then, I showed some photos of Yinchuan's Nanguan Mosque and everyone offered an opinion on which features were typically Chinese and which were local contributions.[4]

A few weeks later, a Chinese colleague came to me with a book she was finishing on provincial tourism markets in the western and southern regions. A Han native of Xinjiang, she was running government-funded initiatives to develop local tourist attractions that would draw middle-class urbanites to small towns and villages in the interior. She was a university professor, an entrepreneur, and a political broker on a mission. Her work traded on ethnic and religious stereotypes, commercial opportunities, and regional rivalries with a gusto that inspired her dozen or so graduate trainees to build a chain of consultancies serving government and business clients nationwide.[5]

I helped her find an editor to prepare an English-language version of her new textbook for international as well as Chinese audiences.

Not all interactions between Islamic and Chinese cultures are so smooth and pleasant. Frictions and contradictions are equally widespread. Ethnocentrism and chauvinism abound in China and one of its nastiest byproducts is a lingering Islamophobia that hard-line security forces stoke to justify wholesale repression against Muslim communities, particularly young Uyghur men.[6] Chinese citizens are well aware of these hatreds and they vigorously debate ethnic and religious issues no matter how much the party state tries to squash discussion. Generations of nationalist leaders have struggled with these problems for over a century during which attitudes and values have changed several times with no final resolution. Nonetheless, the acceptance of religious and racial pluralism has spread more widely than ever across scholarly disciplines and popular audiences.[7]

Understandings of Chineseness are more complex and cosmopolitan than ever, including changing self-perceptions of Han identities. Much of the credit can be traced to ongoing Chinese debates about Islam. Every step in the evolution of Chinese nationalism has been directly shaped by the emergence of modern historical studies, anthropology, archeology, sociology, folklore, philosophy, and comparative religion.[8] In all of these fields, debates over Islamic civilization have sparked rivalries between scientific and ideological factions pressing alternative views of how China should develop as a nation and a member of the world system.

In several cases, nationalist thinkers have used Islamic issues as levers to pry open what they regarded as myths and delusions about Chinese tradition and culture. China's contemporary students of Islamic studies are keenly aware of these contributions. They view themselves as continuing an important tradition of questioning and criticizing both official and popular opinions in light of the best scholarly evidence. Their mentality reflects a number of landmark changes in China's ongoing discovery of Islam at home and around the world.

Coauthoring Chinese Civilization

One of the earliest targets of modern scholarship in China was the ethnocentric myth of Han exclusivism. In many versions, received chronicles portrayed an unbroken Chinese history dominated by a single ancient race with a uniquely homogeneous culture. In this account, Chinese civilization began independently in the Yellow River valley and spread throughout the territories that comprise today's mainland China.[9] A powerful leader in demolishing these views was Gu Jie Gang, a pioneer of interdisciplinary science who combined critical analysis of ancient texts with the study of contemporary folklore.[10] Gu was part of the New Culture Movement inspired by Hu Shi, the famous student of John Dewey, and a proponent of science and democracy as the touchstones of national modernization.[11]

Gu's approach to "doubting antiquity" became a rallying point for resistance to authoritarianism on multiple fronts—Confucian conformism, Nationalist militarism, and Communist dogma.[12] His celebration of popular cultures aimed to mobilize mass opposition to the Japanese occupation, especially among ethnic minorities in the northern borderlands. Gu portrayed the minorities as key contributors to Chinese civilization who had repeatedly rescued Han dynasties from internal rebellion and rekindled creativity whenever the ruling class succumbed to rigid Confucianism.[13]

One of his most frequently cited overviews explained the argument this way. "In the period of the Warring Kingdoms (403–255 B.C.), when there was an influx of many new racial elements, China was unusually vigorous and powerful, but in the Han dynasty, the arbitrary power of the monarchy, and the exclusiveness of Confucian teaching, brought Chinese culture to the verge of extinction. . . . Had it not been for the infusion of new blood from the *wu hu*, or Five Barbarian Tribes of the Chin dynasty (265–419 A.D.), from the Ch'i-tan (eleventh century), from the Ju-chên (twelfth century), and the Mongols (thirteenth century), I fear that the Han race could not have survived. In recent years, each of the great powers of the world has violently encroached upon our sovereignty. But as their civilization is superior to ours, it is futile to expect that they can also be subdued (like the neighboring tribes of earlier times) by assimilation to our culture. . . . . When one looks at the problem from this angle, one is almost forced to conclude that our race has deteriorated, and that its extinction is so near that all we can do is to sit pessimistically waiting for the end."[14]

Gu Jie Gang saw Chinese-speaking Muslims in much the same way that Ibn Khaldun viewed the tribes of North Africa—as half-assimilated primitives whose social solidarity and martial prowess destined them to play a key role in cyclical struggles between semi-pastoral and sedentary societies.[15] The cultural superiority of the Han depended on periodic infusions of vitality from less sophisticated neighbors, but both sides made essential contributions to building a common civilization.

Of course, protracted warfare strongly colored all suggestions that Muslims and other minorities were potential saviors of a Chinese civilization that Han elites had corrupted. The Japanese occupation specifically targeted

Chinese Muslims in efforts to provoke separatist mutinies. During the civil war, Communist troops drifted between Muslim warlords who decimated them from the west and Muslim villagers who gave them refuge in the north.[16] After liberation, Mao's governments continued to cultivate special ties with Chinese-speaking Muslims, creating an official nationality status for them—the Hui category—and co-opting many of their educated youth into prestigious bureaucratic and university positions.[17]

Pluralism and Polycentric Evolution

The new sciences of ethnography and archeology helped to popularize China's self-image as a multiracial society with a rich mix of distinct cultures. Ethnographers highlighted the creativity of non-Han peoples in the frontier areas and archeologists surveyed the multiple centers of Han genesis in the major river valleys.[18] As the two fields overlapped more and more, they began to share a wider geographic coverage. Archeology showed that many non-Han civilizations were older and more advanced than expected while ethnography detailed divergences between Han communities that had been lumped together in conventional histories.[19]

A seminal thinker that shaped both of these fields was Fei Xiao Tong, a student of Bronislaw Malinowski and leader in the study of peasant society. Fei advised the Communist government's controversial project to identify and codify an official listing of Chinese nationalities. His professional image is like a weathered icon that loses and regains its luster at least once every decade. He has been alternatively portrayed as a groundbreaking social scientist who spoke truth to power and as an enabler of tyrants who misused his work and nearly destroyed him.[20]

Fei and his colleagues encouraged an ongoing collaboration between social scientists and politicians that caused constant splits and animosities on both sides. Every incarnation of the nationalities policy has generated widespread anger over alleged arbitrariness and unfairness. Over time, no aspect of the nationalities debates has proved more troublesome than the decision to recognize the Hui as a separate community of Chinese-speaking Muslims—the only group whose ethnicity is defined by religion.[21]

Because Muslims generally believe that their common religion supersedes differences of race and language, China's insistence on Hui nationality seems counterintuitive and demands an explanation. The official account describes the Hui as a melting pot of Muslims who came to China from many places in the Middle East and Central Asia over several centuries. In time, these immigrants supposedly mingled with one another and with indigenous peoples to form a new amalgam that is similar to Han Chinese in most respects while retaining a separate attachment to Islam.[22]

Naturally, there are many other explanations of the Hui category that are far less flattering to its proponents. Many see it as an effort to divide China's Muslims into weak factions that can be manipulated by the state. Splitting Muslims into language groups helps to isolate the Uyghurs in Xinjiang who have repeatedly mounted the strongest resistance to central government control.[23] Others view the Hui's special status as an affirmative action program designed to co-opt a potential swing constituency that has been fabricated by Han elites.[24] There is also a suspicion that China's rulers want to use disputes over the Hui and other minorities to distract attention from simmering cleavages among Han subcultures and regional identities. By stressing the subordination of many non-Han others, the party state allegedly seeks to defuse the explosive potential of open conflicts among the Han themselves.[25]

As China's official pluralist narrative began showing its cracks more openly, Fei and his colleagues tried to repair the damage with various adjustments and compromises. Their most notable contribution was the so-called snowball theory of evolution, which sought to synthesize new findings from ethnology and archeology in a historical panorama that would be palatable to post-Mao rulers. The key trade-off in the theory was emphasizing internal diversity and exchange while minimizing outside influences from beyond China's current borders. As long as the components were confined to the Chinese homeland, their stories could be retold in countless ways that included everyone in the extended family saga.[26]

The snowball analogy is both simple and ambiguous—leaving ample room for interpretation and negotiation. The core of ancient Chinese civilization arose in the central plains of the Yellow River thousands of years ago. It absorbed influences from many racial and cultural groups around a Han nucleus. Then, this composite core spread like a rolling snowball, adding layer after layer as it attracted neighboring communities in its path.[27]

The script allows for multiple centers of ancient Chinese civilization in northern, southern, and central regions that blended into one another after many generations of exchange and competition. Non-Han peoples were involved from the earliest times and numerous variations in Han culture persisted all along. Thus, Chinese civilization is the mutual creation of many races and regions whose interactions form a flourishing ecosystem of human and natural diversity.

All versions of the snowball theory finesse the most difficult questions. Did the Han nucleus assimilate the outer layers, transforming them into a common substance? Did the new elements—Han and non-Han—change everything else into hybrids that evolved together? Or perhaps there are several snowballs in constant motion, fusing and separating in rhythms that are still poorly understood. Fei Xiao Tong's legacy continues to animate all of the current debates over ethnic and religious relations in China.[28] More than anyone, he pushed open the door of empirical investigation and critical thinking to a degree that no authoritarian elite can reverse.

Chinese Universalisms

Discrediting Han chauvinism and promoting multiethnic pluralism have greatly benefitted Chinese writers who want to stress the universal relevance of their civilization for all of humanity. Both before and during Communist rule, the victories of nationalist iconoclasts such as Gu Jie Gang and Fei Xiao Tong ironically paved the way for a recent comeback by Confucian revisionists who seemed to have been cast aside on the mainland.[29] The wave of Confucian revival has looked to Islam—in China and abroad—for an ally in stressing cosmopolitanism over nationalism, especially the importance of ethics and religion as a balance to materialism and atheism.[30]

Bridges between Confucians and Muslims have multiplied since Mao's death. Many of these connections draw inspiration from the earlier writings of Tang Jun Yi, a philosopher and follower of Karl Jaspers who compared Confucianism to the global religions of Islam, Christianity, and Buddhism.[31] Tang believed that Confucian philosophy was an original contribution to humanity that transcended culture and place. Like Jaspers, he suggested that a handful of universal traditions might form the building blocks of a world religion—or global ethic for the more secularly minded—that would unite all peoples.[32]

Tang helped to place Confucian thought at the center of international debates over comparative religion, hermeneutics, and interfaith relations. By globalizing Confucianism instead of touting it as an exclusively Chinese identity, neo-traditionalists were able to assemble an impressive transnational coalition that rivals Beijing's efforts to appropriate or reinvent China's cultural heritage. Competing interpretations of Confucianism are flourishing in China and elsewhere, pushing the party state into constant efforts to co-opt or supersede them.[33] Following Tang's specific interests in Islam, much of the Confucian outreach addresses Muslim audiences at home and abroad.

Chinese scholars have organized several international conferences exploring exchanges between Islam and Confucianism. They showcase mutual borrowings in literature as well as folkloric and mystical parallels between Sufism and Daoism. Many writers treat Islam as the most recent addition to China's traditional belief systems—on a par with Confucianism, Daoism, and Buddhism.[34] More and more Han Chinese scholars have followed the example of Hui and foreign writers who popularized discussions of the Han Kitab. These are well-known works of Chinese Muslims during the Ming and Qing periods that elaborated Islamic concepts with Chinese vocabulary, coining many terms that resonate in Confucian, Daoist, and Buddhist imaginations.[35]

The New Silk Road initiative tries to harness all of these openings to Islam in order to promote China as a Muslim-friendly society that stands apart from European and American tendencies to stigmatize and marginalize Muslims in general.[36] At the same time, however, Beijing is seriously damaging its reputation by repressing Uyghur religious practice and turning Xinjiang into a virtual war zone.[37] This fans Islamophobic sentiment among the Han population, contradicting the government's rhetoric that Islam should be viewed as a national resource instead of an alien menace.[38]

The more ferociously Beijing attacks the Uyghurs, the more desperately it cultivates the special status of the Hui as the supposedly authentic face of Chinese Islam. Promoting the official narrative of Hui patriotism and integration is a top priority for government-supported experts in universities and think tanks. Their efforts include many campaigns directed at the mass media and the school system at all levels. A few examples are particularly helpful in understanding the intent and shortcomings of the wider message.

For several years, there has been an ongoing celebration of Zheng He, the Muslim admiral who built and sailed the Ming dynasty armada of treasure ships on several voyages to the Indian Ocean, the Red Sea, and the east coast of Africa.[39] Zheng He has become a multivocal icon advancing several themes at once for national and foreign audiences. He embodies the faithful Muslim patriot who served his country and spread its glory to distant lands. He is the peaceful ambassador who relied on diplomacy instead of military might even when his forces enjoyed overwhelming superiority.[40] He is the forerunner of China's maritime expansion and its determination to build a blue water navy to protect the seas for all nations. On top of all that, he's also a money-making marketing emblem for sporting goods, household appliances, and travel agencies.[41]

In addition, Chinese history books increasingly treat the Mongol-ruled Yuan dynasty as an indigenous power that connected China to a wider transcontinental empire. Muslim immigrants who served Mongol overlords in governing the Han population are described as absorbing and enhancing Chinese culture—tacitly accepting the superiority of the civilization they once ruled.[42] As a result, both Mongols and Muslims serve a dual role—affirming the self-image of Chinese power and helping to project it into foreign lands. Beijing has consolidated control over the frontier territories where Mongol and Muslim forces once challenged central authority so there is no obstacle to including both groups into the nation and benefitting from their historic ties throughout Eurasia.[43]

One of the most entertaining examples of Islam's appeal in popular culture is the enormous affection for Afanti (阿凡提)—the legendary Sufi folk hero who is also known as Mullah Nasreddin in Turkish and Persian or Goha in Arabic. Afanti is the wise fool that everyone loves for lampooning authority and exposing hypocrisy wherever he finds them.[44] He is a favorite star of cartoons, comic strips, and animated features in the mass media and on the internet. Bookshops are filled with multiple editions of his adventures and wisecracks, which remind people of Zhuangzi's irreverent role in Daoist fables.[45] Han Chinese who hear Afanti stories for the first time almost always recognize them, but can't tell you exactly where they've heard them before. Assuming the tales are Chinese to the core, they are surprised to learn that identical versions tickle the ribs of Muslims in dozens of languages around the world.

Major Themes in China's Islamic Studies

The community of Chinese scholars focusing on Islamic issues is wide-ranging and growing rapidly in both talent and influence. As the field expands, it is increasingly divided between those trained in languages and area studies versus those who focus on social sciences and international relations.[46] Both groups eventually find themselves trying to acquire the additional skills they need to provide integrated and interdisciplinary analysis. Language specialists struggle to learn social science theory and quantitative methods while international relations experts dive into exotic languages with little or no prior exposure. Regardless of which track they follow, Chinese scholars have only limited opportunity to live and travel abroad for extended periods. This puts them at a serious disadvantage when dealing with China's diplomats and top officials who enjoy more personal freedom and greater access to privileged information.

Generational differences are lessened by extensive networking between teachers and former students who collaborate throughout their careers on multiple research projects and training programs across the country. A prime example is the prolific lineage of Zhu Wei Lie, the famous professor of Arabic language studies who has trained most of China's senior Middle Eastern diplomats in addition to several generations of historians, social scientists, and journalists.[47] His protégés are everywhere, running departments and think tanks, staffing government and party research bureaus, and taking up visiting positions at universities in dozens of countries.

One of Zhu's early students was the noted historian Hua Tao, whose career has spanned Turkish, Mongol, and Hui studies, including long involvement in ethnic and religious policies in Xinjiang.[48] Hua stresses Xinjiang's continuing role as a crossroads for multiple cultures and religions—an inseparable part of China, but a pluralistic society where the state has an obligation to see that all groups benefit from economic development. This is a common viewpoint among Chinese scholars that has usually been overshadowed by the preference for military force among security and party officials who set policy.[49] Hua Tao has organized several international meetings featuring Islamic modernists such as Seyyed Hossein Nasr, Neo-Confucians such as Tu Wei Ming, and Christian liberals from several denominations.[50] The common objective is to demonstrate productive interfaith exchanges that contradict expectations about the clash of civilizations. Hua's graduate students include Hui and Uyghur Muslims from across China who often become teachers in their home provinces and in Islamic institutes abroad.

Younger members of Zhu's circle have gone on to lead programs in Arabic, international politics, comparative religion, and economics at top universities in Beijing, Shanghai, Nanjing, and many other cities. Wu Bing is an Arabic teacher who doubles as a leading commentator on Iranian affairs and Shi'ism. Like many area specialists who are trained as linguists, Wu has been pressed into service as a political analyst and official spokesman for policies ranging from backing the Assad regime in the Syrian civil war to criticizing military buildups in the Persian Gulf.[51] Sun De Gang is an international relations theorist who has made original contributions on quasi-alliances, soft military power, and Chinese mediation in Middle East conflicts. Sun is a rare example of a regional expert who not only uses social theory but refashions it to provoke new thinking that is helpful to policymakers and scholars alike.[52] Niu Song is a student of global pilgrimage systems—including the Hajj—who follows their growing impact on international politics. Niu is one of a handful of Chinese writers dealing with transnational religion as an opportunity for exerting diplomatic influence—a field that is frequently labeled "geo-religion" to distinguish it from geopolitics and geoeconomics.[53] Qian Xu Ming focuses on China's Middle East energy suppliers while pursuing interests in commercial relations with Iran and Israel. His work highlights the contradiction between the great powers' pursuit of cooperation in the global economy and their growing military competition in strategic regions.[54]

All of these scholars work on New Silk Road issues from interdisciplinary and trans-regional perspectives. However, the prevailing trend among researchers is toward greater specialization in nationalities institutes, government think tanks, and groups funded by private businesses. Just when China needs more global and transcontinental thinking than ever, many of its best minds are moving in the opposite direction. Religion is being confounded with ethnicity, diplomacy is being eclipsed by military expansion, and development is seen in terms of private business deals.[55]

China is fortunate to have a fertile tradition of Islamic studies that enriches many disciplines and contributes to international knowledge. Chinese minds are far more open today than when the Yellow Emperor was revered as the mythical father of all native races. Nonetheless, ultranationalism is still widespread, and authoritarian rulers find it useful to stir fears of religious extremism when they want to justify curtailing freedom in general.[56]

Chinese and Western Encounters with Islam

China's encounters with the Islamic world have differed widely from Western experiences. China's westward expansion toward Muslim societies gathered momentum just as Europe's maritime empires reached beyond the Mediterranean to pursue trade and conquest in far-flung lands across the Atlantic and Pacific. Western powers attained clear-cut military and economic dominance over Muslim subjects, seldom questioning their inherent superiority as a civilization. In contrast, Sino-Islamic relations were much more varied and ambiguous. Depending on the circumstances, Han Chinese might view Muslims as barbarians or allies, as inferiors or heirs to a sister civilization, as second-class citizens or as indispensable partners in a great nation with worldwide interests.

China refashioned its relations with Muslim societies several times as it passed from a multinational empire to a modern nation-state composed of more than 50 official ethnic groups. Some of the most lasting transformations occurred under non-Han emperors. During the Yuan dynasty (1271–1368),

Mongol rulers reunited China after centuries of division and internal warfare. The Mongols brought thousands of Muslim immigrants to China to serve as junior partners in controlling the predominantly Han population and in running the economy. Many of them intermarried with locals, and their ethnically mixed descendants form the nucleus of what eventually became today's Hui community of Chinese-speaking Muslims.[57] The Qing dynasty (1644–1912), led by the Manchus, doubled the size of China's territories, permanently incorporating northern and northwestern regions occupied by millions of Turkic-speaking Muslims with historic ties to Central Asia, Iran, and Turkey.[58]

Today, China offers to engage Islamic countries in a way that the West never imagined—as coauthors of a trans-hemispheric community that redistributes power and wealth more equitably than ever before. Beijing uses the symbolism of the New Silk Road to portray Chinese attitudes toward Islam as the antithesis of Western colonialism and religious antagonism. Universalist ideals of inclusiveness and tolerance are projected backward as though they flowed seamlessly from past to present and on to a future vision of harmony between civilizations.[59] Such themes can carry considerable appeal for nonwhite and non-Christian citizens in postcolonial societies, particularly as Europe and the United States appear headed in the opposite direction with the rise of racism and Islamophobia.

Nonetheless, China's partners are adept at distinguishing fact from rhetoric and placing interest above emotion. They realize that Silk Road projects are born of hardheaded bargaining over a thousand details with Chinese enterprises committed to maximizing both profits and strategic advantages. They constantly monitor one another's negotiations with Beijing, keeping their eyes open for competing opportunities from China's many rivals and demanding multiple rounds of renegotiation when their deals sour or stall. As foreign partners force Beijing's negotiators to bend to popular pressures on so many fronts, there are growing—but unfulfilled—expectations among younger and educated Chinese citizens that their voices will also reach more deeply into the corridors of power.

CHAPTER 10 | Learning Abroad, Evading at Home

AS THE NEW SILK Road initiatives expose the difficulties of building multiple megaregions and weaving them into a hemispheric network, China's leaders will also have to confront the unfinished business of integrating their own society. Divisions inside China are severe and deepening rapidly. They intersect and aggravate one another, producing more and more groups with grievances that cannot be adequately addressed by a single-party state that chokes public debate and outlaws collective action.

Sooner or later, the ruling elite will have to create more channels for political representation. Chinese society is not being heard. Families and cliques with money and connections are battling to consolidate influence in a system with few fixed laws or property rights. Frustrated citizens are magnifying one another's disdain for authority through social media and the internet. Precisely when China's leaders are inviting the world to join a supposedly more democratic global order, they are trying to shore up a faltering monopoly of power at home.

China has many options for experimenting with inclusive ruling formulas that allow power-sharing without embracing free elections and multiparty pluralism. Since Mao's death, debates over political reform have started and stalled several times—in private discussions of party leaders and in the public arena.[1] As those debates resume, China will increasingly see itself as a changed society with a more prominent position in world affairs. The New Silk Road is likely to encourage both transformations.

China's success in transcontinental politics hinges not on spreading hard-wired infrastructure, but on winning the trust and cooperation of skeptical and self-governing citizens in dozens of developing countries, including the largest and most dynamic nations of the Islamic world. When Chinese listen to these peoples' grievances and respect their needs, they demonstrate a willingness to learn and compromise that opens doors in many directions. In contrast, cutting secret deals with a handful of autocrats sets off chain-reaction protests and self-defeating efforts to contain the fallout. All of these exchanges are occurring under constant examination along the Silk Road, in the global media, and among attentive Chinese audiences. If China's leaders can cultivate skills of mediation and consensus building abroad, then Chinese citizens will expect to see some concrete benefits of that learning translated into greater reciprocity between state and society at home.

In trying to invent Afro-Eurasia and in thwarting domestic reform, China's rulers are experimenting with geography as a tool of statecraft rather than accepting it as a natural or historical given. In different ways, they want to manipulate geography in order to control people. On one hand, they are creating a grand hemispheric canvass on which to magnify China's global influence while, on the other hand, they juggle regional and provincial units to dilute the strength of the party state's would-be rivals within. Beyond China's borders, promoting interconnected megaregions serves to multiply Beijing's power, but, inside China, shuffling jurisdictions aims to divide the strength of independent groups who might wish to challenge that power by acting together.[2]

The multiple visions of the New Silk Road are filled with redundant routes and indefinite timelines. The puzzle has a thousand pieces that can be assembled and rearranged in changing combinations. Each megaregion can reinforce historic flows and identities or try to bend them in this or that direction to suit political conditions. When necessary, new transnational markets and networks can replace or bypass existing ones altogether. Sometimes, preserving familiar labels can help to smooth the process, but, in other cases, a special acronym or hyphenated title can trumpet new alliances and grand coalitions. Xi Jinping's keynote address to the global summit on the Belt and Road Initiative in May 2017 is filled with such references to budding megaregions, real and imagined.[3]

The extensive networks of the Islamic world can both enable and limit these efforts to play with geography. All of China's most important Muslim partners have their own ambitions for translating Silk Road connections into political clout. Their citizens are increasingly pushing government negotiators to exploit their leverage with China in order to maximize national independence and avoid becoming satellites or quasi-colonies. Under these conditions, the greatest obstacles to Chinese initiatives come not from inflexible geographic realities, but from the competing political projects of Beijing's designated partners. It is far easier for Chinese engineers to tunnel through mountains and connect far-flung ports than for Beijing's diplomats to contend with Iran's designs in the Middle East or Indonesia's determination to control its internal waterways.

Disorganizing Society

Inside China, geography plays a defensive role by blocking the influence of social and economic groups that seek to engage in collective action. In allocating resources and authority, party and governmental organizations tend to stress jurisdictions such as provinces and municipalities over functional categories such as entrepreneurs or professionals. Competition between local governments pursuing wider economic activities has encouraged speculation that administrative decentralization has created de facto federalism in China. Some commentators view this a welcome devolution of power and willingness to encourage local initiative, but many people criticize it as opening the door for cronyism and corruption.[4]

Playing regional power centers against one another is a familiar theme in China, but geography has other political uses that are becoming more important. As many types of interest groups become more self-conscious and assertive, there will be greater need to grant them some formal role in decision-making. In modern China, both Nationalist and Communist regimes have tried various ways of organizing group representation in legislative and administrative processes, including corporatist bodies and mixed commissions with appointed and elected members. These techniques are standard practice in authoritarian systems, and we are likely to see more of them in China as political reform resurfaces on the national agenda.[5]

Even these contrived methods of stifling independent expression are usually not enough to satisfy the repressive elites that employ them. Hence, authoritarian regimes usually combine geographic and functional channels in ways that undermine the integrity of both types of representation. When elections are permitted, geographic constituencies are unequally weighted in order to impede majority rule. If functional groups enjoy special quotas, their relative strengths are arbitrarily determined, and their members are appointed or chosen by small groups of electors.

Hong Kong's semi-democracy is encumbered by all of these techniques. Dissident candidates can win the majority of votes and still be outnumbered in the Legislative Council because of gerrymandered districts and reserved seats for contrived social categories. If a few troublesome deputies manage

TABLE 10.1 Hong Kong Legislative Council election results by geographic and functional constituencies, September 4, 2016

DISTRICT/SEATS	REGISTERED VOTERS	VALID VOTES	SHARES OF VOTES IN GEOGRAPHIC DISTRICTS (PERCENT)			
			PRO-BEIJING	PRO-DEMO'CY	LOCAL RULE	OTHER
All Geographic/35	**3,779,085**	**2,163,917**	**30.69**	**31.01**	**15.61**	**22.68**
Hong Kong Island/6	627,807	376,577	39.26	25.84	19.48	15.43
Kowloon West/6	488,129	278,871	36.68	28.89	21.09	13.34
Kowloon East/5	601,567	328,993	30.04	39.53	10.11	20.31
New Terrs. West/9	1,086,511	603,446	26.51	26.62	10.68	36.20
New Terrs. East/9	975,071	580,524	26.61	35.95	18.54	18.89
At Large/5	**3,473,792**	**1,909,968**	**41.88**	**58.02**	—	—

SHARES OF SEATS BY TYPE OF CONSTITUENCY

TYPE OF CONSTITUENCY	PRO-BEIJING	PRO-DEMO'CY	LOCAL RULE*	OTHER	TOTAL
Total	**40**	**23**	**6**	**1**	**70**
Geographic Districts	16	13	6	0	35
At Large	2	3	0	0	5
Functional Groups	22	7	0	1	30

*Includes winning Local Rule candidates who were later prevented from taking their seats.

Author's calculations of data from Hong Kong Special Administrative Region, *2016 Legislative Council Election*, elections.gov.hk, September 6, 2016.

to slip through the obstacle course, they may be barred from taking their seats or expelled after challenges from the executive.[6]

Pro-Beijing politicians control 57 percent of the seats in Hong Kong's Legislative Council even though they won only 31 percent of the 2.1 million votes cast in the elections of September 2016 (Table 10.1). Some of the distortion resulted from electoral laws that handicap independents and small parties. These barriers allowed Pro-Beijing candidates to claim 16 of the 35 geographic seats while losing to Pro-Democracy groups in three of the five electoral regions. But the crux of the regime's power is its domination of the 30 non-geographic seats reserved for small occupational groups that are deemed critically important to Hong Kong's future economic development (Table 10.2). Most of these constituencies are extremely small—24 have fewer than 10,000 registered electors—and about one-third of them are uncontested.[7] Beijing's allies control 22 functional seats, giving them a virtually guaranteed legislative majority based on no more than 140,000 voters regardless of how the total electorate of 3.7 million people decides. In practice, these are appointed positions for special constituencies that can be redrawn at will by the city's Chief Executive.

When discussions of political reform are tolerated on the mainland, the media are filled with proposals to adopt similar mixtures of geographic and functional representation for the entire nation. Elections can be structured in several ways—locally or nationally, with limited or universal suffrage, within a single party or between competing factions. But, as long as the ruling elite shuffles the deck and deals the hands, it can discourage majorities from emerging, and effectively veto them if they do.[8]

Braudel and the River Gods

Students of regionalism who follow Braudel's thinking are often criticized for exaggerating the influence of natural forces and physical barriers while discounting the transformative power of human agents. This perceived imbalance is viewed as increasingly troublesome as state actors acquire powerful new technologies.[9] In contrast, Chinese mythology is filled with ancient gods and ancestors who fostered civilization by changing the flows of rivers and reshaping the contours of lakes and oceans. Miraculous engineering—inspired by compassion for human suffering and aided by artful trickery—compels nature to serve the people in ways that seem to defy the laws of nature.[10]

TABLE 10.2 Functional constituencies represented in the Hong Kong Legislative Council, 30 seats

CONSTITUENCY	REGISTERED BODIES	REGISTERED INDIVIDUALS	CONTESTED/ UNCONTESTED	WINNER'S AFFILIATION
Heung Yee Kuk (rural)		147	Uncontested	Pro-Beijing, BPA
Agriculture and Fisheries	154			Pro-Beijing, DAB
Insurance	134		Uncontested	Independent
Transport	195			Pro-Beijing, Liberal
Education		88,185		Pro-Democracy, PTU
Legal		6,773		Pro-Democracy, Civic
Accountancy		26,008		Pro-Democracy, PC
Medical		11,191		Nonpartisan
Health Services		37,423		Nonpartisan
Engineering		9,406		Pro-Beijing, BPA
Architectural, Planning		7,371		Nonpartisan
Labour (3 seats)	668		Uncontested	Pro-Beijing, FLU, 2 FTU
Social Welfare		13,824		Independent
Real Estate and Const'n	484		Uncontested	Pro-Beijing, BPA
Tourism	1,426	230		Nonpartisan
Commercial (First)	1,086			Pro-Beijing, BPA
Commercial (Second)	618		Uncontested	Nonpartisan

Industrial (First)	544	Uncontested	Pro-Beijing, BPA
Industrial (Second)	769	Uncontested	Nonpartisan
Finance	125	Uncontested	Nonpartisan
Financial Services	622		Pro-Beijing, BPA
Sports, Arts, Publication	2,525		Pro-Beijing, New Forum
Import and Export	865	Uncontested	Pro-Beijing, DAB
Textiles and Garment	2,276		Pro-Beijing, Liberal
Wholesale and Retail	1,853		Pro-Beijing, Liberal
Information Technology	404		Pro-Democracy, PC
Catering	1,004		Pro-Beijing, Liberal
District Council (First)	431	Uncontested	Pro-Beijing, DAB
Total	**15,752**	**223,972**	

Government of the Hong Kong Special Administrative Region, *Voter Registration Statistics*, voterregistration.gov.hk, 2016.

The New Silk Road experience is teaching China's leaders that neither of these approaches addresses their most pressing problem—the need to constantly negotiate trans-regional relations with the people who live on the lands and own their resources. It is easier for Chinese to harness nature and technology than to cultivate relationships, particularly when they have little grasp of the cultural and psychological forces that underpin them. The Islamic world has a rich collection of intercontinental ties and norms that continue to shape modern economic and political behavior. Braudel understood that interpersonal relations were just as important as natural conditions in creating and sustaining human geography.[11] Islamic civilization provides many examples of that insight, including its contemporary centers along the New Silk Road. In this environment, outsiders can only build trust through ongoing involvement with nonofficial society—by cultivating exactly the face-to-face exchanges with ordinary citizens that Chinese leaders typically disavow as unwarranted interference in local affairs.

Negotiating megaregions requires greater inclusion and openness than China and its governmental partners would prefer. The standards are quickly rising as more and more citizens demand information, influence, and tangible benefits. The bargaining process evolves as it spreads—attracting new actors and setting stricter rules. Expected results change dramatically each time the process replays. Simple swaps of infrastructure for resources breed debt and commodity dependence, leading to complaints that China encourages neocolonialism. In response, media and organized interests call for more ambitious development goals, especially long-term commitments to industrialization, technology transfer, and high-value exporting.[12]

If market integration makes promising advances, it often encourages higher-stakes bargaining over plans for free trade areas, treaty organizations, development banks, and currency regimes. As China and cooperating governments try to coordinate the rise of megaregions, they develop new transnational regimes and institutions—the Shanghai Cooperation Organization, the Asian Infrastructure Investment Bank, and the Silk Road Fund. These groups are easily perceived as forming a parallel network of global governance intended to challenge older arrangements inherited from the United States and Europe.[13]

Beijing would like to steer this process indefinitely—remaking the world system one Mediterranean at a time—prodding countries to emulate its economic success and follow its diplomatic lead. But all of the envisioned megaregions depend on at least one key Islamic country where nationalist aspirations and democratic institutions pull in more independent directions. None of these nations wants to be characterized as the nucleus of a Chinese

Mediterranean—an outlying node in a web of connectivity that leads back to a foreign nerve center in China or anywhere else.

The rising powers of the Islamic world already see themselves as transregional actors with global impact. They plan to influence China at least as much as China influences them. In time, they imagine equaling or surpassing China's achievements in poverty eradication, creative arts, and science while avoiding the heavy costs that Chinese people have paid in terms of freedom, family unity, and religious life.[14] This helps to explain why China's Silk Road diplomacy is constantly pressured to move beyond rhetorical endorsements of inclusiveness and to institutionalize reciprocity and coevolution in practice. The most self-confident nations in the Islamic world are telling Beijing precisely what Chinese leaders have been saying to American and European governments for decades—the best way to earn our cooperation is by sharing power instead of trying to be the boss.

Flexible Regions and Deepening Cleavages

In China's domestic statecraft, discussions of regionalism play a very different part from their role in foreign relations. Silk Road campaigns try to spark visions of a more integrated global community, but debates about China's territorial diversity perpetuate images of distinct subcultures with divergent interests and personalities. Acknowledging regional pluralism could encourage power-sharing efforts through federalism or local self-government, but that is not the case in China. Instead, the ruling elite promotes interregional rivalries to prevent challenges to central control.

More important, focusing on jurisdictional interests detracts attention from the far greater problems of inequality and injustice in many other fields, especially the deepening splits between classes, genders, generations, ethnic groups, and religions.[15] The most serious cleavage in Chinese society is the ancient gulf between rural and city life—a kind of internal colonialism that afflicts all regions no matter how much the ruling center boasts about the science it uses to define the units or the connectivity it builds between their privileged capitals.[16]

One of the most worrisome effects of current super-projects in housing and transportation is to partition society by separating people into designated segments. A great deal of new construction amounts to social warehousing—corralling people into controlled environments that are detached from one another and from the congested cores of urban life. Factory workers—often separated from their families—are housed in dormitories of sprawling industrial zones on the edge of metropolitan areas. Universities and high-tech complexes spring up in distant suburbs that used to be farmlands. Former villagers trade their property rights for resettlement in public housing jungles where they can't find jobs to pay the electricity bills for their new air conditioners and washing machines. White-collar commuters are packed into skyscrapers overlooking downtown financial districts where they can barely afford a latte macchiato while running to the train station.[17]

This approach to social engineering is accompanied by a style of political engineering that intentionally distorts normal channels for expressing group demands and opinions. The purpose of formal representation is not to organize citizens but to disorganize them—above all, to prevent them from speaking for themselves. Many of the constituent categories are arbitrary and imposed; most of the organizations are symbolic and powerless. The goal is to thwart collective action by containing it in narrow compartments that make it easier to put out wildfires that might break out in isolated trouble spots.[18]

Ambitious candidates compete to lead a wide range of groups that claim to represent workers, women, students, entrepreneurs, farmers, religions, nationalities, and neighborhoods.[19] But they all understand that the path to access and influence is through co-optation rather than building independent support—rising within instead of challenging from below.[20] Many group activists are opportunists who readily assist state supervision in return for personal advancement and quiet payoffs. Others struggle to become honest mediators of public and private interests, striving for pragmatic compromises to daily problems with little expectation of systemic change. When they succeed, they perform a dual role of gatekeeper and advocate that helps ease the mounting friction between a rigid state and a turbulent society.[21]

When group leaders are forced to maneuver through a system of pervasive co-optation, they commonly try to turn the tables on authoritarian rulers with techniques of regulatory capture—transforming state-sponsored organizations into influential lobbies with privileged access to decision-makers. Their strategy is to embrace government regulation in the short-term so that they can eventually forge private channels for two-way communication and joint action. This might seem like the path of least resistance for cautious activists who doubt that change can arise from China's legislative, party, and media organizations.[22]

With no prospect that China will move toward multiparty democracy, a bureaucratic network of quiet interest group bargaining could appeal to ambitious minorities with the greatest ability to exploit it. The most likely beneficiaries would be educated urbanites. These are the constituencies that crave a stronger voice in decision-making, but that also dread the specter of a one-man one-vote democracy in which poor country folk and migrant workers would outvote them at every turn.[23]

Because of the lingering rural-urban divide, one-half of Chinese society is blocking its own path to greater freedom. Many of these people identify with competing political views, including various shades of Socialism, Liberalism, Confucianism, and assorted hybrids. A large number avoid abstract discussions and concentrate on family and career. To the extent that they share a common social perspective it is a confident nationalism laced with discomfort over the growing intrusion of rural migrants in their midst.[24] By psychologically disengaging from the bottom half of their own society, they have unwittingly fulfilled the most important objective of any authoritarian agenda—letting the citizenry divide itself.

CHAPTER 11 | The Bitter and the Sweet

THE NEW SILK ROAD is filled with contradictions that diminish its idealistic allure because they undercut the core values its proponents claim to represent, particularly universalism, justice, and knowledge. If leaders around the world—and not merely in China—hope to rescue that allure, they will have to join in fashioning more humane political relations with the same energy they devote to pursuing breakthroughs in technology, commerce, and warfare.

The New Silk Road stirs a blend of dreams and disappointment in every land it touches and in many of the distant places it will never reach. Spreading connectivity promotes prosperity and integration, but it also breeds feelings of jealousy and exclusion. Although shrinking the planet heightens exchanges between diverse cultures and civilizations, there is deepening suspicion that these exchanges are inherently unequal and unfair. The grand perspectives of global history and big history spur the sharing of knowledge across disciplines, but the study of politics remains a world apart—more nationalistic and parochial than ever.

Smart Cities and Invisible Citizens

By identifying the New Silk Road so closely with the hardware of railroads, pipelines, and deep-water ports, Chinese planners have made it seem like a soulless feat of engineering with scant regard for ordinary people. Exaggerated attention to physical and economic infrastructure overshadows the greater importance of the social and cultural networks they are supposed to sustain. Concentrating resources in megaprojects and conurbations limits benefits to a thin layer of already privileged citizens. A narrow transcontinental ribbon resting on a chain of wealthy oases would become a long flyover that bypasses invisible hinterlands instead of raising them to greater heights.

China is a poor model for plural societies where competing ethnic and linguistic communities hope to forge a national identity and common destiny. China has long been famous for its vibrant regionalism organized around intricate ladders of market towns reaching out to distant villages and down to poorer strata.[1] Successive campaigns to build nationwide connectivity have strengthened the traditional regions at the top while damaging the roots and branches that sustain the majorities in the countryside. Steady depopulation of the villages and hamlets has made China, for the first time, a half-urban half-rural society.[2] But the cities, in turn, are now split about evenly between underclass newcomers with no rights to education and healthcare and the thriving middle classes who benefit from their labor. Well-wired smart cities plug into a single globalized network, but they also have become more unequal in wealth and influence, more cut off from their rural neighbors, and more internally segregated, both socially and physically.[3]

Within China, the New Silk Road is becoming the preserve of city folk who work in high-rises, shop online, play in super-malls, and live in gated compounds. Meanwhile, it ignores or displaces multitudes of disempowered farmers, fishermen, pastoralists, and mountain people. As markets, the wider regions are more integrated and efficient, but, as communities, they are withered and distorted—increasingly hierarchical and hollowed out. Shortening physical distances widens social and political gaps; the illusory conquest of nature strengthens the dominance of the most advantaged groups and subcultures.

Outside of China, the prospective partners of the New Silk Road view these transformations with both admiration and alarm. Although they are eager to absorb the venture's technological and industrial benefits, they increasingly deplore its social and political side effects. In many of the key gateways and junctions of the Silk Road, national politics is deeply divided by debates over these issues. Particularly in countries with strong democratic traditions and well-organized group networks, discussions in the media and on the campaign trails revolve around demands for greater transparency, power-sharing, and equity between local communities and emerging regions.[4] Time after time, citizens and provincial leaders pressure national governments to rethink and renegotiate Chinese-sponsored projects—not merely to fine-tune their execution, but to redistribute their burdens and advantages. In more open societies, such as Pakistan, Turkey, Indonesia, and Nigeria, these debates have arisen quickly and gained powerful momentum. Even in Iran and Egypt, where freedom is far more limited, they have taken center stage.

In each case, competing visions of the Silk Road are rooted in the coevolution of emerging regions. However, the most urgent conflicts often concern interprovincial and subnational regions instead of the supercontinents and hemispheric visions that tantalize Beijing and its great power rivals. Trains from Xinjiang to the Arabian Sea can take many twists and turns, but will they strengthen Lahore over Peshawar, or both at the expense of Balochistan? Lagos can become an inter-African terminus and a trans-Atlantic springboard, but will it promote a more powerful west with Ibadan and Ilorin or a southern renaissance across the Niger Delta and Igboland?

Similarly, when nationalist leaders imagine projecting power beyond their borders, their ambitions turn first toward local rivals and neighbors of their neighbors before trying to redraw geopolitical maps made in Beijing and Washington. Iranian development can favor the Persian-speaking north or the ethnically mixed west—benefitting the conservative mullahs or their reformist rivals—but both will help spread Iran's influence between the Persian Gulf and the Mediterranean. Indonesia's Muslim politicians can quarrel over the status of their Chinese citizens and the prominence of Java, but their common goal is to leverage Sino-Indian rivalries to their own advantage.

From this perspective, the emergence of the New Silk Road looks like the collision and coevolution of several overlapping regions in the making. Some of these regions grow out of well-formed nuclei—interprovincial communities that are still helping to shape viable nation-states. Others are wider projects of self-confident national coalitions eager to flex their muscles abroad but not necessarily on a global level. China can inspire and nurture these ambitions, but it cannot determine their direction or predict the fallout from their interactions. Most of all, Chinese leaders cannot insulate their own people from the constant criticism that Silk Road initiatives are generating throughout Afro-Eurasia and around the world. China is both the origin and the endpoint of the process—its most powerful component and, potentially, its weakest link.

China and its new partners in the developing world might be learning a valuable lesson—to survive, a Silk Road has to belong to everyone. Ownership should extend beyond the people who build it and pay for it to include those who travel it and rely on it, directly and indirectly. Ownership has to belong also to the communities it displaces and bypasses and to future generations who have no voice in charting its routes and bargaining over its costs. In time, such a Silk Road can grow into a global commons—a shared resource where access is universal as long as its benefits are fairly distributed and its preservation is guaranteed for centuries to come.[5] The alternative would be a world filled with contested commons—dwindling resources and vulnerable routes targeted by rival powers in hostile megaregions with no independent arbiter to resolve disputes.[6]

Islam and Global Community

The New Silk Road joins Chinese and Islamic civilizations more closely than ever and places them both in the forefront of reshaping world politics. But their budding associations are marred by fundamental differences over power-sharing. China views itself as the natural leader of a post-American order and tends to treat smaller nations as—at most—junior partners. In contrast, Muslim nationalists in many countries see China as a useful stepping stone on their own paths to global prominence. Particularly, in Ankara, Jakarta, Tehran, and Abuja, politicians routinely boast about their expectations to match or surpass China's achievements within a generation or two.

In dealing with the Islamic world, Chinese leaders are encountering demands for respect that mirror their own quest for parity with Western nations that dominated most of the planet before the current century. When China's diplomats and scholars promote the dialogue of civilizations, they routinely portray China and Islam as the twin centers of progress that were displaced and humiliated by the sudden rise of European colonialism. Restoring the supposedly natural balance among Western, Chinese, and Islamic civilizations is a standard theme of the revisionist world histories that are so popular in Beijing and many Muslim capitals. Nonetheless, this rhetoric of anti-imperialist solidarity is contradicted by the daily conduct of bilateral relations in which Muslim publics increasingly complain about China's high-handed and overbearing manner.

A common grievance that Muslim writers express about Western scholarship is that it portrays Islamic lands as transmission belts for exchanges between presumably more innovative civilizations along the Atlantic and Pacific shores. In this view, Muslims are forever treated as a lesser people in the middle—possessing territories and riches that powerful outsiders want to exploit, but lacking intrinsic value and dignity as human beings.[7] Inevitably, many Muslims worry that China will follow a similar path. The fear that a growing Chinese Orientalism might replace an older Western version underlies much of the mistrust between Beijing and its Islamic neighbors on the New Silk Road.

It is hardly surprising that some of China's most contentious relations with Muslim nationalists arise in the historic centers of Islamic power and learning. Turkey, Iran, and Pakistan are the successors of Ottoman, Safavid, and Moghul traditions that are just as vibrant for nationalist Muslims as the Confucian and Han legacies are for Chinese patriots. The historical and political importance of these centrally located areas is widely acknowledged by scholars and policymakers alike. Marshall Hodgson described them as the triple gunpowder empires that dominated the Afro-Eurasian landmass before the rise of the West.[8] American strategists of the Cold War era dubbed them the northern tier—a trio of key allies that blocked a Soviet advance toward the Arab world and the Indian Ocean.[9] The leaders and citizens of these three nations are particularly aware of their leverage in world politics—and they regularly remind Chinese negotiators that they have many opportunities to forge alliances with Beijing's competitors. Likewise, in Indonesia and Nigeria, nationalism is increasingly confident and assertive, pushing leaders to stand up to China and other great powers or face political reprisals at home.

In all of these countries, Muslim nationalism is bolstered by a sense of belonging to the much wider community of Islam. In China and in the West, many observers would regard such religious and cultural connections as liabilities rather than assets. In their view, Muslim societies are consumed by religiously inspired violence and reaction—progress depends on abandoning or altering Islam, not on embracing it as a universal ideal. In Beijing and Washington, there is a shared presumption that China and the United States are the center of the universe. Eventually, one of them will achieve preeminence, or perhaps the two can join forces in managing affairs for the rest of the world. Absent from this Sino-American myopia is a serious consideration that both contenders—separately or together—need all the help they can muster to contend with problems that affect the entire planet.[10]

In the most cosmopolitan and rapidly developing Muslim countries, the arch of Islamic history looks far more positive than from Beijing or Washington. The turmoil of revolution and regional conflict appears balanced, if not erased, by important examples of economic growth, democratic resilience, and diplomatic skill. Terrorist movements such as the so-called Islamic State and al-Qaeda are seen as distorting religion, not as capturing its mainstream. Ultraconservative monarchies and police states such as Saudi Arabia and Syria are considered backwaters rather than suitable models for freer and more open societies. For modern Muslims in pluralistic societies, Islam is a flexible set of principles that are constantly adapting to new conditions.[11] It has generated a cosmopolitan civilization that has helped to lay the foundations of modern science, capitalism, and international law.[12] In this view, the leading nations of Islam are ready to reclaim a central role in world politics alongside the formerly dominant West and a newly ascendant China.

Concerning the issues of power-sharing and global governance, there are some clear parallels between China's frustrations with the West and the Islamic world's impatience toward the Chinese. Beijing would like to convince American and European capitals that China will help stabilize the international order rather than overturn it. In a similar manner, Muslim politicians want Chinese leaders to treat the Islamic world as a full partner in building a more inclusive global community that draws on universal values developed by all civilizations. When Muslim leaders and citizens believe that China respects their interests and regards them as equals, they are eager to pursue closer cooperation. On the other hand, when China behaves like an aspiring hegemon—targeting other nations' resources and markets, but disdaining their people and cultures—the protests mount, and Beijing has to correct course or suffer the consequences.

Clashes of Knowledge and Interest

The New Silk Road is a natural magnet for explorers crossing disciplines and cultures. The prospect of creating supercontinents and remixing civilizations demands changes in perspective to grasp many features of growing complexity—longer time frames, faster interactions over wider areas, and more far-reaching side effects. Consequently, students of world history and social science increasingly rely on one another's insights, and both fields look to the life sciences and humanities for guidance in policy and ethics. The most striking exception to this collective approach to knowledge is the study of politics, particularly politics among nations that consider themselves great powers. In that realm, knowledge is still highly constricted by the interests of specific countries, governments, and social groups. In fact, national and partisan influences seem to be spreading in international political studies precisely when universal human problems require greater objectivity and lowered passions.

Commentary and analysis of the New Silk Road does not merely reflect these interests, it exudes and empowers them. In China, international conferences on the initiatives are platforms for government agencies and firms pitching to the foreign press. On the sidelines, a crowd of businesses and consultancies hunt for contracts and contacts.[13] More critical views are percolating through the diplomatic corps, the universities, and business circles. Flashes of these debates arise in the Chinese media, the internet, and the international media, particularly in Hong Kong, Australia, and Japan. Meanwhile, China's digital world and social media are filled with rumors and misinformation about Muslims—attacking them for exploiting minority privileges or lauding them as China's secret weapon for winning global power.[14]

In the United States, a low-keyed discussion of Silk Road issues revolves around the deepening doubts about America's primacy in the global balance of power. Many writers focus on particular megaprojects and countries, concluding that Beijing is wasting its cash on white elephants and showcases with no lasting value. In this view, the New Silk Road is a distraction—it might arouse exaggerated fears of Chinese power or pale before the supposedly greater China threats in economic and military affairs.[15] American commentary emanates primarily from government agencies, partisan think tanks, and pro-business lobbies. More independent scholars and journalists are producing a valuable flow of informed opinion, which is beginning to earn well-deserved attention from the mainstream media. As long as American perspectives of the Silk Road are largely shaped by Washington-based and corporate-funded sources, the conversation will focus on preserving a U.S.-led world order instead of refining the tools of global governance.

Members of the European Union worry that the New Silk Road will accelerate centrifugal tendencies by encouraging member countries to strike separate bilateral deals with China throughout Asia and Africa. Brussels and its supporters are most concerned about overseas investments from Germany, which have often undermined efforts to pursue common European policies toward China on trade, technology transfer, the environment, and human rights.[16] E.U. partisans have plenty of headaches in addition to Berlin. The Arctic Council states are bargaining with Russia and China over access to new shipping routes and natural resources.[17] The debt-ridden economies of the Mediterranean look to Beijing for long-term financial relief and buyers for their risky bonds.[18] The United Kingdom has proclaimed itself China's best friend in Europe, hoping to draw Chinese banks to London as they expand beyond their older outposts in Hong Kong and Singapore.[19] All of these trends point to a loosening of trans-Atlantic ties as Europe fragments and turns toward Pacific markets, with Germany and Britain leading the way.[20]

Some of the worst fears about the New Silk Road come from Japan and India. Japanese government and business leaders see their influence challenged across the Pacific and elsewhere. For decades, Indonesia's markets and resources were Japan's for the taking, but Chinese competition is pushing them into second place or lower in the scramble for commercial advantage. Tokyo faces similar setbacks in many other fast-growing economies where it accuses Beijing of winning unfairly by paying state subsidies to

Chinese companies and giving kickbacks to local politicians.[21] For many in Japan, these challenges seem more like an affront to the nation than a simple test of their business prowess and diplomacy.

India's official and popular discourse is increasingly strident in criticizing Silk Road projects as part of a Chinese effort to colonize Pakistan, isolate New Delhi, and dominate South Asia as a whole. Prime Minister Narendra Modi's government has fanned ultranationalist fears over the military implications of Chinese activities along the Himalayas and across the Indian Ocean.[22] Modi's plans to expand defense spending are drawing criticisms from his own military professionals, who believe he is inserting India's navy into distant Pacific quarrels they cannot control.[23]

In Australia, debates over China and the Silk Road have polarized coalitions of interest groups and politicians from both major parties. Many Australian diplomats and business leaders see their country's future as part of an Asian community powered by Chinese growth. Their views are echoed by a combination of mining, ranching, banking, and higher education groups with widespread influence over public opinion.[24] On the other side, a resurgent nationalist block stresses Australia's unique bonds with the Commonwealth and the United States while denouncing China's supposed desire to gobble up Australian assets. Support for this position runs deep among protectionist, manufacturing, and anti-immigrant groups.[25] The Liberal Party and the Labor Party try to represent both coalitions at the same time, insuring constant divisions within their ranks and incoherence in their programs.

Some of the most intriguing Silk Road debates are developing in Russia—the previous heartland of Eurasian dreamers and grand masters of geopolitics. Vladimir Putin has encouraged both sides in the old argument about whether Russia belongs more to Europe or to Asia. He describes the nation's future as moving toward the Atlantic, then, toward the Pacific, and, then, toward linking the two. The New Silk Road can serve all three visions at once—and that is probably why it is winning at least belated support from most of Russia's rival factions.[26] Another source of Silk Road enthusiasm is the special nature of Russia's Muslim question—or, more accurately, of Moscow's shifting relations with diverse Muslim communities in the vast lands of the former Soviet Union.[27] Putin has warmed to Silk Road cooperation with China more and more as he ponders the steady demographic shift in favor of Muslims over Russian Christians—a trend that is already quite advanced in Russia's military.[28]

An excellent example of growing Sino-Russian coordination is the new bullet train connecting Moscow and Kazan, the capital of the Republic of Tatarstan in the Volga region.[29] Putin's desire to further co-opt Turkic-speaking

Muslims of the Volga stems from fears of renewed troubles with Caucasian Muslims in Dagestan and Chechnya.[30] Beijing is eager to assist in managing Russia's Islamic tensions because it wants to prevent its own religious conflicts from spreading beyond Xinjiang to the rest of China. Leaders in both countries view the Moscow-Kazan line—and the New Silk Road in general—as serving long-standing efforts to segment and incorporate their domestic Muslim populations.[31] The inherent contradiction between strategies of transcontinental connectivity and subnational fragmentation will be difficult to sustain as Muslims everywhere find greater opportunities to strengthen their already substantial networks around the world.

China has merely traveled the first mile of its Silk Road adventure. Most other countries are lining up to participate in one way or another, but the United States remains on the sidelines—skeptical the venture can succeed and fearful that it will. Those who view the New Silk Road from any direction soon realize it rests on an underlying Islamic base with a life and will of its own. The people in the middle—the historic neighbors and coauthors of Atlantic and Pacific civilizations—will set the pace of progress at least as much as anyone else. Outsiders who hope to build and benefit from the New Silk Road will have to earn the trust and support of the people who occupy its lands and own its natural wealth. The story of Chinese statecraft in the Islamic world is an ongoing process of learning and failing to learn the ways of nurturing that cooperation. Their gradual advances and recurring setbacks might also be instructive for leaders of many other countries.

China's political learning is still poorly appreciated in the United States. Many observers of Chinese foreign policy are surprised—even stunned—by the momentum and enthusiasm that propel the New Silk Road toward reshaping the continents and oceans Americans have always seen as natural buffers keeping a turbulent world at arm's length.[32] But this surprise falls far short of a Sputnik moment—a jolt to national self-awareness that spurs renewed commitments in education, science, and outreach across cultures. China's global advance is accelerating precisely at a time when the United States is stepping away from the wider world, so split by race and region that it disinvests in already crumbling transportation, public schooling, and diplomatic services. By the time America's leaders try to regain their role in world affairs, other nations will have moved on. Even if American reengagement is welcomed, it will not be on America's terms. China's leaders are also learning the limits of their new power. The multipolar world they are summoning forth is turning out to be filled with countries whose dreams are at least as lofty as their own, particularly in the lands where Islam and nationalism have forged the strongest partnerships.

NOTES

Introduction

1. John Mearshimer, *The Tragedy of Great Power Politics*, New York-London: Norton, 2003; Robert Kaplan, "How We Would Fight China," *The Atlantic*, June 2005; Ilan Berman, *Winning the Long War: Retaking the Offensive against Radical Islam*, Lanham, MD: Rowman and Littlefield, 2009; Uri Friedman, "The Coming War on 'Radical Islam,'" *The Atlantic*, November 29, 2016; Howard W. French, *Everything under the Heavens: How the Past Helps Shape China's Push for Global Power*, New York: Knopf, 2017; Graham Allison, *Destined for War: Can America and China Escape Thucydides's Trap?* Boston-New York: Houghton Mifflin Harcourt, 2017. In contrast, on the heightened importance of diplomacy in American relations with China and the Islamic world, see David M. Lampton, *The Three Faces of Chinese Power: Might, Money, and Minds*, Berkeley: University of California Press, 2008; Henry Kissinger, *On China*, New York: Penguin Press, 2011; Charles Glaser, "Will China's Rise Lead to War? Why Realism Does Not Mean Pessimism," *Foreign Affairs*, March/April 2011; Vali Nasr, *The Dispensable Nation: American Foreign Policy in Retreat*, New York: Doubleday, 2013; Robert R. Bianchi, *Islamic Globalization: Pilgrimage, Capitalism, Democracy, and Diplomacy*, Singapore-London: World Scientific Publishers, 2013; John Podesta and Brian Kutulis, "Trump's Silent Surge in the Middle East—And the Slippery Slope to War," *Washington Post*, June 20, 2017.

2. Ira Lapidus, "Hierarchies and Networks: A Comparison of Chinese and Islamic Societies," in Frederic Wakeman, Jr. and Carolyn Grant, eds., *Conflict and Control in Late Imperial China*, Berkeley: University of California Press, 1975.

3. Joseph F. Fletcher, *Studies on Chinese and Islamic Inner Asia*, Brookfield, VT: Variorum, 1995.

Chapter 1

1. See the official websites of the Belt and Road Initiative in English and Chinese. The State Council, The People's Republic of China, "The Belt and Road Initiative," *english.gov.cn;* "Zhongguo Yidai Yilu Wang" (China Belt and Road Portal), *yidaiyilu.gov.cn.* Similar websites are planned in Arabic, French, Russian, and Spanish.

A monthly collection of international press coverage of New Silk Road issues is available in English and Chinese at the *Eurasian Vision Newsletter, eurasianvision.com*. For English-language journalistic coverage, see Wade Shepard's articles in *Forbes* and Wade Shepard, *On the New Silk Road: Journeying through China's Artery of Power*, Chicago: University of Chicago Press, 2017.

2. "Will China Encircle the World with Rail?" *Global Construction Review*, October 17, 2014; Kevin Mwanza, "A Chinese-Funded Railway Line to Open Up Central Africa's Hinterland," *AFK Insider*, December 20, 2015; Ryan Kilpatrick, "China's Plans for the Arctic—And a Shipping Centre to Rival Singapore," *South China Morning Post*, November 15, 2016; Atle Staalesen, "Norway, Finland Talk Arctic with China," *The Barents Observer*, April 10, 2017; Fred Pearce, "Mega-canals Could Slice through Continents for Giant Ships," *New Scientist*, April 11, 2017.

3. Liu Yazhou, "Zhong Mei Daguo Boyi: Kaipi Shijie Lishi Xin Shidai" (The Great Game of China and America: The Beginning of a New Historical Era), preface to Liu Ming Fu, *China's Dream: Great Power Thinking and Strategic Posture in a Post-American Era*, Beijing: China Friendship Publishing, 2010; Thomas Fingar, *The New Great Game: China and South and Central Asia in the Era of Reform*, Stanford, CA: Stanford University Press, 2016; Bai Yunyi, "Zhong Mei Xuezhe Yanzhong de Daguo Boyi Yu Nanhai Fenzheng: Zhong Mei Zuizhong Shifou 'Bi You Yi Zhan?'" (The Great Game and the South China Sea Dispute in the Eyes of Chinese and American Scholars: Is a Sino-American War "Inevitable"), *huanqiu.com*, September 28, 2016.

4. Gregory T. Chin, "Beijing's Economic Statecraft," *Current History*, September 2015; Chen Jingpu, "Zhongguo Sichou Zhi Lu Jingji Dai Yu Meiguo TPP: Diyuan Jingji Yu Diyuan Zhengzhi de Jiaoliang" (China's Silk Road Economic Belt and America's TPP: Geoeconomic and Geopolitical Competition), *sciencenet.cn*, October 12, 2015; Hanns Günther Hilpert and Gudrun Wacker, "Geoeconomics Meets Geopolitics: China's New Economic and Foreign Policy Initiatives," *German Institute for International and Security Affairs*, June 2015; Robert D. Blackwill and Jennifer M. Harris, *War by Other Means: Geoeconomics and Statecraft*, Cambridge, MA: Harvard University Press, 2016; Mark Leonard, ed., "Geo-economics with Chinese Characteristics: How China's Economic Might Is Reshaping World Politics," *World Economic Forum*, January 2016; Zou Zhiqiang, "Zhongguo Canyu Zhongdong Diqu Jingji Zhili de Lilun Yu Shijian" (The Theory and Practice of China's Participation in the Economic Governance of the Middle East), *International Outlook*, October 2016; Ling Shengli, "Diyuan Jingji Chongsu Dayangzhou Geju" (Geo-economics Is Reshaping Oceania), *Beijing Review*, March 29, 2017.

5. Yihua Xu, *Zongjiao yu Dangdai Guoji Guanxi (Religion and Contemporary International Relations)*, Shanghai: Shanghai People's Publishing House, 2012; Yihua Xu, "Studies on Religion and China's National Security in the Globalization Era," *Journal of Middle Eastern and Islamic Studies (in Asia)*, vol. 7, no. 3, 2013; He Yafei, "Zongjiao Shi Zhongguo Gonggong Waijiao de Zhongyao Ziyuan" (Religion Is an Important Resource for China's Public Diplomacy), *news.china.com.cn*, March 6, 2015; Yihua Xu and Lei Zou, "Geo-religion and China's Foreign Strategy," in Binhong Shao, ed., *China under Xi Jinping: Its Economic Challenges and Foreign Policy Initiatives*, Leiden: Brill, 2015.

6. Marissa Benavides, "When Soft Power Is Too Soft: Confucius Institutes' Nebulous Role in China's Soft Power Initiative," *Yale Review of International Studies*, August 2012; Joseph S. Nye, Jr., "The Limits of Chinese Soft Power," *Project Syndicate*, July 10, 2015; David Shambaugh, "China's Soft-Power Push: The Search for Respect," *Foreign Affairs*, July/August 2015; Coco Liu and Magdalene Fung, "Towering Figures: Who's Who in the World of Chinese Soft Power?" *South China Morning Post*, March 19, 2017; Justina Crabtree and Cheang Ming, "Why Soft Power Could Be the Real Value of China's Massive Belt and Road Project," *CNBC*, May 22, 2017.

7. Greg Knowler, "China to Dominate Global Shipping by 2030, Shanghai Report Finds," *Journal of Commerce*, June 10, 2015; James Kynge, Chris Campbell, Amy Kazmin, and Farhan Bokhari, "How China Rules the Waves," *Financial Times*, January 12, 2017; Brenda Goh, "Shanghai Port, World's Busiest, Grapples with Traffic Congestion," *Reuters*, April 21, 2017.

8. Andrew Scobell and Andrew J. Nathan, "China's Overstretched Military," *The Washington Quarterly*, Fall 2012; Shane C. Tayloe, "Crossover Point: How China's Naval Modernization Could Reverse the United States' Strategic Advantage," *Journal of Asian Security and International Affairs*, April 10, 2017; Andrew S. Erickson, ed., *Chinese Naval Shipbuilding: An Ambitious and Uncertain Course*, Annapolis, MD: Naval Institute Press, 2016; Yoji Koda, "China's Blue Water Navy Strategy and Its Implications," *Center for a New American Security*, March 2017; Chris Buckley, "China, Sending a Signal, Launches a Home-Built Aircraft Carrier," *New York Times*, April 25, 2017.

9. Ding Xuezhen, "China Eyes Silk Road Countries for Its Beidou Satellite System," *Global Times*, June 17, 2016; Jordan Wilson, "China's Alternative to GPS and Its Implications for the United States," *U.S.-China Economic and Security Review Commission*, January 5, 2017.

10. Rachel Brown, "Beijing's Silk Road Goes Digital," *Council on Foreign Relations*, June 6, 2017.

11. Sebastian Heilmann, Moritz Rudolf, Mikko Huotari, and Johannes Buckow, "China's Shadow Foreign Policy: Parallel Structures Challenge the Established International Order," *Mercator Institute for China Studies*, October 28, 2014; James F. Paradise, "The Role of 'Parallel Institutions' in China's Growing Participation in Global Economic Governance," *Journal of Chinese Political Science*, June 2016; David Lawder, "World Bank Group, China-Led AIIB Agree to Deepen Cooperation," *Reuters*, April 23, 2017; "World Bank, AIIB to Grant $380 Million to Andhra Pradesh Power Project," *The Economic Times*, June 23, 2017.

12. Oliver Pearce, "From Yiwu to Damascus: A New Silk Road Is Born," *Global Times*, June 16, 2009 (on the New Silk Road as China's "Islamic Corridor"); Li Xiguang, "Belt and Road Initiative to Connect Hearts," *China Daily*, April 8, 2015; Baozhong Du and Xuan Li, "China Turns to Islamic Finance to Drive Economic Initiative," *Business Islamica*, June 9, 2016; "Chinese Muslims' Irreplaceable Role in the 'One Belt, One Road' Initiative," *1belt-1road.org*, January 6, 2017; Department of Culture of Ningxia, "A Cultural Gate to China: 'One Belt and One Road' Islamic Customs," *chinaculture.org*, March 31, 2017; Hou Qian, "Will the Belt and Road Initiative Cause Clash of Cultures?" *Xinhua*, May 13, 2017.

13. Ross E. Dunn, *The Adventures of Ibn Battuta: A Muslim Traveler of the 14th Century*, Berkeley: University of California Press, 1986; Richard Foltz, *Religions of the Silk Road: Premodern Patterns of Globalization*, New York: Palgrave Macmillan, 2010; How Man Wong, *Islamic Frontiers of China: Peoples of the Silk Road*, New York: I. B. Tauris, 2011; Hyunhee Park, *Mapping the Chinese and Islamic Worlds: Cross-Cultural Exchange in Pre-modern Asia*, New York: Cambridge University Press, 2012; Gary Paul Nabhan, *Cumin, Camels, and Caravans: A Spice Odyssey*, Berkeley: University of California Press, 2014; Abdul Sheriff and Engseng Ho, *The Indian Ocean: Oceanic Connections and the Creation of New Societies*, London: Hurst, 2014; Anne K. Bang, *Islamic Sufi Networks in the Western Indian Ocean (c. 1880–1940): Ripples of Reform*, Leiden/Boston: Brill, 2014.

14. Zugui Gao, "Zhongguo Yu Yisilan Shijie Guanxi Yanjiu" (A Study of China's Relations with the Islamic World), *Journal of China and International Relations*, vol. 1, no. 2, 2013; Elaine Moore, "Civets, Brics and the Next 11," *Financial Times*, June 8, 2012; Research Centre for Islamic History, Art, and Culture (Turkey), Second International Congress on "China and the Muslim World: Cultural Encounters," ircica.org, February 3–4, 2015; "The Future: A Mostly Muslim World," *The China Post*, April 9, 2015.

15. Adam Taylor, "What Yemen's Crisis Reveals about China's Growing Global Power," *Washington Post*, March 31, 2015; Jonas Parello-Plesner and Mathieu Duchâtel, "China's Strong Arm: Protecting Citizens and Assets Abroad," *International Institute for Security Studies*, Singapore, May 29, 2015; Yan Dongjie, "Chinese Government in Action: Protecting Citizens Overseas," *Xinhua*, January 19, 2016; Syed Ali Shah, "Two Chinese Nationals Kidnapped from Quetta," *Dawn*, May 24, 2017.

16. Scott Kennedy and David A. Parker, "Building China's 'One Belt, One Road,'" *Center for Strategic and International Studies*, April 3, 2015; Saibal Dasgupta, "China's Ambitious 'Silk Road' Plan Faces Hurdles," *Voice of America*, April 15, 2015; "China's 'New Silk Road' Facing Difficulties: Former Official," *South China Morning Post*, April 23, 2016; Arthur Dong, "Ahead of 'Modern Silk Road' Build, China Credit Downgrade Worrisome," *The Hill*, May 25, 2017.

17. This section foreshadows many arguments developed in chapters 3–8. Readers can consult those chapters for detailed evidence and references on each country.

18. For a recent example of popular journalism that explicitly compares democratic turbulence across the Middle East with the aspirations of China's middle classes see Zhou Yi Jun, *Zouchu Zhongdong: Quanqiu Minzhu Langchao de Jianzheng yu Xingsi (Out of the Middle East: Witnessing and Reflecting on the Global Tide of Democracy)*, Beijing: CITIC Publishing Group, 2017.

19. Shamil Shams, "China's Economic Corridor Creating New Conflicts in Pakistan," *Deutsche Welle*, August 29, 2016; Raza Khan, "Dynamics of Ethnic Conflicts in Pakistan," *The Express Tribune*, July 21, 2017.

20. Kunwar Khuldune Shahid, "Trump's Warning to Islamabad Has Formalised the China-Pakistan-Russia Axis," *Huffington Post*, August 30, 2017; Catherine Wong, "China-Pakistan Military Ties Set to Get Even Closer as 'Iron Brothers' Eye New Alliance," *South China Morning Post*, January 7, 2018; Amanda Erickson, "The Long History of Incredibly Fraught Relations between the U.S. and Pakistan," *Washington Post*, January 5, 2018.

21. Lucy Hornby and Piotr Zalewski, "China Accuses Turkey of Aiding Uighurs," *Financial Times*, July 12, 2015; Unal Cevikoz, "Turkey in a Reconnecting Eurasia: Foreign Economic and Security Interests," *Center for Strategic and International Studies*, April 30, 2016; "Turkey Referendum Worries China over Pan-Turkism in Xinjiang," *Financial Express (India)*, April 18, 2017.

22. Callistasia Anggun Wijaya, "Ahok Guilty of Blasphemy, Sentenced to Two Years," *The Jakarta Post*, May 9, 2017; Max Walden, "The Chinese Indonesians with Long Memories and Escape Plans in Case Racial Violence Flares Again—Despite Signs of Tensions Easing," *South China Morning Post*, October 18, 2017; Francis Chan, "Jakarta's New Governor Anies Baswedan Gets Flak for 'Racist' Comments on His First Day in Office," *The Straits Times*, October 18, 2017.

23. Pinak Ranjan Chakravarty, "China and Indonesia: A New Tug-of-War," *Observer Research Foundation Commentaries*, October 13, 2017; Yohanes Sulaiman, "Global Maritime Nexus: Towards a Grand Strategy for Indonesia?" *RSIS Commentaries*, March 23, 2017.

24. Daniel Wagner and Giorgio Cafiero, "China and Nigeria: Neo-colonialism, South-South Solidarity, or Both?" *Huffington Post*, July 19, 2013; Segun Akande, "Is China Taking Advantage of Nigeria with Loans and Grants?" *pulse.ng*, September 10, 2017; "Establish Production Plants in Nigeria to Address Trade Imbalance, Dogara Tells China," *Daily Post*, November 2, 2017.

25. Alex Enumah, "China Renews Commitment to Nigeria's Industrialisation," *This Day*, September 29, 2017; Adelani Adepegba, "China Disburses $30bn Industrialisation Fund to Nigeria, Others," *Punch*, November 3, 2017; "Getting Nigeria's Railways Back on Track with China's Help," *BBC*, December 7, 2017; Felix Onuah and Chijioke Ohuocha, "Nigeria Agrees $550 Million Satellite Deal with China," *Reuters*, January 3, 2018.

26. Rhys Jenkins, "Is Chinese Competition Causing Deindustrialization in Brazil?" *Latin American Perspectives*, July 7, 2015; Kimairis Toogood, "Understanding the Emerging Relationship between China and Africa: The Case of Nigeria," *Stimson Policy Papers*, December 2016.

27. Center for Human Rights in Iran, "Guardians at the Gate: The Expanding State Control over the Internet in Iran," *Center for Human Rights in Iran*, 2018; Bozorgmehr Sharafedin, "Iran Deploys Revolutionary Guards to Quell 'Sedition' in Protest Hotbeds," *Reuters*, January 3, 2018.

28. Stephen Kinzer, "Don't Get Too Excited about the Protests in Iran," *Boston Globe*, January 3, 2018; Haleh Esfandiari, "Despite the Protests, Little Will Change in Iran," *The Hill*, January 3, 2018; Mohammad Ali Kadivar, "Why Haven't Reformists Joined the Protests Sweeping Iran?" *Washington Post*, January 5, 2018.

29. Walid Akef, "5 Years after the Revolution, Egypt's a Hell after a Paradise," *Huffington Post*, January 25, 2016; Saskia Brechenmacher, "Institutionalized Repression in Egypt," in *Civil Society under Assault: Repression and Responses in Russia, Egypt, and Ethiopia*, Washington, DC: Carnegie Endowment for International Peace, May 18, 2017.

30. Luo Jie, "Egypt's Problems," *China Daily*, December 1, 2013; Peter Hessler, "Learning to Speak Lingerie: Chinese Merchants and the Inroads of Globalization," *The New Yorker*, August 10, 2015; Dana Sanchez, "Changing Economics of Canals: Large

Ships Go Around Africa, Bypassing Suez And Panama," *AFK Insider*, June 28, 2016; "Sisi's Dream of New Egypt Capital in Tatters as China Pulls Out," *Middle East Eye*, February 9, 2017; Dorian Geiger, "The Lonely Pyramids of Giza: Egyptian Tourism's Decline," *Al-Jazeera*, June 8, 2017.

31. "China's Xinjiang Tightening Border amid Terrorist Threats," *Jakarta Post*, January 10, 2017; Tom Phillips, "Chinese Troops Stage Show of Force in Xinjiang and Vow to 'Relentlessly Beat' Separatists," *The Guardian*, February 20, 2017; Philip Wen, "Terror Threats Transform China's Uighur Heartland into Security State," *Reuters*, March 30, 2017.

32. "Urban Legend: China's Tiered City System Explained," *South China Morning Post*, October 10, 2016, http://multimedia.scmp.com/2016/cities/; Marcelo Duhalde, "Classifying China's Cities," *South China Morning Post*, March 13, 2017.

33. Ethan Michelson, "Justice from above or Below? Popular Strategies for Resolving Grievances in Rural China," *China Quarterly*, March 2008; Hannah Beech, "Labor Unrest Grows in China, Even in the Historic Heartlands of Revolution," *Time*, April 10, 2016; Te-Ping Chen, "China's Middle Class Vents over Growing List of Grievances," *Wall Street Journal*, May 24, 2016.

34. Clay Shirky, "The Political Power of Social Media: Technology, the Public Sphere, and Political Change," *Foreign Affairs*, January/February 2010; Sina Odugbemi, "The Dictator's Dilemma," *The World Bank*, February 20, 2014; Manuel Castells, *Networks of Outrage and Hope: Social Movements in the Internet Age*, Cambridge: Polity Press, 2015; Jidong Chen and Yiqing Xu, "Why Do Authoritarian Regimes Allow Citizens to Voice Opinions Publicly?" *The Journal of Politics*, vol. 79, no. 3, July 2017.

35. François Jullien, *The Propensity of Things: Toward a History of Efficacy in China*, New York: Zone Books, 1999; Dennis Bloodworth and Ching Ping Bloodworth, *The Chinese Machiavelli: 3000 Years of Chinese Statecraft*, New Brunswick, NJ: Transaction Books, 2007; Yan Xuetong, *Ancient Chinese Thought, Modern Chinese Power*, Princeton, NJ: Princeton University Press, 2011; Wang Gungwu, *Renewal: The Chinese State and the New Global History*, Hong Kong: The Chinese University of Hong Kong, 2013; Suisheng Zhao, ed., "Historical Perspectives on the Rise of China: Chinese Order, Great Harmony, and *Tianxia*," *Journal of Contemporary China*, vol. 24, no. 96, 2015; Feng Zhang, "Confucian Foreign Policy Traditions in Chinese History," *Chinese Journal of International Politics*, April 2015.

36. Ruth Morris, "Parliamentary-Style Debates Take Off in China: Even if Some Topics Are Off Limits," *Public Radio International*, September 5, 2014; Ya-Wen Lei, *The Contentious Public Sphere: Law, Media, and Authoritarian Rule in China*, Princeton, NJ: Princeton University Press, 2017.

37. Michael Anti, "Behind the Great Firewall of China," *TED Global*, June 2012; Emily Parker, "Social Media and the Hong Kong Protests," *The New Yorker*, October 1, 2014; Beina Xu and Eleanor Albert, "Media Censorship in China," *Council on Foreign Relations*, February 17, 2017.

38. Cary Huang, "Paranoia from Soviet Union Collapse Haunts China's Communist Party, 22 Years On," *South China Morning Post*, November 18, 2013; Harry J. Kazianis, "China's Greatest Fear: Dead and Buried Like the Soviet Union," *The National Interest*, March 11, 2016; Roger Garside, "China's Future: Status Quo, Reform, or Chaos?" *Prospect Magazine*, March 26, 2016.

39. Zhu Liqun, "China's Foreign Policy Debates," *European Union Institute for Security Studies*, September 2010; Lai Hongyi, *The Domestic Sources of China's Foreign Policy: Regimes, Leadership, Priorities and Process*, London and New York: Routledge, 2010; Tania Branigan, "China Bans Wordplay in Attempt at Pun Control," *The Guardian*, November 28, 2014; Phil Rosenthal, "Economic Power China Is So Fragile It Orders Pun Control," *Chicago Tribune*, December 2, 2014.

40. Sara Schonhardt, "In Indonesia, Fears Rise among Ethnic Chinese amid Blasphemy Probe," *Wall Street Journal*, November 26, 2016; Shamil Shams, "Istanbul Attack: Why China's Uighurs Are Joining Global Jihadist Groups," *Deutsche Welle*, January 6, 2017.

41. Charles Liu, "Police Brutality Caught on Video at Dongguan Labor Dispute," *The Nanfang*, June 26, 2015; James Pomfret, "Chinese Villagers Describe Police Beatings in 'Wild Crackdown' on Protest," *Reuters*, September 14, 2016.

42. Chai Jing, "Wumai Diaocha: Qiongding Zhi Xia" (Investigating China's Smog: Under the Dome), *youtube.com*, March 1, 2015; Yuan Ren, "Under the Dome: Will This Film Be China's Environmental Awakening?" *The Guardian*, March 5, 2015; Steven Mufson, "This Documentary Went Viral in China. Then It Was Censored. It Won't Be Forgotten," *Washington Post*, March 16, 2015; "China's Citizens Are Complaining More Loudly about Polluted Air: The Government Wants to Silence Them," *The Economist*, March 2, 2017.

43. Li Gan, "Why China Needs to Spend More on Welfare," *CNN*, March 5, 2013; Matthew Carney, "A Generation Left Behind: Millions of Chinese Children Abandoned as Parents Seek Work," *ABC News*, September 13, 2016; Joe McDonald, "China Faces Political Conflicts in Moves to Cut Debt Burden," *US News*, January 25, 2017.

44. Katy N. Lam, *Chinese State-Owned Enterprises in West Africa: Triple-Embedded Globalization*, London and New York: Routledge, 2017; Javier C. Hernández, "In Banning Ivory Trade, China Saw Benefits for Itself, Too," *New York Times*, January 2, 2017.

45. Run Taoyan, "Yisilan? Ta Tongzhi Buliao Zhongguo" (Islam? It Cannot Rule China), *wenxuecity.com*, November 15, 2015; Gao Bai, "Zhongguo Xiehou Yisilan Shijie" (China Encounters the Islamic World), *China Times*, January 23, 2016; Ding Jun, "Lun Zhongguo Yu Yisilan Guojia Jian de 'Minxin Xiangtong'" (On People to People Connections between China and the Islamic World), *globalview.cn*, June 28, 2016.

46. "Got Beef? How One Man Faced Down a 'Noodle Cartel,'" *BBC News*, July 25, 2016; Victor Fung, "New Beef Noodle Restaurant in Shanghai Harassed by Competitors after Violating Unwritten Code," *Shanghailist.com*, July 27, 2016; Emily Feng, "Never the Noodles Shall Meet: A Chinese Treaty Is Tested," *New York Times*, August 31, 2016.

47. Zhang Yiqian, "Halal Hopes," *Global Times*, September 17, 2015; "China Shelves Plan to Regulate Halal Food Preparation," *Hürriyet Daily News*, April 18, 2016; Aza Wee Sile, "Why China Wants a Bite of the Booming Halal Food Market," *CNBC*, August 24, 2015; Li Ruohan, "Halal Food Legislation Violates Constitutional Principle: Expert," *Global Times*, March 7, 2016; Wang Daiyu, "China Considering Nationwide Law on Halal Food," *Islam in China*, April 16, 2016; "Islamic Food, Water,

Toilet Paper Cause Concern about Extremism," *Global Times*, May 9, 2016; Saroja Dorairajoo and Ma Jianfu, "Does Islam Have the Answers to China's Food Safety Problems?" *South China Morning Post*, July 29, 2016.

48. Massoud Hayoun, "Islam with Chinese Characteristics," *The Atlantic*, January 18, 2012; Gao Zhanfu, "Cong Wailai Qiaomin Dao Bentu Guomin: Huizu Yisilan Jiao Zai Zhongguo Bentuhua da Licheng" (From Alien Diaspora to Native Nationals: The Historical Process of the Localization of Hui Islam in China), *360doc.com*, December 24, 2012; Li Leqin, "Qian Tan Yisilan Jiao de Zhongguohua" (On the Sinification of Islam), *chinaislam.net*, February 24, 2016; Duncan Hewitt, "China Calls for Religion to Be 'Localized' to Reduce Foreign 'Infiltration,' Says Party 'Severely Damaged' by Members' Religious Beliefs," *International Business Times*, April 25, 2016; Alice Su, "China's Separation between Mosque and State," *Pulitzer Center*, October 21, 2016.

49. Françoise Aubin, "La Version Chinoise de L'Islam," *European Journal of Sociology*, November 1989; Élisabeth Allès, *Musulmans de Chine, Une Anthropologie des Hui du Henan*, Paris: Éditions de l'EHESS, 2000.

50. Wu Yiye, "Zhongguo Yisilan Jiao de Tedian Ji Qi Yu Alabo Diqu Yisilan Jiao Zhi Bijiao" (The Special Characteristics of Chinese Islam Compared to the Islam of the Arab Region), *Researches on the Hui*, 2, 50, 2003; Zhi Xiang, "Qian Yi Yisilan Jiao de Aiguo Zhuyi" (A Brief Discussion of Islamic Patriotism), *Journal of the Guangzhou Institute of Socialism*, no. 1, 2007.

51. Recently, a number of Western scholars have tried to move beyond the stereotypes of assimilation and syncretism. They still speak of Chinese Islam, but they stress its ongoing ties with mainstream religious currents instead of the divergence of local adaptations. Nonetheless, both Chinese and Western writings continue to overlook the importance of Turkish-speaking Muslims and to underestimate the diversity and discontent of the Hui communities. Roberta Tontini, *Muslim Sanzijing: Shifts and Continuities in the Definition of Islam in China*, Leiden: Brill, 2016; Jonathan Lipman, ed., *Islamic Thought in China: Sino-Muslim Intellectual Evolution from the 17th to the 21st Century*, Edinburgh: Edinburgh University Press, 2016; Zvi Ben-Dor Benite, "Chinese Islam: A Complete Concert," *Cross-Currents: East Asian History and Culture Review*, June 2017; Matthew Erie, *China and Islam: The Prophet, the Party, and Law*, New York: Cambridge University Press, 2017; Tracy You, "Muslim Protesters Clash with Armed SWAT Officers and Order Them to Kneel during a Riot at a Chinese Toll Station," *Daily Mail*, September 4, 2017.

52. Cai Degui, "Yisilan Jiao He Zhongguo Chuantong Wenhua de Ronghe" (The Fusion of Islam and Traditional Chinese Culture), *Arab World*, no. 1, 1996; Dainian Zhang, *Key Concepts in Chinese Philosophy*, translated and edited by Edmund Ryden, New Haven, CT: Yale University Press, 2002; Anita Maria Leopold and Jeppe Sinding Jensen, eds., *Syncretism in Religion: A Reader*, New York: Routledge, 2004; Christine Mollier, *Buddhism and Taoism Face to Face: Scripture, Ritual, and Iconographic Exchange in Medieval China*, Honolulu: University of Hawaii Press, 2008; Janet Alison Hoskins, "An Unjealous God? Christian Elements in a Vietnamese Syncretistic Religion," *Current Anthropology*, December 2014; Peter Berger, "A Mixed Bag, Religious Hybrids," *The American Interest*, June 1, 2016.

53. Maris Boyd Gillette, *Between Mecca and Beijing: Modernization and Consumption among Urban Chinese Muslims*, Stanford, CA: Stanford University Press, 2000;

Mohammed Al-Sudairi, "Chinese Salafism and the Saudi Connection," *The Diplomat*, October 23, 2014; Jonathan Kaiman, "In China, Rise of Salafism Fosters Suspicion and Division among Muslims," *Los Angeles Times*, February 1, 2016; Alice Su, "China Doesn't Mind Islamic Extremists, As Long as They're Not Uighur," *Foreign Policy*, December 16, 2016.

54. Ian Johnson, "China Seeks Tighter Grip in Wake of a Religious Revival," *New York Times*, October 7, 2016; Carey Lodge, "Is Religious Freedom in China Really about to Get Worse?" *Christian Today*, October 6, 2016; Doug Bandow, "Nervous China Ramps Up Religious Persecution," *Japan Times*, April 17, 2017; Ian Johnson, "In China, Unregistered Churches Are Driving a Religious Revolution," *The Atlantic*, April 23, 2017; James Chao, "After a 66-Year Estrangement, Can China and the Catholic Church Kiss and Make Up?" *Newsweek*, May 2, 2017.

55. Liang Chen, "China's Halal Food Exporters Struggle with Ideological, Trade Barriers," *Global Times*, November 26, 2014; Camille Paldi, "Islamic Finance Is Knocking on the Doorsteps of China," *International Finance*, July 15, 2015; Gao Yanqiu, "Huzu Dute Falu Yishi Chengyin Chutan" (A Preliminary Study on the Causes of the Unique Legal Consciousness of the Hui), *Shaanxi Xueqian Normal University Journal*, August 2015; "Kempinski Bets on Ningxia's Hopes to Be Capital of China's New Silk Road," *Jing Daily*, June 19, 2016; Bao Yun, "Publishing House Puts Chinese Books on Middle Eastern Shelves," cgtn.com, April 22, 2017.

56. Ben Hillman, "The Rise of the Community in Rural China: Village Politics, Cultural Identity and Religious Revival in a Hui Hamlet," *The China Journal*, January 2004; Gui Rong, "Huizu Nongcun de 'Quanli Wenhua Wangluo': Yunnan Shadian Hexie Shehui de Zhengzhi Renleixue Yanjiu" (The "Cultural Nexus of Power" of the Rural Hui: The Harmonious Society of Yunnan's Shadian from the Perspective of Political Anthropology), *Journal of Yunnan University of Nationalities*, July 2009; Eric Rudolph, "Kunming, A Melting Pot of Disappearing Culture Where Islam Survives," *The National (UAE)*, February 12, 2013; Luisetta Mudie, "China Deports Hundreds of Uyghur Residents from Yunnan," *Radio Free Asia*, March 12, 2014; Alice Su, "Harmony and Martyrdom among China's Hui Muslims," *The New Yorker*, June 6, 2016.

57. Isabell Côté, "The Enemies Within: Targeting Han Chinese and Hui Minorities in Xinjiang," *Asian Ethnicity*, January 2015; Ahmed Elbenni, "Rift: The Uyghurs and the Hui," *The Yale Globalist*, January 21, 2017; Sophie Williams, "Chinese Muslims Are Banned from Having 'Abnormal' Beards or Wearing Veils as the Nation Calls for a 'People's War' against Islamic Extremism," *Daily Mail*, March 30, 2017; Benjamin Haas, "China Bans Religious Names for Muslim Babies in Xinjiang," *The Guardian*, April 24, 2017.

58. Daniel Bardsley, "Yiwu Is the 'Fastest Growing Muslim Community' in China," *The National (UAE)*, August 12, 2012; Tan Yifan, "Muslims' Spiritual Center in Shenzhen," *Shenzhen Daily*, August 15, 2013; Sun Xiaoling, "Shuoyi, Guojian Yu Rentong: Shenzhen Musilin Yu Shenzhen Shi Da Guannian Rongru Du Diaocha Yanjiu" (Benefit, Build, and Identify: A Survey of the Degree of Shenzhen Muslims' Assimilation of Shenzhen's Ten Great Concepts), *Journal of Qinghai Nationalities Institute*, vol. 42, no. 4, 2016.

59. Wang Yongzhi, Song Jun, Han Xueshuang, and Xue Guifang, "Guanyu Nanhai Duan Xu Xian de Zonghe Tantao" (A Comprehensive Investigation of the Dotted Line in the South China Sea), *Journal of Ocean University of China, Social Sciences Edition*, vol. 8, no. 3, 2008; Guo Peiqing, "Daguo Zhanlue Zhi Bei Ji" (Great Power Strategy Points to the North Pole), 360doc.com, July 7, 2009; "Qingdao-Made LNG Modules to Be Sent to the Arctic," *China Daily*, July 1, 2016; Xie Chuanjiao, "'Blue Economy' Key to Qingdao's Future," *China Daily*, May 27, 2013; Xie Chuanjiao, "Qingdao Set for Leading Role in Global Economy," *The Telegraph*, July 27, 2016; Fan Junmei, "Qingdao Strives to Become Cruise Home Port of Northeast Asia," *China Daily*, February 22, 2017.

60. "Chengdu Report: Four-City Zone to Boost Western Region," *China Daily*, April 23, 2015; Chong Koh Ping, "Chengdu Ranked Top Chinese City for Economic Showing," *Straits Times*, September 17, 2015; Julien Legrand, "The Great Convergence: China's Future Lies in Its West," *Paris Innovation Review*, December 12, 2015; Chen Liubing, "Fastest China-Europe Train Sets Record Time of 10.5 Days," *The Telegraph*, June 21, 2016; Christian Shepherd, "Chengdu Benefits from China's One Belt, One Road Strategy," *Financial Times*, August 18, 2016; "Chengdu to Run 1,000 Cargo Trains to Europe in 2017," *China Daily*, February 20, 2017.

61. Qian Zaijian, "Gonggong Quanli Yunxing Gongkaihua de Xieshang Minzhu Lujing Yanjiu" (The Deliberative Democracy Path to Opening the Operation of Public Power), Nanjing Normal University, Research Center for Local Government and Governance Innovation, *Jianghai Xuekan*, March 10, 2015; LeAnne Graves, "Chinese Investment to Spur Middle East Renewable Energy Ambitions," *The National (UAE)*, December 7, 2015; Partnership for Action on Green Economy, *Transition to a Green Economy in China's Jiangsu Province: A Stocktaking Report*, Nanjing: Ministry of Environmental Protection, 2016; Katrina Hamlin, "China's Zealous Cleantech Firms Risk Burning Cash," *Reuters*, November 15, 2016.

62. Ben Blanchard, "As Trump Stresses 'America First,' China Plays the World Leader," *Reuters*, January 25, 2017; Amitai Etzioni, "China: The Accidental World Leader?" *The Diplomat*, February 13, 2017; Patrick Lawrence, "How China Is Building the Post-Western World," *The Nation*, May 16, 2017; Geoffrey Smith, "Germany and China Position Themselves as World Climate Leaders," *Fortune*, June 1, 2017.

Chapter 2

1. CCTV coverage of the four hour 20 minute 2008 Beijing Olympics opening ceremony is available online. The segment on the Silk Road begins at minute 42 and Zheng He's treasure ships appear at minute 44. https://www.youtube.com/watch?v=8n-gMKtR77g.

2. Randall L. Schweller and Xiaoyu Pu, "After Unipolarity: China's Visions of International Order in an Era of U.S. Decline," *International Security*, Summer 2011; Bart Dessein, ed., *Interpreting China as a Regional and Global Power: Nationalism and Historical Consciousness in World Politics*, New York: Palgrave Macmillan, 2014.

3. Philippe De Lombaerde et al., "The Problem of Comparison in Comparative Regionalism," *Review of International Studies*, July 2010; Zhao Zuoquan, "Zhongguo Juxing Qu Geju," (Megaregions in China, *Urban Development Studies*), vol. 20, no. 2, 2013; Melissa R. McHale et al., "The New Global Urban Realm: Complex, Connected,

Diffuse, and Diverse Social-Ecological Systems," *Sustainability*, vol. 7, no. 5, 2015; Marina Alberti, *Cities That Think Like Planets: Complexity, Resilience, and Innovation in Hybrid Ecosystems*, Seattle: University of Washington Press, 2016.

4. Sylvia Walby, "Complexity Theory, Globalisation and Diversity," *www.leeds. ac.uk*, April 2003; Marc Barthelmy, Patricia Bordin, Henri Berestycki, and Maurizio Gribaudi, "Self-Organization versus Top-Down Planning in the Evolution of a City," *Scientific Reports*, July 2013.

5. Margaret Sleeboom-Faulkner, *The Chinese Academy of Social Sciences (CASS): Shaping the Reforms, Academia and China (1977–2003)*, Leiden and Boston: Brill, 2007; Q. Edward Wang, "World History vs. Global History? The Changing Worldview in Contemporary China," *Chinese Studies in History*, vol. 42, no. 3, 2009; Liu Xincheng, "The Global View of History in China," *Journal of World History*, September 2012; Adrian Wan, "Chinese Academy of Social Sciences Is 'Infiltrated by Foreign Forces': Anti-graft Official," *South China Morning Post*, 2014; "China's President Xi Jinping Calls for Marxism and Intellectual Loyalty," *Agence France-Presse*, May 18, 2016.

6. Françoise Jullien, *The Propensity of Things: Toward a History of Efficacy in China*, New York: Zone Books, 1999; R. James Ferguson and Rosita Dellios, *The Politics and Philosophy of Chinese Power: The Timeless and the Timely*, Lanham, MD: Lexington Books, 2016.

7. Martin W. Lewis, *The Myth of Continents: A Critique of Metageography*, Berkeley: University of California Press, 1997; George Lakoff and Mark Johnson, *Metaphors We Live By*, Chicago: University of Chicago Press, 2003; David Ludden, "Maps in the Mind and the Mobility of Asia," *The Journal of Asian Studies*, November 2003.

8. On efforts to create distinctively Chinese theories of international relations, see Linsay Cunningham-Cross and Peter Marcus Kristensen, "Chinese International Relations Theory," *Oxford Bibliographies*, May 29, 2014; Yaqing Qin, "Recent Developments toward a Chinese School of IR Theory," *E-International Relations*, April 26, 2016.

9. Richard Little, *The Balance of Power in International Relations: Metaphors, Myths, and Models*, New York: Cambridge University Press, 2007; Michael P. Marks, *Metaphors in International Relations Theory*, New York: Palgrave Macmillan, 2011; Michael Hanne, William D. Crano, and Jeffrey Scott Mio, eds., *Warring with Words: Narrative and Metaphor in Politics*, New York and London: Psychology Press, 2014.

10. Zheng Bijian, "China's 'Peaceful Rise' to Great-Power Status," *Foreign Affairs*, September/October 2005; Tang Jin, ed., *Daguo Jueqi: Yi Lishi de Yanguang He Quanqiu de Shiye Jiedu 15 Shiji Yilai 9 Ge Shijiexing Daguo Jueqi de Lishi (The Rise of the Great Powers: In Historical and Global Perspective, Interpreting the History of the Rise of Nine World Powers since the 15th Century)*, Beijing: Renmin Chubanshe, 2006; Bonnie S. Glaser and Evan S. Medeiros, "The Changing Ecology of Foreign Policy-Making in China: The Ascension and Demise of the Theory of "Peaceful Rise," *China Quarterly*, June 2007.

11. Liu Ya, *Zhuanxing Qi Zhengzhi: Jizhi De Tupo Yu Kunrao (Times of Transitional Politics: Breakthroughs and Disruptions)*, Beijing: China Social Science Press, 2011;

Zhang Jianxin, "Hou Xifang Guoji Tixi Yu Dongfang de Xingqi" (The Post-Western International System and the Rise of the East), *World Economics and Politics*, July 9, 2012 (arguing that the eastward shift of world power resembles the collisions of tectonic plates); Liang Guanghe, "Zhongguo Shi Zhongyang Zhi Guo" (China Is the Central Country), *sciencenet.cn*, April 29, 2017 (claiming that China is a center of seismic activity that has shaped the physical contours of Asia).

12. Dai Bingguo, "Zhongguo Qudai Meiguo Cheng Ba Shijie? Na Shi Shenhua" (China Replacing the U.S. as a World Hegemon? That Is a Fairytale), *Beijing Times*, December 8, 2010; Alastair Iain Johnston, "How New and Assertive Is China's New Assertiveness?" *International Security*, Spring 2013; Jian Zhang, "China's New Foreign Policy under Xi Jinping: Towards 'Peaceful Rise 2.0?" *Global Change, Peace and Security*, January 2015; Charles S. Glaser, "A U.S.-China Grand Bargain? The Hard Choice between Military Competition and Accommodation," *International Security*, Spring 2015.

13. For examples of influential foreign policy debates among leading military and academic commentators that promote such metaphors, see Dai Xu, *C Xing Baowei: Neiyou Waihuan Xia de Zhongguo Tuwei (C-Shaped Encirclement: China's Breakout from Internal Troubles and External Aggression)*, Shanghai: Wenhui, 2009; Liu Yazhou, "Xibu Lun" (On the Western Region), *Phoenix Weekly*, August 5, 2010; Dai Xu, "Zhong E Ying Goujian Ouya Da Lianmeng Zuzhi Meiguo Tulu Ruo Guo" (China and Russia Should Establish a Eurasian Alliance to Prevent the United States from Slaughtering Weak Countries), *Global Times*, January 29, 2012; Wang Jisi, "'Xi Jin': Zhongguo Diyuan Zhanlue de Zai Pingheng" ("Marching Westwards": Rebalancing China's Geostrategy), *Global Times Net*, October 17, 2012; Yang Yi, "Zhoubian Anquan Xuyao Quan Fangwei Zhanlue" (Peripheral Security Requires a Comprehensive Strategy), *Global Times*, October 26, 2012; Feng Haiwen, "Zhongguo Daguo Zhuanlue Xuanze: Nan Jin Haishi Xi Jin?" (China's Great Power Strategic Choice: Sail South or March West?), *Global Times*, November 1, 2012; Feng Haiwen, "Meiguo Duihua Zhengce, Huo Cong Ying Weidu Bian Ruan Baowei" (America's Policy of Dialogue, Or from Hard Containment to Soft Encirclement), *Global Net*, January 22, 2013.

14. Hua Zheng, "Cong Daguo Boyi Kan 'Yidai Yilu' Zhanlue" (Viewing "The One Belt, One Road" Strategy in Terms of the Great Game), *Guangming Ribao*, November 29, 2015; Zhai Shui, "Li Xiguang Jiang 'Yidai, Yilu' Yu Daguo Boyi" (Li Xiguang Discusses "One Belt, One Road" and the Great Game), *Siyue Wang, tv.m4.cn*, March 29, 2016; Wang Jisi, "Da Qiju: Guanyu Zhongguo Diyuan Zhanlue de Ruogan Sikao" (The Great Chess Game: Thoughts on China's Geostrategy), *Strategic and International Studies Bulletin*, October 8, 2016; Zhang Baofeng, "Sheke Yuan: 'Yidai Yilu' Chonggou Diyuan Youshi Zhongguo Cheng Boyi Zhongxin" (Social Science Academy: "One Belt, One Road" Will Reshape the Geographic Advantage Making China the Center of the Game), *Dagong Wang*, May 5, 2017.

15. "Selections from the 'Silk Road and China Dream' Speech Contest," *Confucius Institute Magazine*, November 2016; Ma Xiaoning, Zhou Hanbo, Xie Yahong, and Liu Junguo, "Romantic Love Story Brightens Up Silk Road," *Global Times*, May 1, 2017; Xiang Bo, "One Silk Road, One Dream," *Xinhua*, May 6, 2017.

16. Bingdi Wangtian, *Daguo Youxi: Kan Zhongguo Ruhe Ke Ying Shijie* (*The Great Game: How China Can Win the World*), Beijing: World Knowledge, 2009; Liu Tao, *Zhongguo Shiji* (The Chinese Century), Beijing: Xinhua, 2010; Cheng Yawen and Wang Yiwei, *Tian Ming: Yige Xin Lingdaoxing Guojia de Tansheng* (*The Mandate of Heaven: The Birth of a New Leading Country*), Beijing: Qunyan Press, 2015; Wang Fan, *Daguo Waijiao: Cong "Taoguang Yanghui" Dao "Daguo Waijiao," Zhongguo Yao Gaosu Shijie Shenme?* (*Great Power Diplomacy: From "Concealing One's Strength" to "Great Power Diplomacy," What Will China Tell the World?*), Beijing: Beijing United, 2016.

17. Zhu Cuiping, *Yindu Yang Yu Zhongguo* (*The Indian Ocean and China*), Beijing: Social Science, 2014; Li Xiguang, "'Yidai Yilu' Ruhe Zuoguo Zhongdong Zhongya Fengbao Yan" (How "One Belt One Road" Can Pass through the Eye of the Storm in the Middle East and Central Asia), guancha.cn, April 14, 2015; Zhou Chuanbin, "Yingxiang Xiandai Yisilan de San Zhong Sichao" (Three Trends of Influence on Modern Islam), dxw.ifeng.com, January 12, 2016; Yao Liu Changming and Yao Shifan, "'Yidai Yilu' Chengyi Xia Zhongguo de Ouya Yiti Hua Zhanlue Yu Daxiyang Zhuyi" (China's Strategy of Eurasian Integration under "One Belt One Road" and Atlanticism), aisixiang.com, November 12, 2016.

18. H. R. Trevor-Roper, "Fernand Braudel, the Annales, and the Mediterranean," *The Journal of Modern History*, December 1972; Fernand Braudel, *The Mediterranean and the Mediterranean World in the Age of Philip II, Vol. 1*, Berkeley: University of California Press, 1996; Harriet T. Zurndorfer, "Not Bound to China: Étienne Balazs, Fernand Braudel and the Politics of the Study of Chinese History in Post-War France," *Past and Present*, November 2004; André Burguière, *The Annales School: An Intellectual History*, Ithaca, NY: Cornell University Press, 2009.

19. Janet L. Abu-Lughod, *Before European Hegemony: The World System A.D. 1250–1350*, New York: Oxford University Press, 1989; K. N. Chaudhuri, *Asia before Europe: Economy and Civilisation of the Indian Ocean from the Rise of Islam to 1750*, Cambridge: Cambridge University Press, 1990; Philippe Beaujard, "The Indian Ocean in Eurasian and African World-Systems before the Sixteenth Century," *The Journal of World History*, December 2005; Barbara Watson Andaya, "Oceans Unbounded: Transversing Asia across 'Area Studies,'" *Journal of Asian Studies*, November 2006; Peter C. Perdue, "Eurasia in World History: Reflections on Time and Space," *World History Connected*, February 2008; Victor Lieberman, "Protected Rimlands and Exposed Zones: Reconfiguring Premodern Eurasia," *Comparative Studies in Society and History*, July 2008; Sebastian Prange, "Scholars and the Sea: A Historiography of the Indian Ocean," *History Compass*, September 2008; Philippe Beaujard, *Les Mondes de l'Ocean Indien* (*The Worlds of the Indian Ocean*), Paris: Armand Colin, 2012; Patrick Manning, "Africa's Place in Globalization: Africa, Eurasia, and Their Borderlands," *Journal of Globalization Studies*, May 2014.

20. S.A.M. Adshead, *Central Asia in World History*, London: Palgrave Macmillan, 1993; Joseph Fletcher, *Studies on Chinese and Islamic Inner Asia*, Brookfield, VT: Variorum, 1995; Leonard Blussé, "Chinese Century: The Eighteenth Century in the China Sea Region," *Archipel*, vol. 58, no. 3, 1999; Maurice Aymard, "De la Méditerranée à l'Asie: une comparaison nécessarire (commentaire)," *Annales*, no. 1, 2001; R. Bin Wong, "Between Nation and World: Braudelian Regions in Asia," *Review (Fernand Braudel Center)*, vol. 26, no. 1, 2003; Heather Sutherland,

"Southeast Asian History and the Mediterranean Analogy," *Journal of Southeast Asian Studies*, February 2003; Denys Lombard, "Another 'Mediterranean' in Southeast Asia," *The Asia-Pacific Journal*, March 1, 2007; Wang Gungwu, "The China Seas: Becoming an Enlarged Mediterranean," in Angela Schottenhammer, ed., *The East Asian "Mediterranean": Maritime Crossroads of Culture, Commerce and Human Migration*, Wiesbaden: Harrassowitz Verlag, 2008; François Gipouloux, *The Asian Mediterranean: Port Cities and Trading Networks in China, Japan and Southeast Asian, 13th–21st Century*, Cheltenham and Northampton, MA: Edward Elgar, 2011; Yokkaichi Yasuhiro, "The Eurasian Empire or Chinese Empire? The Mongol Impact and the Chinese Centripetal System," in Masaki Mukai and Shiro Momiki, eds., *Empires, Systems, and Maritime Networks*, Osaka: Japan Society for Promotion of Science, 2011; Eric Tagliacozzo and Wen-Chin Chang, eds., *Chinese Circulations: Capital, Commodities, and Networks in Southeast Asia*, Durham, NC: Duke University Press, 2011; Donna R. Gabaccía and Dirk Hoerder, eds., *Connecting Seas and Connected Ocean Rims: Indian, Atlantic, and Pacific Oceans and China Seas Migrations from the 1820s to the 1930s*, Leiden/Boston: Brill, 2011; Roy Bin Wong, "Reflections on Qing Institutions of Governance: Chinese Empire in Comparative Perspective," *Crossroads*, vol. 5, 2012; Pin-tsun Chang, "The Rise of Chinese Mercantile Power in Maritime Southeast Asia, c. 1400–1700," *Crossroads*, vol. 6, 2012; Masaki Mukai, "New Approaches to Premodern Maritime Networks," *Asian Review of World Histories*, July 2016.

21. World History Association, *China in World History, World History from the Center and the Periphery*, Beijing: Capital Normal University, July 2011; China-Japan-Korea Trilateral Research Cooperation Summit, *Relations with the Middle East*, Shanghai: Shanghai International Studies University, November 2015.

22. Ying Tan, *Chinnovation: How Chinese Innovators Are Changing the World*, Hoboken, NJ, Wiley: 2011; Marlène Laruelle and Sébastien Peyrouse, *The Chinese Question in Central Asia: Domestic Order, Social Change, and the Chinese Factor*, London: Hurst, 2012; Juan Pablo Cardenal and Heriberto Araújo, *China's Silent Army: The Pioneers, Traders, Fixers and Workers Who Are Remaking the World in Beijing's Image*, New York: Crown, 2013; Howard French, *China's Second Continent: How a Million Migrants Are Building a New Empire in Africa*, New York: Knopf, 2014; François Godement, "Expanded Ambitions, Shrinking Achievements: How China Sees the Global Order," *European Council on Foreign Relations*, March 2017; Scott Cendrowski, "Alibaba's Jack Ma Expects the World to Experience Decades of 'Pain,'" *Fortune*, April 23, 2017; Tom Miller, *China's Asian Dream: Empire Building along the New Silk Road*, London: Zed Books, 2017; Andreea Brinza, "China's Continent-Spanning Trains Are Running Half-Empty," *Foreign Policy*, June 5, 2017.

23. Catherine Ross, ed., *Megaregions: Planning for Global Competitiveness*, Washington, DC: Island Press, 2012; Alice E. MacGillivray, "A Policy Paradox: Social Complexity Emergence around an Ordered Science Attractor," *Emergence: Complexity and Organization*, November 2015; Ward Rauws, "Embracing Uncertainty without Abandoning Planning," *The Planning Review*, April 2017.

24. John N. Thompson, *The Geographic Mosaic of Coevolution*, Chicago: University of Chicago Press, 2005; Enrico Coen, *Cells to Civilization: The Principles of Change That Shape Life*, Princeton, NJ: Princeton University Press, 2012; Richard Dawkins, *The Selfish Gene*, New York: Oxford University Press, 2016.

25. Steven Manson and David O'Sullivan, "Complexity Theory in the Study of Space and Place," *Environment and Planning*, April 1, 2006; John Duncan, *How Intelligence Happens*, New Haven, CT: Yale University Press, 2010.

26. Zhongqi Pan, ed., *Conceptual Gaps in China-EU Relations: Global Governance, Human Rights and Strategic Partnerships*, London: Palgrave Macmillan, 2012; Maria Adele Carrai, "A Genealogy of Sovereignty in China, 1840–Today," PhD Dissertation, University of Hong Kong, 2015; Zihang Liu, "How the Chinese View International Law," *International Policy Digest*, August 29, 2016.

27. Georg Simmel, *Conflict; The Web of Group-Affiliations*, New York: Free Press, 1964; Lewis A. Coser, *The Functions of Social Conflict*, London: Routledge, 2001.

28. Scott Camazine, Jean-Louis Deneubourg, Nigel R. Franks, James Sneyd, Guy Theraulaz, and Eric Bonabeau, *Self-Organization in Biological Systems*, Princeton, NJ: Princeton University Press, 2003.

29. Craig W. Benkman, Thomas L. Parchman, Amanda Favis, and Adam M. Siepielski, "Reciprocal Selection Causes a Coevolutionary Arms Race between Crossbills and Lodgepole Pine," *The American Naturalist*, August 2003; Judith L. Bronstein, Ulf Dieckmann, and Régis Ferrière, "Coevolutionary Dynamics and the Conservation of Mutualisms," in Régis Ferrière, Ulf Dieckmann, and Denis Couvet, eds., *Evolutionary Conservation Biology*, New York: Cambridge University Press, 2004; Paulo R. Guimarães Jr., Pedro Jordano, and John N. Thompson, "Evolution and Coevolution in Mutualistic Networks," *Ecology Letters*, vol. 14, no. 9, 2011.

30. John N. Thompson, *Relentless Evolution*, Chicago: University of Chicago Press, 2013.

31. R. Gomulkiewicz, D.M Drown, M.F. Dybdahl, W. Godsoe, S.L. Nuismer, K.M. Pepin, B.J. Ridenhour, C.I. Smith, and J.B. Yoder, "Testing the Geographic Mosaic Theory of Coevolution," *Heredity*, vol. 98, no. 5, 2007.

32. Howard French, "China's Quest to End Its Century of Shame," *New York Times*, July 13, 2017.

33. Matthew Dearing, "Nation Building Is Dirty Business," *Foreign Policy*, March 10, 2015; Daniel F. Runde and Conor M. Savory, "Nation Building by Any Other Name," *Center for Strategic and International Studies*, January 23, 2017.

Chapter 3

1. Anatol Lieven, *Pakistan: A Hard Country*, New York: PublicAffairs, 2012; Andrew Small, *The China-Pakistan Axis: Asia's New Geopolitics*, New York: Oxford University Press, 2015.

2. Saeed Shah and Jeremy Page, "China Readies $46 Billion for Pakistan Trade Route," *Wall Street Journal*, April 16, 2015. For details of specific projects see the official CPEC website at, *cpec.gov.pk*. and the several articles collected under "China-Pakistan Economic Corridor" at *wikiwand.com*.

3. Mateen Haider, "Chinese President Cancels Pakistan Trip, India Visit Still On," *Dawn*, September 5, 2014; Faseeh Mangi and Kamran Haider, "Xi Postpones $34 Billion Pakistan Trip amid Protests," *Bloomberg*, September 6, 2014.

4. Shahbaz Rana, "China-Pakistan Economic Corridor: Lines of Development—Not Lines of Divide," *Express Tribune*, May 17, 2015; Shamil Shams, "China's Economic Corridor Creating New Conflicts in Pakistan," *Deutsche Welle*, August 28, 2016.

5. Josh Chin and Liyan Qi, "China Makes Multibillion-Dollar Down-Payment on Silk Road Plans," *Wall Street Journal*, April 21, 2015; Khurram Husain, "CPEC Enclaves," *Dawn*, March 9, 2017.

6. Aditi Phadnis, "Interesting Facts about the Sharif Family and Its Business Interests," *Business Standard* (India), January 2, 2016; Tridivesh Singh Maini, "Shahbaz Sharif's China Visit: Implications for CPEC," *The Diplomat*, August 2, 2016; Aoun Sahi and Shashank Bengali, "Panama Papers Expose Pakistan's Embattled Prime Minister to Allegations of Corruption," *Los Angeles Times*, April 4, 2017.

7. Tahir Khan, "Economic Corridor: Chinese Official Sets Record Straight," *Express Tribune*, March 2, 2015; Farhan Bokhari, Lucy Hornby, and Christian Shepherd, "China Urges Pakistan to Give Army Lead Role in Silk Road Project," *Financial Times*, July 21, 2016; Shafqat Ali, "No Favouratism in CPEC: China," *The Nation*, October 6, 2016.

8. Wu Zhaoli, "Economic Corridor Will Be Lever for All of South Asia," *Global Times*, July 30, 2013; Farman Nawaz, "Proposed Sino-Pakistani Trade Route Misses Areas in Need," *Global Times*, July 30, 2013.

9. "All-Party Conference: Consensus on Trade Route Eludes Confab," awaztoday.pk, May 15, 2015; Muhammad Arif, "CPEC Route, Agreed by APC, Being Implemented in Letter and Spirit: Minister," nihao-salam.com, October 13, 2015; Azam Khan, "Persisting Stalemate: Govt Fails to Assuage APC's Concerns on CPEC," *Express Tribune*, January 11, 2016.

10. Adnan Aamir, "China-Punjab Economic Corridor," *The Nation*, April 24, 2015; Jon Boone and Kiyya Baloch, "A New Shenzhen? Poor Pakistan Fishing Town's Horror at Chinese Plans," *The Guardian*, February 3, 2016.

11. Ahmad Rashid Malik, "Route Alignment Controversy," *The Nation*, February 20, 2015; Mohammad Zafar, "APC Opposes Detours in Economic Corridor Route," *Express Tribune*, May 17, 2015.

12. Qamar Zaman, "Pak-China Economic Corridor: Senators Issue Ominous Warning over Route Change," *Express Tribune*, February 4, 2015; "KP Assembly Threatens to Resist Any Change in Route," *The News International*, February 7, 2015; "KP Assembly Opposes Changes in Economic Corridor Route," *Dawn*, February 7, 2015.

13. "Talking Points: Sikander Reaffirms QWP's Commitment to Developing K-P," *Express Tribune*, November 26, 2015; "CPEC Won't Pass Through KP if Due Share Denied," *Dawn*, January 3, 2016; "CPEC a Matter of Life and Death for Pakhtuns, Says Sherpao," *Pakistan Today*, January 6, 2016.

14. Munir Ghazanfar, "Kalbagh Dam and the Water Debate in Pakistan," *Lahore Journal of Policy Studies*, September 2008; Iram Khalid and Ishrat Begum, "Hydropolitics in Pakistan: Perceptions and Misperceptions," *South Asian Studies*, January–June 2013; Awami National Party, "Pakhtunkhwa's Case against Kalabagh Dam," awaminationalparty.org, May 29, 2013.

15. Umar Farooq, "The Afghan Roots of Pakistan's Zarb-e-Azb Operation," *Foreign Policy*, September 18, 2014; Khaled Ahmed, *Sleepwalking to Surrender: Dealing with Terrorism in Pakistan*, London: Penguin, 2016.

16. Declan Walsh, "Pakistan's Secret Dirty War," *The Guardian*, March 29, 2011; Akbar Ahmed, "Is Pakistan Heading for Disaster in Balochistan?" *Al-Jazeera*, January 15, 2012.

17. Prasun Sonwalkar, "Baloch, Sindhi Leaders in London Protest China-Pak Corridor, Rights Violations," *Hindustan Times*, August 30, 2016.

18. Panos Mourdoukoutas, "Does Karachi Really Want China to Control the Electrical Switch?" *Forbes*, September 5, 2016; Qasim Nauman, "Pakistan Stock Exchange Says Chinese Consortium Has Top Bid for 40% Stake," *Wall Street Journal*, December 22, 2016; International Crisis Group, *Pakistan: Stoking the Fire in Karachi*, Brussels: ICG, February 15, 2017.

19. "RAW at Frontline to Sabotage Economic Corridor, China Warns Pakistan," *Express Tribune*, May 22, 2015; Malik Siraj Akbar, "Tensions Mount between India and Pakistan over Balochistan," *Huffington Post*, March 27, 2016; Malik Siraj Akbar, "Why Modi's Statements Should Be the Least of Our Worries on Balochistan," *Dawn*, August 20, 2016; Vivek Katju, "The Way to Tackle a Rattled China after Modi's Balochistan Barb," *thequint.com*, September 1, 2016.

20. Azam Khan, "China Urges Pakistani Parties to Settle CPEC Differences," *Express Tribune*, January 10, 2016; Baber Aly, "CPEC and Security of Chinese Engineers," *Pakistan Today*, May 9, 2016.

21. "Meeting of Parliamentary Committee CPEC," *nihao-salam.com*, June 30, 2016.

22. "Dark Corridor: Conflict in Balochistan Must Be Resolved for a Trade-Corridor between Pakistan and China to Bring Rewards," *The Economist*, June 6, 2015; Syed Raza Hassan, "To Protect Chinese Investment, Pakistan Military Leaves Little to Chance," *Reuters*, February 7, 2016.

23. Ahmad Noorani, "CPEC Route Controversy Routed," *The News*, January 16, 2016; "Govt Claims 'Total Consensus' among Provinces on CPEC," *Dawn*, January 18, 2017.

24. Raza Habib Raja, "This Is Why I Think Pakistan Needs a Saraiki Province," *Express Tribune*, October 6, 2016; "'I Was Removed for Demanding Seraiki Province': Gilani," *Business Recorder*, December 18, 2016; Imtiyaz Ali, "Chinese Authorities Approve Inclusion of 3 Sindh Projects in CPEC," *Dawn*, December 30, 2016.

25. Farhan Bokhari, "Early Harvest?" *Dawn*, September 7, 2016; "12 Energy Projects under CPEC to Be Completed by 2017–18," *Express Tribune*, January 18, 2017.

26. Adnan Aamir, "Calling CPEC, China-Punjab Economic Corridor Is Not a Mistake," *The Nation*, May 1, 2015; Go Yamada, "Top Marks in 1st Term See Sharif Eyeing 2018 Re-election," *Nikkei Asian Review*, January 13, 2017.

27. Mehreen Zahra-Malik, "Ousted Pakistan Leader Passes Baton to Brother, Shehbaz Sharif," *New York Times*, July 29, 2017; M. Ilyas Khan, "Panama Papers: Controversy behind Ousting of Pakistan PM Nawaz Sharif," *BBC News*, Islamabad, July 28, 2017; Rameez Khan, "Shehbaz Sarif Advised to Stay Put in Punjab," *Express Tribune*, August 2, 2017; Ubaidullah Shaikh and Javed Hussain, "Shahbaz to Be PML-Ns Next Candidate for Prime Minister: Nawaz Sharif," *Dawn*, December 21, 2017.

28. Instead of Shehbaz, it was Nawaz's wife, Kulsoom, who entered a by-election in Lahore and won the safe seat in parliament that Nawaz had been forced to vacate.

Maryam, her daughter, managed the campaign amid reports that the mother was seriously ill and that Maryam herself was being groomed to hold office. Mehreen Zahra-Malik, "In Pakistani Fray, Maryam Sharif Is on the Edge of Power, or Prison," *New York Times*, October 27, 2017; "Nawaz Sharif's Media-Savvy Daughter to Contest Next Election in Pakistan," *Press Trust of India*, January 19, 2018.

29. "General Election 25 July 2018," *Election Commission of Pakistan*, July 29, 2018, https://www.ecp.gov.pk/; "Pakistan Election Headquarters 2018," *Geo Television Network*, July 31, 2018, https://www.geo.tv/election.

30. Uzair M. Younus, "CPEC Questions," *Dawn*, January 3, 2016; Jonathan Hillman, "Mishandled China-Pakistan Economic Corridor Could Misfire," *Nikkei Asian Review*, April 13, 2017.

31. Ali Garewal, "Will Pakistan Forever Be Indebted to China for CPEC?" *Express Tribune*, October 29, 2016; Ishrat Husain, "Financing Burden of CPEC," *Dawn*, February 11, 2017.

32. Editorial, "CPEC Transparency," *Dawn*, November 18, 2015; Fawad Yousafzai, "Experts Concerned over Lack of Transparency in CPEC Projects," *The Nation*, September 21, 2016; "China Denies Allegations of Heavy Charges for CPEC Projects," *The Economic Times (India)*, April 6, 2017.

33. World Bank Group, Public Private Partnership in Infrastructure Resources, "Concessions, Build-Operate-Transfer (BOT) and Design-Build-Operate (DBO) Projects," *worldbank.org*, July 13, 2016.

34. Satyabrata Pal, "The China-Pakistan Corridor Is All about Power—Not Electricity, But the Real Thing," *The Wire*, June 3, 2016; Naveed Butt and Zaheer Abbasi, "CPEC Sovereign Guarantees May Not Augur Well for Budget," *Business Recorder*, January 26, 2017.

35. Frederic Grare, "Balochistan: The State versus the Nation," *The Carnegie Papers*, April 2013; Willem Marx and Marc Wattrelot, *Balochistan: At a Crossroads*, New Delhi: Niyogi Books, 2014.

36. Riaz Haq, "Pak Army Builds over Half of CPEC Western Route in Record Time," *riazhaq.com*, July 1, 2015; Shahbaz Rana, "Army Seeks Role in CPEC Administration," *Express Tribune*, April 16, 2016.

37. Tilak Devasher, "CPEC—A Game Changer or Debt Enhancer for Pakistan?" *Eurasia Review*, February 5, 2017.

38. Amri Wasim, "Kalabagh Dam Controversy Resurfaces in Senate," *Dawn*, June 7, 2016; Siegfried O. Wolf, "China-Pakistan Economic Corridor, Civil-Military Relations and Democracy in Pakistan," *South Asia Democratic Forum*, September 13, 2016.

39. Ahmad Rashid Malik, "Terrifying CPEC, Enemy Trying to Throw a Wrench in the Gears," *Pakistan Today*, June 11, 2016; "China Warns India, Says It Will Intervene if New Delhi Incites Trouble in Balochistan," *Indo-Asian News Service*, August 28, 2016; Zakka Jacob, "Why India Needs to Take Chinese Comments on Balochistan Seriously," *News 18 India*, August 29, 2016.

40. William Dalrymple, *A Deadly Triangle: Afghanistan, Pakistan, and India*, Washington, DC: Brookings, 2013.

41. Catherine Richards, "China-India: An Analysis of the Himalayan Territorial Dispute," *Indo-Pacific Strategic Papers*, Australian Defence College, February 2015; Ralph Jennings, "China Gets Cozier with Pakistan Again and, Yes, India Should Worry," *Forbes*, March 26, 2017.

42. Zeng Xiangyu, "Bajisitan Guada'er Gang Dui Guoji Anquan Taishi de Yingxiang" (The Influence of Pakistan's Gwadar Port on the International Security Situation), *South Asian Studies Quarterly*, September 29, 2009; "Pakistan to Host International Conference on Maritime Economy," *Dunya News*, December 10, 2016; Ananth Krishnan, "China May Station Marines in Gwadar, Say PLA Insiders," *India Today*, March 13, 2017.

43. Mian Abrar, "China Mulling Trade Route with Iran as Pak Leadership Bickers," *Pakistan Today*, January 30, 2016; Usman Shahid, "Balochistan: The Troubled Heart of the CPEC," *The Diplomat*, August 23, 2016; "Balochistan: Where India, China and Pakistan Are Playing the Great Game," newslaundry.com, September 21, 2016.

44. Masood Khan, "Pakistan's Perceived Encirclement by India, Afghanistan, and Iran," *Voice of East*, June 7, 2016; "Economic Corridor-CPEC Could Turn Pakistan into China's 'Client State,'" *Deutsche Welle*, November 14, 2016; Bhaskar Roy, "China: Strategic Encirclement of India's Core Interests," *Eurasia Review*, January 6, 2017.

45. Ahmad Rashid Malik, "The Chabahar Pact, This India-Iran Pact Should Be a Wakeup Call," *Pakistan Today*, June 22, 2016.

46. Subhash Kapila, "Pakistan 2017 Comprehensively Colonized by China," *Uday India*, May 4, 2017.

47. Farhan Zaheer, "Pakistan Imposes Anti-dumping Duty on China's Steel Products," *Express Tribune*, February 9, 2017; Wendy Wu, "China, Pakistan and the Challenges of Silk Road Connectivity," *South China Morning Post*, June 20, 2017.

48. Mathew Cottee, "Sino-Pakistan Civil Nuclear Cooperation: A Growing Challenge to the Global Nuclear Order," *Lowry Institute for International Policy*, July 9, 2015.

49. Shannon Tiezzi, "China Powers Up Pakistan: The Energy Component of the CPEC," *The Diplomat*, January 13, 2016.

50. Navin Singh Khadkha, "Are India and Pakistan Set for Water Wars?" *BBC News*, December 22, 2016; Armin Rosencranz and Merlin Elizabeth Joseph, "By Building the Sawalkot Dam, Is India Using Water as a Weapon against Pakistan?" *The Wire*, March 20, 2017.

51. Brahma Chellaney, "China-Pakistan Water Pincer against India: As Part of CPEC, Mega-dams Are Planned in Gilgit-Baltistan," *Economic Times*, May 16, 2017.

52. Mian Abrar, "China to Build Dams in Pakistan," *Pakistan Today*, May 13, 2017; Zafar Bhutta, "China to Invest $50b to Develop Indus River Cascade," *Express Tribune*, May 13, 2017.

53. Islamabad later rejected China's financial plans for the Diamer-Bhasha Dam, but the project went ahead anyway with Pakistan footing the bill on its own. Liu Zhen, "Pakistan Pulls Plug on Dam Deal over China's 'Too Strict' Conditions in Latest Blow to Belt and Road Plans," *South China Morning Post*, November 16, 2017.

Chapter 4

1. Carter Vaughn Findley, *The Turks in World History*, New York: Oxford University Press, 2004; Halil Inalcik, *The Ottoman Empire and Europe: The Ottoman Empire and Its Place in European History*, Istanbul: Kronik Kitap, 2017.

2. S. A. M. Adshead, *Central Asia in World History*, St. Martin's Press, 1993; David W. Anthony, *The Horse, the Wheel, and Language: How Bronze-Age Riders from the Eurasian Steppes Shaped the Modern World*, Princeton, NJ: Princeton University Press, 2010; Christopher I. Beckwith, *Empires of the Silk Road: A History of Central Eurasia from the Bronze Age to the Present*, Princeton, NJ: Princeton University Press, 2011.

3. Yılmaz Tezkan, *Uzak Ve Eski Komşumuz Çin* (*Our Distant and Ancient Neighbor China*), Istanbul: Ülke Kitapları, 2002; R. Kutay Karaca, *Güç Olma Stratejisi Çin: Soğuk Savaş Sonrası Türkiye-Çin İlişkileri* (*China's Strengthening Strategy: Turkey-China Relations after the Cold War*), Istanbul: IQ Kültür Sanat Yayıncılık, 2008.

4. Arthur Waldron, *The Great Wall of China: From History to Myth*, Cambridge: Cambridge University Press, 1992; Nicola Di Cosmo, *Ancient China and Its Enemies: The Rise of Nomadic Power in East Asian History*, Cambridge: Cambridge University Press, 2002.

5. Herbert Franke and Denis Twitchett, eds., *The Cambridge History of China*, Vol. 6, *Alien Regimes and Border States, 907–1368*, Cambridge: Cambridge University Press, 2008; Don J. Wyatt, *Battlefronts Real and Imagined: War, Border, and Identity in the Chinese Middle Period*, New York: Palgrave Macmillan, 2008; Paul S. Ropp, *China in World History*, New York: Oxford University Press, 2010.

6. Joseph Fletcher, *Studies on Chinese and Islamic Inner Asia*, Brookfield, VT: Variorum, 1995; Morris Rossabi, ed., *Governing China's Multiethnic Frontiers*, Seattle: University of Washington Press, 2004; Mei Zhao Rong, *Super Empire-Chaoji Diguo: Pojie Zhongguo Zui Qianghan Wangchao de Mima* (*Super Empire: Unraveling the Mystery of China's Most Valient Dynasty*), Wuhan: Wuhan University Press, 2006.

7. Wang Zhenping, *Tang China in Multi-Polar Asia: A History of Diplomacy and War*, Honolulu: University of Hawaii Press, 2013.

8. Morris Rossabi, ed., *China among Equals: The Middle Kingdom and Its Neighbors, 10th–14th Centuries*, Berkley: University of California Press, 1983; Zhang Shuangzhi, *Qing Dai Chaojin Zhidu Yanjiu* (*A Study of the Pilgrimage System of the Qing Period*), Beijing: Academy Press, 2010; Zhang Yongjin and Barry Buzan, "The Tributary System as International Society in Theory and Practice, *The Chinese Journal of International Politics*, vol. 5, 2012, 3–36.

9. Morris Rossabi, *Kubilai Khan: His Life and Times*, Berkeley: University of California Press, 2009; Reuven Amitai and Michal Biran, eds., *Nomads as Agents of Cultural Change: The Mongols and Their Eurasian Predecessors*, Honolulu: University of Hawaii Press, 2015.

10. Louise Levathes, *When China Ruled the Seas: The Treasure Fleet of the Dragon Throne, 1400–1433*, New York: Simon and Schuster, 1994; Claudine Salmon and Roderich Ptak, eds., *Zheng He: Images and Perceptions*, Wiesbaden: Harrassowitz, 2005.

11. Dimitris J. Kastritsis, *The Sons of Bayezid: Empire Building and Representation in the Ottoman Civil War of 1402–1413*, Leiden: Brill, 2007; Halil Çetin, *Timur'un Anadolu Seferi ve Ankara Savaşı* (*Timur's Anatolian Campaign and the Battle of Ankara*), Istanbul: Yeditepe Yayınevi, 2012

12. Personal conversation with a former Turkish ambassador.

13. Jacob M. Landau, *Pan-Turkism: From Irredentism to Cooperation*, Bloomington: Indiana University Press, 1995; Hugh Poulton, *Top Hat, Grey Wolf, and Crescent: Turkish Nationalism and the Turkish Republic*, New York: New York University Press, 1997.

14. Man De, "From a 'Wolf Culture' to a 'Lamb Culture'," *chinasource.com*, November 21, 2007; Jiang Rong, *Wolf Totem*, New York: Penguin, 2008.

15. John Feffer, "Stealth Superpower: How Turkey Is Chasing China in Bid to Become the Next Big Thing," *tomdispatch.com*, January 13, 2010; Marlène Laruelle and Sébastien Peyrouse, *The Chinese Question in Central Asia: Domestic Order, Social Change and the Chinese Factor*, London: Hurst, 2012.

16. Hüseyin Bağci, "Turkey, Central Asia and Islam," *Hürriyet Daily News*, June 29, 2000; Bayram Balci, "Turkey's Religious Outreach in Central Asia and the Caucasus," *Carnegie Endowment*, January 27, 2014; Farkhad Alimukhamedov, "Turkey's Central Asia Policy in the Changing World: Priorities, Policies and Actions," *South-East European Journal of Political Science*, January–June, 2016.

17. Barış Adıbelli, "Türkiye'nin Avrasya Politikasi Çöktü!" (Turkey's Eurasia Policy Has Collapsed!), *Radikal*, August 16, 2008; Armando Cordoba, "China Looks to Kurdistan as Growing Oil Partner," *rudaw.net*, July 29, 2013; Helena Smith, "Chinese Carrier Cosco Is Transforming Piraeus—And Has Eyes on Thessaloniki," *The Guardian*, June 29 2014.

18. Arturas Jurgelevicius, "Friendship of Interests: Turkey and China," *bilgesam.org*, May 20, 2010; Robert M. Cutler, "Turkey's Erdogan Pushes into Eurasia," *Asia Times*, May 31, 2012; Ilia Roubanis, "Energy and Turkey's South Caucasus Policy: The EU Regionalization Catalyst," *The New Turkey*, December 16, 2016.

19. Eşref Yalınkılıçlı, "A Tale of Becoming an Energy Hub in Eurasia: Russian-Turkish Cooperation on the South Stream," *Daily Sabah*, December 7, 2014; Begüm Tunakan, "Turkey Goes from a Transit Country to an Energy Hub," *Daily Sabah*, November 20, 2015; Firat Kayakiran, "Oil Flows through Turkey Energy Corridor Unhindered as Coup Ends," *Bloomberg*, July 16, 2016.

20. Ahmet Davutoğlu, "Naturalizing the Flow of History," *Al-Jazeera*, March 16, 2011; Ahmet Davutoğlu, "Global Governance," *Center for Strategic Research, Ministry of Foreign Affairs*, March 2012.

21. "Turkish President Wraps Up Visit in China," *Hürriyet Daily News*, June 28, 2009; Şafak Timur, "Local Uighurs Skeptical about Gül's Visit," *Hürriyet Daily News*, June 29, 2009.

22. "Turkish PM Erdogan Likens Xinjiang Violence to 'Genocide,'" *Agence France-Presse*, July 10, 2009; Mo Lingjiao, "Turkey, Another Axis of Evil?" *Global Times*, July 10, 2009; Igor Torbakov and Matti Nojonen, "China, Turkey and Xinjiang: A Frayed Relationship," *Open Democracy*, August 5, 2009.

23. Anshel Pfeffer, "Growing Ties between Turkey, China, Iran Worry Israel and U.S.," *Ha'aretz*, October 7, 2010; Jim Wolf, "China Mounts Air Exercise with Turkey, U.S. Says," *Reuters*, October 8, 2010; Ibrahim Kiras, "Çin Bilmecesi" (The Chinese Puzzle), *haber10.com*, October 9, 2010.

24. Keith Bradsher, "China Plans a New Silk Road, But Trade Partners Are Wary," *New York Times*, December 25, 2015.

25. Kadri Gürsel, "Erdogan Serious about Turkey's Bid for Shanghai 5 Membership," *Al-Monitor*, January 31, 2013; Joshua Kucera, "Erdogan to Putin: Let Us into SCO!," *eurasianet.org*, November 23, 2013.

26. "China Willing to Consider Turkey's Membership to Shanghai Security Pact," *Daily Sabah*, December 29, 2016.

27. Pelin Turgut, "Turkey No Longer a Safe Haven for Chinese Uighurs," *Time*, July 27, 2009; "BBP Genel Sekreteri Destici, Çin Büyükelçiliği 1. Musteşari Junzheng İle Görüstü" (BBP General Secretary Destici Speaks with Chinese Embassy Undersecretary Junzheng), *medya73.com*, June 24, 2010; Abdullah Bozkurt, "China Seeks Further Engagement from Turkey in Xinjiang Region," *Today's Zaman*, April 1, 2012.

28. "Çin Büyükelçisi Yu Hongyang'dan Destici'ye Ziyaret" (Chinese Ambassador Yu Hongyang Visits Destici), *olay53.com*, July 22, 2015.

29. Barry Neild, "Kunming Rail Station Attack: China Horrified as Mass Stabbings Leave Dozens Dead," *The Guardian*, March 2, 2014; Andrea Chen, "Three Given Death Penalty over Kunming Rail Station Attack," *South China Morning Post*, September 12, 2014; James Millward, "China's Fruitless Repression of the Uighurs," *New York Times*, September 28, 2014.

30. "China Rebukes Turkey for Offer to Shelter Uighur Refugees," *Reuters*, November 28, 2014; "Turkey's Diplomatic Steps Save Lives of Uyghur Refugees in Thailand," *Daily Sabah*, December 28, 2014; "Muslim Uigurs Escape Chinese Persecution; Seek Refuge in Turkey," *World Bulletin*, January 15, 2015.

31. Muammer Elveren, "Turkey Should Look After Turks in Thailand, Says Head of Uighurs," *Hürriyet Daily News*, December 22, 2014; "Turkey's Diplomatic Steps Save Lives of Uyghur Refugees in Thailand," *Daily Sabah*, December 28, 2014; "Anti-China Protests in Turkey Take Toll on Economic Ties," *Today's Zaman*, July 6, 2015.

32. Thomas Monzon, "Thai Consulate in Turkey Attacked following Deportation of Uighurs," *UPI*, July 9, 2015; Matt Schiavenza, "Why Thailand Forced Uighurs to Return to China," *The Atlantic*, July 12, 2015; Edward Wong, "Ethnic Tensions Complicate Turkey's Relationship with China," *New York Times*, July 29, 2015.

33. Jeremy Page and Emre Peker, "As Muslim Uighurs Flee, China Sees Jihad Risk," *Wall Street Journal*, January 30, 2015; Fergus Ryan, "Islamic State Hostage Killing: China Vows Justice after Confirming Death," *The Guardian*, November 18, 2015; Ben Blanchard, "Syria Says up to 5,000 Chinese Uighurs Fighting in Militant Groups," *Reuters*, May 8, 2017.

34. Altay Atlı, "Questioning Turkey's China Trade," *Turkish Policy Quarterly*, November 2011; Satuk Bugra Kutlugun and Gokhan Kurtaran, "Erdogan Wants Turkey-China Trade Imbalance Tackled," *World Bulletin*, July 31, 2015; "Turkey's Erdogan Urges Russia, China and Iran to Trade in Local Currencies," *RT News*, December 5, 2016.

35. Can Erimtan, "The New Silk Road: China Looks West, Turkey Looks East," *RT News*, March 19, 2014; Bien Perez, "China's ZTE Takes Over Netas for $101m, Eyes Expansion in Turkey," *South China Morning Post*, December 6, 2016; "China, An Ocean of Opportunities for Turkey," *Daily Sabah*, December 22, 2016; Gila Benmayor, "Dragon and Crescent in the Asian Century," *Hurriyet Daily News*, December 27, 2016.

36. George Marshall Lerner, "In Turkey, U.S. Loss Is China's Gain," *The Diplomat*, January 31, 2017; Patrick Kingsley, "Erdogan Claims Vast Powers in Turkey after Narrow Victory in Referendum," *New York Times*, April 16, 2017.

37. Kemal Kirişci, "The Transformation of Turkish Foreign Policy: The Rise of the Trading State," *New Perspectives on Turkey*, no. 40, 2009; Pinar Tremblay, "Clash of the Anatolian Tigers," *Al-Monitor*, April 28, 2014.

38. "Turkey among Top 5 Violators of ILO Conventions: DİSK," *Hürriyet Daily News*, June 1, 2016; Walton Pantland, "Unions in Turkey: Holding the Line for Workers," *industriall-union.org*, June 8, 2016.

39. Fulya Ozerkan, "Recep Tayyip Erdogan Sparks Furor in Turkey by Saying He Wants to 'Raise a Religious Youth,'" *Reuters*, February 9, 2012; Ayça Alemdaroğlu, "From Cynicism to Protest: Reflections on Youth and Politics in Turkey," *jadaliyya.com*, July 18, 2013; Gözde Böcü, "The 'Gezi Generation': Youth, Polarization and the 'New Turkey,'" in Isabel Schäfer, ed., *Youth, Revolt, Recognition: The Young Generation during and after the "Arab Spring*,*"* Berlin: Mediterranean Institute Berlin, 2015.

40. Damia Aras, "Turkey's Ambassadors vs. Erdoğan," *The Middle East Quarterly*, vol. 18, no. 1, Winter 2011; Doğan Gürpınar, *Ottoman Imperial Diplomacy, A Political, Social and Cultural History*, London: I. B. Tauris, 2014.

41. Pelin Telseren Kadercan and Burak Kadercan, "The Turkish Military as a Political Actor: Its Rise and Fall," *Middle East Policy*, Fall 2016; Peter Müller and Maximillian Popp, "Purges Have Weakened Once Mighty Turkish Military," *Spiegel*, January 18, 2017.

42. "Turkey to Chair 2017 Energy Club of Shanghai Cooperation Organization," *Daily Sabah*, November 23, 2016; Altay Atli, "Does Turkey Have to Choose between Brussels and Shanghai?" *Asia Times*, November 29, 2016; Zhou Bo, "Could Turkey Serve as a Bridge between NATO and SCO?" *China-U.S. Focus*, December 19, 2016.

43. "Nuclear Power in Turkey," *World Nuclear Association*, June 21, 2017.

44. Bruce Pannier, "The Trans-Caspian Pipeline: Technically Possible, Politically Difficult," *Radio Free Europe Radio Liberty*, May 24, 2015; Haluk Direskeneli, *Eurasian Review*, "Trans-Caspian Subsea Gas Pipeline Project Vital for Turkey," February 24, 2017.

45. Tulay Karadeniz and Daren Butler, "Turkey Confirms Cancellation of $3.4 Billion Missile Defence Project," *Reuters*, November 18, 2005.

46. "Turkey Opens Part of Real Estate Market to Chinese Nationals," *Xinhua*, August 24, 2012; "Bank of China to Start Operation in Turkey by End of This Year," *China Daily*, November 7, 2016; Altay Atli, "China and Turkey Rev Up Efforts to Strengthen Ties," *Asia Times*, November 8, 2016; "Could Turkey Be the Next Investment Hotspot for Chinese Buyers?" *juwai.com*, March 9, 2017.

47. Ben Meyer, "COSCO Pacific to Acquire Istanbul Container Terminal for $940m," *American Shipper*, September 17, 2015.

48. Bahar Bayhan, "Kanal İstanbul'da İkinci Haliç Planı" (The Second Bosporus Plan of Kanal Istanbul), *Arkitera*, November 17, 2016; Mustafa Sonmez, "Canal Istanbul: Still Hyped, Still 'Crazy,'" *Al-Monitor*, February 22, 2017.

49. "Turkey Builds Massive High-Speed Railway to Mark Centennial Anniversary," *Xinhua*, May 14, 2017.

50. Selim Koru and Timur Kaymaz, "Turkey: Perspectives on Eurasian Integration," *European Council on Foreign Relations*, June 8, 2016; George Marshall Lerner, "In Turkey, U.S. Loss Is China's Gain," *The Diplomat*, January 31, 2017; William Armstrong, "Eurasianism in Modern Turkey," *Hürriyet Daily News*, May 18, 2017.

Chapter 5

1. Denys Lombard, *Le carrefour javanais, Essai d'histoire globale*, Paris: Éditions de l'École des Hautes Études en Sciences Sociales, 1990; Barbara Watson Andaya, "Oceans Unbounded: Transversing Asia across 'Area Studies,'" *Journal of Asian Studies*, vol. 65, no. 4, November 2006, 669–690.

2. Wang Gungwu, *The Chinese Overseas: From Earthbound China to the Quest for Autonomy*, Cambridge, MA: Harvard University Press, 2002; Leo Suryadinata, ed., *Ethnic Chinese in Contemporary Indonesia*, Singapore: Chinese Heritage Centre and Institute of Southeast Asian Studies, 2008.

3. Krithika Varagur, "Amidst Protests, Tense Times for Chinese Indonesians," *Voice of America*, November 15, 2016; Oliver Holmes, "Jakarta's Violent Identity Crisis: Behind the Vilification of Chinese-Indonesians," *The Guardian*, November 25, 2016; Chow Chung-Yan, "The Plight of Chinese Indonesians: Distrusted in Jakarta, Forgotten in China," *South China Morning Post*, February 25, 2017.

4. Leo Suryadinata, ed., *Southeast Asia's Chinese Businesses in an Era of Globalization: Coping with the Rise of China*, Singapore: Institute of Southeast Asian Studies, 2006.

5. Denys Lombard and Claudine Salmon, "Islam and Chineseness," *Indonesia*, vol. 57, April 1993, 115–132; Muhamad Ali, "Chinese Muslims in Colonial and Postcolonial Indonesia," *Explorations*, vol. 7, 2, Spring 2007; Hew Wai-Weng, "Marketing the Chinese Face of Islam," *Inside Indonesia*, December 1, 2009; Aubrey Belford, "Chinese Preachers Bridge Indonesia's Ethnic Gap," *New York Times*, July 14, 2010.

6. Sahil Nagpal, "Chinese-Indonesian Muslims Criticize China over Urumqi Unrest," *TopNews.in*, July 10, 2009; Patung, "Chinese Uighurs and Xinjiang Province Riots," *IndonesiaMatters.com*, July 16, 2009.

7. Mo Hang'e, "Indonesia Keen to Tap More Chinese Tourists during Spring Festival Holiday," *Xinhua*, December 28, 2016; Farida Susanty and Nurul Fitri Ramadhani, "Indonesia's Love of Mecca Boosts Lucrative 'Umrah' Business," *Jakarta Post*, January 21, 2017.

8. "The Chinese Community in Indonesia: A Force to Be Reckoned With," stirringtroubleinternationally.com, August 6, 2008; Christine Susanna Tjhin, "Indonesia's Relations with China: Productive and Pragmatic, But Not Yet a Strategic Partnership," *China Report* vol. 48, no. 3, 2012, 303–315.

9. "Thousands of Members from Muslim Youth Organization Banser Ready to Guard Churches on Christmas," *Coconuts Jakarta*, December 21, 2016; Tajudin Buano and Gunawan, "Muslim Youths Helped Keep Indonesia's Christmas Peaceful," *Benarnews.org*, December 27, 2016.

10. Oliver Holmes, "Fears over Violence in Jakarta as Hardline Islamists Protest Governor's 'Blasphemy,'" *The Guardian*, November 2, 2016; Krithika Varagur,

"Evicted Jakarta Residents Join Hardline Rally against Governor," *Voice of America*, December 2, 2016.

11. "Indonesia Protest: Jakarta Anti-governor Rally Turns Violent," *BBC News*, November 4, 2017; "Hard-Line Muslim Protest against Christian Jakarta Governor Ends in Violence," *Voice of America*, November 4, 2016; Corry Elyda, "Anti-Ahok Protest Causes Huge Financial Losses: Kadin," *Jakarta Post*, November 5, 2016.

12. Jewel Topsfield, "Pluralism in Peril: Is Indonesia's Religious Tolerance under Threat?" *Sydney Morning Herald*, December 24, 2016.

13. Joe Cochrane, "In Indonesia, an Islamic Edict Seeks to Keep Santa Hats off Muslims," *New York Times*, December 23, 2016; Callistasia Anggun Wijaya, "Ahok Confused about Muhammadiyah Youth Wing Accusation," *Jakarta Post*, January 10, 2017; Haeril Halim, "Muhammadiyah Pushes Jokowi to Suspend Ahok," *Jakarta Post*, February 21, 2017.

14. Hila Japi, "Prof Buya Syafi'i Maarif: Ahok Tidak Menghina Al Quran" (Professor Buya Shafi'i Maarif: Ahok Did Not Insult the Quran), *netralnews.com*, November 6, 2016.

15. Ina Parlina, "Jokowi Changes Tune in Handling Rally," *Jakarta Post*, December 3, 2016.

16. Adam Harvey, "Jakarta Election: Agus Yudhoyono Campaigns as Champion of the Poor, With Dynasty in Mind," *Australian Broadcasting Corporation*, February 8, 2017; Jewel Topsfield, "Agus Yudhoyono Protests Explosive Allegations against His Father on Eve of Election," *Sydney Morning Herald*, February 15, 2017.

17. Anies, who is an American educated political scientist, rated the comparative advantages of Indonesia's pro-Muslim parties in an article based on his doctoral dissertation. Anies Baswedan, "Political Islam in Indonesia: Present and Future Trajectory," *Asian Survey*, vol. 44 no. 5, September/October 2004, 669–690.

18. Ahmad Junaidi, "Contemplating a Syariah-Influenced Indonesian Capital," *The Star Online (Malaysia)*, March 26, 2017; Kate Lamb, "Jakarta Election Challenger Anies Accused of Courting Islamic Vote amid Religious Divide," *The Guardian*, April 14, 2017.

19. Robin Bush, "Regional 'Sharia' Regulations in Indonesia: Anomaly or Symptom?" in Greg Fealy and Sally White, eds., *Expressing Islam: Religious Life and Politics in Indonesia*, Singapore: Institute of Southeast Asian Studies, 2008, pp. 174–191; Krithika Varagur, "Majority of Religion School Teachers in Indonesia Support Sharia Law," *Voice of America*, December 27, 2016.

20. Komisi Pemilihan Umum, *Pilkada Provinsi DKI Jakarta (Putaran Kedua)* (General Election Commission, *Governor's Election for the Province of Jakarta, Second Round*), Jakarta: April 19, 2017. https://pilkada2017.kpu.go.id/hasil/2/t1/dki_jakarta.

21. Alexander R. Arifianto, "Jakarta Governor Election Results in a Victory for Prejudice over Pluralism," *Jakarta Globe*, April 19, 2017; Nurul Fitri Ramadhani, Safrin La Batu and Indra Budiari, "Anies Rides Islamist Wave," *Jakarta Post*, April 20, 2017; "Anies' Victory Raises Muslim Dignity in Politics: PKS," *Jakarta Post*, April 26, 2017.

22. Krithika Varagur, "As Jakarta Sinks, Government Pins Hopes on Bird-Shaped Sea Wall," *Voice of America*, January 10, 2017; Joe Cochrane, "Jakarta Governor Concedes Defeat in Religiously Tinged Election," *New York Times*, April 19, 2017;

Rendi A. Witular, "Losing Jakarta: How Will It Impact Jokowi's 2019 Reelection Bid?" *Jakarta Post*, April 21, 2017; Michael Kimmelman, "Jakarta Is Sinking So Fast, It Could End Up Underwater," *New York Times*, December 21, 2017.

23. Marty Natalegawa, "An Indonesian Perspective on the Indo-Pacific," *Jakarta Post*, May 20, 2013; Greta Nabbs-Keller, "The Very Public Flaying of Marty Natalagawa," *The Interpreter*, September 19, 2014.

24. Sara Schonhardt and Anita Rachman, "Indonesian President Joko Widodo Shakes Up Cabinet," *Wall Street Journal*, July 27, 2016; Stephen Wright, "New Indonesian Cabinet Includes Reformer, Rights Abuser," *Associated Press*, July 28, 2016.

25. Keith Johnson, "Can Indonesia Afford a Fish War with China?" *Foreign Policy*, July 8, 2016; Karlis Salna and Yudith Ho, "Jokowi Taps Ex-Generals amid Terrorism Threat, China Tensions," *Bloomberg*, July 27, 2016.

26. Leo Timm, "Indonesia to Bolster Defense at 'Front Door' after South China Sea Ruling," *Epoch Times*, July 14, 2016.

27. Trefor Moss, "Indonesia Blows Up 23 Foreign Fishing Boats to Send a Message," *Wall Street Journal*, April 5, 2016.

28. Vasudevan Sridharan, "Indonesian President Holds Cabinet Meeting on Board Warship in South China Sea," *International Business Times*, June 23, 2016.

29. Prashanth Parameswaran, "Indonesia and China's AIIB," *The Diplomat*, July 26, 2016.

30. Christopher Hill, "China's Bad-Neighbor Policy Is Bad Business," *Project Syndicate*, June 30, 2016; Evelyn Cheng, "Asia Pacific Nations Are Tilting Closer toward China as Trump Declares 'America First,'" *CNBC*, January 31, 2017.

31. Ben Otto, "ASEAN Looks for Wiggle Room to Skirt South China Sea Impasse," *Wall Street Journal*, July 24, 2016; David Tweed and Norman P. Aquino, "Duterte's Tilt toward China Upsets U.S. Strategy in Asia," *Chicago Tribune*, September 15, 2016.

32. Vibhanshu Shekhar and Joseph Chinyong Liow, "Indonesia as a Maritime Power: Jokowi's Vision, Strategies, and Obstacles Ahead," *Brookings*, November 7, 2014; Emanuel Bria, "Why Do Indonesia, ASEAN Matter to China?" *The Straits Times*, January 6, 2017.

33. Klaus Heinrich Raditio, "Indonesia 'Speaks Chinese' in South China Sea," *Jakarta Post*, July 18, 2016; Evan A. Laksmana, "Why International Law Cannot Rule over the South China Sea," *Jakarta Post*, July 25, 2016.

34. Paul Keating, "Forget the West, Our Future Is to the North, *Brisbane Times*, November 15, 2012; Michael Fullilove, "Time for a Larger Australia," *The National Interest*, March 20, 2014; Malcolm Fraser, "America: Australia's Dangerous Ally," *The National Interest*, December 16, 2014.

35. "More Jakarta Means More Trouble for Tony Abbott," *The Economist*, November 23, 2013.

36. Hugh White, *The China Choice: Why America Should Share Power*, Carlton, Australia: Black, 2013.

37. Kevin Rudd, "A Subtle Defrosting in China's Chilly War with America," *Financial Times*, June 10, 2013.

38. John Garnaut, "Australia and India to Strengthen Military Ties," *Sydney Morning Herald*, July 1, 2014.

39. Stuart Rollo, "Australia Needs a New Foreign Policy, Tillerson's Remarks on China Make It Urgent," *The Guardian*, January 12, 2017; Primrose Riordan, "Tillerson Comments Show Australia Will Have to Wade into South China Sea Dispute," *Financial Review*, January 12, 2017; Conor Friedersdorf, "Donald Trump's Blunder Down Under," *The Atlantic*, February 2, 2017.

40. C. Raja Mohan, *Samudra Manthan: Sino-Indian Rivalry in the Indo-Pacific*, Washington, DC: Carnegie Endowment for International Peace, 2012; Rory Medcalf, "Reimagining Asia: From Asia-Pacific to Indo-Pacific," *The ASAN Forum*, June 26, 2015.

41. Evelyn Goh, "Great Powers and Southeast Asian Regional Security Strategies: Omni-enmeshment, Balancing and Hierarchical Order," *Institute of Defense and Strategic Studies, Singapore*, July 2005; Amitav Acharya and Barry Buzan, eds., *Non-Western International Relations Theory: Perspectives on and beyond Asia*, New York: Routledge, 2010; Robert Yates, "ASEAN as the 'Regional Conductor': Understanding ASEAN's Role in Asia-Pacific Order," *The Pacific Review*, December 9, 2016.

42. Rizal Sukma, "A Post-ASEAN Foreign Policy for a Post-G8 World," *Jakarta Post*, October 5, 2009; A. Ibrahim Almuttaqi, "ASEAN Still the Cornerstone of Indonesia's Foreign Policy," *Jakarta Post*, March 17, 2017.

43. Fedina S. Sundaryani, "Indonesia Must Diversify China Trade," *Jakarta Post*, September 14, 2016; "Why Indonesia Is Chasing China's Billions," *Bloomberg*, October 31, 2016; Biman Mukherji, "Indonesian Nickel Exports a Boon for China," *Wall Street Journal*, January 17, 2017.

44. Li Wannan and Wen Beiyan, "Shixi Hou Suhatuo Shidai Yinni Dui Hua Zhengce de Bianhua" (Examining Changes in Indonesia's Policy toward China in the Post-Suharto Period), *Southeast Asian Studies*, June 2009; Iain Marlow, "The Next China? Indonesia Emerging as a New Asian Powerhouse," *The Globe and Mail*, January 16, 2015; Ma Bo, "'Yidai Yilu' Yu Yinni 'Quanqiu Hai Shang Zhidian' de Zhanlue Duijie Yanjiu" (Joint Study of "One Belt One Road" and Indonesia's Global Maritime Axis Strategy), *International Outlook*, September 15, 2015; Greg Fealy and Hugh White, "Indonesia's 'Great Power' Aspirations: A Critical View," *Asia and the Pacific Policy Studies*, vol. 3, no. 1, 2016, pp. 92–100.

45. Phila Siu, "What Indonesia Can Do to Be in China's Belt and Road Loop," *South China Morning Post*, April 29, 2017; "China's Positive Response to Indonesia's Investment Offer," netralnews.com, May 19, 2017; "Indonesia Seeks to Draw $28b Investment from China's Belt and Road Forum: Minister," *Jakarta Globe*, May 24, 2017; Oliviana Handayani, "Government to Channel Chinese Investment into Special Economic Zone," *Indonesia Expat*, May 31, 2017.

46. Eveline Danubrata and Gayatri Suroyo, "In Indonesia, Labor Friction and Politics Fan Anti-Chinese Sentiment," *Reuters*, April 18, 2017.

47. "Trade Union Rejects Chinese Unskilled Workers," *Jakarta Post*, February 9, 2016; Amirullah, "Labor Union Demands Free-Visa Policy to Be Dropped," *Tempo*, December 27, 2016.

48. Eveline Danubrata and Gayatri Suroyo, "In Indonesia, Labor Friction and Politics Fan Anti-Chinese Sentiment," *Reuters*, April 18, 2017.

49. "Indonesia: From Vigilantism to Terrorism in Cirebon," *International Crisis Group*, January 26, 2012; Laurens Bakker, "Illegality for the General Good? Vigilantism and Social Responsibility in Contemporary Indonesia," *Critique of Anthropology*, March 3, 2015; Krithika Varagur, "Crackdowns Have Indonesia Gay Community on Edge," *Voice of America*, May 31, 2017.

50. Anton Hermansyah, "Jakarta-Bandung High Speed Railway to Get Chinese Loan," *Jakarta Post*, November 10, 2016.

51. "Indonesia's Bullet Train Deal with China: 'Delusional,' No Coordination," *rappler.com*, October 8, 2015.

52. Tao Kong and Pierre van der Eng, "Mixed Messages of Chinese Investment in Indonesia," *East Asia Forum*, May 18, 2017; "Investment by China Not as Heavy as Indonesian Opponents Fear," *m.todayonline*, June 16, 2017.

53. "China's Investment Reaches US$1.6 Billion in Indonesia," *Jakarta Post*, January 20, 2017; Wataru Suzuki and Erwida Maulia, "China Overtakes Japan in Indonesia Direct Investment," *Nikkei Asian Review*, January 25, 2017.

54. Thomas Kutty Abraham, "Why Indonesia Is Chasing China's Billions," *Bloomberg*, October 31, 2016.

55. Farida Susanty, "China Strengthens Grip on Indonesia," *Jakarta Post*, November 24, 2016; Tara MacIsaac, "Indonesia's Last Stand for a Coal Industry in Peril," *Mongabay*, February 13, 2017.

Chapter 6

1. "Chinese Scholar Describes Internal Debate over Iran Policy," *Wikileaks Cables, U.S. Embassy, Beijing China*, Canonical ID: 07BEIJING5902_a, September 10, 2007; Michael D. Swaine, "Beijing's Tightrope Walk on Iran," *Carnegie Endowment China Leadership Monitor*, March 1, 2010; Joel Wuthnow, *Chinese Diplomacy and the U.N. Security Council: Beyond the Veto*, New York: Routledge, 2013.

2. Flynt Leverett and Hillary Mann Leverett, "U.S. Sanctions and China's Iran Policy," *Monthly Review*, July 30, 2011; "U.S. Threatens Sanctions on China Banks over Iran," *Agence France-Presse*, September 28, 2011; Ilan I. Berman, "To Stop Iran, Lean On China," *New York Times*, November 8, 2011; "Geithner, In Beijing for Talks, Faces Struggle to Gain China's Cooperation on Iran Sanctions," *Associated Press*, January 10, 2012; Richard Weitz, "China Balances between Iran and U.S.," *World Politics Review*, August 13, 2013.

3. Willem Van Kemenade, "Iran's Relations with China and the West: Cooperation and Confrontation in Asia," *Netherlands Institute of International Relations "Clingendael,"* November 2009; Joel Wuthnow, "China and the Iran Nuclear Issue: Beyond the Limited Partnership," *Testimony before the U.S.-China Security and Economic Review Commission*, June 6, 2013.

4. Henry Hoyle, "Chinese Think Tank Official: Change the Terms of the Iran Debate," *Foreign Policy Association*, March 8, 2010; Zhao Hong, "China's Dilemma on Iran: Between Energy Security and a Responsible Rising Power," *Journal of Contemporary China*, January 2014; Peter Ford, "Iran Nuclear Talks: What China Brings to the Negotiating Table," *Christian Science Monitor*, March 30, 2015.

5. Christopher Bodeen, "China, Key Iran Ally, Backs Nuclear Sanctions," *Associated Press*, June 10, 2010.

6. Ma Ping, "Bosi Yilsilan Wenming Dui Zhongguo Yisilan Wenming de Gongxian Ji Qi Shenyuan Yingxiang" (The Contribution and Deep Influence of Persian Islamic Civilization on Chinese Islamic Civilization), *Journal of Hui Muslim Minority Studies*, no. 3, 2004; David Morgan, "Persian as a *Lingua Franca* in the Mongol Empire," in Brian Spooner and William L. Hanaway, eds., *Literacy in the Persianate World: Writing and the Social Order*, Philadelphia: University of Pennsylvania Press, 2012; Zhao Xinying, "Interest Growing in Study of Persian Language, History," *China Daily*, January 25, 2016.

7. Ministry of Foreign Affairs of the People's Republic of China, "Chinese Ambassadors to Iran," *fmprc.gov.cn*, May 2014.

8. Hua Liming, "Yilang He Wenti Yu Zhongguo de Waijiao Xuanze" (The Iranian Nuclear Issue and China's Diplomatic Options), *Guoji Wenti Yanjiu (Journal of International Studies)* January 2007; Wen Yi, "Interview with Former Chinese Ambassador Hua Liming," *chinaculture.org*, September 15, 2009 (including a concluding segment in which Hua recites a poem of Saadi in Persian); Yang Xingli, "Xin Zhongguo Yu Yilang Guanxi Liushi Nian" (Sixty Years of Relations between the New China and Iran), *Xiya Feizhou (Western Asia and Africa)*, no. 4, 2010; Antoaneta Bezlova, "Sanctions Give China an Advantage in Iran," *Iran Review*, August 2, 2010.

9. Nathan Beauchamp-Mustafaga, "China-Iran Relations: China's Hawks Condemn U.S. Influence," *European Council on Foreign Relations*, October 2013; "China Plays Key Broker Role in Iran Nuclear Deal," *Reuters*, November 25, 2013.

10. "Chinese Special Envoy on the Middle East Issue Wang Shijie Talks about His Middle East Tour," *chinaconsulatesf.org*, November 30, 2004; "Sun Bigan to Be Special Envoy on Middle East Issues," *china.org.cn*, March 30, 2006; Ming Pao, "Zhongguo Qian Zhongdong Teshi Cheng Zhongdong Jiaojin Jaiju Zhong Mei Fenqi" (China's Former Middle East Envoy Said Mideast Competition Has Intensified Differences between China and the United States), *boxun.com*, October 7, 2009 (on Sun Bigan's statement that Sino-American conflict in the Middle East was inevitable).

11. Liu Zhentang, *Zhongguo Zhu Zhongdong Dashi Hua Zhongdong: Libanen (China's Middle East Ambassadors Discuss the Middle East: Lebanon)*, Beijing: World Knowledge Press, 2009; Ministry of Foreign Affairs of the People's Republic of China, "Special Envoy of the Chinese Government on Syrian Issue Xie Xiaoyan Visits Egypt," *fmprc.gov.cn*, April 24, 2017.

12. Omar Nashabe, "China's Ambassador in Lebanon: Hezbollah Arms a Trade Matter," *Al-Akhbar*, May 4, 2012.

13. "Lalejin, Iran's Pottery Capital," *payvand.com*, June 19, 2010; "Varedat Gul Az Chin, Gusht Az Pakistan" (Importing Flowers from China, Meat from Pakistan), *icana.ir*, July 31, 2011; "Some Died in the Hospital from Fake Chinese Anesthetics," *peykeiran.com*, August 22, 2011; "China Floods Iran with Cheap Consumer Goods in Exchange for Oil," *The Guardian*, February 20, 2013.

14. Luke Pachymuthu and Seng Li Peng, "China's Top Oil Firms Sell Gasoline to Iran," *Reuters*, April 14, 2010; "China Imports More Iran Crude, Refinery Plan Stalls," *Trend (Azerbaijian)*, August 5, 2011.

15. "Iranians Not Too Happy with Their Made-In-China Qurans," *Shanghailist.com*, August 31, 2011.

16. Yin Gang, "Yilang Yiwei Qianying, Biding Beiju Shouchang" (Iran's Blind Intransigence, Bound to End in Tragedy), *Global Times*, February 20, 2010; Peter Lee, "China Fine-Tunes Its Iran Strategy," *Asia Times*, February 25, 2010; Yossi Melman, "China Will Not Stop Israel if It Decides to Attack Iran," *Haaretz*, September 22, 2011.

17. "A History of Iran's Nuclear Program," *Iran Watch*, August 9, 2016.

18. Joel Wuthnow, "Posing Problems without an Alliance: China-Iran Relations after the Nuclear Deal," *INSS Strategic Forum*, February 2016.

19. Scott Harold and Alireza Nader, "China and Iran: Economic, Political, and Military Relations," *RAND Center for Middle East Public Policy*, 2012.

20. Richard Frye, *The Heritage of Central Asia from Antiquity to the Turkish Expansion*, Princeton, NJ: Markus Wiener, 1996; Richard Eaton, "Revisiting the Persian Cosmopolis," *Asia Times Online*, July 19, 2013.

21. F. Gregory Cause, III, "Beyond Sectarianism: The New Middle East Cold War," *Brookings Doha Center*, July 2014; Jonathan Spyer, "Is It Iran's Middle East Now?" *Fathom*, Autumn 2015.

22. Wu Bing Bing, *Shiye Pai Xiandai Yisilan Zhuyi de Xingqi* (*The Rise of Modern Shi'i Islamism*), Beijing: Chinese Academy of Social Science Press, 2004; Itamar Y. Lee, "Chasing the Rising Red Crescent: Sino-Shi'i Relations in Post-Cold War Era China," *Comparative Islamic Studies*, vol. 7, no. 1–2, 2011; Nadia Helmy, "Chinese Scholarship on Iran and the Middle East," *Iranian Review of Foreign Affairs*, vol. 4, no. 3, Fall 2013; Karim Alwadi, *Zhenshi de Libanen Zhenzhudang* (The Real Story of Hezbollah), Beijing: World Knowledge, 2015.

23. Vali Nasr, *The Shia Revival: How Conflicts within Islam Will Shape the Future*, New York: Norton, 2006; Ali Hashem, "Why Iran Wants Palestine Back on Regional Agenda," *Al-Monitor*, February 24, 2017; Arhama Siddiqa, "The Sunni Allies of Tehran," *The Nation (Pakistan)*, May 20, 2017.

24. Jamsheed K. Choksy, "A Sino-Persian Grab for the Indian Ocean?" *Small Wars Journal*, July 7, 2011; Christina Lin, "China's Strategic Shift towards the Region of the Four Seas: The Middle Kingdom Arrives in the Middle East," *ISPSW Strategy Series*, April 2013.

25. Kayhan Barzegar, "The Balance of Power in the Persian Gulf: An Iranian View," *Middle East Policy*, Fall 2010; Hua Liming, "Yilan He Wenti Yu Zhongguo Zhongdong Waijiao" (The Iran Nuclear Issue and China's Middle East Diplomacy), *Arab World Studies*, no. 6, 2014.

26. Kristine Kwok, "Is Xi Jinping the Man to Defuse Tensions in the Middle East?" *South China Morning Post*, January 14, 2016; Michael Martina, "China's Xi to Visit Saudi, Iran in New Diplomacy Push," *Reuters*, January 15, 2016.

27. Nicola Slawson, "Saudi Execution of Shia Cleric Sparks Outrage in Middle East," *The Guardian*, January 2, 2016.

28. Jane Perlez, "President Xi Jinping of China Is All Business in Middle East Visit," *New York Times*, January 30, 2016.

29. Geoffrey F. Gresh, "China's Emerging Twin Pillar Policy in the Gulf," *Foreign Policy*, November 7, 2011; Thomas L. Friedman, "Global Oil War Underway between US-Saudi Arabia and Russia-Iran?" *New York Times*, October 15, 2014.

30. Giulia C. Romano and Jean-François Meglio, *China's Energy Security: A Multidimensional Perspective*, New York: Routledge, 2016; Janis Mackey Frayer, "China Ventures into America's Backyard: Latin America," *NBC News*, April 5, 2017.

31. Stephen Fidler, Te-Ping Chen, and Lingling Wei, "China's Xi Jinping Seizes Role as Leader on Globalization," *Wall Street Journal*, January 17, 2017; "The New Davos Man: Xi Jinping Portrays China as a Rock of Stability," *The Economist*, January 21, 2017.

32. "Full Text of Xi Jinping Keynote at the World Economic Forum," america.cgtn.com, January 17, 2017.

33. Bessa Momani, "Xi Jinping's Davos Speech Showed the World Has Turned Upside Down," *Newsweek*, January 18, 2017; Shaheli Das, "China Treads Its Way to Global Governance," *Forbes*, February 8, 2017.

34. Irina Kobrinskaya, "Is Russia Coming to Terms with China's 'Silk Road'?" *PONARS Eurasia*, September 2, 2016; Raghida Dergham, "Russia's Interests and the Iranian Project in the Region," *Huffington Post*, January 9, 2017; "Iran Vows Full Throttle Dedication to China's Silk Road," presstv.ir, May 13, 2017.

35. Charles Clover, "In Moscow, A New Eurasianism," *Journal of International Security Affairs*, Fall/Winter 2014; Mark Bassin, Sergey Glebov, and Marlene Laruelle, eds., *Between Europe and Asia: The Origins, Theories, and Legacies of Russian Eurasianism*, Pittsburgh, PA: University of Pittsburgh Press, 2015; Charles Clover, *Black Wind, White Snow: The Rise of Russia's New Nationalism*, New Haven, CT: Yale University Press, 2016; Timofei Bordachev, "To Russia's Friends in Asia and Beyond," Valdaiclub.com, February 15, 2017.

36. "Iran: The Revolution Is Over," *The Economist*, October 30, 2014; Emma Ashford, "The Trump Administration's Iran Policy Is Dangerous and Flawed," *The Guardian*, May 23, 2017.

37. David Axe, "Donald Trump Is Handing China the World," *Daily Beast*, January 30, 2017; David Nakamura, "As Trump Pursues 'America First,' China's Xi Sees Opening for Primacy in Asia," *Washington Post*, April 4, 2017; James Palmer, "What Trump Calls Strength, China Calls Stupidity," *Foreign Policy*, April 7, 2017; Jeffrey D. Sachs, "Eurasia Is on the Rise, Will the US Be Left on the Sidelines?" *Boston Globe*, April 9, 2017.

38. Asa Fitch and Benoit Faucon, "Foreign Investors Flock to Iran as U.S. Firms Watch on the Sidelines," *Wall Street Journal*, March 27, 2017; Stanley Reed, "Even Bold Foreign Investors Tiptoe in Iran," *New York Times*, March 31, 2017.

39. David E. Sanger, "Iran Sticks to Terms of Nuclear Deal, but Defies the U.S. in Other Ways," *New York Times*, July 13, 2016; Antony J. Blinken, "Why the Iran Nuclear Deal Must Stand," *New York Times*, February 17, 2017.

40. Dave Ernsberger, "China's Approach to Global Markets Is One to Follow: Fuel for Thought," platts.com, November 14, 2016; Greg Price, "New Iran Sanctions Coming, But None for Russia, Committee Leaders Say," *Newsweek*, May 2, 2017.

41. Pepe Escobar, "Trump Will Try to Smash the China-Russia-Iran Triangle . . . Here's Why He Will Fail," *South China Morning Post*, January 22, 2017; Joe McDonald, Munir Ahmed, and Gillian Wong, "'Silk Road' Plan Stirs Unease over China's Strategic Goals," *Associated Press*, May 11, 2017.

42. Mohammed Turki Al-Sudairi, "Sino-Saudi Relations: An Economic History," *GRC Gulf Papers*, August 2012; Fahad Nazer, "Saudi Arabia's New Best Friend: China?" *The National Interest*, September 2, 2015.

43. Robert R. Bianchi, "Reimagining the Hajj," *Social Sciences*, vol. 6, no. 2, 2017.

44. Yao Chunjun, "Dui Xinjiang Weiwuer Zu Zongjiao Xinyangzhe Chaojin Wenti de Xinli Tanxi" (Psychological Analysis of Xinjiang Uyghur Muslims' Hajj), *Xinjiang Social Science*, April 2009; Han Shuyun, "Nu Haji Yu Tongguo Yishi Jiyu Qinghai Xun Hua Musilin Nuxing Chaojinzhe de Diaocha Yanjiu" (On Women Hajjis and Their Rites of Passage: Survey Research on Women Muslim Hajjis in Xunhua, Qinghai Province), *Journal of Beifang Ethnic University*, no. 2, 2010; Robert R. Bianchi, "The Hajj and Politics in China," in Babak Rahimi and Peyman Eshagi, eds., *Muslim Pilgrimage in the Modern World*, Durham: North Carolina University Press, 2018.

45. Ulf Laessing, "Saudi Arabia Opens Chinese-Built Haj Pilgrimage Train," *Reuters*, November 14, 2010.

46. Wu Lei, "Goujian 'Xin Sichou Zhi Lu': Zhongguo Yu Zhongdong Guanxi Fazhan de Xin Neihan" (Constructing "the New Silk Road": New Meanings of Developing Sino-Middle East Relations), *West Asia and Africa*, no. 3, 2014; Sun Degang and He Shaoxiong, "From a By-stander to a Constructor: China and the Middle East Security Governance," *Journal of Middle Eastern and Islamic Studies (in Asia)*, vol. 9, no. 3, 2015; Li Xiaokun, "China Takes on Mediation Role," *China Daily*, December 24, 2015.

47. Julian Borger, "Medvedev: Sanctions against Iran's Nuclear Programme 'May Be Inevitable', Russia and China Called Upon by Gulf Countries to Use Economic Leverage to Prevent Nuclear Advances," *The Guardian*, September 24, 2009; "Mei Yaoqiu Zhongdong Mengyou Zengjia Dui Hua Gong You, You Shi Zhongguo Shuyuan Yilang" (U.S. Asks Middle East Allies to Increase Oil Sales to China in Order to Induce It to Isolate Iran), *Global Times*, October 20, 2009.

48. Shenaz Kermali, "Who's Afraid of Iran?" *Al-Jazeera*, July 30, 2008; Simeon Kerr, "Qatar Fund Aims to Diversity through Asia," *Financial Times*, November 2, 2009; Zheng Lifei and Yang Huiwen, "Qatar Seeks $5 Billion China QFII Quota," *Bloomberg*, June 24, 2012.

49. Philip Gater-Smith, "Qatar Crisis Impacts China's Ambitious Foreign Policy," *International Policy Digest*, June 13, 2017; Cary Huang, "How the Qatar Crisis Could Turn into a Disaster for Beijing," *South China Morning Post*, June 18, 2017.

50. Greg Jaffe and Thomas Gibbons-Neff, "For Qataris, A U.S. Air Base Is Best Defense against Trump Attacks," *Washington Post*, June 6, 2017; "Qatar Blockade: Iran Sends Five Planeloads of Food," *BBC News*, June 11, 2017; Noah Browning and Tom Finn, "Qatar Willing to Listen to Gulf Concerns, Kuwait Says," *Reuters*, June 11, 2017; Ercan Gurses and Aziz El Yaakoubi, "Turkish President Says Qatar Isolation Violates Islamic Values," *Reuters*, June 13, 2017; Peter Beaumont, "Turkish Troops Take Part in Joint Military Exercises in Qatar," *The Guardian*, June 19, 2017.

51. John Davison, "Gulf Crisis a 'Blessing in Disguise' for Qatar Seaport," *Reuters*, June 16, 2017.

52. Julia Hollingsworth, "Why Qatar Matters to China in Spite of Gulf Isolation," *South China Morning Post*, June 7, 2017.

53. Catherine Wong, "Arab States' Rift with Qatar Clouds China's Plans for Gulf Free-Trade Deal," *South China Morning Post*, June 6, 2017.

54. Stéphane A. Dudoignon, *The Baluch, Sunnism and the State in Iran: From Tribal to Global*, London: Hurst, 2017; James Dorsey, "The U.S.-Saudi Plot for Iran That Spells Trouble for China's New Silk Road," *South China Morning Post*, May 27, 2017.

55. Somak Ghoshal, "The Qatar Crisis and How It Affects India," *Huffington Post*, June 6, 2017; Mu Xuequan, "Iran Blames Saudi Arabia of 'Sponsoring Terrorism,'" *Xinhua*, June 15, 2017; "Explosives Seized from Terrorist Cell in Chabahar," *Mehr News Agency*, June 15, 2017.

56. Ting Shi, "Qatar Standoff Tests China's Neutrality on Saudi-Iran Feud," *Bloomberg*, June 7, 2017; "China Tells Iran That Given the Crisis with Qatar, Stability in the Gulf Is for the Best," *Reuters*, June 9, 2017.

57. Tania Branigan, "China Welcomes Binyamin Netanyahu," *The Guardian*, May 8, 2013; Qian Shanming, "Can China Be an Important Mediator in Mid-East Peace?" *CRIEnglish.com*, May 9, 2013.

58. Emma Scott, "Defying Expectations: China's Iran Trade and Investments," *Middle East Institute*, April 6, 2016; Camilia Razavi and Daniel Khalessi, "China Looks towards Iran," *Huffington Post*, May 6, 2016.

59. David Rogers, "Iran's Railway Revolution," *Global Construction Review*, December 14, 2015; Brendon Hong, "China's Plans to Railroad the West (Literally)," *Daily Beast*, July 13, 2016; Najmeh Bozorgmehr, "First Freight Trains from China Arrive in Tehran," *Financial Times*, May 9, 2016; "Iran Signs €2.2bn Rail Deal with China's CMC," *Global Construction Review*, May 22, 2017.

60. Ministry of Interior, *Natayej Tafsili Entekhabat Riyasat Jomhori (Detailed Results of the Presidential Elections)*, Islamic Republic of Iran, 2013 and 2017.

61. Marc Champion, "Iran Is Stuck with China to Finance Its Oil Dreams," *Bloomberg*, October 12, 2016; Wang Jin, "U.S. Sanctions on Iran: Good or Bad News for China?" *The Diplomat*, February 7, 2017.

62. "Angry Protestors Force Rouhani to Flee Rally in Tehran," *Center for Human Rights in Iran*, June 23, 2017; "Iran's President Rouhani and Iranian Revolutionary Guard Continue Their Feud," *Iran News Update*, June 28, 2017.

63. Saeed Kamali Dehghan, "Rift between Iran's Ayatollah and Re-elected President Widens," *The Guardian*, June 22, 2017.

64. Saeed Kamali Dehghan, "What's in a Ring? Iran's Khamenei Sends Mixed Election Messages," *The Guardian*, May 19, 2017.

65. "Street Protests Hit Iran for Third Straight Day as Pro-government Rallies Held," *Reuters*, December 30, 2017; "Na'aramiha Dar Sharhai Mokhtalef Iran Baraye Sevomin Ruz Peyapei" (Unrest in Several Cities of Iran for the Third Day in a Row), *BBC Persian Service*, December 30, 2017; Farideh Farhi, "Here's What Makes Iran's Anti-regime Protests Different This Time," *NPR*, January 4, 2018.

Chapter 7

1. Adewale Maja-Pearce, "Nigeria's China Connection," *New York Times*, May 7, 2014; Howard W. French, *China's Second Continent: How a Million Migrants Are Building a New Empire in Africa*, New York: Vintage, 2015; Allen Hai Xiao, "In the

Shadow of the States: The Informalities of Chinese Petty Entrepreneurship in Nigeria," *Journal of Current Chinese Affairs*, no. 44, vol. 1, 2015, 75–105.

2. Elliott Young, *Alien Nation: Chinese Migration in the Americas from the Coolie Era through World War II*, Chapel Hill: University of North Carolina Press, 2014; Bruce A. Elleman and Stephen Kotkin, eds., *Manchurian Railways and the Opening of China: An International History*, New York: Routledge, 2015.

3. Salem Solomon and Falastine Iman, "New African Railways Ride on Chinese Loans," *Voice of America*, January 24, 2017; Andrew Jacobs, "Joyous Africans Take to the Rails, With China's Help," *New York Times*, February 7, 2017.

4. Rasheed Bisiriyu, "Nigerian Railway: A Tale of Failed Contracts, Dashed Hope," *Punch*, February 4, 2016; Oye Abioye, Kadom Shubber, and John Koenigsberger, "Evaluating the Role and Impact of Railway Transport in the Nigerian Economy, Options and Choices: Case of Nigerian Railway Corporation," *AshEse Journal of Economics*, October 2016.

5. "Abuja-Kano Light Rail Project 'Dumped,'" *Railways Africa*, December 19, 2010; "Amaechi: Work on Lagos-Kano Rail Line to Begin This Year," *The News (Lagos)*, April, 25, 2016.

6. Oyekanmi Abioye, *Privatisation of the Nigerian Railway Corporation: An Evaluation of Critical Choices*, Doctoral Dissertation, Cardiff Metropolitan University, April 2016; "Need to Repeal Colonial Rail Monopoly Law," *Ships and Ports*, June 27, 2016; Ayo Teriba, "Nigeria's Economic Outlook in 2017," *SSRN*, March 23, 2017.

7. Leke Salaudeen, "Obasanjo's $8.3b Rail Deal Unsettles Yar'Adua," *Nigerian Muse*, March 19, 2008; Gregory Mthembu-Salter, "Elephants, Ants and Superpowers: Nigeria's Relations with China," *South Africa Institute of International Affairs, Occasional Paper No. 42*, September 2009.

8. Olivia Archdeacon, "China Adds Nigeria to Its African Empire," *capx.com*, April 14, 2016; Francis Arinze Iloani, "Nigeria: China, Nigeria Trade Imbalance Hits N1.67 Trillion in Five Years," *Daily Trust*, July 5, 2016; Aminu Adamu, "Nigeria Secures $7.5 Billion Loan from China for Rail Project—Amaechi," *Premium Times*, February 6, 2017; Maggie Fick, "Nigeria's Ruling Politicians Jostle for Power in Buhari's Absence," *Financial Times*, February 23, 2017.

9. Morgan Winsor, "China Slowdown Worsens Nigeria's Economic Woes amid Buhari's War on Corruption, Boko Haram," *International Business Times*, August 27, 2015; "Nigeria to Borrow $2.3 Billion from World Bank and China, Finance Minister," *Reuters*, February 21, 2017.

10. Chuka Odittah, "China Gives Stringent Conditions for $20bn Loan to Nigeria," *The Guardian*, August 14, 2016.

11. Chuka Odittah, "Hope Dims on N170 Billion Abuja-Kaduna Rail Project," *The Guardian*, January 27, 2016.

12. William Wallis, "Africa Told to View China as Competitor," *Financial Times*, March 12, 2013.

13. Lamido Sanusi, "Africa Must Get Real about Chinese Ties," *Financial Times*, March 11, 2013.

14. Ibid.

15. Ibid.

16. Solomon Ibrahim Hari, "The Evolution of Social Protest in Nigeria: The Role of Social Media in the '#OccupyNigeria' Protest," *International Journal of Humanities and Social Science Invention*, September 2014; Lafenwa Stephen Akinyemi, "Civil Society and the Anti-corruption Struggle in Nigeria," *International Journal of Business and Social Science*, March 2016.

17. Omoyele Sowore, "Nigerians Still Waiting for Their 'African Spring,'" *cnn.com*, January 14, 2013; Scott Baldauf, "Chinua Achebe on Corruption and Hope in Nigeria," *Christian Science Monitor*, March 22, 2013.

18. Joy Ekeke, "Nigeria Has No Long-Term Roadmap for Rail Transport-Comrade Esan," *Daily Times*, September 16, 2016.

19. Kingsley Nwezeh, "Nigeria: Fake Drugs-China Apologises to the Government," *This Day*, September 21, 2009; Adie Vanessa Offiong, "Nigeria: 'Africans Order for Low Quality Products from China,'" *Daily Trust*, December 7, 2015.

20. Keith Bradsher and Adam Nossiter, "In Nigeria, Chinese Investment Comes with a Downside," *New York Times*, December 5, 2015.

21. "Nigerian Anger over China Deaths," *BBC News*, September 25, 2009; Eric Olander and Cobus van Staden, "Nigerian in China: Why Are People Here So Racist towards Black People?" *The Huffington Post*, June 27, 2016.

22. "Fake Plastic Rice Seized in Nigeria amid Rocketing Food Prices," *Agence France-Presse*, December 21, 2016; Alex Linder, "Nigeria Says Seized 'Plastic Rice' Is Not Actually Fake but also Isn't Fit for Human Consumption," *shanghailist.com*, January 3, 2017.

23. Pauline Bax, "Chinese Furniture Fashion Ravages West Africa's Savannas," *Bloomberg*, August 1, 2016; Tunde Alao, "Buhari, Conservationists Decry Illegal Logging in Nigeria," *Nigerian Tribune*, January 4, 2017.

24. Solape Renner and Tope Alake, "Solar Power May Get Boost from Africa's Biggest Oil Exporter," *Bloomberg*, March 6, 2017; Tina Casey, "Nigeria Debates $20 Million for Diesel-Killing, Off-Grid Solar Power," *cleantechnica.com*, March 8, 2017.

25. Joseph Undu, "Nigerian Allegedly Defrauds Chinese Firm of N165m," *Vanguard*, December 28, 2016.

26. Ann M. Simmons, "Meet the Pangolin, the Most Poached Mammal in the World," *Los Angeles Times*, September 1, 2016; Camila Domonoske, "China Announces Its Largest-Ever Seizure of Trafficked Pangolin Scales," *NPR*, December 28, 2016.

27. Jenni Marsh, "Afro-Chinese Marriages Boom in Guangzhou: But Will It Be 'Til Death Do Us Part'?" *South China Morning Post*, July 2, 2014.

28. Jerrywright Ukwu, "China to Invest $750bn in Nigeria-Ambassador," *naij.com*, April 12, 2016; Olawale Ajimotokan, "China's Support for Nigeria's Digital Switch Over Project Exciting, Says Lai Mohammed," *This Day*, July 6, 2016; Ambassador Zhou Pingjian, "Made in Nigeria—With China," *This Day*, November 28, 2016; Victoria Ojeme, "NASS Moves to Enhance Technology Transfer between China, Nigeria," *Vanguard*, January 30, 2017.

29. Jacob Kushner, *China's Congo Plan: What the Next World Power Sees in the World's Poorest Nation*, Washington, DC: Pulitzer Center, March 28, 2013; Ken Moriyasu, "China-Aided Trans-Africa Railway Line Likely to Transform Regional Trade," *Nikkei Asian Review*, August 25, 2014; "Ethiopia-Djibouti Railway a First Step to Trans-Africa Railway?" *Africa Business Forum*, January 22, 2017.

30. Brian Wang, "China Moving Ahead with Trans-African Rail Line, New Silk Road Part of Global Land Bridge Vision," *Next Big Future*, October 17, 2014; Liezel Hill, "Africa's $30 Billion Rail Renaissance Holds Ticket for Trade," *Bloomberg*, April 7, 2016.

31. Wayne Jumat, "Quadrilateral Cooperation: Angola, Brazil, Nigeria and South Africa," *Institute for Global Dialogue*, May 29, 2014.

32. Analúcia Danilevicz Pereira, "The South Atlantic, Southern Africa and South America: Cooperation and Development," *Austral: Brazilian Journal of Strategy and International Relations*, July–December, 2013, pp. 31–45. "Transformation in the South Atlantic," *Atlantic Future*, July 24, 2013; Adriana Erthal Abdenur and Danilo Marcondes de Souza Neto, "China's Growing Influence in the South Atlantic," *BRICS Policy Center*, October 2013.

33. Deborah Brautigam, *Will Africa Feed China?* New York: Oxford University Press, 2015; Dani Rodrik, "Premature Deindustrialization," *Journal of Economic Growth*, vol. 21, 2016; Kevin P. Gallagher, *The China Triangle: Latin America's China Boom and the Fate of the Washington Consensus*, New York: Oxford University Press, 2016; Riordan Roett and Guadalupe Paz, *Latin America and the Asian Giants: Evolving Ties with China and India*, Washington, DC: Brookings, 2016.

34. Barbara Tasch, "China's $10 Billion Railway across South America Is Either Bold or Insane," *Business Insider*, June 10, 2015; Simon Romero, "China's Ambitious Rail Projects Crash into Harsh Realities in Latin America," *New York Times*, October 3, 2015; Jonathan Watts, "Nicaragua Canal: In a Sleepy Pacific Port, Something Stirs," *The Guardian*, November 24, 2016.

35. Richard L. Sklar, "An Elusive Target: Nigeria Fends Off Sanctions," in Kunle Amuwo, Daniel C. Bach, and Yann Lebeau, eds., *Nigeria during the Abacha Years, 1993–1998*, Institut français de recherche en Afrique, 2001; Dipo Kolawole, "From Isolation to Globalization: Transformation of Nigeria's Foreign Policy from the Abacha Regime to the Obasanjo Administration," *Pakistan Journal of Social Sciences*, vol. 3, no. 6, 2005.

36. "We've Potentials to Replicate Commercial Success of Chinese Economy in Anambra-Ubah," *Vanguard*, February 7, 2017; Okaekwu Chinaemelum, "China Plans Visa Office in Anambra as Chinese Deputy Consul-General Visits Obiano," *anambrastate.gov.ng*, April 28, 2017.

37. David H. Shinn and Joshua Eisenman, *China and Africa: A Century of Engagement*, Philadelphia: University of Pennsylvania Press, 2012.

38. Patrick Boehler, "China Pledges Help to Nigeria's Hunt for Boko Haram Militants," *Agence France-Presse*, May 8, 2014; Helene Cooperjan, "Rifts between U.S. and Nigeria Impeding Fight against Boko Haram," *New York Times*, January 24, 2015; Ashley Cowburn, "Two-Thirds of African Countries Now Using Chinese Military Equipment, Report Reveals," *Independent*, March 1, 2016; Senator Iroegbu, "To Finish Off Boko Haram, FG Looks to China for More Weapons," *This Day*, May 13, 2016.

39. Paul Wallace, "Nigeria Presidency Approves Borrowing from World Bank, China," *Bloomberg*, September 8, 2016.

40. "China 'Backs' Nigeria for Permanent U.N. Seat," *thecable.ng*, August 31, 2015; Brendan Scott, Ting Shi, and Yinka Ibukun, "Nigeria Snubs Taiwan as China Pledges $40 Billion Investment," *Bloomberg*, January 12, 2017.

41. Wang Wen and Chen Xiaochen, "Who Supports China in the South China Sea and Why," *The Diplomat*, July 27, 2016.

42. Drew Hinshaw, "West Africa Rising: Nigeria Shifting Currency Reserves from Dollars to Chinese Yuan," *Christian Science Monitor*, September 6, 2011; "Nigeria Bank Chief Sees Yuan Becoming Reserve Currency," *Xinhua*, September 6, 2011; Tobi Soniyi and Zacheaus Somorin, "Nigeria Offered $6bn Chinese Loan, Agrees Currency Swap to Shore Up Naira," *This Day*, April 13, 2016; Joe Uche Uwaleke, "Nigeria-China Currency Swap Deal at a Glance," *Punch*, April 19, 2016.

43. Simon Shen, "Why Nigeria Prefers China to the West," *Hong Kong Economic Journal*, May 4, 2016; Bhaso Ndzendze, "The Contours of China-Africa Relations," *Modern Diplomacy*, April 29, 2017; Brook Larmer, "Is China the World's New Colonial Power?" *New York Times*, May 2, 2017.

44. Chimamanda Ngozi Adichie, "A Nigerian Revolution: The Political Awakening of My Country's Young People Could Transform Nigeria's Rotten Democracy," *The Guardian*, March 16, 2011; Chika Oduah, "Nigeria—A Fractured Giant?" *Huffington Post*, October 15, 2014.

45. Jideofor Adibe, "Reality Check—Nigeria's Sense of Entitlement Cannot Stand Empirical Examination," *ynaija.com*, January 27, 2017.

46. Ibid.

47. Bassey Udo, "As U.S. Gradually Closes Door, Nigeria Turns to China to Boost Economy," *Premium Times*, July 4, 2013.

48. Ikechukwu Onyewuchi, "Nigeria/China: Still a Long Way to Go," *Saturday Magazine*, April 24, 2016.

49. Tolu Ogunlesi, "Nigeria and China Deals: What's the Benefit for Us?" *Financial Times*, December 4, 2015.

50. Damian Zane, "Nigeria's Goodluck Jonathan: Five Reasons Why He Lost," *BBC News*, March 31, 2015; "Nigeria's Goodluck Jonathan, Profile of a Defeated President," *BBC News*, March 31, 2015; Max Siollun, "How Goodluck Jonathan Lost the Nigerian Election," *The Guardian*, April 1, 2015.

51. "Chinese Sign US $12bn Contract to Build Nigerian Coastal Railway," *Railway Gazette*, November 20, 2014.

52. Danny Schechter, "#OccupyNigeria Shows the Movement's Global Face," *Al-Jazeera*, January 23, 2012.

53. Ovetta Sampson, "Occupy Nigeria Victory: President to Cut Fuel Prices," *Christian Science Monitor*, January 16, 2012; Katrin Matthaei, "Goodluck Jonathan: A Powerless President," *Deutsche Welle*, July 5, 2014.

54. Mayowa Tijani, "Buhari: I'm Committed to Jonathan's China Deal," *The Cable*, April 10, 2016; Gboyega Akinsanmi and Benneth Oghifo, "Nigeria: Govt, China to Finalise $11 Billion Lagos-Calabar Rail Deal in June," *All Africa*, March 8, 2017; Felix Onuah and Paul Carsten, "Nigeria Awards $1.79 Bln Railway Contract to Chinese State Firm CCECC," *Reuters*, March 22, 2017.

55. Aminu Adamu, "Nigeria Secures $7.5 Billion Loan from China for Rail Project," *Premium Times*, February 6, 2017.

56. Hassan Adebayo, "Buhari Writes Senate, Hands Over to Vice President Osinbajo," *Premium Times*, June 7, 2016.

57. Reno Omokri, "When an Acting President Acts Well," *This Day*, February 18, 2017; "With Buhari Away, Osinbajo Comes Out of the Shadows," *The Guardian*, February 25, 2017.

58. Dionne Searcey and Tony Iyare, "President Buhari Returns to Nigeria, Facing Serious Challenges," *New York Times*, August 21, 2017.

Chapter 8

1. Robert R. Bianchi, *Unruly Corporatism: Associational Life in Twentieth-Century Egypt*, New York: Oxford University Press, 1989.

2. Tarek Osman, *Egypt on the Brink: From Nasser to the Muslim Brotherhood*, New Haven, CT: Yale University Press, 2013.

3. Ding Ying, "Egypt's Diplomatic Balancing Act," *Beijing Review*, September 6, 2012; Fahmi Huwaidi, "Morsi in Beijing and Tehran," *Middle East Monitor*, January 25, 2014.

4. Lin Noueihed and Ali Abdelaty, "China's Xi Visits Egypt, Offers Financial, Political Support," *Reuters*, January 21, 2016; Julian Pecquet, "What Happened to the Billions the U.S. Gave to Egypt?" *U.S. News*, May 13, 2016.

5. Peter Hessler, "Egypt's Failed Revolution," *The New Yorker*, January 2, 2017; Zeinab Abul-Magd, *Militarizing the Nation: The Army, Business, and Revolution in Egypt*, New York: Columbia University Press, 2017.

6. Charles Tiefer, "As U.S. Resumes Military Aid to Egypt, Reports Show How Little We Know on How It's Being Used," *Forbes*, April 7, 2015; Aya Nader, "U.S. Resumes Military Aid to Egypt despite Human Rights Situation," *Daily News Egypt*, April 14, 2015.

7. Maria Golia, "Dark Waters," *The National* (Egypt), November 26, 2009.

8. Ben Flanagan, "Higher Tolls 'Risky' after $4bn Suez Canal Expansion," *Al-Arabiya News*, August 7, 2014.

9. Andrew R. Thomas, "Suez and Panama: A Healthy Competition," *Industry Week*, May 10, 2015; Jack O'Connell, "Canal Wars," *Maritime Executive*, October 31, 2016.

10. Mohamed Ahmed, "Future of Suez Canal Revenues Hostage to International Currencies Struggle," *Daily News* (Egypt), February 21, 2016; Chris Baraniuk, "Cheap Oil Is Taking Shipping Routes Back to the 1880s," *BBC*, March 4, 2016.

11. Blair Cunningham, "New Rail Freight Link Could Become 'Israel's Suez Canal,'" *Haaretz*, February 14, 2014; Mordechai Chaziza, "The Red-Med Railway: New Opportunities for China, Israel, and the Middle East," *Begin-Sadat Center for Strategic Studies*, December 11, 2016; Michael Tanchum, "China's One Belt, One Road Reshapes Mideast," *Jerusalem Post*, January 24, 2017.

12. "China Wants to Divert Its Ships from Egypt's Suez Canal to New Arctic Route," *Egyptian Streets*, April 21, 2016; Eddy Bekkers et al., "Melting Ice Caps and the Economic Impact of Opening the Northern Sea Route," *The Economic Journal*, December 16, 2016; David Trilling, "Arctic Melt Boosts Northern Trade Routes, Hurts Suez," *Journalist's Resource*, March 6, 2017.

13. Greg Lebedev and Ana C. Rold, "The New Suez Canal: How Egypt Is Charting a Brand New Future for Itself and The Region," *Diplomatic Courier*, September 1, 2015; Ismael El-Kholy, "One Year On, Are 'New' Suez Canal Revenues Sinking?" *Almonitor*, August 10, 2016.

14. Nesma Nowar, Stefan Weichert, and Mona El-Fiqi, "Egypt's Dwindling Foreign Currency Resources," *Al-Ahram Weekly*, March 23, 2016.

15. Ahmed Aleem, "Egypt Hopes Chinese Visitors Can Make Up for Russian Tourism Decline," *Al-Monitor*, March 6, 2017.

16. Amira Salah-Ahmed and Isabel Esterman, "Crowdfunding the Canal?" *madamasr.com*, August 31, 2014.

17. Maria Golia, "The New Suez Canal Project and Egypt's Economic Future," *Middle East Institute*, December 19, 2014.

18. Hiba Safi, "Maximum Wage in Egypt: Who Pays the Bill?" *Center for International Private Enterprise*, May 6, 2015; Patrick Werr, "Egypt Caught Up in a Vicious Circle with Its Finances," *The National*, April 27, 2016.

19. Steven A. Cook, "Egypt's Solvency Crisis," *Council on Foreign Relations*, April 2014; "A Dollar Crisis Threatens Egypt's Economy," *Stratfor*, March 10, 2016; Tarek El-Tablawy, "Egypt Moves Closer to IMF Loan with China Currency Swap Deal," *Bloomberg*, October 30, 2016.

20. Daria Solovieva, "Suez Canal: Egyptian Military Takes Charge of Economic Development," *International Business Times*, April 3, 2014; John Daly, "Egypt's Upgraded Suez Canal Is Bold Bid on the Future," *The Arab Weekly*, August 14, 2015; Mahmoud Fouly, "Interview: China Largest Investor in Egypt's Suez Canal Region with Earnest, Win-Win Partnership: Official," *Xinhua*, March 16, 2017.

21. Samar Samir, "32 Chinese Firms Invest in 1st Phase of Suez Canal Area with $426 m: Xi," *The Cairo Post*, January 21, 2016; Shannon Tiezzi, "The Belt and Road and Suez Canal: China-Egypt Relations under Xi Jinping," *China Policy Institute*, February 2, 2016; "Egypt Turning towards China for Investment," *African Business Magazine*, October 18, 2016.

22. "Chinese Company to Spend US$20 billion on Egypt's New Capital East of Cairo," *South China Morning Post*, October 4, 2016; "Sisi's Dream of New Egypt Capital in Tatters as China Pulls Out," *Middle East Eye*, February 9, 2017.

23. "Egyptian Contractors to Build Ministerial District in New Capital after Failed Chinese Deal," *Ahram Online*, February 6, 2017; Eric Knecht, "Egypt's Capital Project Hits Latest Snag as Chinese Pull Out," *Reuters*, February 8, 2017.

24. Ahmed Feteha, "Egypt, China Sign $2.6B Currency Swap Boosting Pound Flotation," *Bloomberg*, December 6, 2016; "China to Contribute US$64 Million to 'Egypt Sat 2' Project," *Al-Masry Al-Youm*, March 21, 2017; "China Jushi's Expansion in Egypt Is Ahead of Schedule," *Composites World*, March 27, 2017; "Egypt Announces New Chinese Investments in Textile," *China Daily*, April 5, 2017.

25. Ahmed El-Sayed Al-Naggar, "Egypt and China: The Potential for Stronger Economic Ties," *Al-Ahram Online*, October 21, 2016; Zaynab El-Bernoussi, "China Making Big Diplomat Gains in Egypt," *Japan Times*, December 10, 2016; Kyle Haddad-Fonda, "Egypt and Other Arab States Embrace a Chinese Model of Development," *World Politics Review*, March 16, 2017.

26. Jack Farchy et al., "One Belt, One Road: A Ribbon of Road, Rail and Energy Projects to Help Increase Trade," *Financial Times*, September 14, 2016; Brian Wang, "Megacities and One Belt, One Road Are Core to China's 100 Year Economic Strategy," *nextbigfuture.com*, April 1, 2017; Tony Semerad, "Changing China: The Nation Places a Heavy Bet on One Belt, One Road," *Salt Lake Tribune*, April 17, 2017.

27. Shana Marshall, "The Egyptian Armed Forces and the Remaking of an Economic Empire," *Carnegie Middle East Center*, 2015.

28. Peter Bellwood, *First Farmers: The Origins of Agricultural Societies*, Malden, MA: Wiley-Blackwell, 2004; Randa El Bedawy, "Water Resources Management: Alarming Crisis for Egypt," *Journal of Management and Sustainability*, vol. 4, August 2014; Mohie El Din M. Omar and Ahmed M. A. Moussa, "Water Management in Egypt For Facing the Future Challenges," *Journal of Advanced Research*, vol. 7, May 2016.

29. Sayed A. Selim et al., "Groundwater Rising as Environmental Problem, Causes and Solutions: Case Study from Aswan City, Upper Egypt," *Open Journal of Geology*, vol. 4, July 2014.

30. Jano Charbel, "Nile Delta's Increasing Salinity and Rising Sea Levels May Make Egypt Uninhabitable by 2100," *madamasr.com*, March 16, 2017.

31. Andre Fecteau, "On Toshka New Valley's Mega-Failure," *Egypt Independent*, April 26, 2012; Peter Schwartzstein, "Forget ISIS, Egypt's Population Boom Is Its Biggest Threat," *Newsweek*, March 20, 2017; Bushra Azhar, "Egypt's Toshka New Valley Project: A Failure of Planning or a Failure of Implementation," *greenprophet.com*, May 6, 2012.

32. Edson Mpyisi, *Egypt: National Drainage Programme*, African Development Bank Group, April 2015; Masayoshi Satoh and Samir Aboulroos, eds., *Irrigated Agriculture in Egypt: Past, Present and Future*, Cham, Switzerland: Springer, 2017.

33. Santiago Herrera et al., "Reshaping Egypt's Economic Geography: Domestic Integration as a Development Platform," *World Bank*, June 2012; "Egypt's Farmers: Sowing the Seeds of an Agricultural Revolution," *International Labor Organization*, February 7, 2013; Eduardo Amaral Haddad et al., "Regional Analysis of Domestic Integration in Egypt: An Interregional CGE Approach," *Journal of Economic Structures*, vol. 5, no. 25, 2016.

34. Yamen M. Hegazy et al., "Ruminant Brucellosis in the Kafr El Sheikh Governorate of the Nile Delta, Egypt: Prevalence of a Neglected Zoonosis," *Public Library of Science: Neglected Tropical Diseases*, January 11, 2011.

35. Egypt Network for Integrated Development, *Promoting Manufacturing in Upper Egypt*, Policy Brief 16, Cairo, 2013; Hafez Ghanem, *Improving Regional and Rural Development for Inclusive Growth in Egypt*, Brookings Global Economy and Development Working Paper 67, January 2014; International Fund for Agricultural Development, *Investing in Rural People in Egypt*, IFAD, Rome, April 2017.

36. Robert R. Bianchi, "Urban Backlash against Democracy: Battling the Tyranny of the Majority or the Rise of Rural Power?," in Roman Stadnicki, ed., *City and Revolution in Egypt*, Cairo: Le Centre d'Études et de Documentation Économiques, Juridiques et Sociales, 2014, pp. 67–82.

37. Robert R. Bianchi, "Egypt's Revolutionary Elections," *The Singapore Middle East Papers*, vol. 2, Summer 2012, pp. 14–19.

38. Ibid. pp. 19–21.

39. Robert R. Bianchi, "Urban Backlash against Democracy: Battling the Tyranny of the Majority or the Rise of Rural Power?," in Roman Stadnicki, ed., *City and Revolution in Egypt*, Cairo: Le Centre d'Études et de Documentation Économiques, Juridiques et Sociales, 2014, pp. 70–74.

40. Declan Walsh, "Egyptian Prosecutor Orders Release of Hosni Mubarak, President Toppled in 2011," *New York Times*, March 13, 2017.

41. Eddie Cheng, "Alabo de Tian'anmen He Zhongguo de Molihua" (The Arab Tiananmen and the Chinese Jasmine), *tiananmenduizhi.com*, February 27, 2011; Qian Xuewen, "The January Revolution and the Future of Egypt," *Journal of Middle Eastern and Islamic Studies (in Asia)* vol. 6, no. 2, 2012; Jackson Diehl, "Sissi's Teeming Prisons," *Al-Jazeera*, September 27, 2015; Amr Darrag, "Sissi's Brutality Is Feeding the Islamic State's New Front in Egypt," *Washington Post*, November 5, 2015; Jack Shenker, "State Repression in Egypt Worst in Decades, Says Activist," *The Guardian*, January 24, 2016; H. A. Hellyer, "Is Another Egyptian Uprising un the Way?" *The Globe and Mail*, January 25, 2016.

42. Xue Li and Zheng Yuwen, "The Future of China's Diplomacy in the Middle East," *The Diplomat*, July 26, 2016; Abdourahim Arteh, "Djibouti Breaks Ground on Massive Chinese-Backed Free Trade Zone," *Reuters*, January 16, 2017.

43. American Enterprise Institute, "China Global Investment Tracker," aei.org, 2017.

44. Nicholas Mehling, "15 Major Chinese Companies Meet with Egypt before G20 Summit," *Daily News Egypt*, July 9, 2016; Sudeshna Sarkar, "Egypt Turning toward China for Investment," *African Business Magazine*, October 18, 2016.

45. Ahmed El-Sayed Al-Naggar, "Egypt and China: The Potential for Stronger Economic Ties," *Al-Ahram*, October 21, 2016.

46. Ahmed Kamel, "Chinese Project to Build New Egyptian Capital Revived," *Nikkei Asian Review*, May 26, 2017.

47. Finbarr Bermingham, "Chinese Banks Pump Money into Egypt," *Global Trade Review*, April 25, 2017; "Spotlight: Figures Show Growth in Egypt, China Cooperation on Belt and Road Initiative," *Xinhua*, May 3, 2017.

48. Charley Locke, "Go inside China's Bizarre Theme Park in the Egyptian Desert," *Wired*, October 24, 2016.

49. Fatima Ramadan and Amr Adly, "Low-Cost Authoritarianism: The Egyptian Regime and Labor Movement since 2013," *Carnegie Middle East Center*, September 17, 2015; "Egypt Witnessed Hundreds of Labour Protests in 2015: Report," *Middle East Eye*, January 12, 2016; Brian Rohan, "Hard Times in Egypt Stoke Labor Unrest, Showdown Ahead," *Associated Press*, June 11, 2016.

50. Nour Youssef, "Egyptian Police Detain Uighurs and Deport Them to China," *New York Times*, July 6, 2017; "To Appease China, Egypt Arrests 500 Turkestani Students Studying in Al-Azhar," *Middle East Observer*, July 6, 2017; "Egypt Arrests Chinese Muslim Students amid Police Sweep," *Al-Jazeera*, July 7, 2017.

Chapter 9

1. "8 Great Places to Break Fast during Ramadan in Shanghai," *shanghailist.com*, June 10, 2016; Liu Dong, Huang Jingjing, and Xie Wenting, "Shanghai Muslims'

Outdoor Prayers Show Urban Integration," *english.sina.com*, July 8, 2016; Lena Scheen, "Islam in China," *International Institute for Asian Studies Newsletter*, Autumn 2016 (http://iias.asia/the-newsletter/article/islam-china).

2. Robyn Iredale, Naran Bilik, and Fei Guo, eds., *China's Minorities on the Move: Selected Case Studies*, London: M. E. Sharpe, 2003; Björn Gustafsson and Xiuna Yang, "Are China's Ethnic Minorities Less Likely to Move?" *IZA Discussion Paper Series*, Bonn: April 2015; Zheng Wang, Fangzhu Zhang, and Fulong Wu, "Social Trust between Rural Migrants and Urban Locals in China—Exploring the Effects of Residential Diversity and Neighborhood Deprivation," *Population, Space and Place*, December 11, 2015.

3. Lisa Movius, "New Museum on Silk Road Breaks the Chinese Mould, Islam Is the Focus of North-West China's First Contemporary Art Institution," *theartnewspaper.com*, August 27, 2015; Andrew Jacobs, "Light Government Touch Lets China's Hui Practice Islam in the Open," *New York Times*, February 1, 2016; Yan Cong, "Life in the Hui Culture Park," *chinafile.com*, May 5, 2016; "Muslim Communist Theme Park Set for China to Bolster Ties with Middle East," *rt.com*, May 13, 2016; "For Allah, Beijing and Marx: Young Imams in China Espouse Islam through Prism of Party Line," *Japan Times*, May 23, 2016.

4. Daniel Bardsley, "China Shifts to More 'Authentic' Arabian-Style Mosques," *The National (UAE)*, July 12, 2012; Sun Dazhang and Qiu Yulan, *Islamic Buildings: The Architecture of Islamic Mosques in China*, Beijing: CN Times Books, 2015; Nancy Shatzman Steinhardt, *China's Early Mosques*, Edinburgh: Edinburgh University Press, 2016.

5. Tim Oakes, "China's Provincial Identities: Reviving Regionalism and Reinventing 'Chineseness,'" *Journal of Asian Studies*, vol. 59, no. 3, August 2000; Tim Oakes and Donald S. Sutton, eds., *Faiths on Display: Religion, Tourism, and the Chinese State*, Lanham, MD: Rowman & Littlefield, 2010; Edward Wong, "Mongolian Warriors and Communist Soldiers: A Frontier Town in China," *New York Times*, June 18, 2017.

6. James Leibold, "Creeping Islamophobia: China's Hui Muslims in the Firing Line," *Jamestown China Brief*, June 20, 2016; Matthew S. Erie, "In China, Fears of 'Creeping Sharia' Proliferate Online," *Foreign Policy*, September 15, 2016; Massoud Hayoun, "Surrealism Abounds in China's Uyghur Crackdown," *Pacific Standard*, May 3, 2017.

7. Mayfair Mei-hui Yang, ed., *Chinese Religiosities: Afflictions of Modernity and State Formation*, Berkeley: University of California Press, 2008; Yoshiko Ashiwa and David L. Wank, *Making Religion, Making the State: The Politics of Religion in Modern China*, Stanford, CA: Stanford University Press, 2009; John Lagerwey, *China: A Religious State*, Hong Kong: Hong Kong University Press, 2010; Vincent Goossaert and David A. Palmer, *The Religious Question in Modern China*, Chicago: University of Chicago Press, 2011; Ian Johnson, *The Souls of China: The Return of Religion after Mao*, New York: Pantheon/Knopf, 2017.

8. Vera Schwarcz, *The Chinese Enlightenment: Intellectuals and the Legacy of the May Fourth Movement of 1919*, Berkeley: University of California Press, 1986.

9. Frank Dikötter, *The Discourse of Race in Modern China*, Stanford, CA: Stanford University Press, 1992; Prasenjit Duara, *Rescuing History from the Nation: Questioning*

Narratives of Modern China, Chicago: University of Chicago Press, 1995; Barry Sautman, "Peking Man and the Politics of Paleoanthropological Nationalism in China," *Journal of Asian Studies*, vol. 60, 2001; James Leibold, "Competing Narratives of Racial Unity in Republican China: From the Yellow Emperor to Peking Man," *Modern China*, April, 2006.

10. Arthur Hummel, trans., *The Autobiography of a Chinese Historian*, Taipei: Ch'eng Wen, 1966; Laurence Schneider, *Ku Chieh-kang and China's New History: Nationalism and the Quest for Alternative Traditions*, Berkeley: University of California Press, 1971; Ursula Richter, "Gu Jiegang: His Last Thirty Years," *China Quarterly*, June 1982.

11. David L. Hall and Roger T. Ames, *The Democracy of the Dead: Dewey, Confucius, and the Hope for Democracy in China*, Chicago: Open Court, 1999; Sor-Hoon Tan, *Confucian Democracy: A Deweyan Reconstruction*, Albany: State University of New York Press, 2003; Joseph Grange, *John Dewey, Confucius, and Global Philosophy*, Albany: State University of New York Press, 2004; Jessica Ching-Sze Wang, *John Dewey in China: To Teach and to Learn*, Albany: State University of New York Press, 2007; Stephen T. Asma, "From China, With Pragmatism," *New York Times*, June 8, 2014.

12. Ursula Richter, "Historical Scepticism in the New Culture Era: Gu Jiegang and the 'Debate on Ancient History,'" *Studies of Modern Chinese History*, no. 23, June 1994; Edward L. Shaughnessy, *Rewriting Early Chinese Texts*, Albany: State University of New York Press, 2006; Yuri Pines, "Political Mythology and Dynastic Legitimacy in the Rong Cheng shi Manuscript," *Bulletin of SOAS*, vol. 73, no. 3, 2010; Li Feng, *Early China: A Social and Cultural History*, Cambridge: Cambridge University Press, 2013.

13. Tze-Ki Hon, "Ethnic and Cultural Pluralism: Gu Jiegang's Vision of a New China in His Studies of Ancient History," *Modern China*, vol. 22, 1996; Wang Hongliang, "Gu Jiegang yu Minguo Shiqi de Bianzheng Yanjiu" (Gu Jiegang and Frontier Political Studies in the Republican Period), *Qilu Journal*, no. 232, 2013.

14. Arthur Hummel, trans., *The Autobiography of a Chinese Historian*, Taipei: Ch'eng Wen, 1966, pp. 166–167.

15. Ibid. pp. 167–168; Muhsin Mahdi, *Ibn Khaldun's Philosophy of History: A Study in the Philosophic Foundation of the Science of Culture*, Chicago: University of Chicago Press, 1964; Linda T. Darling, "Social Cohesion ('Asabiyya') and Justice in the Late Medieval Middle East," *Comparative Studies in Society and History*, vol. 49, April 2007.

16. Andrew D. W. Forbes, *Warlords and Muslims in Chinese Central Asia: A Political History of Republican Sinkiang 1911–1949*, New York: Cambridge University Press, 1986; Jonathan N. Lipman, *Familiar Strangers: A History of Muslims in Northwest China*, Seattle: University of Washington Press, 1997; Françoise Aubin, "Islam on the Wings of Nationalism: The Case of Muslim Intellectuals in Republican China," in Stéphane A. Dudoignon, Komatsu Hisao, and Dosugi Yaushi, eds, *Intellectuals in the Modern Islamic World: Transmission, Transformation, Communication*, London: Routledge, 2006.

17. Dru C. Gladney, *Muslim Chinese: Ethnic Nationalism in the People's Republic*, Cambridge, MA: Council on East Asian Studies, Harvard University, 1996; Ma Ping, "Zhongguo Huizu Musilin de Shehui Wangluo Jiegou" (The Structure of Social Networks of Chinese Hui Muslims), *Journal of Hui Muslim Minority Studies*, no. 1, 2008.

18. K. C. Chang, "Xia Nai (1910–1985)," *American Anthropologist*, vol. 88, June 1986; Wang Tao, "Establishing the Chinese Archaeological School: Su Bingqi and Contemporary Chinese Archaeology," *SOAS Antiquity*, vol. 71, 1997; Michael Puett, "China in Early Eurasian History: A Brief Review of Recent Scholarship on the Issue," in Victor H. Mair, ed., *The Bronze Age and Early Iron Age Peoples of Eastern Central Asia, Vol. 2*, Washington, DC: Institute for the Study of Man, 1998; Xingcan Chen, "Archaeological Discoveries in the People's Republic of China and Their Contribution to the Understanding of Chinese History," *Bulletin of the History of Archaeology*, vol. 19, November 2009.

19. Clayton D. Brown, "Making the Majority: Defining Han Identity in Chinese Ethnology and Archaeology," PhD dissertation, Department of History, University of Pittsburgh, 2008.

20. Fei Hsiao-tung, "The New Outlook of Rural China: Kaishienkung Revisited after Half a Century," *RAIN (Royal Anthropological Institute of Great Britain and Ireland)*, February 1982; Fei Xiaotong, "Toward a People's Anthropology," in Thomas Weaver, ed., *The Dynamics of Applied Anthropology in the Twentieth Century: The Malinowski Award Papers*, Oklahoma City, OK: Society for Applied Anthropology, 2002; Gary Hamilton and Xiangqun Chang, "China and World Anthropology: A Conversation on the Legacy of Fei Xiaotong (1910–2005)," *Anthropology Today*, December 2011.

21. Dru C. Gladney, *Dislocating China: Muslims, Minorities, and Other Subaltern Subjects*, Chicago: University of Chicago Press, 2004; Thomas Mullaney, *Coming to Terms with the Nation: Ethnic Classification in Modern China*, Berkeley: University of California Press, 2010.

22. Susan K. McCarthy, *Chinese Multiculturalism: Ethnic Revival in Southwest China*, Seattle: University of Washington Press, 2009.

23. Justin Jon Rudelson, *Oasis Identities: Uyghur Nationalism along China's Silk Road*, New York: Columbia University Press, 1997; Gardner Bovingdon, *The Uyghurs: Strangers in Their Own Land*, New York: Columbia University Press, 2010.

24. Jonathan N. Lipman, "White Hats, Oil Cakes, and Common Blood: The Hui in the Contemporary Chinese State," in *Governing China's Multiethnic Frontiers*, Morris Rossabi, ed., Seattle: University of Washington Press, 2004.

25. Dru C. Gladney, *Dislocating China: Muslims, Minorities, and Other Subaltern Subjects*, Chicago: University of Chicago Press, 2004; James Leibold, *Ethnic Policy in China: Is Reform Inevitable?* Honolulu, HA: East-West Center, 2013.

26. Fei Xiaotong, *Plurality and Unity in the Configuration of the Chinese People*, Hong Kong: The Chinese University of Hong Kong, November 1988.

27. Xu Jiexun, *Xueqiu: Han Minzude Renleixue Fenxi (Snowball: An Anthropological Analysis of Han Nationality)*, Shanghai: Shanghai People's Publishers, 1999.

28. James Leibold, "In Search of Han: Early Twentieth-Century Narratives on Chinese Origins and Development," *China Heritage Quarterly*, September 2009; Xu Jiexun, "Understanding the Snowball Theory of the Han Nationality," in Thomas S. Mullaney, James Leibold, Stéphane Gros, and Eric Vanden Bussche, eds., *Critical Han Studies: The History, Representation, and Identity of China's Majority*, Berkeley: University of California Press, 2012.

29. Arif Dirlik, "Confucius in the Borderlands: Global Capitalism and the Reinvention of Confucianism," *Boundary*, Autumn 1995; Robert Neville, *Boston

Confucianism, Albany: State University of New York Press, 2000; Gloria Davies, *Worrying about China: The Language of Chinese Critical Inquiry*, Cambridge, MA: Harvard University Press, 2007; John Makeham, *Lost Soul: "Confucianism" in Contemporary Chinese Academic Discourse*, Harvard-Yenching Institute, 2008.

30. Osman Bakar, ed., *Islam and Confucianism: A Civilizational Dialogue*, Kuala Lumpur: University of Malaysia Press, 1997; Sachiko Murata, William C. Chittick, and Weiming Tu, *The Sage Learning of Liu Zhi: Islamic Thought in Confucian Terms*, Cambridge, MA: Harvard University Asia Center, 2009.

31. Zhang Rong, "Xin Rujia Shijie xia de Yisilan Wenming: Cong Tang Jun Yi dao Du Wei Ming" (Islamic Civilization from the Perspective of Neo-Confucianism: From Tang Junyi to Du Weiming), *Journal of Hui Muslim Minority Studies*, no. 4, 2004.

32. Sin Yee Chan, "Tang Junyi: Moral Idealism and Chinese Culture," in Chung-Ying Cheng and Nicholas Bunnin, eds., *Contemporary Chinese Philosophy*, Malden, MA: Blackwell, 2002.

33. Daniel A. Bell, *China's New Confucianism: Politics and Everyday Life in a Changing Society*, Princeton, NJ: Princeton University Press, 2008; Sun Shuyun, "Chicken Broth for the Soul? No Thanks," *The Guardian*, May 16, 2009; Yuan-Kang Wang, *Harmony and War: Confucian Culture and Chinese Power Politics*, New York: Columbia University Press, 2010.

34. George Saliba, "China and Islamic Civilization: Exchange of Techniques and Scientific Ideas," *The Silk Road*, Summer 2008; Richard Foltz, *Religions of the Silk Road: Premodern Patterns of Globalization*, New York: Palgrave Macmillan, 2010; Xinru Liu, "A Silk Road Legacy: The Spread of Buddhism and Islam," *Journal of World History*, March 2011; Johan Elverskog, *Buddhism and Islam on the Silk Road*, Philadelphia: University of Pennsylvania Press, 2011; Zhuying Shi, "When Confucius Meets Rumi: Chinese, Turkish Scholars Discuss Academic Cooperation in Istanbul," Wordpress.com, May 23, 2012; Arun Bala and Prasenjit Duara, eds., *The Bright Dark Ages: Comparative and Connective Perspectives*, Leiden/Boston: Brill, 2016; Toshihiko Izutsu, *Sufism and Taoism: A Comparative Study of Key Philosophical Concepts*, Berkeley: University of California Press, 2016.

35. Liang Xiangming, *Liu Zhi: Jiqi Yisilan Sixiang Yanjiu* (*Liu Zhi: A Study of His Islamic Ethics*), Lanzhou: Lanzhou Daxue Chubanshe, 2004; Gao Zhanfu, "Cong 'Tianfang Dianli' Zhanshi de 'Yi Rui Quanjing' Sixiang Kan Yisilan Jiao Zai Zhongguo de Bentuhua" (From "Arabian Rituals" to "Explaining Islamic Classics with Confucianism": The Localization of Islam in China), *Hui Nationality Studies*, no. 3, 2010; Liang Xiangming, *Mingmo Qingchu Huizu San Da Hanwen Yizhejia Lunli Sixiang Yanjiu* (*The Ethics of Three Hui Chinese Translators during the Late Ming Dynasty to the Early Qing Dynasty*), Beijing: Guangming Ribao Chubanshe, 2010; Liang Xiangming, *Huizu Chuantong Lunli Sixiang Yanjiu* (*Traditional Hui Ethics*), Yinchuan: Yangguang Chubanshe, 2014; Jonathan Lipman, ed., *Islamic Thought in China: Sino-Muslim Intellectual Evolution from the 17th to the 21st Century*, Edinburgh: Edinburgh University Press, 2016.

36. Sun Degang and Yahia H. Zoubir, eds., *Building a New Silk Road: China and the Middle East in the 21st Century*, Beijing: World Affairs Press, 2014.

37. Joshua Tschantret, "How China's Repression in Xinjiang Can Backfire, Again," *Asia and the Pacific Policy Society Forum*, December 12, 2016; Michael Martina, "China

Holds Massive Police Rally in Xinjiang as Hundreds Sent to Anti-terror 'Frontline,'" *Reuters*, February 29, 2017; "The Extraordinary Ways in Which China Humiliates Muslims," *The Economist*, May 4, 2017.

38. Mu Chunshan, "Anti-Muslim Sentiment Is Taking Over China's Social Media Scene," *The Diplomat*, September 13, 2016; Viola Zhou, "'When Are You Going Back to Arabia?': How Chinese Muslims Became the Target of Online Hate," *South China Morning Post*, March 12, 2017.

39. Wang Tian You and Wan Ming, *Zhenghe Yanjiu Bainian Lunwen Xuan (100 Years of Zheng He Studies: Selected Writings)*, Beijing University Press, 2004; Wang Gungwu, "China's Cautious Pride in an Ancient Mariner," *Yale Global*, August 4, 2005; Tan Ta Sen, *Cheng Ho and Islam in Southeast Asia*, Singapore: Institute of Southeast Asian Studies, 2009; Ying Liu, Zhongping Chen, and Gregory Blue, eds., *Zheng He's Maritime Voyages (1405–1433) and China's Relations with the Indian Ocean World*, Leiden/Boston: Brill, 2014.

40. In China and elsewhere, historians frequently revive debates about the significance of Zheng He's voyages and their many political interpretations. Chinese writers usually cast the expeditions as peaceful explorations that demonstrated the Ming emperor's grandeur and goodwill. Some foreign commentators are more skeptical, arguing that the fleets carried overwhelming military power, which they brandished to intimidate weaker states and to crush would-be opponents. These two faces of Zheng He—the quiet diplomat and the rugged admiral—increasingly emerge during heated arguments over China's determination to build an all-ocean navy that is outfitted for both peacekeeping and war making. Geoff Wade, *The Zheng He Voyages: A Reassessment*, Asia Research Institute, National University of Singapore, October 2004; Edward L. Dreyer, *Zheng He: China and the Oceans in the Early Ming Dynasty, 1405–1433*, Old Tappan, NJ: Pearson Longman, 2006.

41. "Shipping News: Zheng He's Sexcentenary," *China Heritage Newsletter*, June 2005; "Bronze Statue of Zhen He Inaugurated in Quanzhou," *People's Daily*, July 12, 2005; Bjoern Moritz, "Admiral Zheng He, The Columbus from the Far East!" *Maritime Topics on Stamps*, 2006; Edward Wong, "Celebrating the Legacy of a Chinese Explorer," *New York Times*, December 18, 2014.

42. James C. Y. Watt, ed., *The World of Khubilai Khan: Chinese Art in the Yuan Dynasty*, New York: Metropolitan Museum of Art, 2010; Pan Guxi, ed., *Buildings of the Yuan-Ming Period*, Reading, UK: Paths International Ltd., 2013.

43. "China's Islamic Heritage," *China Heritage Newsletter*, March 2006; Alice Su, "Meet China's State-Approved Muslims," *Foreign Policy*, November 2, 2016; Lily Hindy, "A Rising China Eyes the Middle East," *The Century Foundation*, April 6, 2017.

44. Idries Shah, *The Pleasantries of the Incredible Mulla Nasrudin*, New York: Penguin, 1993; Aikebaier Wulamu and Zhao Shijie, *Malu Shang de Zhizhe: Afanti de Da Zhihui (Sage on a Donkey: The Wisdom of Afanti)*, Urumuqi: Xinjiang Youth Publishing House, 2006; Aikebair Wulamu, *Jiangbuwan de Afanti Gushi: Fengci Gushi (Endless Tales of Afanti: Satirical Stories)*, Urumqi: Xinjiang Youth Publishing House, 2012.

45. Cai Zhizhong, *Manhua Daojia Sixiang: Zhuang Zi Shuo (Daoist Thought in Cartoons: Sayings of Zhuang Zi)*, Beijing: Shangwu Yinshuguan Chuban, 2009; Cai Zhizhong, *Cai Gen Tan Xin Jing: Rensheng de Ziwei (The Roots of Wisdom Heart Sutra: The Flavor of Life)*, Beijing: Xiandai Chubanshe, 2013.

46. Su Shiqun, Ding Xieqin, and Qi Cheng, "Lun Zhongguo Yisilan Jiao de Shehui Gongneng" (On The Social Functions of Chinese Islam), *Chinese Muslim*, no. 3, 1999; Zhou Chuan Bin, "Ta Shan Zhi Shi: Xifang Xuejie Dui Zhongguo Huizu Yisilan Jiao de Yanjiu Shuping" (Stones from Other Hills [May Help to Polish the Jade of This One]: A Review of Western Academic Studies on the Islam of China's Hui Community), *Northwest Nationalities Studies*, January 2005; Degang Sun, "Six Decades of Chinese Middle East Studies: A Review," *Bustan: The Middle East Book Review*, vol. 2, no. 1, 2011; Jin Wang, "Middle East Studies in China: Achievements and Problems," *Rubin Center Research in International Affairs*, September 5, 2016; Haiyun Ma and I-wei Jennifer Chang, "China's Strategic Middle Eastern Languages," *Middle East Research and Information Project*, Spring 2016.

47. Zhu Weilie, "Yisilan Wenming Yu Shijie" (Islamic Civilization and the World), *World Economy and Politics*, July 2007; Zhu Wei Lie, "Bawo Jiyu, Xuan Zhun Lujing, Shixian Ningxia Xin Tengfei" (Seize the Opportunity, Choose the Right Road, Achieve Ningxia's New Takeoff), *Hui Minority Studies*, no. 4, 2010; Zhu Wei Lie, "Shilun Zhongguo Yu Zhongdong Yisilan Guojia de Zhanluexing Guanxi" (On the Strategic Relationship between China and Islamic Countries in the Middle East), *Journal of Sino-Western Communications*, July 2011.

48. Hua Tao, "Wenhua Duihua Yu Zhongguo Chuantong Wenhua Fanshi Zhong de Zhang'ai" (Cultural Dialogue and Obstacles in the Paradigms of Traditional Chinese Culture), *Nanjing University Journal*, no. 1, 2003; Hua Tao, "Tanxi Xinjiang de Lishi, Wenhua Yu Minzu" (Exploring Xinjiang's History, Culture, and Nationalities), *Nanjing Library Lectures*, August 28, 2010.

49. Robyn Iredale, Naran Bilik, and Fei Guo, eds., *China's Minorities on the Move: Selected Case Studies*, London: M. E. Sharpe, 2003; Shan Wei, "Explaining Ethnic Protests and Ethnic Policy Changes in China," *International Journal of China Studies*, October 2010; Ma Rong, "A New Perspective in Guiding Ethnic Relations in the 21st Century: 'De-politicization' of Ethnicity in China," *Procedia-Social and Behavioral Sciences*, vol. 2, no. 5, 2010; "To De-politicize and Enculturalize Ethnicity? What's Wrong with China's Ethnic Relations," *Xinjiang Review*, November 1, 2011.

50. "Opening of the Fourth Nanjing University-Harvard Yanjing International Academic Conference on the Dialogue of Civilizations," iwr.cass.cn, Nanjing, June 11–14, 2010; Ding Kejia, "Wenhua Duihua Shijiao Xia de Hui-Rui Duihua" (Hui-Confucian Dialogue from the Perspective of the Dialogue of Civilizations), *Arab World Studies*, May 2011; Jonathan Hall-Eastman, "Professor Hua Tao on Islam in China," *SAIS Observer*, May 3, 2016.

51. Wu Bingbing, "Strategy and Politics in the Gulf as Seen from China," in Bryce Wakefield and Susan Levenstein, eds., *China and the Persian Gulf: Implications for the United States*, Washington, DC: Woodrow Wilson Center, 2011; Ye Hailin, Wu Bingbing, and Christophe Bahuet, "'New Silk Road' Can Be Tailored for Each Side," *Global Times*, March 31, 2014; Wu Bingbing and Li Weijian, "U.S. Focus Unchanged After Syria Attack," *Global Times*, April 16, 2017.

52. Sun Degang, *Duoyuan Pingheng Yu "Zhun Lianmeng" Lilun Yanjiu (Multipolarity and the Theory of "Quasi-alliances")*, Current Events Press, 2007; Degang Sun, "China's Soft Military Presence in the Middle East," *Middle East Institute Blog*, March 11, 2015.

53. Xu Yihua and Zou Lei, "Geo-religion and China's Foreign Strategies," *China Inernational Studies*, January/February, 2013; Niu Song and Rawya Gamil Metwally, "The Hajj and Its Impact on International Relations," *Journal of Middle Eastern and Islamic Studies (in Asia)*, vol. 10, no. 3, 2016.

54. Qian Xuming, *"Yidai Yilu" Zhanlue Beijing Xia Yu Zhongdong de Nengyuan Hezuo (The Belt and Road Initiatives and China-Middle East Energy Cooperation)*, Beijing: Shishi Chubanshe, 2015.

55. James G. McGann, "Chinese Think Tanks, Policy Advice and Global Governance," *Indiana University Research Center for Chinese Politics and Business*, March 2012; Xufeng Zhu, *The Rise of Think Tanks in China*, London and New York: Routledge, 2013; Xiaowei Zang and Chien-wen Kou, eds., *Elites and Governance in China*, Milton Park, Abingdon, Oxon: Routledge, 2013; Jérôme Doyon, François Godement, Angela Stanzel, and Abigaël Vasselier, "A Hundred Think Tanks Bloom in China," *European Council on Foreign Relations*, August 25, 2016.

56. Charles Horner and Eric Brown, "Beijing's Islamic Complex," *Wall Street Journal*, June 2, 2010; Shirong Chen, "China Scholars Warn of Growing National Arrogance," *BBC News*, August 11, 2010; Ye Hailin, Yang Rui, Du Ping, and Zhang Yiwu, "Cong Wu Du Dao Wu Du" (From Misreading to Poisoning), *Guoji Xianqui Daobao*, August 13, 2010; Rowan Callick, "Xi Jinping Push for 'Unyielding Atheists' Worries Religious Groups," *The Australian*, April 27, 2016.

57. Morris Rossabi, "China and the Islamic World," *Comparative Civilizations Review*: vol. 13, no. 13, 1985; Morris Rossabi, ed., *Eurasian Influences on Yuan China*, Singapore: Institute of Southeast Asian Studies, 2013.

58. Pamela Kyle Crossley, ed., *Empire at the Margins: Culture, Ethnicity, and Frontier in Early Modern China*, Berkeley: University of California Press, 2006; Peter C. Perdue, *China Marches West: The Qing Conquest of Central Eurasia*, Cambridge, MA: Harvard University Press, 2010.

59. Harm Langenkamp, "Conflicting Dreams of Global Harmony in US-PRC Silk Road Diplomacy," in Rebekah Ahrendt, Mark Ferraguto, and Damien Mahiet, eds., *Music and Diplomacy from the Early Modern Era to the Present*, New York: Palgrave Macmillan, 2014; Pepe Escobar, "Peace, Harmony and Happiness, Plus a Deluge of Yuan," *Asia Times*, May 15, 2017; Yang Yang, "Chinese, Foreign Experts Talk of Shared Values of Silk Road Program," *China Daily*, July 28, 2017.

Chapter 10

1. For examples of influential reform debates under Xi Jinping's predecessors see Zi Zhongyun, "Neng Fanxing Lishi de Minzu Cai You Guangming de Weilai" (Only a Nation That Can Reflect on Its History Will Have a Bright Future), *view.news.qq.com*, February 2, 2009; Li Rui, Hu Jiwei et al., "Zhixing Xianfa Di 35 Tiao, Feichu Yushen Zhi, Duixian Gongmin de Yanlun Chuban Ziyou!" (Implement Article 35 of the Constitution, Abolish Censorship, Honor the Citizenry's Speech and Press Freedoms!), *boxun.com*, October 11, 2010; David Bandurski, "Open Letter from Party Elders Calls for Free Speech," *China Media Project*, October 13, 2010; Zi Zhongyun, "Qimeng Yu Zhishi Fenzi de Chuantong" (Enlightenment and the Tradition of the Intellectuals), *aisixiang.com*, November 14, 2011; Zhang Lifan, "Zai Zhongguo Gaige Luntan de Fayin" (Pronouncement of the China Reform Forum), *cn.rfi.fr*, February 1,

2012; Deng Yuwen, "Hu Wen de Zhengzhi Yichan" (The Political Legacy of Hu and Wen), *caijing.com.cn*, September 5, 2012.

2. G. William Skinner, "Presidential Address: The Structure of Chinese History," *Journal of Asian Studies*, February 1985; Mark Henderson, G. William Skinner, and Lawrence W. Crissman, "A Hierarchical Regional Space Model for Contemporary China," Paper prepared for the Geoinformatics 1999 Conference, University of Michigan, June 20, 1999; Lawrence W. Crissman, "G. William Skinner's Spatial Analysis of Complex Societies: Its Importance for Anthropology," *Taiwan Journal of Anthropology*, vol. 8, no. 1, 2010; Meg E. Rithmire, "China's 'New Regionalism': Subnational Analysis in Chinese Political Economy," *World Politics*, January 2014.

3. The Chinese text and English translation of the speech are available from Xinhua. Xi Jinping, "Xieshou Tuijin 'Yi Dai Yi Lu' Jianshe" (Work Together to Build the Silk Road Economic Belt and the Twenty-First Century Maritime Silk Road), *Xinhua*, May 16, 2017. In this version, Xi calls for building six major economic corridors across Asia, Europe, Africa, and the Americas, but he avoids mentioning the specific routes by name.

4. Yongnian Zheng, *De Facto Federalism in China: Reforms and Dynamics of Central-Local Relations*, Singapore: World Scientific, 2007; Andrew Wedeman, *Double Paradox: Rapid Growth and Rising Corruption in China*, Ithaca, NY: Cornell University Press, 2012; Nan-Hie In, "In China, A Tug of War between Local States and Beijing to Curb Organized Crime," *Forbes*, January 25, 2016.

5. Bruce J. Dickson, "Cooptation and Corporatism in China: The Logic of Party Adaptation," *Political Science Quarterly*, Winter, 2000–2001; Jude Howell, "Civil Society, Corporatism and Capitalism in China," *Journal of Comparative Asian Development*, October 2012; Jennifer Y. J. Hsu and Reza Hasmath, eds., *The Chinese Corporatist State: Adaptation, Survival and Resistance*, London and New York: Routledge, 2013; Jonathan Unger and Anita Chan, "State Corporatism and Business Associations in China: A Comparison with Earlier Emerging Economies of East Asia," *International Journal of Emerging Markets*, vol. 10, no. 2, 2015.

6. Joshua Steimle, "How China Can Lead the World, And Why Hong Kong Is the Key," *Forbes*, September 10, 2013; Ma Jian, "Hong Kong: The River of Democracy Will Flow to Tiananmen Square," *The Guardian*, October 3, 2014; Eric X. Li, "The Umbrella Revolution Won't Give Hong Kong Democracy," *Washington Post*, October 6, 2014; Peter Guy, "Hong Kong's (Dys)functional Constituencies Simply Help Big Business Defend the Status Quo and Oppress the Economy," *South China Morning Post*, October 20, 2016; Antony Dapiran et al., "Is Hong Kong on Its Way to Becoming Just Another City in the P.R.C?" *ChinaFile.com*, March 31, 2017.

7. Tanna Chong, "Legco Election 2016: How a Handful of Voters Elect 30 Hong Kong Lawmakers," *South China Morning Post*, February 6, 2014; Jeffie Lam and Joyce Ng, "Dubious Voters for Hong Kong's Legislative Council Functional Constituencies Revealed," *South China Morning Post*, July 4, 2016; Kris Cheng, "12 LegCo Functional Constituency Seats Automatically Filled as Nominees Stand Uncontested," *Hong Kong Free Press*, July 30, 2016; James Griffiths and Vivian Kam, "Hong Kong Votes: Is This the World's Weirdest Election?" *CNN*, September 2016.

8. Bryan Ho, "Village Democracy Shrugs in Rural China," *East Asia Forum*, July 22, 2014; "The Power of Fish: A Peculiar Distortion in Hong Kong's Political Structure," *The Economist*, March 5, 2015; Salvatore Babones, "A Rural Incubator for China's Political Reform?" *Foreign Affairs*, October 14, 2015; Clifford Coonan, "China Goes to Polls in Strictly Controlled Local Elections," *The Irish Times*, November 17, 2016.

9. Peregrine Horden and Nicholas Purcell, *The Corrupting Sea: A Study of Mediterranean History*, Oxford: Blackwell, 2000; Gabriel Piterberg, Teofilo F. Ruiz, and Geoffrey Symcox, eds., *Braudel Revisited: The Mediterranean World, 1600–1800*, Toronto: University of Toronto Press, 2010.

10. Mark Edward Lewis, *The Flood Myths of Early China*, Albany: State University of New York Press: 2006; Dennis Normile, "Massive Flood May Have Led to China's Earliest Empire," *Science*, August 4, 2016; David R. Montgomery, "What Science Can—And Can't—Tell Us about Legendary Ancient Figures Like China's Emperor Yu," *Washington Post*, August 5, 2016; Qinglong Wu, et al., "Outburst Flood at 1920 BCE Supports Historicity of China's Great Flood and the Xia Dynasty," *Science*, August 5, 2016.

11. Fernand Braudel, *The Mediterranean and the Mediterranean World in the Age of Philip II, Vol. 1*, Berkeley: University of California Press, 1996; Christopher Chase-Dunn and Salvatore J. Babones, eds., *Global Social Change: Historical and Comparative Perspectives*, Baltimore: Johns Hopkins University Press, 2006; Richard E. Lee, ed., *The Longue Duree and World-Systems Analysis*, Albany: State University of New York Press, 2012.

12. "More Than Minerals: Chinese Trade with Africa Keeps Growing: Fears of Neocolonialism Are Overdone," *The Economist*, March 23, 2013; "Neo-colonialism or De-colonialism? China's Economic Engagement in Africa and the Implications for World Order," *African Journal of Political Science and International Relations*, October 2014; Rafael Salazar, "Chinese Investment in Latin America: A Poisoned Chalice?" *Huffington Post*, June 19, 2015; David Roman, "China Is Transforming Southeast Asia Faster than Ever," *Bloomberg*, December 5, 2016.

13. Mark Hanrahan, "Asian Infrastructure Investment Bank Opposed by U.S., Seen as Attempt to Boost Chinese Influence," *International Business Times*, October 9, 2014; Sebastian Heilmann, Moritz Rudolf, Middo Huotari, and Johannes Buckow, "China's Shadow Foreign Policy: Parallel Structures Challenge the Established International Order," *MERICS China Monitor*, October 28, 2014; James F. Paradise, "The Role of 'Parallel Institutions' in China's Growing Participation in Global Economic Governance," *Journal of Chinese Political Science*, June 2016.

14. Soner Cagaptay, *The Rise of Turkey: The Twenty-First Century's First Muslim Power*, Herndon, VA: Potomac Books, 2014; Bruce Gilley and Andrew O'Neil, eds., *Middle Powers and the Rise of China*, Washington DC: Georgetown University Press, 2014; Robert W. Jordan, "Iran Could Become an Economic Superpower," *Time*, July 16, 2015; Vikram Nehru, "Indonesia: The Reluctant Giant," *The National Interest*, February 11, 2016; Kamal Alam, "Asia's Quiet Superpower: Pakistan Army's Teetering Balance between Saudi and Iran," *Middle East Eye*, March 2, 2017; Liesl Louw-Vaudran, "Nigeria Will Be Africa's First Global Superpower," *Mail and Guardian (South Africa)*,

May 29, 2017; Suzy Hansen and Norman Behrendt, "Reading Erdogan's Ambitions in Turkey's New Mosques," *New York Times*, June 14, 2017.

15. Chris Buckley, "Studies Point to Inequalities That Could Strain Chinese Society," *New York Times*, January 27, 2016.

16. Joe Zhang, "The Disintegration of Rural China," *New York Times*, November 28, 2014.

17. Ian Johnson, "China's Great Uprooting: Moving 250 Million into Cities," *New York Times*, June 15, 2013; Ian Johnson, "New China Cities: Shoddy Homes, Broken Hope," *New York Times*, November 9, 2013.

18. Deng Yuwen, "Seven Spheres of Interest," china.org, May 4, 2013; Stephen Harner, "Why David Shambaugh's 'Coming Chinese Crackup' Case Is Wrong," *Forbes*, March 10, 2015; Orville Schell, "China's Once and Future Democracy," *Wall Street Journal*, March 31, 2017; Anders Corr, "Waiting for China to Democratize? Holding Your Breath May Be Fatal," *Forbes*, April 3, 2017.

19. Chloé Froissart, "The Rise of Social Movements among Migrant Workers: Uncertain Strivings for Autonomy," *China Perspectives*, no. 61, 2005; Kevin J. O'Brien and Lianjiang Li, *Rightful Resistance in Rural China*, Cambridge: Cambridge University Press, 2006; Scott Kennedy, *The Business of Lobbying in China*, Cambridge, MA, Harvard University Press, 2008; Jonathan Benney and Peter Marolt, "Introduction: Modes of Activism and Engagement in the Chinese Public Sphere," *Asian Studies Review*, vol. 39, no. 1, 2015; Cynthia Estlund, *A New Deal for China's Workers?* Cambridge, MA: Harvard University Press, 2017.

20. Diana Fu, "Disguised Collective Action in China," *Comparative Political Studies*, February 2016; Yuen Yuen Ang, "Co-optation and Clientelism: Nested Distributive Politics in China's Single-Party Dictatorship," *Studies in Comparative International Development*, September 2016; Xiaoying Qi, "Social Movements in China: Augmenting Mainstream Theory with *Guanxi*," *Sociology*, February 1, 2017.

21. Yu-Wen Chen, "Internet and Interest Articulation in China, A Theoretical Re-examination," *First Monday*, January 2, 2012; Junko Oikawa, "China's Struggle for Civil Society: A New Perspective on Social Development," *The Tokyo Foundation*, September 26, 2013; "China Encourages Environmental Groups to Sue Polluters," *The Guardian*, January 7, 2015; Scott Wilson, "China's NGO Regulations and Uneven Civil Society Development," *China Policy Institute*, February 15, 2017.

22. Guosheng Deng and Scott Kennedy, "Big Business and Industry Association Lobbying in China: The Paradox of Contrasting Styles," *The China Journal*, January 2010; David A. Steinberg and Victor C. Shih, "Interest Group Influence in Authoritarian States: The Political Determinants of Chinese Exchange Rate Policy," *Comparative Political Studies*, November 2012; He Wei Ping, "Regulatory Capture in China's Banking Sector," *Journal of Banking Regulation*, January 2013; Simon Denyer, "A Young Man Died in Police Custody, and Middle-Class Chinese Are Outraged," *New York Times*, December 31, 2016; Simon Denyer, "Stop Making Our Children Sick: Beijing Parents Force Government Action over Smog," *New York Times*, January 6, 2017.

23. Wei Cheng, *Suowei Zhongchan: Yingguo "Jinrong Shibao" Zhongwen Wang Dui Zhongguo Zhongchan Jieceng de Diaocha (China's Emerging Middle Class: A Survey by FTChinese.com)*, Guangzhou: Nanfang Ribao Chubanshe, 2007; Minxin Pei, "China's

Middle Class Is about to Demand Big Changes," *Fortune*, May 26, 2016; Mandy Zuo, "China's Middle Class to Rise to More than Third of Population by 2030, Research Firm Says," *South China Morning Post*, November 3, 2016.

24. "The Rural-Urban Divide: Ending Apartheid," *The Economist*, April 19, 2014; Karoline Kan, "Shanghai's Move to Curb International Programs in Schools Worries Parents," *New York Times*, December 29, 2016; Lauren Teixeira, "China's Middle Class Anger at Its Education System Is Growing," *Foreign Policy*, February 6, 2017; Rowan Callick, "Meet China's Middle Class," *The Australian*, May 4, 2017.

Chapter 11

1. G. William Skinner, ed., *The City in Late Imperial China*, Stanford, CA: Stanford University Press, 1977; G. William Skinner, *Marketing and Social Structure in Rural China*, Ann Arbor, MI: Association for Asian Studies, 2001.

2. Zheng Yongnian, Zhao Litao, and Sarah Y. Tong, eds., *China's Great Urbanization*, New York: Routledge, 2017.

3. Michael Totty, "The Rise of the Smart City," *Wall Street Journal*, April 16, 2017; Hatem Zeine, "The Problems with Smart Cities," *Forbes*, June 19, 2017; Oliver Wainwright, "The City Is Ours Review—Will Vertical Forests and Smart Street Lights Really Save the Planet?" *The Guardian*, July 13, 2017.

4. Wang Xinsong, "One Belt, One Road's Governance Deficit Problem: How China Can Ensure Transparency and Accountability," *Foreign Affairs*, November 17, 2017.

5. Elinor Ostrom, "Managing Resources in the Global Commons," *Journal of Business Administration and Policy Analysis*, vol. 30—31, 2002; Gerald Stang, "Global Commons: Between Cooperation and Competition," *European Union Institute for Security Studies*, April 2013.

6. Michael T. Klare, *Resource Wars: The New Landscape of Global Conflict*, New York: Metropolitan Books, 2001; Pranab Bardhan and Isha Ray, eds., *The Contested Commons: Conversations between Economists and Anthropologists*, Malden, MA: Blackwell, 2008.

7. In contrast, for discussions of Islamic civilization's dual role in both authoring and disseminating innovation, see John M. Hobson, *The Eastern Origins of Western Civilisation*, New York: Cambridge University Press, 2004; Chris Lowney, *A Vanished World: Muslims, Christians, and Jews in Medieval Spain*, New York: Oxford University Press, 2006.

8. Marshall G. S. Hodgson, *The Venture of Islam: Conscience and History in a World Civilization*, Chicago: University of Chicago Press, 1974.

9. Michael J. Cohen, *Strategy and Politics in the Middle East, 1954–1960: Defending the Northern Tier*, London and New York: Frank Cass, 2005.

10. Henry A. Kissinger, "The Future of U.S.-Chinese Relations: Conflict Is a Choice, Not a Necessity," *Foreign Affairs*, March/April 2012; Ramon Pacheco Pardo, "Return of the G2: Can US and China Run the World?" *The Telegraph*, November 12, 2014; Robert Kahn, "China and the United States: A G2 within the G20," *Council on Foreign Relations*, April 2016.

11. Muhammad Iqbal, *The Reconstruction of Religious Thought in Islam*, London: Oxford University Press, 1934; Ali Shariati, *Hajj*, Bedford, OH: Free Islamic Literatures, 1977; Fazlur Rahman, *Islam and Modernity: Transformation of an*

Intellectual Tradition, Chicago: University of Chicago Press, 1982; Leonard Binder, *Islamic Liberalism: A Critique of Development Ideologies,* Chicago: University of Chicago Press, 1988; Charles Kurzman, ed., *Liberal Islam: A Source Book*, New York: Oxford University Press, 1998; Mohammed Arkoun, *The Unthought in Contemporary Islamic Thought*, London: Saqi Books, 2002.

12. Peter Gran, *Islamic Roots of Capitalism: Egypt, 1760–1840*, Austin: University of Texas Press, 1979; Abdullahi Ahmed An-Na'im, *Toward an Islamic Reformation: Civil Liberties, Human Rights, and International Law*, Syracuse, NY: Syracuse University Press, 1996; George Saliba, *Islamic Science and the Making of the European Renaissance*, Cambridge, MA: The MIT Press, 2007.

13. Ben Blanchard and Sue-Lin Wong, "China's New Silk Road Promises Trade and Riches, With President Xi at Helm," *Reuters*, May 14, 2017; James Griffiths, "China's New World Order: Xi, Putin and Others Meet for Belt and Road Forum," *CNN*, May 14, 2017; Tetsushi Takahashi, "Belt and Road Conference Is Xi's Time to Shine," *Nikkei Asian Review*, May 16, 2017.

14. Alix Culbertson, "Chinese Mock Europe for 'Being Taken Over by Muslims'—As More Mosques Are Built in China," *Express*, September 14, 2016; Gerry Shih, "Islamophobia in China on the Rise Fueled By Online Hate Speech," *The Independent*, April 10, 2017.

15. "America Is Wrong to Obstruct China's Asian-Infrastructure Bank," *The Economist*, March 19, 2015; Ben Blanchard, "China Says All Welcome at Silk Road Forum After U.S. Complains over North Korea," *Reuters*, May 13, 2017; Richard Javad Heydarian, "China's Silk Road Project: A Trap or an Opportunity?" *Al-Jazeera*, May 17, 2017.

16. "Merkel: Germany, China Must Expand Partnership in 'Times of Global Uncertainty,'" *Deutsche Welle*, June 1, 2017; Ben Blanchard, "West Underestimates China's New Silk Road, German Envoy Says," *Reuters*, June 8, 2017.

17. Marc Lanteigne, "China and Norway: Cold Shoulder No More, Following Diplomatic Thaw," *Arctic Deeply*, January 3, 2017; Timothy Gardner, "Hidden Tensions between the U.S., China, and Russia Emerge at Arctic Council Meeting Hosted by Rex Tillerson," *Reuters*, May 12, 2017.

18. Tobias Buck, "China's Migrants Thrive in Spain's Financial Crisis," *Financial Times*, October 9, 2014; Stephanie Kirchgaessner, "Italy Seeks to Reassure Asian Tourists with Imported Chinese Police," *The Guardian*, May 4, 2016; Jessie Pang, "De Yiwu a Madrid. Conoce la línea de tren más larga del mundo," *Estrella Digital*, November 20, 2016; Douglas Bulloch, "Textile Wars: Will 'Made in Italy' Replace 'Made in China'?" *Forbes*, February 16, 2017; Jason Horowitz and Liz Alderman, "Chastised by E.U., a Resentful Greece Embraces China's Cash and Interests," *New York Times*, August 26, 2017.

19. Tom Phillips, "Britain Has Made 'Visionary' Choice to Become China's Best Friend, Says Xi," *The Guardian*, October 18, 2015; Jacob Dryer, "Could China Be the New Best Friend for a Post-Brexit Britain?" *New Statesman*, July 6, 2017.

20. Tim Sculthorpe, "David Cameron Is Given Special Permission to Take a New Job Brokering Talks between Britain and China," *Daily Mail*, December 17, 2017; Bruno Maçães, "David Cameron Didn't Just Sell Out to China," *Foreign Policy*, December 20, 2017.

21. Tridivesh Singh Maini, "Japan's Effort to Counter China's Silk Road," *The Globalist*, April 6, 2016; Wade Shepard, "Japan Ups Its Game against China's Belt and Road," *Forbes*, December 1, 2016.

22. Prem Shankar Jha, "Modi's Beijing Policy Is Like Cutting Off India's Nose to Spite China's Face," *The Wire*, May 12, 2017; Sanjeev Miglani, "India Cool on Beijing Summit as 'Silk Road' Stirs Unease," *Reuters*, May 13, 2017.

23. Franz-Stefan Gady, "Indian Navy Practices Sinking Chinese Subs in Largest-Ever Military Exercise," *The Diplomat*, February 10, 2017; Abhijit Iyer-Mitra, "The Problem with India's Naval Build-Up," *Live Mint*, March 15, 2017.

24. Greg Earl, "Opinion Poll Reveals Australians Split over What to Do about the U.S. and China," *Australian Financial Review*, June 10, 2016; Peter Williams, "Clear Air for China's Silk Road Project," *The West Australian*, May 19, 2017; "2017 Lowy Institute Poll," *Lowy Institute for International Policy*, June 22, 2017.

25. Eric DuVall, "Australia Eyeing Tough New Anti-immigrant Legislation to Combat 'People Smuggling,'" *United Press International*, October 29, 2016; Philip Wen, "Australia Receptive to China's Silk Road, But National Interest First," *Reuters*, May 14, 2017; Merriden Varrall, "A Chinese Threat to Australian Openness," *New York Times*, July 31, 2017.

26. Natasha Kuhrt, "Russia and Asia-Pacific: Diversification or Sinocentrism?" in David Cadier and Margot Light, eds, *Russia's Foreign Policy: Ideas, Domestic Politics and External Relations*, London: Palgrave Macmillan, 2015; Joshua Kucera, "Is Russia in Europe or Asia? Why Not Both?" *Slate*, February 13, 2017.

27. Rinat Mukhametov, "Russian Muslims and Foreign Policy," *Global Affairs*, October 7, 2012; Alexey Malashenko and Alexey Starostin, "The Rise of Nontraditional Islam in the Urals," *Carnegie Moscow Center*, September 30, 2015; Alexey Malashenko, "Divisions and Defiance among Russia's Muslims," *Carnegie Moscow Center*, November 20, 2015.

28. Robert D. Crews, "Moscow and the Mosque: Co-opting Muslims in Putin's Russia," *Foreign Affairs*, March/April, 2014; Vasily Rudich, "Russia's Muslim Reality," *Foreign Affairs*, May/June, 2014; Julia Ioffe, "Putin Is Down with Polygamy," *Foreign Policy*, July 24, 2015.

29. Wade Shepard, "Investors from East and West Eager to Get a Piece of Russian High-Speed Rail Action," *Forbes*, November 15, 2016; Eva Grey, "Moscow-Kazan Rail Project Advances Hopes for Eurasian Connectivity," *Railway Technology*, November 21, 2016; "Russia, China to Build High-Speed Rail Link," *Sputnik*, February 10, 2017; "Russia Asks China to Boost Moscow-Kazan Fast-Speed Rail Project Financing," *TASS*, May 18, 2017.

30. Ruslan Kurbanov, "Tatarstan: Smooth Islamization Sprinkled with Blood," *Islam.ru*, February 27, 2013; Ronan Keenan, "Tatarstan: The Battle over Islam in Russia's Heartland," *World Policy Institute*, Summer 2013; Ildar Gabidullin and Maxim Edwards, "Crimea Crisis: The Tatarstan Factor," *Al-Jazeera*, March 15, 2014; Egor Lazarev and Anna Biryukova, "Are Russia's 20 Million Muslims Seething about Putin Bombing Syria?" *Washington Post*, March 7, 2016.

31. Paul Goble, "A 'Hybrid Islam' Is Emerging in Russia, Malashenko Says," *The Interpreter*, October 29, 2014.

32. Nadège Rolland, *China's Eurasian Century? Political and Strategic Implications of the Belt and Road Initiative*, Washington, DC: National Bureau of Asian Research, May 2017; Lazaro Gamio and Erica Pandey, "The Staggering Scale of China's Belt and Road Initiative," *Axios*, January 19, 2018; Ely Ratner, "Geostrategic and Military Drivers and Implications of the Belt and Road Initiative," *Council on Foreign Relations*, January 25, 2018.

SELECTED BIBLIOGRAPHY

"A Dollar Crisis Threatens Egypt's Economy." *Stratfor*, March 10, 2016.
"A History of Iran's Nuclear Program." *Iran Watch*, August 9, 2016.
Aamir, Adnan. "China-Punjab Economic Corridor." *The Nation*, April 24, 2015.
Aamir, Adnan. "Calling CPEC, China-Punjab Economic Corridor Is Not a Mistake." *The Nation*, May 1, 2015.
Abdenur, Adriana Erthal and Danilo Marcondes de Souza Neto. "China's Growing Influence in the South Atlantic." *BRICS Policy Center*, October 2013.
Abioye, Oye, Kadom Shubber, and John Koenigsberger. "Evaluating the Role and Impact of Railway Transport in the Nigerian Economy, Options and Choices: Case of Nigerian Railway Corporation." *AshEse Journal of Economics*, October 2016.
Abioye, Oyekanmi. *Privatisation of the Nigerian Railway Corporation: An Evaluation of Critical Choices*. Doctoral Dissertation, Cardiff Metropolitan University, April 2016.
Abraham, Thomas Kutty. "Why Indonesia Is Chasing China's Billions." *Bloomberg*, October 31, 2016.
Abrar, Mian. "China Mulling Trade Route with Iran as Pak Leadership Bickers." *Pakistan Today*, January 30, 2016.
Abrar, Mian. "China to Build Dams in Pakistan." *Pakistan Today*, May 13, 2017.
"Abuja-Kano Light Rail Project 'Dumped.'" *Railways Africa*, December 19, 2010.
Abul-Magd, Zeinab. *Militarizing the Nation: The Army, Business, and Revolution in Egypt*. New York: Columbia University Press, 2017.
Abu-Lughod, Janet L. *Before European Hegemony: The World System A.D. 1250–1350*. New York: Oxford University Press, 1989.
Acharya, Amitav and Barry Buzan, eds. *Non-Western International Relations Theory: Perspectives on and Beyond Asia*. New York: Routledge, 2010.
Adamu, Aminu. "Nigeria Secures $7.5 Billion Loan from China for Rail Project—Amaechi." *Premium Times*, February 6, 2017.
Adebayo, Hassan. "Buhari Writes Senate, Hands Over to Vice President Osinbajo." *Premium Times*, June 7, 2016.

Adepegba, Adelani. "China Disburses $30bn Industrialisation Fund to Nigeria, Others." *Punch*, November 3, 2017.

Adibe, Jideofor. "Reality Check—Nigeria's Sense of Entitlement Cannot Stand Empirical Examination." *ynaija.com*, January 27, 2017.

Adıbelli, Barış, "Türkiye'nin Avrasya Politikasi Çöktü!" (Turkey's Eurasia Policy Has Collapsed!). *Radikal*, August 16, 2008.

Adichie, Chimamanda Ngozi. "A Nigerian Revolution: The Political Awakening of My Country's Young People Could Transform Nigeria's Rotten Democracy." *The Guardian*, March 16, 2011.

Adshead, S.A.M. *Central Asia in World History*. London: St. Martin's Press, 1993.

Ahmed, Akbar. "Is Pakistan Heading for Disaster in Balochistan?" *Al-Jazeera*, January 15, 2012.

Ahmed, Khaled. *Sleepwalking to Surrender: Dealing with Terrorism in Pakistan*. London: Penguin, 2016.

Ahmed, Mohamed. "Future of Suez Canal Revenues Hostage to International Currencies Struggle." *Daily News (Egypt)*, February 21, 2016.

Ajimotokan, Olawale. "China's Support for Nigeria's Digital Switch Over Project Exciting, Says Lai Mohammed." *This Day*, July 6, 2016.

Akande, Segun. "Is China Taking Advantage of Nigeria with Loans and Grants?" *pulse.ng*, September 10, 2017.

Akbar, Malik Siraj. "Tensions Mount between India and Pakistan over Balochistan." *Huffington Post*, March 27, 2016.

Akbar, Malik Siraj. "Why Modi's Statements Should Be the Least of Our Worries on Balochistan." *Dawn*, August 20, 2016.

Akef, Walid. "5 Years after the Revolution, Egypt's a Hell after a Paradise." *Huffington Post*, January 25, 2016.

Akinsanmi, Gboyega and Benneth Oghifo. "Nigeria: Govt, China to Finalise $11 Billion Lagos-Calabar Rail Deal in June." *All Africa*, March 8, 2017.

Akinyemi, Lafenwa Stephen. "Civil Society and the Anti-Corruption Struggle in Nigeria." *International Journal of Business and Social Science*, March 2016, 115–127.

Alam, Kamal. "Asia's Quiet Superpower: Pakistan Army's Teetering Balance between Saudi and Iran." *Middle East Eye*, March 2, 2017.

Alao, Tunde. "Buhari, Conservationists Decry Illegal Logging in Nigeria." *Nigerian Tribune*, January 4, 2017.

Alberti, Marina. *Cities That Think Like Planets: Complexity, Resilience, and Innovation in Hybrid Ecosystems*. Seattle: University of Washington Press, 2016.

Aleem, Ahmed. "Egypt Hopes Chinese Visitors Can Make Up for Russian Tourism Decline." *Al-Monitor*, March 6, 2017.

Alemdaroğlu, Ayça. "From Cynicism to Protest: Reflections on Youth and Politics in Turkey." *jadaliyya.com*, July 18, 2013.

Ali, Muhamad. "Chinese Muslims in Colonial and Postcolonial Indonesia." *Explorations*, vol. 7, no. 2, Spring 2007, 1–22.

Ali, Shafqat. "No Favouratism in CPEC: China." *The Nation*, October 6, 2016.

Alimukhamedov, Farkhad. "Turkey's Central Asia Policy in the Changing World: Priorities, Policies and Actions." *South-East European Journal of Political Science*, January–June 2016.

"All-Party Conference: Consensus on Trade Route Eludes Confab." *awaztoday.pk*, May 15, 2015.

Allès, Élisabeth. *Musulmans de Chine, Une Anthropologie des Hui du Henan*. Paris: Éditions de l'EHESS, 2000.

Allison, Graham. *Destined for War: Can America and China Escape Thucydides's Trap?* Boston and New York: Houghton Mifflin Harcourt, 2017.

Almuttaqi, A. Ibrahim. "ASEAN Still the Cornerstone of Indonesia's Foreign Policy." *Jakarta Post*, March 17, 2017.

Al-Naggar, Ahmed El-Sayed. "Egypt and China: The Potential for Stronger Economic Ties." *Al-Ahram Online*, October 21, 2016.

Al-Sudairi, Mohammed Turki. "Sino-Saudi Relations: An Economic History." *GRC Gulf Papers*, August 2012.

Al-Sudairi, Mohammed. "Chinese Salafism and the Saudi Connection." *The Diplomat*, October 23, 2014.

Alwadi, Karim. *Zhenshi de Libanen Zhenzhudang* (The Real Story of Hezbollah). Beijing: World Knowledge Publishers, 2015.

Aly, Baber. "CPEC and Security of Chinese Engineers." *Pakistan Today*, May 9, 2016.

"Amaechi: Work on Lagos-Kano Rail Line to Begin This Year." *The News (Lagos)*, April, 25, 2016.

"America Is Wrong to Obstruct China's Asian-Infrastructure Bank." *The Economist*, March 19, 2015.

American Enterprise Institute. "China Global Investment Tracker." *aei.org*, 2017.

Amirullah. "Labor Union Demands Free-Visa Policy to Be Dropped." *Tempo*, December 27, 2016.

Amitai, Reuven and Michal Biran, eds. *Nomads as Agents of Cultural Change: The Mongols and Their Eurasian Predecessors*. Honolulu: University of Hawaii Press, 2015.

Andaya, Barbara Watson. "Oceans Unbounded: Transversing Asia across 'Area Studies.'" *Journal of Asian Studies*, vol. 65, no. 4, November 2006, 669–690.

Ang, Yuen Yuen. "Co-optation and Clientelism: Nested Distributive Politics in China's Single-Party Dictatorship." *Studies in Comparative International Development*, September 2016, 235–256.

"Angry Protestors Force Rouhani to Flee Rally in Tehran." *Center for Human Rights in Iran*, June 23, 2017.

"Anies' Victory Raises Muslim Dignity in Politics: PKS." *Jakarta Post*, April 26, 2017.

An-Na'im, Abdullahi Ahmed. *Toward an Islamic Reformation: Civil Liberties, Human Rights, and International Law*. Syracuse, NY: Syracuse University Press, 1996.

Anthony, David W. *The Horse, the Wheel, and Language: How Bronze-Age Riders from the Eurasian Steppes Shaped the Modern World*. Princeton, NJ: Princeton University Press, 2010.

Anti, Michael. "Behind the Great Firewall of China." *TED Global*, June 2012.

"Anti-China Protests in Turkey Take Toll on Economic Ties." *Today's Zaman*, July 6, 2015.

Aras, Damia. "Turkey's Ambassadors vs. Erdoğan." *The Middle East Quarterly*, vol. 18, no. 1, Winter 2011.

Archdeacon, Olivia. "China Adds Nigeria to Its African Empire." *capx.com*, April 14, 2016.
Arif, Muhammad. "CPEC Route, Agreed by APC, Being Implemented in Letter and Spirit: Minister." *nihao-salam.com*, October 13, 2015.
Arifianto, Alexander R. "Jakarta Governor Election Results in a Victory for Prejudice over Pluralism." *Jakarta Globe*, April 19, 2017.
Arinze Iloani, Francis. "Nigeria: China, Nigeria Trade Imbalance Hits N1.67 Trillion in Five Years." *Daily Trust*, July 5, 2016.
Arkoun, Mohammed. *The Unthought in Contemporary Islamic Thought*. London: Saqi Books, 2002.
Armstrong, William. "Eurasianism in Modern Turkey." *Hürriyet Daily News*, May 18, 2017.
Arteh, Abdourahim. "Djibouti Breaks Ground on Massive Chinese-Backed Free Trade Zone." *Reuters*, January 16, 2017.
Ashford, Emma. "The Trump Administration's Iran Policy Is Dangerous and Flawed." *The Guardian*, May 23, 2017.
Ashiwa, Yoshiko and David L. Wank. *Making Religion, Making the State: The Politics of Religion in Modern China*. Stanford, CA: Stanford University Press, 2009.
Asma, Stephen T. "From China, With Pragmatism." *New York Times*, June 8, 2014.
Atlı, Altay. "Questioning Turkey's China Trade." *Turkish Policy Quarterly*, November 2011, 107–116.
Atli, Altay. "China and Turkey Rev Up Efforts to Strengthen Ties." *Asia Times*, November 8, 2016.
Atli, Altay. "Does Turkey Have to Choose between Brussels and Shanghai?" *Asia Times*, November 29, 2016.
Aubin, Françoise. "La Version Chinoise de L'Islam." *European Journal of Sociology*, November 1989, 192–220.
Aubin, Françoise. "Islam on the Wings of Nationalism: The Case of Muslim Intellectuals in Republican China." In Stéphane A. Dudoignon, Komatsu Hisao, and Dosugi Yaushi, eds. *Intellectuals in the Modern Islamic World: Transmission, Transformation, Communication*. London: Routledge, 2006, 241–272.
Awami National Party. "Pakhtunkhwa's Case Against Kalabagh Dam." *awaminationalparty.org*, May 29, 2013.
Axe, David. "Donald Trump Is Handing China the World." *Daily Beast*, January 30, 2017.
Aymard, Maurice. "De la Méditerranée à l'Asie: une comparaison nécessarire (commentaire)." *Annales*, no. 1, 2001, 43–50.
Azhar, Bushra. "Egypt's Toshka New Valley Project: A Failure of Planning or a Failure of Implementation." *greenprophet.com*, May 6, 2012.
Babones, Salvatore. "A Rural Incubator for China's Political Reform?" *Foreign Affairs*, October 14, 2015.
Bağci, Hüseyin. "Turkey, Central Asia and Islam." *Hürriyet Daily News*, June 29, 2000.
Bai, Gao. "Zhongguo Xiehou Yisilan Shijie" (China Encounters the Islamic World). *China Times*, January 23, 2016.
Bai, Yunyi. "Zhong Mei Xuezhe Yanzhong de Daguo Boyi Yu Nanhai Fenzheng: Zhong Mei Zuizhong Shifou 'Bi You Yi Zhan?' " (The Great Game and the South China

Sea Dispute in the Eyes of Chinese and American Scholars: Is a Sino-American War "Inevitable"?). *huanqiu.com*, September 28, 2016.

Bakar, Osman, ed. *Islam and Confucianism: A Civilizational Dialogue*. Kuala Lumpur: University of Malaysia Press, 1997.

Bakker, Laurens. "Illegality for the General Good? Vigilantism and Social Responsibility in Contemporary Indonesia." *Critique of Anthropology*, March 3, 2015, 78–93.

Bala, Arun and Prasenjit Duara, eds. *The Bright Dark Ages: Comparative and Connective Perspectives*. Leiden/Boston: Brill, 2016.

Baldauf, Scott. "Chinua Achebe on Corruption and Hope in Nigeria." *Christian Science Monitor*, March 22, 2013.

"Balochistan: Where India, China and Pakistan Are Playing the Great Game." *newslaundry.com*, September 21, 2016.

Bandow, Doug. "Nervous China Ramps Up Religious Persecution." *Japan Times*, April 17, 2017.

Bandurski, David. "Open Letter from Party Elders Calls for Free Speech." *China Media Project*, October 13, 2010.

Bang, Anne K. *Islamic Sufi Networks in the Western Indian Ocean (c. 1880–1940): Ripples of Reform*. Leiden/Boston: Brill, 2014.

"Bank of China to Start Operation in Turkey by End of This Year." *China Daily*, November 7, 2016.

Baraniuk, Chris. "Cheap Oil Is Taking Shipping Routes Back to the 1880s." *BBC*, March 4, 2016.

Bardhan, Pranab and Isha Ray, eds. *The Contested Commons: Conversations between Economists and Anthropologists*. Malden, MA: Blackwell, 2008.

Bardsley, Daniel. "China Shifts to More 'Authentic' Arabian-Style Mosques." *The National (UAE)*, July 12, 2012.

Bardsley, Daniel. "Yiwu Is the 'Fastest Growing Muslim Community' in China." *The National (UAE)*, August 12, 2012.

Barthelmy, Marc, Patricia Bordin, Henri Berestycki, and Maurizio Gribaudi. "Self-Organization versus Top-down Planning in the Evolution of a City." *Scientific Reports*, July 2013, 1–12.

Barzegar, Kayhan. "The Balance of Power in the Persian Gulf: An Iranian View." *Middle East Policy*, Fall 2010, 74–87.

Bassin, Mark, Sergey Glebov, and Marlene Laruelle, eds. *Between Europe and Asia: The Origins, Theories, and Legacies of Russian Eurasianism*. Pittsburgh, PA: University of Pittsburgh Press, 2015.

Baswedan, Anies. "Political Islam in Indonesia: Present and Future Trajectory." *Asian Survey*, vol. 44, no. 5, September/October 2004, 669–690.

Bayhan, Bahar. "Kanal İstanbul'da İkinci Haliç Planı" (The Second Bosporus Plan of Kanal Istanbul). *Arkitera*, November 17, 2016.

Bax, Pauline. "Chinese Furniture Fashion Ravages West Africa's Savannas." *Bloomberg*, August 1, 2016.

"BBP Genel Sekreteri Destici, Çin Büyükelçiliği 1. Musteşari Junzheng İle Görüstü" (BBP General Secretary Destici Speaks with Chinese Embassy Undersecretary Junzheng). *medya73.com*, June 24, 2010.

Beauchamp-Mustafaga, Nathan. "China-Iran Relations: China's Hawks Condemn U.S. Influence." *European Council on Foreign Relations*, October 2013.

Beaujard, Philippe. "The Indian Ocean in Eurasian and African World-Systems before the Sixteenth Century." *The Journal of World History*, December 2005, 411–465.

Beaujard, Philippe. *Les Mondes de l'Ocean Indien (The Worlds of the Indian Ocean)*. Paris: Armand Colin, 2012.

Beaumont, Peter. "Turkish Troops Take Part in Joint Military Exercises in Qatar." *The Guardian*, June 19, 2017.

Beckwith, Christopher I. *Empires of the Silk Road: A History of Central Eurasia from the Bronze Age to the Present*. Princeton, NJ: Princeton University Press, 2011.

Beech, Hannah. "Labor Unrest Grows in China, Even in the Historic Heartlands of Revolution." *Time*, April 10, 2016.

Bekkers, Eddy et al., "Melting Ice Caps and the Economic Impact of Opening the Northern Sea Route." *The Economic Journal*, December 16, 2016.

Belford, Aubrey. "Chinese Preachers Bridge Indonesia's Ethnic Gap." *New York Times*, July 14, 2010.

Bell, Daniel A. *China's New Confucianism: Politics and Everyday Life in a Changing Society*. Princeton, NJ: Princeton University Press, 2008.

Bellwood, Peter. *First Farmers: The Origins of Agricultural Societies*. Malden, MA: Wiley-Blackwell, 2004.

Benavides, Marissa. "When Soft Power Is Too Soft: Confucius Institutes' Nebulous Role in China's Soft Power Initiative." *Yale Review of International Studies*, August 2012.

Benite, Zvi Ben-Dor. "Chinese Islam: A Complete Concert." *Cross-Currents: East Asian History and Culture Review*, June 2017, 170–203.

Benkman, Craig W., Thomas L. Parchman, Amanda Favis, and Adam M. Siepielski. "Reciprocal Selection Causes a Coevolutionary Arms Race between Crossbills and Lodgepole Pine." *The American Naturalist*, August 2003, 182–194.

Benmayor, Gila. "Dragon and Crescent in the Asian Century." *Hurriyet Daily News*, December 27, 2016.

Benney, Jonathan and Peter Marolt. "Introduction: Modes of Activism and Engagement in the Chinese Public Sphere." *Asian Studies Review*, vol. 39, no. 1, 2015, 88–99.

Berger, Peter. "A Mixed Bag, Religious Hybrids." *The American Interest*, June 1, 2016.

Berman, Ilan. *Winning the Long War: Retaking the Offensive against Radical Islam*. Lanham, MD.: Rowman and Littlefield, 2009.

Berman, Ilan I. "To Stop Iran, Lean on China." *New York Times*, November 8, 2011.

Bermingham, Finbarr. "Chinese Banks Pump Money into Egypt." *Global Trade Review*, April 25, 2017.

Bezlova, Antoaneta. "Sanctions Give China an Advantage in Iran." *Iran Review*, August 2, 2010.

Bhutta, Zafar. "China to Invest $50b to Develop Indus River Cascade." *Express Tribune*, May 13, 2017.

Bianchi, Robert R. *Unruly Corporatism: Associational Life in Twentieth-Century Egypt*. New York: Oxford University Press, 1989.

Bianchi, Robert R. *Egypt's Revolutionary Elections*. The Singapore Middle East Papers, vol. 2, Summer 2012.

Bianchi, Robert R. *Islamic Globalization: Pilgrimage, Capitalism, Democracy, and Diplomacy*. Singapore and London: World Scientific, 2013.

Bianchi, Robert R. "Urban Backlash against Democracy: Battling the Tyranny of the Majority or the Rise of Rural Power?" In Roman Stadnicki, ed., *City and Revolution in Egypt*. Cairo: Le Centre d'Études et de Documentation Économiques, Juridiques et Sociales, 2014, 67–82.

Bianchi, Robert R. "Reimagining the Hajj." *Social Sciences*, vol. 6, no. 2, 2017, 1–26.

Bianchi, Robert R. "The Hajj and Politics in China." In Babak Rahimi and Peyman Eshagi, eds. *Muslim Pilgrimage in the Modern World*. Durham: North Carolina University Press, 2018.

Binder, Leonard. *Islamic Liberalism: A Critique of Development Ideologies*. Chicago: University of Chicago Press, 1988.

Bingdi, Wangtian. *Daguo Youxi: Kan Zhongguo Ruhe Ke Ying Shijie (The Great Game: How China Can Win the World)*. Beijing: World Knowledge, 2009.

Bisiriyu, Rasheed. "Nigerian Railway: A Tale of Failed Contracts, Dashed Hope." Punch, February 4, 2016.

Blackwill, Robert D. and Jennifer M. Harris. *War by Other Means: Geoeconomics and Statecraft*. Cambridge, MA: Harvard University Press, 2016.

Blanchard, Ben. "As Trump Stresses 'America First,' China Plays the World Leader." *Reuters*, January 25, 2017.

Blanchard, Ben. "Syria Says up to 5,000 Chinese Uighurs Fighting in Militant Groups." *Reuters*, May 8, 2017.

Blanchard, Ben. "China Says All Welcome at Silk Road Forum after U.S. Complains over North Korea." *Reuters*, May 13, 2017.

Blanchard, Ben. "West Underestimates China's New Silk Road, German Envoy Says." *Reuters*, June 8, 2017.

Blanchard, Ben and Sue-Lin Wong. "China's New Silk Road Promises Trade and Riches, With President Xi at Helm." *Reuters*, May 14, 2017.

Blinken, Antony J. "Why the Iran Nuclear Deal Must Stand." *New York Times*, February 17, 2017.

Bloodworth, Dennis and Ching Ping Bloodworth. *The Chinese Machiavelli: 3000 Years of Chinese Statecraft*. New Brunswick, NJ: Transaction Books, 2007.

Blussé, Leonard. "Chinese Century: The Eighteenth Century in the China Sea Region." *Archipel*, vol. 58, no. 3, 1999, 107–129.

Bo, Xiang. "One Silk Road, One Dream." *Xinhua*, May 6, 2017.

Bodeen, Christopher. "China, Key Iran Ally, Backs Nuclear Sanctions." *Associated Press*, June 10, 2010.

Boehler, Patrick. "China Pledges Help to Nigeria's Hunt for Boko Haram Militants." *Agence France-Presse*, May 8, 2014.

Bokhari, Farhan, Lucy Hornby, and Christian Shepherd. "China Urges Pakistan to Give Army Lead Role in Silk Road Project." *Financial Times*, July 21, 2016.

Boone, Jon and Kiyya Baloch. "A New Shenzhen? Poor Pakistan Fishing Town's Horror at Chinese Plans." *The Guardian*, February 3, 2016.

Bordachev, Timofei. "To Russia's Friends in Asia and Beyond." *Valdaiclub.com*, February 15, 2017.

Bovingdon, Gardner. *The Uyghurs: Strangers in Their Own Land*. New York: Columbia University Press, 2010.

Bozkurt, Abdullah. "China Seeks Further Engagement from Turkey in Xinjiang Region." *Today's Zaman*, April 1, 2012.

Bozorgmehr, Najmeh. "First Freight Trains from China Arrive in Tehran." *Financial Times*, May 9, 2016.

Böcü, Gözde. "The 'Gezi Generation': Youth, Polarization and the 'New Turkey.'" In Isabel Schäfer, ed. *Youth, Revolt, Recognition: The Young Generation During and After the "Arab Spring."* Berlin: Mediterranean Institute Berlin, 2015, 52–61.

Bradsher, Keith. "China Plans a New Silk Road, But Trade Partners Are Wary." *New York Times*, December 25, 2015.

Bradsher, Keith and Adam Nossiter. "In Nigeria, Chinese Investment Comes with a Downside." *New York Times*, December 5, 2015.

Branigan, Tania. "China Welcomes Binyamin Netanyahu." *The Guardian*, May 8, 2013.

Branigan, Tania. "China Bans Wordplay in Attempt at Pun Control." *The Guardian*, November 28, 2014.

Braudel, Fernand. *The Mediterranean and the Mediterranean World in the Age of Philip II*, Vol. 1. Berkeley: University of California Press, 1996.

Brautigam, Deborah. *Will Africa Feed China?* New York: Oxford University Press, 2015.

Brechenmacher, Saskia. "Institutionalized Repression in Egypt." In *Civil Society under Assault: Repression and Responses in Russia, Egypt, and Ethiopia*, Saskia Brechenmacher, ed. Washington, DC: Carnegie Endowment for International Peace, May 18, 2017.

Bria, Emanuel. "Why Do Indonesia, ASEAN Matter to China?" *The Straits Times*, January 6, 2017.

Brinza, Andreea. "China's Continent-Spanning Trains Are Running Half-Empty." *Foreign Policy*, June 5, 2017.

Bronstein, Judith L., Ulf Dieckmann, and Régis Ferrière. "Coevolutionary Dynamics and the Conservation of Mutualisms." In Régis Ferrière, Ulf Dieckmann, and Denis Couvet, eds. *Evolutionary Conservation Biology*. New York: Cambridge University Press, 2004, 305–326.

"Bronze Statue of Zhen He Inaugurated in Quanzhou." *People's Daily*, July 12, 2005.

Brown, Clayton D. "Making the Majority: Defining Han Identity in Chinese Ethnology and Archaeology." PhD dissertation, Department of History, University of Pittsburgh, 2008.

Brown, Rachel. "Beijing's Silk Road Goes Digital." *Council on Foreign Relations*, June 6, 2017.

Browning, Noah and Tom Finn. "Qatar Willing to Listen to Gulf Concerns, Kuwait Says." *Reuters*, June 11, 2017.

Buano, Tajudin and Gunawan, "Muslim Youths Helped Keep Indonesia's Christmas Peaceful." *Benarnews.org*, December 27, 2016.

Buck, Tobias. "China's Migrants Thrive in Spain's Financial Crisis." *Financial Times*, October 9, 2014.

Buckley, Chris. "Studies Point to Inequalities That Could Strain Chinese Society." *New York Times*, January 27, 2016.

Buckley, Chris. "China, Sending a Signal, Launches a Home-Built Aircraft Carrier." *New York Times*, April 25, 2017.

Bulloch, Douglas. "Textile Wars: Will 'Made in Italy' Replace 'Made in China'?" *Forbes*, February 16, 2017.

Burguière, André. *The Annales School: An Intellectual History*. Ithaca, NY: Cornell University Press, 2009.

Bush, Robin. "Regional 'Sharia' Regulations in Indonesia: Anomaly or Symptom?" In Greg Fealy and Sally White, eds., *Expressing Islam: Religious Life and Politics in Indonesia*. Singapore: Institute of Southeast Asian Studies, 2008, 174–191.

Butt, Naveed and Zaheer Abbasi. "CPEC Sovereign Guarantees May Not Augur Well for Budget." *Business Recorder*, January 26, 2017.

Cagaptay, Soner. *The Rise of Turkey: The Twenty-First Century's First Muslim Power*. Herndon, VA: Potomac Books, 2014.

Cai, Degui. "Yisilan Jiao He Zhongguo Chuantong Wenhua de Ronghe" (The Fusion of Islam and Traditional Chinese Culture). *Arab World*, no. 1, 1996, 63–69.

Cai, Zhizhong. *Manhua Daojia Sixiang: Zhuang Zi Shuo (Daoist Thought in Cartoons: Sayings of Zhuang Zi)*. Beijing: Shangwu Yinshuguan Chuban, 2009.

Cai, Zhizhong. *Cai Gen Tan Xin Jing: Rensheng de Ziwei (The Roots of Wisdom Heart Sutra: The Flavor of Life)*. Beijing: Xiandai Chubanshe, 2013.

Callick, Rowan. "Xi Jinping Push for 'Unyielding Atheists' Worries Religious Groups." *The Australian*, April 27, 2016.

Callick, Rowan. "Meet China's Middle Class." *The Australian*, May 4, 2017.

Calvino, Italo. *Invisible Cities*. Translated by William Weaver. London: Vintage Books, 1972.

Camazine, Scott, Jean-Louis Deneubourg, Nigel R. Franks, James Sneyd, Guy Theraulaz, and Eric Bonabeau, *Self-Organization in Biological Systems*. Princeton, NJ: Princeton University Press, 2003.

Cardenal, Juan Pablo and Heriberto Araújo. *China's Silent Army: The Pioneers, Traders, Fixers and Workers Who Are Remaking the World in Beijing's Image*. New York: Crown, 2013.

Carney, Matthew. "A Generation Left Behind: Millions of Chinese Children Abandoned as Parents Seek Work." *ABC News*, September 13, 2016.

Carrai, Maria Adele. "A Genealogy of Sovereignty in China, 1840–Today." PhD Dissertation, University of Hong Kong, 2015.

Casey, Tina. "Nigeria Debates $20 Million For Diesel-Killing, Off-Grid Solar Power." *cleantechnica.com*, March 8, 2017.

Castells, Manuel. *Networks of Outrage and Hope: Social Movements in the Internet Age*. Cambridge: Polity Press, 2015.

Cendrowski, Scott. "Alibaba's Jack Ma Expects the World to Experience Decades of 'Pain.'" *Fortune*, April 23, 2017.

Center for Human Rights in Iran. "Guardians at the Gate: The Expanding State Control over the Internet in Iran." *Center for Human Rights in Iran*, 2018.

Cevikoz, Unal. "Turkey in a Reconnecting Eurasia: Foreign Economic and Security Interests." *Center for Strategic and International Studies*, April 30, 2016.

Chakravarty, Pinak Ranjan. "China and Indonesia: A New Tug-of-War." *Observer Research Foundation Commentaries*, October 13, 2017.

Champion, Marc. "Iran Is Stuck with China to Finance Its Oil Dreams." *Bloomberg*, October 12, 2016.

Chan, Francis. "Jakarta's New Governor Anies Baswedan Gets Flak for 'Racist' Comments on His First Day in Office." *The Straits Times*, October 18, 2017.

Chan, Sin Yee. "Tang Junyi: Moral Idealism and Chinese Culture." In Chung-Ying Cheng and Nicholas Bunnin, eds. *Contemporary Chinese Philosophy*, Malden, MA: Blackwell, 2002, 305–326.

Chang, K.C. "Xia Nai (1910–1985)." *American Anthropologist*, vol. 88, June 1986, 442–444.

Chang, Pin-tsun. "The Rise of Chinese Mercantile Power in Maritime Southeast Asia, c. 1400–1700." *Crossroads*, vol. 6, 2012, 205–230.

Changming, Yao Liu and Yao Shifan. "'Yidai Yilu' Chengyi Xia Zhongguo de Ouya Yiti Hua Zhanlue Yu Daxiyang Zhuyi" (China's Strategy of Eurasian Integration under 'One Belt One Road' and Atlanticism). *aisixiang.com*, November 12, 2016.

Chao, James. "After a 66-year Estrangement, Can China and the Catholic Church Kiss and Make Up?" *Newsweek*, May 2, 2017.

Charbel, Jano. "Nile Delta's Increasing Salinity and Rising Sea Levels May Make Egypt Uninhabitable by 2100." *madamasr.com*, March 16, 2017.

Chaudhuri, K. N. *Asia before Europe: Economy and Civilisation of the Indian Ocean from the Rise of Islam to 1750*. Cambridge: Cambridge University Press, 1990.

Chase-Dunn, Christopher and Salvatore J. Babones, eds. *Global Social Change: Historical and Comparative Perspectives*. Baltimore: Johns Hopkins University Press, 2006.

Chaziza, Mordechai. "The Red-Med Railway: New Opportunities for China, Israel, and the Middle East." *Begin-Sadat Center for Strategic Studies*, December 11, 2016.

Chellaney, Brahma. "China-Pakistan Water Pincer against India: As Part of CPEC, Mega-dams Are Planned in Gilgit-Baltistan." *Economic Times*, May 16, 2017.

Chen, Andrea. "Three Given Death Penalty over Kunming Rail Station Attack." *South China Morning Post*, September 12, 2014.

Chen, Jidong and Yiqing Xu. "Why Do Authoritarian Regimes Allow Citizens to Voice Opinions Publicly?" *The Journal of Politics*, vol. 79, no. 3, July 2017, 792–803.

Chen, Jingpu. "Zhongguo Sichou Zhi Lu Jingji Dai Yu Meiguo TPP: Diyuan Jingji Yu Diyuan Zhengzhi de Jiaoliang" (China's Silk Road Economic Belt and America's TPP: Geoeconomic and Geopolitical Competition). *sciencenet.cn*, October 12, 2015.

Chen, Liang. "China's Halal Food Exporters Struggle with Ideological, Trade Barriers." *Global Times*, November 26, 2014.

Chen, Liubing. "Fastest China-Europe Train Sets Record Time of 10.5 Days." *The Telegraph*, June 21, 2016.

Chen, Shirong. "China Scholars Warn of Growing National Arrogance." *BBC News*, August 11, 2010.

Chen, Te-Ping Chen. "China's Middle Class Vents over Growing List of Grievances." *Wall Street Journal*, May 24, 2016.

Chen, Xingcan. "Archaeological Discoveries in the People's Republic of China and Their Contribution to the Understanding of Chinese History." *Bulletin of the History of Archaeology*, vol. 19, no. 2, November 2009, 4–13.

Chen, Yu-Wen. "Internet and Interest Articulation in China a Theoretical Re-examination." *First Monday*, January 2, 2012.

Cheng, Eddie. "Alabo de Tian'anmen He Zhongguo de Molihua" (The Arab Tiananmen and the Chinese Jasmine). *tiananmenduizhi.com*, February 27, 2011.

Cheng, Evelyn. "Asia Pacific Nations Are Tilting Closer toward China as Trump Declares 'America First.'" *CNBC*, January 31, 2017.

Cheng, Kris. "12 LegCo Functional Constituency Seats Automatically Filled as Nominees Stand Uncontested." *Hong Kong Free Press*, July 30, 2016.

Cheng, Wei. *Suowei Zhongchan: Yingguo 'Jinrong Shibao' Zhongwen Wang Dui Zhongguo Zhongchan Jieceng de Diaocha (China's Emerging Middle Class: A Survey by FTChinese.com)*. Guangzhou: Nanfang Ribao Chubanshe, 2007.

Cheng, Yawen and Wang Yiwei. *Tian Ming: Yige Xin Lingdaoxing Guojia de Tansheng (The Mandate of Heaven: The Birth of a New Leading Country)*. Beijing: Qunyan Press, 2015.

"Chengdu Report: Four-City Zone to Boost Western Region." *China Daily*, April 23, 2015.

"Chengdu to Run 1,000 Cargo Trains to Europe in 2017." *China Daily*, February 20, 2017.

Chin, Gregory T. "Beijing's Economic Statecraft." *Current History*, vol. 114, no. 773, September 2015, 217.

Chin, Josh and Liyan Qi. "China Makes Multibillion-Dollar Down-Payment on Silk Road Plans." *Wall Street Journal*, April 21, 2015.

Chin, Tamara. "The Invention of the Silk Road, 1877." *Critical Inquiry*, vol. 40, no. 1, Autumn 2013, 194–219.

"China, An Ocean of Opportunities for Turkey." *Daily Sabah*, December 22, 2016.

"China 'Backs' Nigeria for Permanent U.N. Seat." *thecable.ng*, August 31, 2015.

"China Denies Allegations of Heavy Charges for CPEC Projects." *The Economic Times (India)*, April 6, 2017.

"China Encourages Environmental Groups to Sue Polluters." *The Guardian*, January 7, 2015.

"China Floods Iran with Cheap Consumer Goods in Exchange for Oil." *The Guardian*, February 20, 2013.

"China Imports More Iran Crude, Refinery Plan Stalls." *Trend (Azerbaijian)*, August 5, 2011.

China-Japan-Korea Trilateral Research Cooperation Summit. *Relations with the Middle East*. Shanghai: Shanghai International Studies University, November 2015.

"China Jushi's Expansion in Egypt Is Ahead of Schedule." *Composites World*, March 27, 2017.

"China Plays Key Broker Role in Iran Nuclear Deal." *Reuters*, November 25, 2013.

"China Rebukes Turkey for Offer to Shelter Uighur Refugees." *Reuters*, November 28, 2014.

"China Tells Iran That Given the Crisis with Qatar, Stability in the Gulf Is for the Best." *Reuters*, June 9, 2017.

"China to Contribute US$64 Million to 'Egypt Sat 2' Project." *Al-Masry Al-Youm,* March 21, 2017.

"China Wants to Divert Its Ships from Egypt's Suez Canal to New Arctic Route." *Egyptian Streets,* April 21, 2016.

"China Warns India, Says It Will Intervene if New Delhi Incites Trouble in Balochistan." *Indo-Asian News Service,* August 28, 2016.

"China Willing to Consider Turkey's Membership to Shanghai Security Pact." *Daily Sabah,* December 29, 2016.

"China's Citizens Are Complaining More Loudly about Polluted Air: The Government Wants to Silence Them." *The Economist,* March 2, 2017.

"China's Investment Reaches US$1.6 Billion in Indonesia." *Jakarta Post,* January 20, 2017.

"China's Islamic Heritage." *China Heritage Newsletter,* March 2006.

"China's 'New Silk Road' Facing Difficulties: Former Official." *South China Morning Post,* April 23, 2016.

"China's Positive Response to Indonesia's Investment Offer." *netralnews.com,* May 19, 2017.

"China's President Xi Jinping Calls for Marxism and Intellectual Loyalty." *Agence France-Presse,* May 18, 2016.

Chinaemelum, Okaekwu. "China Plans Visa Office in Anambra as Chinese Deputy Consul-General Visits Obiano." *anambrastate.gov.ng,* April 28, 2017.

"China Shelves Plan to Regulate Halal Food Preparation." *Hürriyet Daily News,* April 18, 2016.

"Chinese Company to Spend US$20 Billion on Egypt's New Capital East of Cairo." *South China Morning Post,* October 4, 2016.

"Chinese Muslims' Irreplaceable Role in the 'One Belt, One Road' Initiative." *1belt-1road.org,* January 6, 2017.

"Chinese Scholar Describes Internal Debate over Iran Policy." *Wikileaks Cables, U.S. Embassy, Beijing China.* Canonical ID: 07BEIJING5902_a, September 10, 2007.

"Chinese Sign US $12bn Contract to Build Nigerian Coastal Railway." *Railway Gazette,* November 20, 2014.

"Chinese Special Envoy on the Middle East Issue Wang Shijie Talks about His Middle East Tour." *chinaconsulatesf.org,* November 30, 2004.

Choksy, Jamsheed K. "A Sino-Persian Grab for the Indian Ocean?" *Small Wars Journal,* July 7, 2011.

Chong, Koh Ping. "Chengdu Ranked Top Chinese City for Economic Showing." *Straits Times,* September 17, 2015.

Chong, Tanna. "Legco Election 2016: How a Handful of Voters Elect 30 Hong Kong Lawmakers." *South China Morning Post,* February 6, 2014.

Chow, Chung-Yan. "The Plight of Chinese Indonesians: Distrusted in Jakarta, Forgotten in China." *South China Morning Post,* February 25, 2017.

Christian, David. "Silk Roads or Steppe Roads? The Silk Roads in World History." *Journal of World History,* vol. 11, no. 1, Spring 2000, 1–26.

Clover, Charles. "In Moscow, A New Eurasianism." *Journal of International Security Affairs,* Fall/Winter 2014.

Clover, Charles. *Black Wind, White Snow: The Rise of Russia's New Nationalism*. New Haven, CT: Yale University Press, 2016.
Cochrane, Joe. "In Indonesia, an Islamic Edict Seeks to Keep Santa Hats Off Muslims." *New York Times*, December 23, 2016.
Cochrane, Joe. "Jakarta Governor Concedes Defeat in Religiously Tinged Election." *New York Times*, April 19, 2017.
Coen, Enrico. *Cells to Civilization: The Principles of Change That Shape Life*. Princeton, NJ: Princeton University Press, 2012.
Cohen, Michael J. *Strategy and Politics in the Middle East, 1954–1960: Defending the Northern Tier*. London and New York: Frank Cass, 2005.
Cong, Yan. "Life in the Hui Culture Park." *chinafile.com*, May 5, 2016.
Cook, Steven A. "Egypt's Solvency Crisis." *Council on Foreign Relations*, April 2014.
Coonan, Clifford. "China Goes to Polls in Strictly Controlled Local Elections." *The Irish Times*, November 17, 2016.
Cooperjan, Helene. "Rifts between U.S. and Nigeria Impeding Fight against Boko Haram." *New York Times*, January 24, 2015.
Cordoba, Armando. "China Looks to Kurdistan as Growing Oil Partner." *rudaw.net*, July 29, 2013.
Corr, Anders. "Waiting for China to Democratize? Holding Your Breath May Be Fatal." *Forbes*, April 3, 2017.
Coser, Lewis A. *The Functions of Social Conflict*. London: Routledge, 2001.
Côté, Isabell. "The Enemies Within: Targeting Han Chinese and Hui Minorities in Xinjiang." *Asian Ethnicity*, vol. 16, no. 2, January 2015, 136–151.
Cottee, Mathew. "Sino-Pakistan Civil Nuclear Cooperation: A Growing Challenge to the Global Nuclear Order." *Lowry Institute for International Policy*, July 9, 2015.
"Could Turkey Be the Next Investment Hotspot for Chinese Buyers?" *juwai.com*, March 9, 2017.
Cowburn, Ashley. "Two-Thirds of African Countries Now Using Chinese Military Equipment, Report Reveals." *Independent*, March 1, 2016.
Crabtree, Justina and Cheang Ming. "Why Soft Power Could Be the Real Value of China's Massive Belt and Road Project." *CNBC*, May 22, 2017.
"CPEC a Matter of Life and Death for Pakhtuns, Says Sherpao." *Pakistan Today*, January 6, 2016.
"CPEC Won't Pass Through KP if Due Share Denied." *Dawn*, January 3, 2016.
Crews, Robert D. "Moscow and the Mosque: Co-opting Muslims in Putin's Russia." *Foreign Affairs*, March/April, 2014, 125–134.
Crissman, Lawrence W. "G. William Skinner's Spatial Analysis of Complex Societies: Its Importance for Anthropology." *Taiwan Journal of Anthropology*, vol. 8, no. 1, 2010, 27–45.
Crossley, Pamela Kyle, ed. *Empire at the Margins: Culture, Ethnicity, and Frontier in Early Modern China*. Berkeley: University of California Press, 2006.
Culbertson, Alix. "Chinese Mock Europe for 'Being Taken Over by Muslims'—As More Mosques Are Built in China." *Express*, September 14, 2016.
Cunningham, Blair. "New Rail Freight Link Could Become 'Israel's Suez Canal'." *Haaretz*, February 14, 2014.

Cunningham-Cross, Linsay and Peter Marcus Kristensen. "Chinese International Relations Theory." *Oxford Bibliographies*, May 29, 2014.

Cutler, Robert M. "Turkey's Erdogan Pushes into Eurasia." *Asia Times*, May 31, 2012.

Çetin, Halil. *Timur'un Anadolu Seferi ve Ankara Savaşı (Timur's Anatolian Campaign and The Battle of Ankara)*. Istanbul: Yeditepe Yayınevi, 2012.

"Çin Büyükelçisi Yu Hongyang'dan Destici'ye Ziyaret" (Chinese Ambassador Yu Hongyang Visits Destici). *olay53.com*, July 22, 2015.

Dai, Bingguo. "Zhongguo Qudai Meiguo Cheng Ba Shijie? Na Shi Shenhua" (China Replacing the U.S. as a World Hegemon? That Is a Fairytale). *Beijing Times*, December 8, 2010.

Dai, Xu. *C Xing Baowei: Neiyou Waihuan Xia de Zhongguo Tuwei (C-Shaped Encirclement: China's Breakout from Internal Troubles and External Aggression)*. Shanghai: Wenhui, 2009.

Dai, Xu. "Zhong E Ying Goujian Ouya Da Lianmeng Zuzhi Meiguo Tulu Ruo Guo" (China and Russia Should Establish a Eurasian Alliance to Prevent the United States from Slaughtering Weak Countries). *Global Times*, January 29, 2012.

Dalrymple, William. *A Deadly Triangle: Afghanistan, Pakistan, and India*. Washington, DC: Brookings, 2013.

Daly, John. "Egypt's Upgraded Suez Canal Is Bold Bid on the Future." *The Arab Weekly*, August 14, 2015.

Danubrata, Eveline and Gayatri Suroyo. "In Indonesia, Labor Friction and Politics Fan Anti-Chinese Sentiment." *Reuters*, April 18, 2017.

Dapiran, Antony et al. "Is Hong Kong on Its Way to Becoming Just Another City in the P.R.C?" *ChinaFile.com*, March 31, 2017.

Daraca, R. Kutay. *Güç Olma Stratejisi Çin: Soğuk Savaş Sonrası Türkiye-Çin İlişkileri (China's Strengthening Strategy: Turkey-China Relations after the Cold War)*. Istanbul: IQ Kültür Sanat Yayıncılık, 2008.

"Dark Corridor: Conflict in Balochistan Must Be Resolved for a Trade-Corridor between Pakistan and China to Bring Rewards." *The Economist*, June 6, 2015.

Darling, Linda T. "Social Cohesion ('Asabiyya) and Justice in the Late Medieval Middle East." *Comparative Studies in Society and History*, vol. 49, no. 2, April 2007, 329–357.

Darrag, Amr. "Sissi's Brutality Is Feeding the Islamic State's New Front in Egypt." *Washington Post*, November 5, 2015;

Das, Shaheli. "China Treads Its Way to Global Governance." *Forbes*, February 8, 2017.

Dasgupta, Saibal. "China's Ambitious 'Silk Road' Plan Faces Hurdles." *Voice of America*, April 15, 2015.

Davies, Gloria. *Worrying about China: The Language of Chinese Critical Inquiry*. Cambridge, MA: Harvard University Press, 2007.

Davison, John. "Gulf Crisis a 'Blessing in Disguise' for Qatar Seaport." *Reuters*, June 16, 2017.

Davutoğlu, Ahmet. "Naturalizing the Flow of History." *Al-Jazeera*, March 16, 2011.

Davutoğlu, Ahmet. "Global Governance." *Center for Strategic Research, Ministry of Foreign Affairs*, March 2012.

Dawkins, Richard. *The Selfish Gene*. New York: Oxford University Press, 2016.

De, Man. "From a 'Wolf Culture' to a 'Lamb Culture.'" *chinasource.com*, November 21, 2007.

Dearing, Matthew. "Nation Building Is Dirty Business." *Foreign Policy*, March 10, 2015.

Dehghan, Saeed Kamali. "What's in a Ring? Iran's Khamenei Sends Mixed Election Messages." *The Guardian*, May 19, 2017.

Dehghan, Saeed Kamali. "Rift between Iran's Ayatollah and Re-elected President Widens." *The Guardian*, June 22, 2017.

De Lombaerde, Philippe et al. "The Problem of Comparison in Comparative Regionalism." *Review of International Studies*, vol. 36, no. 3, July 2010, 731–753.

Deng, Guosheng and Scott Kennedy. "Big Business and Industry Association Lobbying in China: The Paradox of Contrasting Styles." *The China Journal*, January 2010.

Deng, Yuwen. "Hu Wen de Zhengzhi Yichan" (The Political Legacy of Hu and Wen). *caijing.com.cn*, September 5, 2012.

Deng, Yuwen. "Seven Spheres of Interest." *china.org*, May 4, 2013.

Denyer, Simon. "A Young Man Died in Police Custody, and Middle-Class Chinese Are Outraged." *New York Times*, December 31, 2016.

Denyer, Simon. "Stop Making Our Children Sick: Beijing Parents Force Government Action over Smog." *New York Times*, January 6, 2017.

Department of Culture of Ningxia. "A Cultural Gate to China: 'One Belt and One Road' Islamic Customs." *chinaculture.org*, March 31, 2017.

Dergham, Raghida. "Russia's Interests and the Iranian Project in the Region." *Huffington Post*, January 9, 2017.

Dessein, Bart, ed. *Interpreting China as a Regional and Global Power: Nationalism and Historical Consciousness in World Politics*. New York: Palgrave Macmillan, 2014.

Devasher, Tilak. "CPEC-A Game Changer or Debt Enhancer for Pakistan?" *Eurasia Review*, February 5, 2017.

Di Cosmo, Nicola. *Ancient China and Its Enemies: The Rise of Nomadic Power in East Asian History*. Cambridge: Cambridge University Press, 2002.

Dickson, Bruce J. "Cooptation and Corporatism in China: The Logic of Party Adaptation." *Political Science Quarterly*, vol. 115, no. 4, Winter, 2000–2001, 517–540.

Diehl, Jackson. "Sissi's Teeming Prisons." *Al-Jazeera*, September 27, 2015.

Dikötter, Frank. *The Discourse of Race in Modern China*. Stanford, CA: Stanford University Press, 1992.

Ding, Jun. "Lun Zhongguo Yu Yisilan Guojia Jian de 'Minxin Xiangtong'" (On People to People Connections between China and the Islamic World). *globalview.cn*, June 28, 2016.

Ding, Kejia. "Wenhua Duihua Shijiao Xia de Hui-Rui Duihua" (Hui-Confucian Dialogue from the Perspective of the Dialogue of Civilizations). *Arab World Studies*, vol. 30, no. 3, May 2011, 73–80.

Ding, Xuezhen. "China Eyes Silk Road Countries for its Beidou Satellite System." *Global Times*, June 17, 2016.

Direskeneli, Haluk. "Trans-Caspian Subsea Gas Pipeline Project Vital for Turkey." *Eurasian Review*, February 24, 2017.

Dirlik, Arif. "Confucius in the Borderlands: Global Capitalism and the Reinvention of Confucianism." *Boundary*, vol. 22, no. 3, Autumn 1995, 229–273.

Domonoske, Camila. "China Announces Its Largest-Ever Seizure of Trafficked Pangolin Scales." *NPR*, December 28, 2016.

Dorairajoo, Saroja and Ma Jianfu. "Does Islam Have the Answers to China's Food Safety Problems?" *South China Morning Post*, July 29, 2016.

Dorsey, James. "The U.S.-Saudi Plot for Iran That Spells Trouble for China's New Silk Road." *South China Morning Post*, May 27, 2017.

Doyon, Jérôme, François Godement, Angela Stanzel, and Abigaël Vasselier. "A Hundred Think Tanks Bloom in China." *European Council on Foreign Relations*, August 25, 2016.

Dryer, Jacob. "Could China Be the New Best Friend for a Post-Brexit Britain?" *New Statesman*, July 6, 2017.

Du, Baozhong and Xuan Li. "China Turns to Islamic Finance to Drive Economic Initiative." *Business Islamica*, June 9, 2016.

Duara, Prasenjit. *Rescuing History from the Nation: Questioning Narratives of Modern China*. Chicago: University of Chicago Press, 1995.

Dudoignon, Stéphane A. *The Baluch, Sunnism and the State in Iran: From Tribal to Global*, London: Hurst, 2017.

Duhalde, Marcelo. "Classifying China's Cities." *South China Morning Post*, March 13, 2017.

Duncan, John. *How Intelligence Happens*. New Haven, CT: Yale University Press, 2010.

Dunn, Ross E. *The Adventures of Ibn Battuta: A Muslim Traveler of the 14th Century*. Berkeley: University of California Press, 1986.

DuVall, Eric. "Australia Eyeing Tough New Anti-immigrant Legislation to Combat 'People Smuggling.'" *United Press International*, October 29, 2016.

Earl, Greg. "Opinion Poll Reveals Australians Split over What to Do about the U.S. and China." *Australian Financial Review*, June 10, 2016.

Eaton, Richard. "Revisiting the Persian Cosmopolis." *Asia Times Online*, July 19, 2013.

"Economic Corridor-CPEC Could Turn Pakistan into China's 'Client State.'" *Deutsche Welle*, November 14, 2016.

Editorial. "CPEC Transparency." *Dawn*, November 18, 2015.

"8 Great Places to Break Fast during Ramadan in Shanghai." *shanghailist.com*, June 10, 2016.

"Egypt Announces New Chinese Investments in Textile." *China Daily*, April 5, 2017.

"Egypt Arrests Chinese Muslim Students amid Police Sweep." *Al-Jazeera*, July 7, 2017.

Egypt Network for Integrated Development, "Promoting Manufacturing in Upper Egypt." *ENID Policy Brief 16*, 2013.

"Egypt Turning towards China for Investment." *African Business Magazine*, October 18, 2016.

"Egypt Witnessed Hundreds of Labour Protests in 2015: Report." *Middle East Eye*, January 12, 2016.

"Egypt's Farmers: Sowing the Seeds of an Agricultural Revolution." *International Labor Organization*, February 7, 2013.

"Egyptian Contractors to Build Ministerial District in New Capital after Failed Chinese Deal." *Ahram Online*, February 6, 2017.

Ekeke, Joy. "Nigeria Has No Long-Term Roadmap for Rail Transport-Comrade Esan." *Daily Times*, September 16, 2016.

El Bedawy, Randa. "Water Resources Management: Alarming Crisis for Egypt." *Journal of Management and Sustainability*, vol. 4, no. 3, August 2014, 113–122.

Elbenni, Ahmed. "Rift: The Uyghurs and the Hui." *The Yale Globalist*, January 21, 2017.

El-Bernoussi, Zaynab. "China Making Big Diplomat Gains in Egypt." *Japan Times*, December 10, 2016.

El-Kholy, Ismael. "One Year On, Are 'New' Suez Canal Revenues Sinking?" *Almonitor*, August 10, 2016.

El-Tablawy, Tarek. "Egypt Moves Closer to IMF Loan with China Currency Swap Deal." *Bloomberg*, October 30, 2016.

Elleman, Bruce A. and Stephen Kotkin, eds. *Manchurian Railways and the Opening of China: An International History*. New York: Routledge, 2015.

Elveren, Muammer. "Turkey Should Look After Turks in Thailand, Says Head of Uighurs." *Hürriyet Daily News*, December 22, 2014.

Elverskog, Johan. *Buddhism and Islam on the Silk Road*. Philadelphia: University of Pennsylvania Press, 2011.

Elyda, Corry. "Anti-Ahok Protest Causes Huge Financial Losses: Kadin." *Jakarta Post*, November 5, 2016.

Enumah, Alex. "China Renews Commitment to Nigeria's Industrialisation." *This Day*, September 29, 2017.

Erickson, Amanda. "The Long History of Incredibly Fraught Relations between the U.S. and Pakistan." *Washington Post*, January 5, 2018.

Erickson, Andrew S. ed. *Chinese Naval Shipbuilding: An Ambitious and Uncertain Course*. Annapolis, MD: Naval Institute Press, 2016.

Erie, Matthew S. "In China, Fears of 'Creeping Sharia' Proliferate Online." *Foreign Policy*, September 15, 2016.

Erie, Matthew. *China and Islam: The Prophet, the Party, and Law*. New York: Cambridge University Press, 2017.

Erimtan, Can. "The New Silk Road: China Looks West, Turkey Looks East." *RT News*, March 19, 2014.

Ernsberger, Dave. "China's Approach to Global Markets Is One to Follow: Fuel for Thought." *platts.com*, November 14, 2016.

Escobar, Pepe. "Trump Will Try to Smash the China-Russia-Iran Triangle . . . Here's Why He Will Fail." *South China Morning Post*, January 22, 2017.

Escobar, Pepe. "Peace, Harmony and Happiness, Plus a Deluge of Yuan." *Asia Times*, May 15, 2017.

Esfandiari, Haleh. "Despite the Protests, Little Will Change in Iran." *The Hill*, January 3, 2018.

"Establish Production Plants in Nigeria to Address Trade Imbalance, Dogara Tells China." *Daily Post*, November 2, 2017.

Estlund, Cynthia. *A New Deal for China's Workers?* Cambridge, MA: Harvard University Press, 2017.

"Ethiopia-Djibouti Railway a First Step to Trans-Africa Railway?" *Africa Business Forum*, January 22, 2017.

Etzioni, Amitai. "China: The Accidental World Leader?" *The Diplomat*, February 13, 2017.
"Explosives Seized from Terrorist Cell in Chabahar." *Mehr News Agency*, June 15, 2017.
"Fake Plastic Rice Seized in Nigeria amid Rocketing Food Prices." *Agence France-Presse*, December 21, 2016.
Fan, Junmei. "Qingdao Strives to Become Cruise Home Port of Northeast Asia." *China Daily*, February 22, 2017.
Farchy, Jack et al. "One Belt, One Road: A Ribbon of Road, Rail and Energy Projects to Help Increase Trade." *Financial Times*, September 14, 2016.
Farhi, Farideh. "Here's What Makes Iran's Anti-regime Protests Different This Time." *NPR*, January 4, 2018.
Farooq, Umar. "The Afghan Roots of Pakistan's Zarb-e-Azb Operation." *Foreign Policy*, September 18, 2014.
Fealy, Greg and Hugh White. "Indonesia's 'Great Power' Aspirations: A Critical View." *Asia and the Pacific Policy Studies*, vol. 3, no. 1, 2016, pp. 92–100.
Fecteau, Andre. "On Toshka New Valley's Mega-failure." *Egypt Independent*, April 26, 2012.
Feffer, John. "Stealth Superpower: How Turkey Is Chasing China in Bid to Become the Next Big Thing." *tomdispatch.com*, January 13, 2010.
Fei, Hsiao-tung. "The New Outlook of Rural China: Kaishienkung Revisited after Half a Century." *RAIN (Royal Anthropological Institute of Great Britain and Ireland)*, no. 48, February 1982, 4–8.
Fei, Xiaotong. *Plurality and Unity in the Configuration of the Chinese People*. Hong Kong: The Chinese University of Hong Kong, November 1988.
Fei, Xiaotong. "Toward a People's Anthropology." In Thomas Weaver, ed. *The Dynamics of Applied Anthropology in the Twentieth Century: The Malinowski Award Papers*. Oklahoma City, OK: Society for Applied Anthropology, 2002.
Feng, Emily. "Never the Noodles Shall Meet: A Chinese Treaty Is Tested." *New York Times*, August 31, 2016.
Feng, Haiwen. "Zhongguo Daguo Zhuanlue Xuanze: Nan Jin Haishi Xi Jin?" (China's Great Power Strategic Choice: Sail South or March West?). *Global Times*, November 1, 2012.
Feng, Haiwen. "Meiguo Duihua Zhengce Huo Cong Ying Weidu Bian Ruan Baowei" (America's Policy of Dialogue or from Hard Containment to Soft Encirclement). *Global Net*, January 22, 2013.
Feng, Li. *Early China: A Social and Cultural History*. Cambridge: Cambridge University Press, 2013.
Ferguson, R. James and Rosita Dellios. *The Politics and Philosophy of Chinese Power: The Timeless and the Timely*. Lanham, MD: Lexington Books, 2016.
Feteha, Ahmed. "Egypt, China Sign $2.6B Currency Swap Boosting Pound Flotation." *Bloomberg*, December 6, 2016.
Fick, Maggie Fick. "Nigeria's Ruling Politicians Jostle for Power in Buhari's Absence." *Financial Times*, February 23, 2017.
Fidler, Stephen, Te-Ping Chen, and Lingling Wei. "China's Xi Jinping Seizes Role as Leader on Globalization." *Wall Street Journal*, January 17, 2017.

Findley, Carter Vaughn. *The Turks in World History*. New York: Oxford University Press, 2004.

Fingar, Thomas. *The New Great Game: China and South and Central Asia in the Era of Reform*. Stanford, CA: Stanford University Press, 2016.

Fitch, Asa and Benoit Faucon. "Foreign Investors Flock to Iran as U.S. Firms Watch on the Sidelines." *Wall Street Journal*, March 27, 2017.

Flanagan, Ben. "Higher Tolls 'Risky' after $4bn Suez Canal Expansion." *Al-Arabiya News*, August 7, 2014.

Fletcher, Joseph F. "China and Central Asia, 1368–1884," in John King Fairbank, ed., *The Chinese World Order: Traditional China's Foreign Relations*, Cambridge, MA: Harvard University Press, 1968.

Fletcher, Joseph F. *Studies on Chinese and Islamic Inner Asia*. Brookfield, VT: Variorum, 1995.

Foltz, Richard. *Religions of the Silk Road: Premodern Patterns of Globalization*. New York: Palgrave Macmillan, 2010.

"For Allah, Beijing and Marx: Young Imams in China Espouse Islam through Prism of Party Line." *Japan Times*, May 23, 2016.

Forbes, Andrew D.W. *Warlords and Muslims in Chinese Central Asia: A Political History of Republican Sinkiang 1911–1949*. New York: Cambridge University Press, 1986.

Ford, Peter. "Iran Nuclear Talks: What China Brings to the Negotiating Table." *Christian Science Monitor*, March 30, 2015.

Fouly, Mahmoud. "Interview: China Largest Investor in Egypt's Suez Canal Region with Earnest, Win-Win Partnership: Official." *Xinhua*, March 16, 2017.

Franke, Herbert and Denis Twitchett, eds. *The Cambridge History of China, Vol. 6, Alien Regimes and Border States, 907–1368*. Cambridge: Cambridge University Press, 2008.

Fraser, Malcolm. "America: Australia's Dangerous Ally." *The National Interest*, December 16, 2014.

Frayer, Janis Mackey. "China Ventures into America's Backyard: Latin America." *NBC News*, April 5, 2017.

French, Howard W. *China's Second Continent: How a Million Migrants Are Building a New Empire in Africa*. New York: Vintage, 2015.

French, Howard W. *Everything under the Heavens: How the Past Helps Shape China's Push for Global Power*. New York, Knopf, 2017.

French, Howard W. "China's Quest to End Its Century of Shame." *New York Times*, July 13, 2017.

Friedersdorf, Conor. "Donald Trump's Blunder Down Under." *The Atlantic*, February 2, 2017.

Friedman, Thomas L. "Global Oil War Underway between US-Saudi Arabia and Russia-Iran?" *New York Times*, October 15, 2014.

Froissart, Chloé. "The Rise of Social Movements among Migrant Workers: Uncertain Strivings for Autonomy." *China Perspectives*, no. 61, September-October 2005, 30–40.

Frye, Richard. *The Heritage of Central Asia from Antiquity to the Turkish Expansion*. Princeton, NJ: Markus Wiener, 1996.

Fu, Diana. "Disguised Collective Action in China." *Comparative Political Studies*, February 2016, 1–29.

"Full Text of Xi Jinping Keynote at the World Economic Forum." *america.cgtn.com*, January 17, 2017.

Fullilove, Michael. "Time for a Larger Australia." *The National Interest*, March 20, 2014.

Fung, Victor. "New Beef Noodle Restaurant in Shanghai Harassed by Competitors after Violating Unwritten Code." *Shanghailist.com*, July 27, 2016.

Gabaccía, Donna R. and Dirk Hoerder, eds. *Connecting Seas and Connected Ocean Rims: Indian, Atlantic, and Pacific Oceans and China Seas Migrations from the 1820s to the 1930s*. Leiden/Boston: Brill, 2011.

Gabidullin, Ildar and Maxim Edwards. "Crimea Crisis: The Tatarstan Factor." *Al-Jazeera*, March 15, 2014.

Gady, Franz-Stefan. "Indian Navy Practices Sinking Chinese Subs in Largest-Ever Military Exercise." *The Diplomat*, February 10, 2017.

Gallagher, Kevin P. *The China Triangle: Latin America's China Boom and the Fate of the Washington Consensus*. New York: Oxford University Press, 2016.

Gamio, Lazaro and Erica Pandey. "The Staggering Scale of China's Belt and Road Initiative." *Axios*, January 19, 2018.

Garewal, Ali. "Will Pakistan Forever Be Indebted to China for CPEC?" *Express Tribune*, October 29, 2016.

Gao, Yanqiu. "Huzu Dute Falu Yishi Chengyin Chutan" (A Preliminary Study on the Causes of the Unique Legal Consciousness of the Hui). *Shaanxi Xueqian Normal University Journal*, no. 4, August 2015, 105–109.

Gao, Zhanfu. "Cong 'Tianfang Dianli' Zhanshi de 'Yi Rui Quanjing' Sixiang Kan Yisilan Jiao Zai Zhongguo de Bentuhua" (From "Arabian Rituals" to "Explaining Islamic Classics with Confucianism": The Localization of Islam in China). *Hui Nationality Studies*, no. 3, 2010, 42–47.

Gao, Zhanfu. "Cong Wailai Qiaomin Dao Bentu Guomin: Huizu Yisilan Jiao Zai Zhongguo Bentuhua da Licheng" (From Alien Diaspora to Native Nationals: The Historical Process of the Localization of Hui Islam in China). *360doc.com*, December 24, 2012.

Gao, Zugui. "Zhongguo Yu Yisilan Shijie Guanxi Yanjiu" (A Study of China's Relations with the Islamic World). *Journal of China and International Relations*, vol. 1, no. 2, 2013, 28–36.

Gardner, Timothy. "Hidden Tensions between the U.S., China, and Russia Emerge at Arctic Council Meeting Hosted by Rex Tillerson." *Reuters*, May 12, 2017.

Garnaut, John. "Australia and India to Strengthen Military Ties." *Sydney Morning Herald*, July 1, 2014.

Garside, Roger. "China's Future: Status Quo, Reform, or Chaos?" *Prospect Magazine*, March 26, 2016.

Gater-Smith, Philip. "Qatar Crisis Impacts China's Ambitious Foreign Policy." *International Policy Digest*, June 13, 2017.

Gause, F. Gregory, III. "Beyond Sectarianism: The New Middle East Cold War." *Brookings Doha Center*, July 2014.

Geiger, Dorian. "The Lonely Pyramids of Giza: Egyptian Tourism's Decline." *Al-Jazeera*, June 8, 2017.
"Geithner, In Beijing for Talks, Faces Struggle to Gain China's Cooperation on Iran Sanctions." *Associated Press*, January 10, 2012.
"Getting Nigeria's Railways Back on Track with China's Help." *BBC*, December 7, 2017.
"General Election 25 July 2018," *Election Commission of Pakistan*, July 29, 2018, https://www.ecp.gov.pk/.
Ghanem, Hafez. "Improving Regional and Rural Development for Inclusive Growth in Egypt." *Brookings Global Economy and Development Working Paper 67*, January 2014.
Ghazanfar, Munir. "Kalbagh Dam and the Water Debate in Pakistan." *Lahore Journal of Policy Studies*, vol. 2, no. 1, September 2008, 153–180.
Ghoshal, Somak. "The Qatar Crisis and How It Affects India." *Huffington Post*, June 6, 2017.
Gillette, Maris Boyd. *Between Mecca and Beijing: Modernization and Consumption among Urban Chinese Muslims*. Stanford, CA: Stanford University Press, 2000.
Gilley, Bruce and Andrew O'Neil, eds. *Middle Powers and the Rise of China*. Washington DC: Georgetown University Press, 2014.
Gipouloux, François. *The Asian Mediterranean: Port Cities and Trading Networks in China, Japan and Southeast Asian, 13th–21st Century*. Cheltenham and Northampton, MA: Edward Elgar, 2011.
Gladney, Dru C. *Muslim Chinese: Ethnic Nationalism in the People's Republic*. Cambridge, MA: Council on East Asian Studies, Harvard University, 1996.
Gladney, Dru C. *Dislocating China: Muslims, Minorities, and Other Subaltern Subjects*. Chicago: University of Chicago Press, 2004.
Glaser, Bonnie S. and Evan S. Medeiros. "The Changing Ecology of Foreign Policy-making in China: The Ascension and Demise of the Theory of "Peaceful Rise." *China Quarterly*, vol. 190, June 2007, 291–310.
Glaser, Charles. "Will China's Rise Lead to War? Why Realism Does Not Mean Pessimism." *Foreign Affairs*, March/April 2011.
Glaser, Charles S. "A U.S.-China Grand Bargain? The Hard Choice between Military Competition and Accommodation." *International Security*, vol. 39, no. 4, Spring 2015, 49–90.
Goble, Paul. "A 'Hybrid Islam' Is Emerging in Russia, Malashenko Says." *The Interpreter*, October 29, 2014.
Godement, François. "Expanded Ambitions, Shrinking Achievements: How China Sees the Global Order." *European Council on Foreign Relations*, March 2017.
Goh, Brenda. "Shanghai Port, World's Busiest, Grapples with Traffic Congestion." *Reuters*, April 21, 2017.
Goh, Evelyn. "Great Powers and Southeast Asian Regional Security Strategies: Omni-enmeshment, Balancing and Hierarchical Order." *Institute of Defense and Strategic Studies, Singapore*, July 2005.
Golia, Maria. "Dark Waters." *The National (Egypt)*, November 26, 2009.
Golia, Maria. "The New Suez Canal Project and Egypt's Economic Future." *Middle East Institute*, December 19, 2014.

Gomulkiewicz, R., D.M Drown, M.F. Dybdahl, W. Godsoe, S.L. Nuismer, K.M. Pepin, B.J. Ridenhour, C.I. Smith, and J.B. Yoder. "Testing the Geographic Mosaic Theory of Coevolution." *Heredity*, vol. 98, no. 5, 2007, 249–258.

Goossaert, Vincent and David A. Palmer. *The Religious Question in Modern China*. Chicago: University of Chicago Press, 2011.

"Got Beef? How One Man Faced Down a 'Noodle Cartel.'" *BBC News*, July 25, 2016.

"Govt Claims 'Total Consensus' among Provinces on CPEC." *Dawn*, January 18, 2017.

Gran, Peter. *Islamic Roots of Capitalism: Egypt, 1760–1840*. Austin: University of Texas Press, 1979.

Grange, Joseph. *John Dewey, Confucius, and Global Philosophy*. Albany: Southern University of New York Press, 2004.

Grare, Frederic. "Balochistan: The State versus the Nation." *The Carnegie Papers*, April 2013.

Graves, LeAnne. "Chinese Investment to Spur Middle East Renewable Energy Ambitions." *The National (UAE)*, December 7, 2015.

Gresh, Geoffrey F. "China's Emerging Twin Pillar Policy in the Gulf." *Foreign Policy*, November 7, 2011.

Grey, Eva. "Moscow-Kazan Rail Project Advances Hopes for Eurasian Connectivity." *Railway Technology*, November 21, 2016.

Griffiths, James. "China's New World Order: Xi, Putin and Others Meet for Belt and Road Forum." *CNN*, May 14, 2017.

Griffiths, James and Vivian Kam. "Hong Kong Votes: Is This the World's Weirdest Election?" *CNN*, September 2016.

Guimarães, Paulo R. Jr., Pedro Jordano, and John N. Thompson. "Evolution and Coevolution in Mutualistic Networks." *Ecology Letters*, vol. 14, 2011, 877–885.

Gürpınar, Doğan. *Ottoman Imperial Diplomacy, A Political, Social and Cultural History*. London: I.B. Tauris, 2014.

Gürsel, Kadri. "Erdogan Serious about Turkey's Bid for Shanghai 5 Membership." *Al-Monitor*, January 31, 2013.

Guo, Peiqing. "Daguo Zhanlue Zhi Bei Ji" (Great Power Strategy Points to the North Pole). *360doc.com*, October 27, 2011.

Gurses, Ercan and Aziz El Yaakoubi. "Turkish President Says Qatar Isolation Violates Islamic Values." *Reuters*, June 13, 2017.

Gustafsson, Björn and Xiuna Yang. "Are China's Ethnic Minorities Less Likely to Move?" *IZA Discussion Paper Series*, Bonn: April 2015.

Guy, Peter. "Hong Kong's (Dys)functional Constituencies Simply Help Big Business Defend the Status Quo and Oppress the Economy." *South China Morning Post*, October 20, 2016.

Haas, Benjamin. "China Bans Religious Names for Muslim Babies in Xinjiang." *The Guardian*, April 24, 2017.

Haddad, Eduardo Amaral et al. "Regional Analysis of Domestic Integration in Egypt: An Interregional CGE Approach." *Journal of Economic Structures*, vol. 5, no. 1, 2016, 1–33.

Haddad-Fonda, Kyle. "Egypt and Other Arab States Embrace a Chinese Model of Development." *World Politics Review*, March 16, 2017.

Hai Xiao, Allen. "In the Shadow of the States: The Informalities of Chinese Petty Entrepreneurship in Nigeria." *Journal of Current Chinese Affairs*, vol. 44, no. 1, 2015, 75–105.

Haider, Mateen. "Chinese President Cancels Pakistan Trip, India Visit Still On." *Dawn*, September 5, 2014.

Halim, Haeril. "Muhammadiyah Pushes Jokowi to Suspend Ahok." *Jakarta Post*, February 21, 2017.

Hall, David L. and Roger T. Ames, *The Democracy of the Dead: Dewey, Confucius, and the Hope for Democracy in China*. Chicago: Open Court, 1999.

Hall-Eastman, Jonathan. "Professor Hua Tao on Islam in China." *SAIS Observer*, May 3, 2016.

Hamilton, Gary and Xiangqun Chang. "China and World Anthropology: A Conversation on the Legacy of Fei Xiaotong (1910–2005)." *Anthropology Today*, vol. 27, no. 6, December 2011, 20–23.

Hamlin, Katrina. "China's Zealous Cleantech Firms Risk Burning Cash." *Reuters*, November 15, 2016.

Han, Shuyun. "Nu Haji Yu Tongguo Yishi Jiyu Qinghai Xun Hua Musilin Nuxing Chaojinzhe de Diaocha Yanjiu" (On Women Hajjis and Their Rites of Passage: Survey Research on Women Muslim Hajjis in Xunhua, Qinghai Province). *Journal of Beifang Ethnic University*, no. 2, 2010, 70–74.

Handayani, Oliviana. "Government to Channel Chinese Investment into Special Economic Zone." *Indonesia Expat*, May 31, 2017.

Hang'e, Mo. "Indonesia Keen to Tap More Chinese Tourists during Spring Festival Holiday." *Xinhua*, December 28, 2016.

Hanne, Michael, William D. Crano, and Jeffrey Scott Mio, eds. *Warring with Words: Narrative and Metaphor in Politics*. New York and London: Psychology Press, 2014.

Hanrahan, Mark. "Asian Infrastructure Investment Bank Opposed by US, Seen as Attempt to Boost Chinese Influence." *International Business Times*, October 9, 2014.

Hansen, Suzy and Norman Behrendt. "Reading Erdogan's Ambitions in Turkey's New Mosques." *New York Times*, June 14, 2017.

Haq, Riaz. "Pak Army Builds over Half of CPEC Western Route in Record Time." *riazhaq.com*, July 1, 2015.

"Hard-Line Muslim Protest against Christian Jakarta Governor Ends in Violence." *Voice of America*, November 4, 2016.

Hari, Solomon Ibrahim. "The Evolution of Social Protest in Nigeria: The Role of Social Media in the '#OccupyNigeria' Protest." *International Journal of Humanities and Social Science Invention*, vol. 3, no. 9, September 2014, 33–39.

Harner, Stephen. "Why David Shambaugh's 'Coming Chinese Crackup' Case Is Wrong." *Forbes*, March 10, 2015.

Harold, Scott and Alireza Nader. "China and Iran: Economic, Political, and Military Relations." *RAND Center for Middle East Public Policy*, 2012.

Harvey, Adam. "Jakarta Election: Agus Yudhoyono Campaigns as Champion of the Poor, With Dynasty in Mind." *Australian Broadcasting Corporation*, February 8, 2017.

Hashen, Ali Hashem. "Why Iran Wants Palestine Back on Regional Agenda." *Al-Monitor*, February 24, 2017.

Hassan, Syed Raza. "To Protect Chinese Investment, Pakistan Military Leaves Little to Chance." *Reuters*, February 7, 2016.

Hayoun, Massoud. "Islam with Chinese Characteristics." *The Atlantic*, January 18, 2012.

Hayoun, Massoud. "Surrealism Abounds in China's Uyghur Crackdown." *Pacific Standard*, May 3, 2017.

He, Yafei. "Zongjiao Shi Zhongguo Gonggong Waijiao de Zhongyao Ziyuan" (Religion Is an Important Resource for China's Public Diplomacy). news.china.com.cn, March 6, 2015.

Hegazy, Yamen M. et al. "Ruminant Brucellosis in the Kafr El Sheikh Governorate of the Nile Delta, Egypt: Prevalence of a Neglected Zoonosis." *Public Library of Science: Neglected Tropical Diseases*, vol. 5, no. 1, January 11, 2011.

Heilmann, Sebastian, Moritz Rudolf, Middo Huotari, and Johannes Buckow. "China's Shadow Foreign Policy: Parallel Structures Challenge the Established International Order." *MERICS China Monitor*, October 28, 2014.

Hellyer, H. A. "Is Another Egyptian Uprising on the Way?" *The Globe and Mail*, January 25, 2016.

Helmy, Nadia. "Chinese Scholarship on Iran and the Middle East." *Iranian Review of Foreign Affairs*, vol. 4, no. 3, Fall 2013, 5–32.

Henderson, Mark G., William Skinner, and Lawrence W. Crissman. "A Hierarchical Regional Space Model for Contemporary China." Paper Prepared for the Geoinformatics '99 Conference, University of Michigan, June 20, 1999.

Hermansyah, Anton. "Jakarta-Bandung High Speed Railway to Get Chinese Loan." *Jakarta Post*, November 10, 2016.

Hernández, Javier C. "In Banning Ivory Trade, China Saw Benefits for Itself, Too." *New York Times*, January 2, 2017.

Herrera, Santiago Herrera et al. "Reshaping Egypt's Economic Geography: Domestic Integration as a Development Platform." *World Bank*, June 2012.

Hessler, Peter. "Learning to Speak Lingerie: Chinese Merchants and the Inroads of Globalization." *The New Yorker*, August 10, 2015.

Hessler, Peter. "Egypt's Failed Revolution." *The New Yorker*, January 2, 2017.

Hew, Wai-Weng. "Marketing the Chinese Face of Islam." *Inside Indonesia*, December 1, 2009.

Hewitt, Duncan. "China Calls for Religion to Be 'Localized' to Reduce Foreign 'Infiltration,' Says Party 'Severely Damaged' by Members' Religious Beliefs." *International Business Times*, April 25, 2016.

Heydarian, Richard Javad. "China's Silk Road Project: A Trap or an Opportunity?" *Al-Jazeera*, May 17, 2017.

Hill, Christopher. "China's Bad-Neighbor Policy Is Bad Business." *Project Syndicate*, June 30, 2016.

Hill, Liezel. "Africa's $30 Billion Rail Renaissance Holds Ticket for Trade." *Bloomberg*, April 7, 2016.

Hillman, Ben. "The Rise of the Community in Rural China: Village Politics, Cultural Identity and Religious Revival in a Hui Hamlet." *The China Journal*, no. 51, January 2004, 53–73.

Hillman, Jonathan. "Mishandled China-Pakistan Economic Corridor Could Misfire." *Nikkei Asian Review*, April 13, 2017.

Hilpert, Hanns Günther and Gudrun Wacker. "Geoeconomics Meets Geopolitics: China's New Economic and Foreign Policy Initiatives." *German Institute for International and Security Affairs*, June 2015.

Hindy, Lily. "A Rising China Eyes the Middle East." *The Century Foundation*, April 6, 2017.

Hinshaw, Drew. "West Africa Rising: Nigeria Shifting Currency Reserves from Dollars to Chinese Yuan." *Christian Science Monitor*, September 6, 2011.

Ho, Bryan. "Village Democracy Shrugs in Rural China." *East Asia Forum*, July 22, 2014.

Hobson, John M. *The Eastern Origins of Western Civilisation*. New York: Cambridge University Press, 2004.

Hodgson, Marshall G. S. *The Venture of Islam: Conscience and History in a World Civilization*. Chicago: University of Chicago Press, 1974.

Hollingsworth, Julia. "Why Qatar Matters to China in Spite of Gulf Isolation." *South China Morning Post*, June 7, 2017.

Holmes, Oliver. "Fears over Violence in Jakarta as Hardline Islamists Protest Governor's 'Blasphemy.'" *The Guardian*, November 2, 2016.

Holmes, Oliver. "Jakarta's Violent Identity Crisis: Behind the Vilification of Chinese-Indonesians." *The Guardian*, November 25, 2016.

Hon, Tze-Ki. "Ethnic and Cultural Pluralism: Gu Jiegang's Vision of a New China in His Studies of Ancient History." *Modern China*, vol. 22, no. 3, July 1996, 315–339.

Hong, Brendon. "China's Plans to Railroad the West (Literally)." *Daily Beast*, July 13, 2016.

Horden, Peregrine and Nicholas Purcell. *The Corrupting Sea: A Study of Mediterranean History*. Oxford: Blackwell, 2000.

Hornby, Lucy and Piotr Zalewski. "China Accuses Turkey of Aiding Uighurs." *Financial Times*, July 12, 2015.

Horner, Charles and Eric Brown. "Beijing's Islamic Complex." *Wall Street Journal*, June 2, 2010.

Hoskins, Janet Alison. "An Unjealous God? Christian Elements in a Vietnamese Syncretistic Religion." *Current Anthropology*, vol. 55, no. 10, December 2014, 5302–5311.

Howell, Jude, "Civil Society, Corporatism and Capitalism in China." *Journal of Comparative Asian Development*, vol. 11, no. 3, October 2012, 271–297.

Hoyle, Henry. "Chinese Think Tank Official: Change the Terms of the Iran Debate." *Foreign Policy Association*, March 8, 2010.

Hsu, Jennifer Y. J. and Reza Hasmath, eds. *The Chinese Corporatist State: Adaptation, Survival and Resistance*. London and New York: Routledge, 2013.

Hua, Liming. "Yilang He Wenti Yu Zhongguo de Waijiao Xuanze" (The Iranian Nuclear Issue and China's Diplomatic Options). *Guoji Wenti Yanjiu (Journal of International Studies)*, no. 1, January 2007, 58–62.

Hua, Liming. "Yilan He Wenti Yu Zhongguo Zhongdong Waijiao" (The Iran Nuclear Issue and China's Middle East Diplomacy). *Arab World Studies*, no. 6, November 2014, 4–16.

Hua, Tao. "Wenhua Duihua Yu Zhongguo Chuantong Wenhua Fanshi Zhong de Zhang'ai" (Cultural Dialogue and Obstacles in the Paradigms of Traditional Chinese Culture). Nanjing University Journal, no. 1, 2003.

Hua, Tao. "Tanxi Xinjiang de Lishi, Wenhua Yu Minzu" (Exploring Xinjiang's History, Culture, and Nationalities). *Nanjing Library Lectures*, August 28, 2010.

Huang, Cary. "Paranoia from Soviet Union Collapse Haunts China's Communist Party, 22 Years On." *South China Morning Post*, November 18, 2013.

Huang, Cary. "How the Qatar Crisis Could Turn into a Disaster for Beijing." *South China Morning Post*, June 18, 2017.

Hummel, Arthur, trans. *The Autobiography of a Chinese Historian*. Taipei: Ch'eng Wen, 1966.

Husain, Ishrat. "Financing Burden of CPEC." *Dawn*, February 11, 2017.

Husain, Khurram. "CPEC Enclaves." *Dawn*, March 9, 2017.

Huwaidi, Fahmi. "Morsi in Beijing and Tehran." *Middle East Monitor*, January 25, 2014.

"'I Was Removed for Demanding Seraiki Province': Gilani." *Business Recorder*, December 18, 2016.

In, Nan-Hie. "In China, A Tug of War between Local States and Beijing to Curb Organized Crime." *Forbes*, January 25, 2016.

Inalcik, Halil. *The Ottoman Empire and Europe: The Ottoman Empire and Its Place in European History*. Istanbul: Kronik Kitap, 2017.

"Indonesia: From Vigilantism to Terrorism in Cirebon." *International Crisis Group*, January 26, 2012.

"Indonesia Protest: Jakarta Anti-Governor Rally Turns Violent." *BBC News*, November 4, 2017.

"Indonesia Seeks to Draw $28b Investment from China's Belt and Road Forum: Minister." *Jakarta Globe*, May 24, 2017.

"Indonesia's Bullet Train Deal with China: 'Delusional,' No Coordination." *rappler.com*, October 8, 2015.

International Crisis Group. *Pakistan: Stoking the Fire in Karachi*. Brussels: ICG, February 15, 2017.

International Fund for Agricultural Development. "Investing in Rural People in Egypt." *IFAD*, Rome, April 2017.

"Investment by China Not as Heavy as Indonesian Opponents Fear." *m.todayonline*, June 16, 2017.

Ioffe, Julia. "Putin Is Down with Polygamy." *Foreign Policy*, July 24, 2015.

Iqbal, Muhammad. *The Reconstruction of Religious Thought in Islam*. London: Oxford University Press, 1934.

"Iran Signs €2.2bn Rail Deal with China's CMC." *Global Construction Review*, May 22, 2017.

"Iran: The Revolution Is Over." *The Economist*, October 30, 2014.

"Iran Vows Full Throttle Dedication to China's Silk Road." *presstv.ir*, May 13, 2017.

"Iranians Not Too Happy with Their Made-In-China Qurans." *Shanghailist.com*, August 31, 2011.

Iredale, Robyn, Naran Bilik, and Fei Guo, eds. *China's Minorities on the Move: Selected Case Studies*. London: M.E. Sharpe, 2003.

Iroegbu, Senator. "To Finish Off Boko Haram, FG Looks to China for More Weapons." *This Day*, May 13, 2016.

"Islamic Food, Water, Toilet Paper Cause Concern about Extremism." *Global Times*, May 9, 2016.

Iyer-Mitra, Abhijit. "The Problem with India's Naval Build-Up." *Live Mint*, March 15, 2017.

Izutsu, Toshihiko. *Sufism and Taoism: A Comparative Study of Key Philosophical Concepts*. Berkeley: University of California Press, 2016.

Jacob, Zakka. "Why India Needs to Take Chinese Comments on Balochistan Seriously." *News 18 India*, August 29, 2016.

Jacobs, Andrew. "Light Government Touch Lets China's Hui Practice Islam in the Open." *New York Times*, February 1, 2016.

Jacobs, Andrew. "Joyous Africans Take to the Rails, With China's Help." *New York Times*, February 7, 2017.

Jaffe, Greg and Thomas Gibbons-Neff. "For Qataris, A U.S. Air Base Is Best Defense against Trump Attacks." *Washington Post*, June 6, 2017.

Japi, Hila. "Prof Buya Syafi'i Maarif: Ahok Tidak Menghina Al Quran" (Professor Buya Shafi'i Maarif: Ahok Did Not Insult the Quran). netralnews.com, November 6, 2016.

Jenkins, Rhys. "Is Chinese Competition Causing Deindustrialization in Brazil?" *Latin American Perspectives*, vol. 42, no. 6, July 7, 2015, 42–63.

Jennings, Ralph. "China Gets Cozier with Pakistan Again And, Yes, India Should Worry." *Forbes*, March 26, 2017.

Jha, Prem Shankar. "Modi's Beijing Policy Is Like Cutting Off India's Nose to Spite China's Face." *The Wire*, May 12, 2017.

Jie, Luo. "Egypt's Problems." *China Daily*, December 1, 2013.

Jin, Tang, ed. *Daguo Jueqi: Yi Lishi de Yanguang He Quanqiu de Shiye Jiedu 15 Shiji Yilai 9 Ge Shijiexing Daguo Jueqi de Lishi (The Rise of the Great Powers: In Historical and Global Perspective, Interpreting the History of the Rise of Nine World Powers Since the 15th Century)*. Beijing: Renmin Chubanshe, 2006.

Jing, Chai. "Wumai Diaocha: Qiongding Zhi Xia" (Investigating China's Smog: Under the Dome). youtube.com, March 1, 2015.

Johnson, Ian. "China's Great Uprooting: Moving 250 Million into Cities." *New York Times*, June 15, 2013.

Johnson, Ian. "New China Cities: Shoddy Homes, Broken Hope." *New York Times*, November 9, 2013.

Johnson, Ian. "China Seeks Tighter Grip in Wake of a Religious Revival." *New York Times*, October 7, 2016.

Johnson, Ian. "In China, Unregistered Churches Are Driving a Religious Revolution." *The Atlantic*, April 23, 2017.

Johnson, Ian. *The Souls of China: The Return of Religion after Mao*. New York: Pantheon/Knopf, 2017.

Johnson, Keith. "Can Indonesia Afford a Fish War with China?" *Foreign Policy*, July 8, 2016.

Johnston, Alastair Iain. "How New and Assertive Is China's New Assertiveness?" *International Security*, vol. 37, no. 4, Spring 2013, 7–48.

Jordan, Robert W. "Iran Could Become an Economic Superpower." *Time*, July 16, 2015.

Jullien, François. *The Propensity of Things: Toward a History of Efficacy in China*. New York: Zone Books, 1999.

Jumat, Wayne. "Quadrilateral Cooperation: Angola, Brazil, Nigeria and South Africa." *Institute for Global Dialogue*, May 29, 2014.

Junaidi, Ahmad. "Contemplating a Syariah-Influenced Indonesian Capital." *The Star Online (Malaysia)*, March 26, 2017.

Jurgelevicius, Arturas. "Friendship of Interests: Turkey and China." *bilgesam.org*, May 20, 2010.

Kadercan, Pelin Telseren and Burak Kadercan. "The Turkish Military as a Political Actor: Its Rise and Fall." *Middle East Policy*, Fall 2016.

Kadivar, Mohammad Ali. "Why Haven't Reformists Joined the Protests Sweeping Iran?" *Washington Post*, January 5, 2018.

Kahn, Robert. "China and the United States: A G2 within the G20." *Council on Foreign Relations*, April 2016.

Kaiman, Jonathan. "In China, Rise of Salafism Fosters Suspicion and Division among Muslims." *Los Angeles Times*, February 1, 2016.

Kamel, Ahmed. "Chinese Project to Build New Egyptian Capital Revived." *Nikkei Asian Review*, May 26, 2017.

Kan, Karoline. "Shanghai's Move to Curb International Programs in Schools Worries Parents." *New York Times*, December 29, 2016.

Kapila, Subhash. "Pakistan 2017 Comprehensively Colonized by China." *Uday India*, May 4, 2017.

Kaplan, Robert. "How We Would Fight China." *The Atlantic*, June 2005.

Karadeniz, Tulay and Daren Butler. "Turkey Confirms Cancellation of $3.4 Billion Missile Defence Project." *Reuters*, November 18, 2005.

Kastritsis, Dimitris J. *The Sons of Bayezid: Empire Building and Representation in the Ottoman Civil War of 1402–1413*. Leiden: Brill, 2007.

Katju, Vivek. "The Way to Tackle a Rattled China after Modi's Balochistan Barb." *thequint.com*, September 1, 2016.

Kayakiran, Firat. "Oil Flows through Turkey Energy Corridor Unhindered as Coup Ends." *Bloomberg*, July 16, 2016.

Kazianis, Harry J. "China's Greatest Fear: Dead and Buried Like the Soviet Union." *The National Interest*, March 11, 2016.

Keating, Paul. "Forget the West, Our Future Is to the North." *Brisbane Times*, November 15, 2012.

Keenan, Ronan. "Tatarstan: The Battle over Islam in Russia's Heartland." *World Policy Institute*, Summer 2013.

"Kempinski Bets on Ningxia's Hopes to Be Capital of China's New Silk Road." *Jing Daily*, June 19, 2016.

Kennedy, Scott. *The Business of Lobbying in China*. Cambridge, MA, Harvard University Press, 2008.

Kennedy, Scott and David A. Parker. "Building China's 'One Belt, One Road'." *Center for Strategic and International Studies*, April 3, 2015.

Kermali, Shenaz. "Who's Afraid of Iran?" *Al-Jazeera*, July 30, 2008.

Kerr, Simeon. "Qatar Fund Aims to Diversity through Asia." *Financial Times*, November 2, 2009.

Khadkha, Navin Singh. "Are India and Pakistan Set for Water Wars?" *BBC News*, December 22, 2016.

Khalid, Iram and Ishrat Begum. "Hydro-politics in Pakistan: Perceptions and Misperceptions." *South Asian Studies*, vol. 28, no. 1, January-June 2013, 7–23.

Khan, Azam. "China Urges Pakistani Parties to Settle CPEC Differences." *Express Tribune*, January 10, 2016.

Khan, Azam. "Persisting Stalemate: Govt Gails to Assuage APC's Concerns on CPEC." *Express Tribune*, January 11, 2016.

Khan, Masood. "Pakistan's Perceived Encirclement by India, Afghanistan, and Iran." *Voice of East*, June 7, 2016.

Khan, Rameez. "Shehbaz Sarif Advised to Stay Put in Punjab." *Express Tribune*, August 2, 2017.

Khan, Raza. "Dynamics of Ethnic Conflicts in Pakistan." *The Express Tribune*, July 21, 2017.

Khan, Tahir Khan. "Economic Corridor: Chinese Official Sets Record Straight." *Express Tribune*, March 2, 2015.

Kilpatrick, Ryan. "China's Plans for the Arctic—And a Shipping Centre to Rival Singapore." *South China Morning Post*, November 15, 2016.

Kimmelman, Michael. "Jakarta Is Sinking So Fast, It Could End Up Underwater." *New York Times*, December 21, 2017.

Kingsley, Patrick. "Erdogan Claims Vast Powers in Turkey after Narrow Victory in Referendum." *New York Times*, April 16, 2017.

Kinzer, Stephen. "Don't Get Too Excited about the Protests in Iran." *Boston Globe*, January 3, 2018.

Kiras, Ibrahim. "Çin Bilmecesi" (The Chinese Puzzle). *haber10.com*, October 9, 2010.

Kirchgaessner, Stephanie. "Italy Seeks to Reassure Asian Tourists with Imported Chinese Police." *The Guardian*, May 4, 2016.

Kirişci, Kemal. "The Transformation of Turkish Foreign Policy: The Rise of the Trading State." *New Perspectives on Turkey*, no. 40, Spring 2009, 29–56.

Kissinger, Henry. *On China*. New York: Penguin Press, 2011.

Kissinger, Henry A. "The Future of U.S.-Chinese Relations: Conflict Is a Choice, Not a Necessity." *Foreign Affairs*, vol. 91, no. 2, March/April 2012, 44–55.

Klare, Michael T. *Resource Wars: The New Landscape of Global Conflict*. New York: Metropolitan Books, 2001.

Knecht, Eric. "Egypt's Capital Project Hits Latest Snag as Chinese Pull Out." *Reuters*, February 8, 2017.

Knowler, Greg. "China to Dominate Global Shipping by 2030, Shanghai Report Finds." *Journal of Commerce*, June 10, 2015.

Kobrinskaya, Irina. "Is Russia Coming to Terms with China's 'Silk Road'?" *PONARS Eurasia*, September 2, 2016, 1–4.

Koda, Yoji. "China's Blue Water Navy Strategy and Its Implications." *Center for a New American Security*, March 2017.

Kolawole, Dipo. "From Isolation to Globalization: Transformation of Nigeria's Foreign Policy from the Abacha Regime to the Obasanjo Administration." *Pakistan Journal of Social Sciences*, vol. 3, no. 6, 2005, 873–879.

Komisi Pemilihan Umum, *Pilkada Provinsi DKI Jakarta (Putaran Kedua)* (General Election Commission, *Governor's Election for the Province of Jakarta, Second Round*). Jakarta: April 19, 2017. https://pilkada2017.kpu.go.id/hasil/2/t1/dki_jakarta.

Kong, Tao and Pierre van der Eng. "Mixed Messages of Chinese Investment in Indonesia." *East Asia Forum*, May 18, 2017.

Koru, Selim and Timur Kaymaz. "Turkey: Perspectives on Eurasian Integration." *European Council on Foreign Relations*, June 8, 2016.

"KP Assembly Opposes Changes in Economic Corridor Route." *Dawn*, February 7, 2015.

"KP Assembly Threatens to Resist Any Change in Route." *The News International*, February 7, 2015.

Krishnan, Ananth. "China May Station Marines in Gwadar, Say PLA Insiders." *India Today*, March 13, 2017.

Kucera, Joshua. "Erdogan to Putin: Let Us into SCO!" *eurasianet.org*, November 23, 2013.

Kucera, Joshua. "Is Russia in Europe or Asia? Why Not Both?" *Slate*, February 13, 2017.

Kuhrt, Natasha. "Russia and Asia-Pacific: Diversification or Sinocentrism?" In David Cadier and Margot Light, eds. *Russia's Foreign Policy: Ideas, Domestic Politics and External Relations*. London: Palgrave Macmillan, 2015, 175–188.

Kurbanov, Ruslan. "Tatarstan: Smooth Islamization Sprinkled with Blood." *Islam.ru*, February 27, 2013.

Kurzman, Charles, ed. *Liberal Islam: A Source Book*. New York: Oxford University Press, 1998.

Kushner, Jacob. *China's Congo Plan: What the Next World Power Sees in the World's Poorest Nation*. Washington, DC: Pulitzer Center, March 28, 2013.

Kutlugun, Satuk Bugra and Gokhan Kurtaran. "Erdogan Wants Turkey-China Trade Imbalance Tackled." *World Bulletin*, July 31, 2015.

Kwok, Kristine. "Is Xi Jinping the Man to Defuse Tensions in the Middle East?" *South China Morning Post*, January 14, 2016.

Kynge, James, Chris Campbell, Amy Kazmin, and Farhan Bokhari. "How China Rules the Waves." *Financial Times*, January 12, 2017.

Laessing, Ulf. "Saudi Arabia Opens Chinese-Built Haj Pilgrimage Train." *Reuters*, November 14, 2010.

Lagerwey, John. *China: A Religious State*. Hong Kong: Hong Kong University Press, 2010.

Lai, Hongyi. *The Domestic Sources of China's Foreign Policy: Regimes, Leadership, Priorities and Process*. London and New York: Routledge, 2010.

Lakoff, George and Mark Johnson. *Metaphors We Live By*. Chicago: University of Chicago Press, 2003.

Laksmana, Evan A. "Why International Law Cannot Rule over the South China Sea." *Jakarta Post*, July 25, 2016.

"Lalejin, Iran's Pottery Capital." *payvand.com*, June 19, 2010.

Lam, Jeffie and Joyce Ng. "Dubious Voters for Hong Kong's Legislative Council Functional Constituencies Revealed." *South China Morning Post*, July 4, 2016.

Lam, Katy N. *Chinese State-Owned Enterprises in West Africa: Triple-Embedded Globalization*. London and New York: Routledge, 2017.

Lamb, Kate. "Jakarta Election Challenger Anies Accused of Courting Islamic Vote amid Religious Divide." *The Guardian*, April 14, 2017.

Lampton, David M. *The Three Faces of Chinese Power: Might, Money, and Minds*. Berkeley: University of California Press, 2008.

Landau, Jacob M. *Pan-Turkism: From Irredentism to Cooperation*. Bloomington: Indiana University Press, 1995.

Langenkamp, Harm. "Conflicting Dreams of Global Harmony in US-PRC Silk Road Diplomacy." In Rebekah Ahrendt, Mark Ferraguto, and Damien Mahiet, eds. *Music and Diplomacy from the Early Modern Era to the Present*. New York: Palgrave Macmillan, 2014, 83–100.

Lanteigne, Marc. "China and Norway: Cold Shoulder No More, Following Diplomatic Thaw." *Arctic Deeply*, January 3, 2017.

Lapidus, Ira. "Hierarchies and Networks: A Comparison of Chinese and Islamic Societies." In Frederic WakemanJr. and Carolyn Grant, eds. *Conflict and Control in Late Imperial China*. Berkeley: University of California Press, 1975, 26–42.

Larmer, Brook. "Is China the World's New Colonial Power?" *New York Times*, May 2, 2017.

Laruell, Marlène and Sébastien Peyrouse. *The Chinese Question in Central Asia: Domestic Order, Social Change and the Chinese Factor*. London: Hurst and Co., 2012.

Lawder, David. "World Bank Group, China-Led AIIB Agree to Deepen Cooperation." *Reuters*, April 23, 2017.

Lawrence, Patrick. "How China Is Building the Post-Western World." *The Nation*, May 16, 2017.

Lazarev, Egor and Anna Biryukova. "Are Russia's 20 Million Muslims Seething about Putin Bombing Syrian?" *Washington Post*, March 7, 2016.

Lebedev, Greg and Ana C. Rold. "The New Suez Canal: How Egypt Is Charting a Brand New Future for Itself and the Region." *Diplomatic Courier*, September 1, 2015.

Lee, Itamar Y. "Chasing the Rising Red Crescent: Sino-Shi'i Relations in Post-Cold War Era China." *Comparative Islamic Studies*, vol. 7, no. 1–2, 2011, 313–347.

Lee, Peter. "China Fine-Tunes Its Iran Strategy." *Asia Times*, February 25, 2010.

Lee, Richard E., ed. *The Longue Duree and World-Systems Analysis*. Albany: State University of New York Press, 2012.

Legrand, Julien. "The Great Convergence: China's Future Lies in Its West." *Paris Innovation Review*, December 12, 2015.

Lerner, George Marshall. "In Turkey, U.S. Loss is China's Gain." *The Diplomat*, January 31, 2017.

Levathes, Louise. *When China Ruled the Seas: The Treasure Fleet of the Dragon Throne, 1400–1433*. New York: Simon and Schuster, 1994.

Leverett, Flynt and Hillary Mann Leverett. "U.S. Sanctions and China's Iran Policy." *Monthly Review*, July 30, 2011.

Lewis, Mark Edward. *The Flood Myths of Early China*. Albany: State University of New York Press: 2006.

Li, Xiaokun. "China Takes on Mediation Role." *China Daily*, December 24, 2015.

Li, Xue and Zheng Yuwen. "The Future of China's Diplomacy in the Middle East." *The Diplomat*, July 26, 2016.

Liang, Xiangming. *Liu Zhi: Jiqi Yisilan Sixiang Yanjiu* (*Liu Zhi: A Study of His Islamic Ethics*). Lanzhou: Lanzhou Daxue Chubanshe, 2004.

Liang, Xiangming. *Mingmo Qingchu Huizu San Da Hanwen Yizhejia Lunli Sixiang Yanjiu* (*The Ethics of Three Hui Chinese Translators during the Late Ming Dynasty to the Early Qing Dynasty*). Beijing: Guangming Ribao Chubanshe, 2010.

Liang, Xiangming. *Huizu Chuantong Lunli Sixiang Yanjiu* (*Traditional Hui Ethics*). Yinchuan: Yangguang Chubanshe, 2014.

Lei, Ya-Wen. *The Contentious Public Sphere: Law, Media, and Authoritarian Rule in China*. Princeton, NJ: Princeton University Press, 2017.

Lieberman, Victor. "Protected Rimlands and Exposed Zones: Reconfiguring Premodern Eurasia." *Comparative Studies in Society and History*, vol. 50, no. 3, July 2008, 692–723.

Leibold, James. "Competing Narratives of Racial Unity in Republican China: From the Yellow Emperor to Peking Man." *Modern China*, vol. 32, no. 2, April, 2006, 181–220.

Leibold, James. "In Search of Han: Early Twentieth-Century Narratives on Chinese Origins and Development." *China Heritage Quarterly*, no. 19, September 2009.

Leibold, James. *Ethnic Policy in China: Is Reform Inevitable?* Honolulu, HA: East-West Center, 2013.

Leibold, James. "Creeping Islamophobia: China's Hui Muslims in the Firing Line." *Jamestown China Brief*, June 20, 2016.

Leonard, Mark, ed. "Geo-economics with Chinese Characteristics: How China's Economic Might Is Reshaping World Politics." *World Economic Forum*, January 2016.

Leopold, Anita Maria and Jeppe Sinding Jensen, eds. *Syncretism in Religion: A Reader*. New York: Routledge, 2004.

Lewis, Martin W. *The Myth of Continents: A Critique of Metageography*. Berkeley: University of California Press, 1997.

Li, Eric X. "The Umbrella Revolution Won't Give Hong Kong Democracy." *Washington Post*, October 6, 2014.

Li, Gan. "Why China Needs to Spend More on Welfare." *CNN*, March 5, 2013.

Li, Leqin. "Qian Tan Yisilan Jiao de Zhongguohua" (On the Sinification of Islam). chinaislam.net, February 24, 2016.

Li, Rui, Hu Jiwei et al. "Zhixing Xianfa Di 35 Tiao, Feichu Yushen Zhi, Duixian Gongmin de Yanlun Chuban Ziyou!" (Implement Article 35 of the Constitution, Abolish Censorship, Honor the Citizenry's Speech and Press Freedoms!) boxun. com, October 11, 2010.

Li, Ruohan. "Halal Food Legislation Violates Constitutional Principle: Expert." *Global Times*, March 7, 2016.

Li, Wannan and Beiyan Wen. "Shixi Hou Suhatuo Shidai Yinni Dui Hua Zhengce de Bianhua" (Examining Changes in Indonesia's Policy Toward China in the Post-Suharto Period). *Southeast Asian Studies*, no. 3, June 2009, 57–67.

Li, Xiguang. "Belt and Road Initiative to Connect Hearts." *China Daily*, April 8, 2015.

Li, Xiguang. "'Yidai Yilu' Ruhe Zuoguo Zhongdong Zhongya Fengbao Yan" (How 'One Belt One Road' Can Pass through the Eye of the Storm in the Middle East and Central Asia). *guancha.cn*, April 14, 2015.

Liang, Guanghe. "Zhongguo Shi Zhongyang Zhi Guo" (China Is the Central Country). *sciencenet.cn*, April 29, 2017.

Lieven, Anatol. *Pakistan: A Hard Country*. New York: PublicAffairs, 2012.

Lin, Christina. "China's Strategic Shift towards the Region of the Four Seas: The Middle Kingdom Arrives in the Middle East." *ISPSW Strategy Series*, April 2013.

Linder, Alex. "Nigeria Says Seized 'Plastic Rice' Is Not Actually Fake but also Isn't Fit for Human Consumption." *shanghailist.com*, January 3, 2017.

Ling, Shengli. "Diyuan Jingji Chongsu Dayangzhou Geju" (Geo-economics Is Reshaping Oceania). *Beijing Review*, March 29, 2017.

Lipman, Jonathan N. *Familiar Strangers: A History of Muslims in Northwest China*. Seattle: University of Washington Press, 1997.

Lipman, Jonathan N. "White Hats, Oil Cakes, and Common Blood: The Hui in the Contemporary Chinese State." In Morris Rossabi, ed. *Governing China's Multiethnic Frontiers*. Seattle: University of Washington Press, 2004, 19–52.

Lipman, Jonathan, ed. *Islamic Thought in China: Sino-Muslim Intellectual Evolution from the 17th to the 21st Century*. Edinburgh: Edinburgh University Press, 2016.

Little, Richard. *The Balance of Power in International Relations: Metaphors, Myths, and Models*. New York: Cambridge University Press, 2007.

Liu, Charles. "Police Brutality Caught on Video at Dongguan Labor Dispute." *The Nanfang*, June 26, 2015.

Liu, Coco and Magdalene Fung. "Towering Figures: Who's Who in the World of Chinese Soft Power?" *South China Morning Post*, March 19, 2017.

Liu, Dong, Huang Jingjing, and Xie Wenting. "Shanghai Muslims' Outdoor Prayers Show Urban Integration." *english.sina.com*, July 8, 2016.

Liu, Tao. *Zhongguo Shiji* (The Chinese Century). Beijing: Xinhua, 2010.

Liu, Xincheng. "The Global View of History in China." *Journal of World History*, September 2012.

Liu, Xinru. "A Silk Road Legacy: The Spread of Buddhism and Islam." *Journal of World History*, vol. 22, no. 1, March 2011, 55–81.

Liu, Ya. *Zhuanxing Qi Zhengzhi: Jizhi De Tupo Yu Kunrao* (Times of Transitional Politics: Breakthroughs and Disruptions). Beijing: China Social Science Press, 2011.

Liu, Yazhou. "Xibu Lun" (On the Western Region). *Phoenix Weekly*, August 5, 2010.

Liu, Yazhou. "Zhong Mei Daguo Boyi: Kaipi Shijie Lishi Xin Shidai" (The Great Game of China and America: The Beginning of a New Historical Era). Preface to Liu Ming Fu, *China's Dream: Great Power Thinking and Strategic Posture in a Post-American Era*. Beijing: China Friendship, 2010.

Liu, Ying, Zhongping Chen, and Gregory Blue, eds. *Zheng He's Maritime Voyages (1405–1433) and China's Relations with the Indian Ocean World*. Leiden/Boston, Brill, 2014.

Liu, Zhentang. *Zhongguo Zhu Zhongdong Dashi Hua Zhongdong: Libanen* (*China's Middle East Ambassadors Discuss the Middle East: Lebanon*). Beijing: World Knowledge Press, 2009.

Liu, Zihang. "How the Chinese View International Law." *International Policy Digest*, August 29, 2016.

Locke, Charley. "Go Inside China's Bizarre Theme Park in the Egyptian Desert." *Wired*, October 24, 2016.

Lodge, Carey. "Is Religious Freedom in China Really about to Get Worse?" *Christian Today*, October 6, 2016.

Lombard, Denys. *Le carrefour javanais, Essai d'histoire globale*. Paris: Éditions de l'École des Hautes Études en Sciences Sociales, 1990.

Lombard, Denys. "Another 'Mediterranean' in Southeast Asia." *The Asia-Pacific Journal*, vol. 5, no. 3, March 1, 2007, 1–13.

Lombard Denys and Claudine Salmon. "Islam and Chineseness." *Indonesia*, vol. 57, April 1993, 115–132.

Louw-Vaudran, Liesl. "Nigeria Will Be Africa's First Global Superpower." *Mail and Guardian (South Africa)*, May 29, 2017.

Lowney, Chris. *A Vanished World: Muslims, Christians, and Jews in Medieval Spain*. New York: Oxford University Press, 2006.

Ludden, David. "Maps in the Mind and the Mobility of Asia." *The Journal of Asian Studies*, vol. 62, no. 4, November 2003, 1057–1078.

Ma, Bo. "'Yidai Yilu' Yu Yinni 'Quanqiu Hai Shang Zhidian' de Zhanlue Duijie Yanjiu" (Joint Study of "One Belt One Road" and Indonesia's Global Maritime Axis Strategy). *International Outlook*, September 15, 2015.

Ma, Haiyun and I-wei Jennifer Chang. "China's Strategic Middle Eastern Languages." *Middle East Research and Information Project*, no. 270, Spring 2014, 26–27.

Ma, Jian. "Hong Kong: The River of Democracy Will Flow to Tiananmen Square." *The Guardian*, October 3, 2014.

Ma, Ping. "Bosi Yilsilan Wenming Dui Zhongguo Yisilan Wenming de Gongxian Ji Qi Shenyuan Yingxiang" (The Contribution and Deep Influence of Persian Islamic Civilization on Chinese Islamic Civilization). *Journal of Hui Muslim Minority Studies*, no. 3, 2004, 100–103.

Ma Ping, "Zhongguo Huizu Musilin de Shehui Wangluo Jiegou" (The Structure of Social Networks of Chinese Hui Muslims), *Journal of Hui Muslim Minority Studies*, no. 1, 2008, 5–10.

Ma, Rong. "A New Perspective in Guiding Ethnic Relations in the 21st Century: 'Depoliticization' of Ethnicity in China." *Procedia-Social and Behavioral Sciences*, vol. 2, no. 5, 2010, 6831–6845.

Ma, Xiaoning, Zhou Hanbo, Xie Yahong, and Liu Junguo. "Romantic Love Story Brightens Up Silk Road." *Global Times*, May 1, 2017.

MacGillivray, Alice E. "A Policy Paradox: Social Complexity Emergence Around an Ordered Science Attractor." *Emergence: Complexity and Organization*, vol. 14, no. 4, November 2015, 1–18.

MacIsaac, Tara. "Indonesia's Last Stand for a Coal Industry In Peril." *Mongabay*, February 13, 2017.

Mahdi, Muhsin. *Ibn Khaldun's Philosophy of History: A Study in the Philosophic Foundation of the Science of Culture*. Chicago: University of Chicago Press, 1964.

Maini, Tridivesh. "Shahbaz Sharif's China Visit: Implications for CPEC." *The Diplomat*, August 2, 2016.

Maini, Tridivesh Singh. "Japan's Effort to Counter China's Silk Road." *The Globalist*, April 6, 2016.

Maja-Pearce, Adewale. "Nigeria's China Connection." *New York Times*, May 7, 2014.

Makeham, John. *Lost Soul: "Confucianism" in Contemporary Chinese Academic Discourse*. Harvard-Yenching Institute, 2008.

Malashenko, Alexey. "Divisions and Defiance among Russia's Muslims." *Carnegie Moscow Center*, November 20, 2015.

Malashenko, Alexey and Alexey Starostin. "The Rise of Nontraditional Islam in the Urals." *Carnegie Moscow Center*, September 30, 2015.

Malik, Ahmad Rashid. "Route Alignment Controversy." *The Nation*, February 20, 2015.

Malik, Ahmad Rashid. "Terrifying CPEC, Enemy Trying to Throw a Wrench in the Gears." *Pakistan Today*, June 11, 2016.

Malik, Ahmad Rashid. "The Chabahar Pact, This India-Iran Pact Should Be a Wakeup Call." *Pakistan Today*, June 22, 2016.

Mangi, Faseeh and Kamran Haider. "Xi Postpones $34 Billion Pakistan Trip amid Protests." *Bloomberg*, September 6, 2014.

Manning, Patrick. "Africa's Place in Globalization: Africa, Eurasia, and Their Borderlands." *Journal of Globalization Studies*, vol. 5, no. 1, May 2014, 65–81.

Manson, Steven and David O'Sullivan. "Complexity Theory in the Study of Space and Place." *Environment and Planning*, vol. 38, no. 4, April 1, 2006, 677–692.

Marks, Michael P. *Metaphors in International Relations Theory*. London: Palgrave Macmillan, 2011.

Marlow, Iain. "The Next China? Indonesia Emerging as a New Asian Powerhouse." *The Globe and Mail*, January 16, 2015.

Marsh, Jenni. "Afro-Chinese Marriages Boom in Guangzhou: But Will It Be 'Til Death Do Us Part'?" *South China Morning Post*, July 2, 2014.

Marshall, Shana. "The Egyptian Armed Forces and the Remaking of an Economic Empire," *Carnegie Middle East Center*, 2015.

Martina, Michael. "China's Xi to Visit Saudi, Iran in New Diplomacy Push." *Reuters*, January 15, 2016.

Martina, Michael. "China Holds Massive Police Rally in Xinjiang as Hundreds Sent to Anti-terror 'Frontline.'" *Reuters*, February 29, 2017.

Marx, Willem and Marc Wattrelot. *Balochistan: At a Crossroads*. New Delhi: Niyogi Books, 2014.

Matthaei, Katrin. "Goodluck Jonathan: A Powerless President." *Deutsche Welle*, July 5, 2014.

McCarthy, Susan K. *Chinese Multiculturalism: Ethnic Revival in Southwest China*. Seattle: University of Washington Press, 2009.

McDonald, Joe. "China Faces Political Conflicts in Moves to Cut Debt Burden." *US News*, January 25, 2017.

McDonald, Joe, Munir Ahmed, and Gillian Wong. "'Silk Road' Plan Stirs Unease over China's Strategic Goals." *Associated Press*, May 11, 2017.

McGann, James G. "Chinese Think Tanks, Policy Advice and Global Governance." *Indiana University Research Center for Chinese Politics and Business*, March 2012.

McHale, Melissa R. McHale et al. "The New Global Urban Realm: Complex, Connected, Diffuse, and Diverse Social-Ecological Systems." *Sustainability*, vol. 7, no. 5, 2015, 5211–5240.

Mearshimer, John. *The Tragedy of Great Power Politics*. New York-London: Norton, 2003.

Medcalf, Rory. "Reimagining Asia: From Asia-Pacific to Indo-Pacific." *The ASAN Forum*, June 26, 2015.

"Meeting of Parliamentary Committee CPEC." *nihao-salam.com*, June 30, 2016.

Mehling, Nicholas. "15 Major Chinese Companies Meet with Egypt before G20 Summit." *Daily News Egypt*, July 9, 2016.

"Mei Yaoqiu Zhongdong Mengyou Zengjia Dui Hua Gong You, You Shi Zhongguo Shuyuan Yilang" (U.S. Asks Middle East Allies to Increase Oil Sales to China in Order to Induce It to Isolate Iran). *Global Times*, October 20, 2009.

Melman, Yossi. "China Will Not Stop Israel if It Decides to Attack Iran." *Haaretz*, September 22, 2011.

"Merkel: Germany, China Must Expand Partnership in 'Times of Global Uncertainty.'" *Deutsche Welle*, June 1, 2017.

Meyer, Ben. "COSCO Pacific to Acquire Istanbul Container Terminal for $940m." *American Shipper*, September 17, 2015.

Michelson, Ethan. "Justice from Above or Below? Popular Strategies for Resolving Grievances in Rural China." *China Quarterly*, vol. 193, March 2008, 43–64.

Miglani, Sanjeev. "India Cool on Beijing Summit as 'Silk Road' Stirs Unease." *Reuters*, May 13, 2017.

Miller, Tom. *China's Asian Dream: Empire Building along the New Silk Road*. London: Zed Books, 2017.

Millward, James. "China's Fruitless Repression of the Uighurs." *New York Times*, September 28, 2014.

Ming, Pao. "Zhongguo Qian Zhongdong Teshi Cheng Zhongdong Jiaojin Jaiju Zhong Mei Fenqi" (China's Former Middle East Envoy Said Mideast Competition Has Intensified Differences between China and the United States). *boxun.com*, October 7, 2009.

Ministry of Foreign Affairs of the People's Republic of China. "Chinese Ambassadors to Iran." *fmprc.gov.cn*, May 2014.

Ministry of Foreign Affairs of the People's Republic of China. "Special Envoy of the Chinese Government on Syrian Issue Xie Xiaoyan Visits Egypt." *fmprc.gov.cn*, April 24, 2017.

Ministry of Interior Islamic Republic of Iran. *Natayej Tafsili Entekhabat Riyasat Jomhori (Detailed Results of the Presidential Elections)*. Tehran: Ministry of Interior, 2013 and 2017.

MIT Media Lab. "Observatory of Economic Complexity." *atlas.media.mit.edu*, 2017.

Mo, Lingjiao. "Turkey, Another Axis of Evil?" *Global Times*, July 10, 2009.

Mohan, C. Raja. *Samudra Manthan: Sino-Indian Rivalry in the Indo-Pacific*. Washington, DC: Carnegie Endowment for International Peace, 2012.

Mollier, Christine. *Buddhism and Taoism Face to Face: Scripture, Ritual, and Iconographic Exchange in Medieval China.* Honolulu: University of Hawaii Press, 2008.

Momani, Bessa. "Xi Jinping's Davos Speech Showed the World Has Turned Upside Down." *Newsweek*, January 18, 2017.

Montgomery, David R. "What Science Can—And Can't—Tell Us about Legendary Ancient Figures Like China's Emperor Yu." *Washington Post*, August 5, 2016.

Monzon, Thomas. "Thai Consulate in Turkey Attacked Following Deportation of Uighurs." *UPI*, July 9, 2015.

Moore, Elaine. "Civets, Brics and the Next 11." *Financial Times*, June 8, 2012.

"More Jakarta Means More Trouble for Tony Abbott." *The Economist*, November 23, 2013.

"More than Minerals: Chinese Trade with Africa Keeps Growing: Fears of Neocolonialism Are Overdone." *The Economist*, March 23, 2013.

Morgan, David. "Persian as a *Lingua Franca* in the Mongol Empire." In Brian Spooner and William L. Hanaway, eds. *Literacy in the Persianate World: Writing and the Social Order.* Philadelphia: University of Pennsylvania Press, 2012, 160–170.

Moriyasu, Ken. "China-Aided Trans-Africa Railway Line Likely to Transform Regional Trade." *Nikkei Asian Review*, August 25, 2014.

Moritz, Bjoern. "Admiral Zheng He, The Columbus from the Far East!" *Maritime Topics on Stamps*, 2006.

Morris, Ruth. "Parliamentary-Style Debates Take Off in China: Even if Some Topics Are Off Limits." *Public Radio International*, September 5, 2014.

Moss, Trefor. "Indonesia Blows Up 23 Foreign Fishing Boats to Send a Message." *Wall Street Journal*, April 5, 2016.

Mourdoukoutas, Panos. "Does Karachi Really Want China to Control the Electrical Switch?" *Forbes*, September 5, 2016.

Movius, Lisa. "New Museum on Silk Road Breaks the Chinese Mould, Islam Is the Focus of North-West China's First Contemporary Art Institution." *theartnewspaper.com*, August 27, 2015.

Mpyisi, Edson. *Egypt: National Drainage Programme.* African Development Bank Group, April 2015.

Mthembu-Salter, Gregory. "Elephants, Ants and Superpowers: Nigeria's Relations with China." *South Africa Institute of International Affairs, Occasional Paper No. 42*, September 2009.

Mu, Chunshan. "Anti-Muslim Sentiment Is Taking Over China's Social Media Scene." *The Diplomat*, September 13, 2016.

Mu, Xuequan. "Iran Blames Saudi Arabia of 'Sponsoring Terrorism.'" *Xinhua*, June 15, 2017.

Mudie, Luisetta. "China Deports Hundreds of Uyghur Residents from Yunnan." *Radio Free Asia*, March 12, 2014.

Mufson, Steven. "This Documentary Went Viral in China. Then It Was Censored. It Won't Be Forgotten." *Washington Post*, March 16, 2015.

Mukai, Masaki. "New Approaches to Pre-modern Maritime Networks." *Asian Review of World Histories*, vol. 4, no. 2, July 2016, 179–189.

Mukhametov, Rinat. "Russian Muslims and Foreign Policy." *Global Affairs*, October 7, 2012.

Mukherji, Biman. "Indonesian Nickel Exports a Boon for China." *Wall Street Journal*, January 17, 2017.

Mullaney, Thomas. *Coming to Terms with the Nation: Ethnic Classification in Modern China*. Berkeley: University of California Press, 2010.

Murata, Sachiko, William C. Chittick, and Weiming Tu. *The Sage Learning of Liu Zhi: Islamic Thought in Confucian Terms*. Cambridge, MA: Harvard University Asia Center, 2009.

"Muslim Communist Theme Park Set for China to Bolster Ties with Middle East." rt.com, May 13, 2016.

"Muslim Uigurs Escape Chinese Persecution; Seek Refuge in Turkey." *World Bulletin*, January 15, 2015.

Müller, Peter and Maximillian Popp. "Purges Have Weakened Once Mighty Turkish Military." *Spiegel*, January 18, 2017.

Mwanza, Kevin. "A Chinese-Funded Railway Line to Open Up Central Africa's Hinterland." *AFK Insider*, December 20, 2015.

"Na'aramiha Dar Sharhai Mokhtalef Iran Baraye Sevomin Ruz Peyapei" (Unrest in Several Cities of Iran for the Third Day in a Row). *BBC Persian Service*, December 30, 2017.

Nabbs-Keller, Greta. "The Very Public Flaying of Marty Natalagawa." *The Interpreter*, September 19, 2014.

Nabhan, Gary Paul. *Cumin, Camels, and Caravans: A Spice Odyssey*. Berkeley: University of California Press, 2014.

Nader, Aya. "U.S. Resumes Military Aid to Egypt despite Human Rights Situation." *Daily News Egypt*, April 14, 2015.

Nagpal, Sahil. "Chinese-Indonesian Muslims Criticize China over Urumqi Unrest." *TopNews.in*, July 10, 2009.

Nakamura, David. "As Trump Pursues 'America First,' China's Xi Sees Opening for Primacy in Asia." *Washington Post*, April 4, 2017.

Nashabe, Omar. "China's Ambassador in Lebanon: Hezbollah Arms a Trade Matter." *Al-Akhbar*, May 4, 2012.

Nasr, Vali. *The Shia Revival: How Conflicts within Islam Will Shape the Future*. New York: Norton, 2006.

Nasr, Vali. *The Dispensable Nation: American Foreign Policy in Retreat*. New York: Doubleday, 2013.

Natalegawa, Marty. "An Indonesian Perspective on the Indo-Pacific." *Jakarta Post*, May 20, 2013.

Nauman, Qasim. "Pakistan Stock Exchange Says Chinese Consortium Has Top Bid for 40% Stake." *Wall Street Journal*, December 22, 2016.

Nawaz, Farman. "Proposed Sino-Pakistani Trade Route Misses Areas in Need." *Global Times*, July 30, 2013.

"Nawaz Sharif's Media-Savvy Daughter to Contest Next Election in Pakistan." *Press Trust of India*, January 19, 2018.

Nazer, Fahad. "Saudi Arabia's New Best Friend: China?" *The National Interest*, September 2, 2015.

Ndzendze, Bhaso. "The Contours of China-Africa Relations." *Modern Diplomacy*, April 29, 2017.

"Need to Repeal Colonial Rail Monopoly Law." *Ships and Ports*, June 27, 2016.
Nehru, Vikram. "Indonesia: The Reluctant Giant." *The National Interest*, February 11, 2016.
Neild, Barry. "Kunming Rail Station Attack: China Horrified as Mass Stabbings Leave Dozens Dead." *The Guardian*, March 2, 2014.
"Neo-colonialism or De-colonialism? China's Economic Engagement in Africa and the Implications for World Order." *African Journal of Political Science and International Relations*, vol. 8, no. 7, October 2014, 185–201.
Neville, Robert. *Boston Confucianism*. Albany: State University of New York Press, 2000.
"Nigeria Bank Chief Sees Yuan Becoming Reserve Currency." *Xinhua*, September 6, 2011.
"Nigeria to Borrow $2.3 Billion from World Bank and China, Finance Minister." *Reuters*, February 21, 2017.
"Nigerian Anger over China Deaths." *BBC News*, September 25, 2009.
"Nigeria's Goodluck Jonathan, Profile of a Defeated President." *BBC News*, March 31, 2015.
Noorani, Ahmad. "CPEC Route Controversy Routed." *The News*, January 16, 2016.
Normile, Dennis. "Massive Flood May Have Led to China's Earliest Empire." *Science*, August 4, 2016.
Noueihed, Lin and Ali Abdelaty. "China's Xi Visits Egypt, Offers Financial, Political Support." *Reuters*, January 21, 2016.
Nowar, Nesma, Stefan Weichert, and Mona El-Fiqi. "Egypt's Dwindling Foreign Currency Resources." *Al-Ahram Weekly*, March 23, 2016.
"Nuclear Power in Turkey." *World Nuclear Association*, June 21, 2017.
Nwezeh, Kingsley. "Nigeria: Fake Drugs—China Apologises to the Government." *This Day*, September 21, 2009.
Nye, Joseph S. Jr. "The Limits of Chinese Soft Power." *Project Syndicate*, July 10, 2015.
Oakes, Tim. "China's Provincial Identities: Reviving Regionalism and Reinventing 'Chineseness.'" *Journal of Asian Studies*, vol. 59, no. 3, August 2000, 667–692.
Oakes, Tim and Donald S. Sutton, eds. *Faiths on Display: Religion, Tourism, and the Chinese State*. Lanham, MD: Rowman & Littlefield, 2010.
O'Brien, Kevin J. and Lianjiang Li. *Rightful Resistance in Rural China*. Cambridge: Cambridge University Press, 2006.
O'Connell, Jack. "Canal Wars." *Maritime Executive*, October 31, 2016.
Odittah, Chuka. "Hope Dims on N170 Billion Abuja-Kaduna Rail Project." *The Guardian*, January 27, 2016.
Odittah, Chuka. "China Gives Stringent Conditions for $20bn Loan to Nigeria." *The Guardian*, August 14, 2016.
Oduah, Chika. "Nigeria—A Fractured Giant?" *Huffington Post*, October 15, 2014.
Odugbemi, Sina. "The Dictator's Dilemma." *The World Bank*, February 20, 2014.
Offiong, Adie Vanessa. "Nigeria: 'Africans Order for Low Quality Products from China.'" *Daily Trust*, December 7, 2015.
Ogunlesi, Tolu. "Nigeria and China Deals: What's the Benefit for Us?" *Financial Times*, December 4, 2015.

Oikawa, Junko. "China's Struggle for Civil Society: A New Perspective on Social Development." *The Tokyo Foundation*, September 26, 2013.

Ojeme, Victoria. "NASS Moves to Enhance Technology Transfer between China, Nigeria." *Vanguard*, January 30, 2017.

Olander, Eric and Cobus van Staden. "Nigerian in China: Why Are People Here So Racist towards Black People?" *The Huffington Post*, June 27, 2016.

Omar, Mohie El Din M. and Ahmed M. A. Moussa. "Water Management in Egypt for Facing the Future Challenges." *Journal of Advanced Research*, vol. 7, no. 3, May 2016, 403–412.

Omokri, Reno. "When an Acting President Acts Well." *This Day*, February 18, 2017.

Onuah, Felix and Paul Carsten. "Nigeria Awards $1.79 Bln Railway Contract to Chinese State Firm CCECC." *Reuters*, March 22, 2017.

Onuah, Felix and Chijioke Ohuocha. "Nigeria Agrees $550 Million Satellite Deal with China." *Reuters*, January 3, 2018.

Onyewuchi, Ikechukwu. "Nigeria/China: Still a Long Way to Go." *Saturday Magazine*, April 24, 2016.

"Opening of the Fourth Nanjing University-Harvard Yanjing International Academic Conference on the Dialogue of Civilizations." *iwr.cass.cn*, Nanjing, June 11–14, 2010.

Osman, Tarek. *Egypt on the Brink: From Nasser to the Muslim Brotherhood*. New Haven: CT: Yale University Press, 2013.

Ostrom, Elinor. "Managing Resources in the Global Commons." *Journal of Business Administration and Policy Analysis*, vol. 30–31, 2002, 401–413.

Otto, Ben. "ASEAN Looks for Wiggle Room to Skirt South China Sea Impasse." *Wall Street Journal*, July 24, 2016.

Ozerkan, Fulya. "Recep Tayyip Erdogan Sparks Furor in Turkey by Saying He Wants to 'Raise a Religious Youth.'" *Reuters*, February 9, 2012.

Pachymuthu, Luke and Seng Li Peng. "China's Top Oil Firms Sell Gasoline to Iran." *Reuters*, April 14, 2010.

Page, Jeremy and Emre Peker. "As Muslim Uighurs Flee, China Sees Jihad Risk." *Wall Street Journal*, January 30, 2015.

"Pakistan Election Headquarters 2018," *Geo Television Network*, July 31, 2018, https://www.geo.tv/election.

"Pakistan to Host International Conference on Maritime Economy." *Dunya News*, December 10, 2016.

Pal, Satyabrata. "The China-Pakistan Corridor Is All About Power—Not Electricity, But the Real Thing." *The Wire*, June 3, 2016.

Paldi, Camille. "Islamic Finance Is Knocking on the Doorsteps of China." *International Finance*, July 15, 2015.

Palmer, James. "What Trump Calls Strength, China Calls Stupidity." *Foreign Policy*, April 7, 2017.

Pan, Guxi, ed. *Buildings of the Yuan-Ming Period*. Reading, UK: Paths International, 2013.

Pan, Zhongqi, ed. *Conceptual Gaps in China-EU Relations: Global Governance, Human Rights and Strategic Partnerships*." London: Palgrave Macmillan, 2012.

Pang, Jessie. "De Yiwu a Madrid. Conoce la línea de tren más larga del mundo." *Estrella Digital*, November 20, 2016.

Pannier, Bruce. "The Trans-Caspian Pipeline: Technically Possible, Politically Difficult." *Radio Free Europe Radio Liberty*, May 24, 2015.

Pantland, Walton. "Unions in Turkey: Holding the Line for Workers." *industriall-union.org*, June 8, 2016.

Paradise, James F. "The Role of 'Parallel Institutions' in China's Growing Participation in Global Economic Governance." *Journal of Chinese Political Science*, vol. 21, no. 2, June 2016, 149–175.

Parameswaran, Prashanth. "Indonesia and China's AIIB." *The Diplomat*, July 26, 2016.

Pardo, Ramon Pacheco. "Return of the G2: Can US and China Run the World?" *The Telegraph*, November 12, 2014.

Parello-Plesner, Jonas and Mathieu Duchâtel. "China's Strong Arm: Protecting Citizens and Assets Abroad." *International Institute for Security Studies, Singapore*, May 29, 2015.

Park, Hyunhee. *Mapping the Chinese and Islamic Worlds: Cross-Cultural Exchange in Pre-modern Asia*. New York: Cambridge University Press, 2012.

Parker, Emily. "Social Media and the Hong Kong Protests." *The New Yorker*, October 1, 2014.

Parlina, Ina. "Jokowi Changes Tune in Handling Rally." *Jakarta Post*, December 3, 2016.

Partnership for Action on Green Economy. *Transition to a Green Economy in China's Jiangsu Province: A Stocktaking Report*. Nanjing: Ministry of Environmental Protection, 2016.

Patung, "Chinese Uighurs and Xinjiang Province Riots." *IndonesiaMatters.com*, July 16, 2009.

Pearce, Fred. "Mega-canals Could Slice through Continents for Giant Ships." *New Scientist*, April 11, 2017.

Pearce, Oliver. "From Yiwu to Damascus: A New Silk Road Is Born." *Global Times*, June 16, 2009.

Pecquet, Julian. "What Happened to the Billions the U.S. Gave to Egypt?" *U.S. News*, May 13, 2016.

Pei, Minxin. "China's Middle Class Is About to Demand Big Changes." *Fortune*, May 26, 2016.

Perdue, Peter C. "Eurasia in World History: Reflections on Time and Space." *World History Connected*, vol. 5, no. 2, February 2008.

Perdue, Peter C. *China Marches West: The Qing Conquest of Central Eurasia*. Cambridge, MA: Harvard University Press, 2010.

Pereira, Analúcia Danilevicz. "The South Atlantic, Southern Africa and South America: Cooperation and Development." *Austral: Brazilian Journal of Strategy and International Relations*, vol. 2, no. 4, July-December, 2013, 31–45.

Perez, Bien. "China's ZTE Takes Over Netas for $101m, Eyes Expansion in Turkey." *South China Morning Post*, December 6, 2016.

Perlez, Jane. "President Xi Jinping of China Is All Business in Middle East Visit." *New York Times*, January 30, 2016.

Pfeffer, Anshel. "Growing Ties between Turkey, China, Iran Worry Israel and U.S." *Ha'aretz*, October 7, 2010.

Phadnis, Aditi. "Interesting Facts about the Sharif Family and Its Business Interests." *Business Standard* (India), January 2, 2016.

Phillips, Tom. "Britain Has Made 'Visionary' Choice to Become China's Best Friend, Says Xi." *The Guardian*, October 18, 2015.

Phillips, Tom. "Chinese Troops Stage Show of Force in Xinjiang and Vow to'Relentlessly Beat' Separatists." *The Guardian*, February 20, 2017.

Pines, Yuri. "Political Mythology and Dynastic Legitimacy in the Rong Cheng shi Manuscript." *Bulletin of SOAS*, vol. 73, no. 3, 2010, 503–529.

Ping, He Wei. "Regulatory Capture in China's Banking Sector." *Journal of Banking Regulation*, vol. 14, no. 1, January 2013, 80–90.

Piterberg, Gabriel, Teofilo F. Ruiz, and Geoffrey Symcox, eds. *Braudel Revisited: The Mediterranean World, 1600–1800*. Toronto: University of Toronto Press, 2010.

Podesta, John and Brian Kutulis. "Trump's Silent Surge in the Middle East—And the Slippery Slope to War." *Washington Post*, June 20, 2017.

Pomfret, James. "Chinese Villagers Describe Police Beatings in 'Wild Crackdown' on Protest." *Reuters*, September 14, 2016.

Poulton, Hugh. *Top Hat, Grey Wolf, and Crescent: Turkish Nationalism and the Turkish Republic*. New York: New York University Press, 1997.

Prange, Sebastian. "Scholars and the Sea: A Historiography of the Indian Ocean." *History Compass*, vol. 6, no. 5, September 2008, 1382–1393.

Price, Greg. "New Iran Sanctions Coming, But None for Russia, Committee Leaders Say." *Newsweek*, May 2, 2017.

Puett, Michael. "China in Early Eurasian History: A Brief Review of Recent Scholarship on the Issue." In Victor H. Mair, ed. *The Bronze Age and Early Iron Age Peoples of Eastern Central Asia, Vol. 2*. Washington, DC: Institute for the Study of Man, 1998, 699–715.

"Qatar Blockade: Iran Sends Five Planeloads of Food." *BBC News*, June 11, 2017.

Qi, Xiaoying. "Social Movements in China: Augmenting Mainstream Theory with Guanxi." *Sociology*, vol. 51, no. 1, February 1, 2017, 111–126.

Qian, Hou. "Will the Belt and Road Initiative Cause Clash of Cultures?" *Xinhua*, May 13, 2017.

Qian, Shanming. "Can China Be an Important Mediator in Mid-East Peace?" CRIEnglish.com, May 9, 2013.

Qian, Xuewen. "The January Revolution and the Future of Egypt." *Journal of Middle Eastern and Islamic Studies (in Asia)* vol. 6, no. 2, 2012, 49–61.

Qian, Xuming. "*Yidai Yilu*" *Zhanlue Beijing Xia Yu Zhongdong de Nengyuan Hezuo (The Belt and Road Initiatives and China-Middle East Energy Cooperation)*. Beijing: Shishi Chubanshe, 2015.

Qian, Zaijian. "Gonggong Quanli Yunxing Gongkaihua de Xieshang Minzhu Lujing Yanjiu" (The Deliberative Democracy Path to Opening the Operation of Public Power). Nanjing Normal University, Research Center for Local Government and Governance Innovation, *Jianghai Xuekan*, March 10, 2015.

Qin, Yaqing. "Recent Developments toward a Chinese School of IR Theory." *E-International Relations*, April 26, 2016.

"Qingdao-made LNG Modules to Be Sent to the Arctic." *China Daily*, July 1, 2016.

Raditio, Klaus Heinrich. "Indonesia 'Speaks Chinese' in South China Sea." *Jakarta Post*, July 18, 2016.

Rahman, Fazlur. *Islam and Modernity: Transformation of an Intellectual Tradition*. Chicago: University of Chicago Press, 1982.

Raja, Raza Habib. "This Is Why I Think Pakistan Needs a Saraiki Province." *Express Tribune*, October 6, 2016.

Ramadan, Fatima and Amr Adly, "Low-Cost Authoritarianism: The Egyptian Regime and Labor Movement since 2013." *Carnegie Middle East Center*, September 17, 2015.

Ramadhani, Nurul Fitri, Safrin La Batu, and Indra Budiari, "Anies Rides Islamist Wave." *Jakarta Post*, April 20, 2017.

Rana, Shahbaz. "China-Pakistan Economic Corridor: Lines of Development—Not Lines of Divide." *Express Tribune*, May 17, 2015.

Rana, Shahbaz. "Army Seeks Role in CPEC Administration." *Express Tribune*, April 16, 2016.

Ratner, Ely. "Geostrategic and Military Drivers and Implications of the Belt and Road Initiative." *Council on Foreign Relations*, January 25, 2018.

Rauws, Ward. "Embracing Uncertainty without Abandoning Planning." *The Planning Review*, vol. 53, no. 1, April 2017, 32–45.

"RAW at Frontline to Sabotage Economic Corridor, China Warns Pakistan." *Express Tribune*, May 22, 2015.

Razavi, Camilia and Daniel Khalessi. "China Looks towards Iran." *Huffington Post*, May 6, 2016.

Reed, Stanley. "Even Bold Foreign Investors Tiptoe in Iran." *New York Times*, March 31, 2017.

Ren, Yuan. "Under the Dome: Will This Film Be China's Environmental Awakening?" *The Guardian*, March 5, 2015.

Renner, Solape and Tope Alake. "Solar Power May Get Boost from Africa's Biggest Oil Exporter." *Bloomberg*, March 6, 2017.

Research Centre for Islamic History, Art, and Culture (Turkey). Second International Congress on "China and the Muslim World: Cultural Encounters." ircica.org, February 3–4, 2015.

Richards, Catherine. "China-India: An Analysis of the Himalayan Territorial Dispute." *Indo-Pacific Strategic Papers*, Australian Defence College, February 2015.

Richter, Ursula. "Gu Jiegang: His Last Thirty Years." *China Quarterly*, vol. 90, June 1982, 286–295.

Richter, Ursula. "Historical Scepticism in the New Culture Era: Gu Jiegang and the 'Debate on Ancient History.'" *Studies of Modern Chinese History*, no. 23, June 1994, 353–389.

Riordan, Primrose. "Tillerson Comments Show Australia Will Have to Wade into South China Sea Dispute." *Financial Review*, January 12, 2017.

Rithmire, Meg E. "China's 'New Regionalism': Subnational Analysis in Chinese Political Economy." *World Politics*, vol. 66, no. 1, January 2014, 165–194.

Rodrik, Dani. "Premature Deindustialization." *Journal of Economic Growth*, vol. 21, no. 1, March 2016, 1–33.

Roett, Riordan and Guadalupe Paz. *Latin America and the Asian Giants: Evolving Ties with China and India*. Washington, DC: Brookings, 2016.

Rogers, David. "Iran's Railway Revolution." *Global Construction Review*, December 14, 2015.

Rohan, Brian. "Hard Times in Egypt Stoke Labor Unrest, Showdown Ahead." *Associated Press*, June 11, 2016.

Rolland, Nadège. *China's Eurasian Century? Political and Strategic Implications of the Belt and Road Initiative*. Washington, DC: National Bureau of Asian Research, May 2017.

Rollo, Stuart. "Australia Needs a New Foreign Policy, Tillerson's Remarks on China Make It Urgent." The *Guardian*, January 12, 2017.

Roman, David. "China Is Transforming Southeast Asia Faster than Ever." *Bloomberg*, December 5, 2016.

Romano, Giulia C. and Jean-François Meglio. *China's Energy Security: A Multidimensional Perspective*. New York: Routledge, 2016.

Romero, Simon. "China's Ambitious Rail Projects Crash into Harsh Realities in Latin America." *New York Times*, October 3, 2015.

Rong, Gui. "Huizu Nongcun de 'Quanli Wenhua Wangluo': Yunnan Shadian Hexie Shehui de Zhengzhi Renleixue Yanjiu" (The "Cultural Nexus of Power" of the Rural Hui: The Harmonious Society of Yunnan's Shadian from the Perspective of Political Anthropology). *Journal of Yunnan University of Nationalities*, vol. 27, no. 4, July 2009, 49–52.

Rong, Jiang. *Wolf Totem*. New York: Penguin, 2008.

Rong, Mei Zhao, *Super Empire-Chaoji Diguo: Pojie Zhongguo Zui Qianghan Wangchao de Mima* (*Super Empire: Unraveling the Mystery of China's Most Valient Dynasty*). Wuhan: Wuhan University Press, 2006.

Rong, Zhang. "Xin Rujia Shijie xia de Yisilan Wenming: Cong Tang Jun Yi dao Du Wei Ming" (Islamic Civilization from the Perspective of Neo-Confucianism: from Tang Junyi to Du Weiming). *Journal of Hui Muslim Minority Studies*, no. 4, 2004, 19–26.

Ropp, Paul S. *China in World History*. New York: Oxford University Press, 2010.

Rosencranz, Armin and Merlin Elizabeth Joseph. "By Building the Sawalkot Dam, Is India Using Water as a Weapon against Pakistan?" *The Wire*, March 20, 2017.

Rosenthal, Phil. "Economic Power China Is So Fragile It Orders Pun Control." *Chicago Tribune*, December 2, 2014.

Ross, Catherine, ed. *Megaregions: Planning for Global Competitiveness*. Washington, DC: Island Press, 2012.

Rossabi, Morris. "China and the Islamic World." *Comparative Civilizations Review*: vol. 13, no. 13, 1985, 269–283.

Rossabi, Morris. *Kubilai Khan: His Life and Times*. Berkeley: University of California Press, 2009.

Rossabi, Morris, ed. *China among Equals: The Middle Kingdom and Its Neighbors, 10th–14th Centuries*. Berkley: University of California Press, 1983.

Rossabi, Morris, ed. *Governing China's Multiethnic Frontiers*. Seattle: University of Washington Press, 2004.

Rossabi, Morris, ed. *Eurasian Influences on Yuan China*. Singapore: Institute of Southeast Asian Studies, 2013.

Roubanis, Ilia. "Energy and Turkey's South Caucasus Policy: The EU Regionalization Catalyst." *The New Turkey*, December 16, 2016.

Roy, Bhaskar. "China: Strategic Encirclement of India's Core Interests." *Eurasia Review*, January 6, 2017.

Rudd, Kevin. "A Subtle Defrosting in China's Chilly War with America." *Financial Times*, June 10, 2013.

Rudelson, Justin Jon. *Oasis Identities: Uyghur Nationalism Along China's Silk Road*. New York: Columbia University Press, 1997.

Rudich, Vasily. "Russia's Muslim Reality." *Foreign Affairs*, vol. 93, no. 3, May/June, 2014, 199–200.

Rudolph, Eric. "Kunming, A Melting Pot of Disappearing Culture Where Islam Survives." *The National (UAE)*, February 12, 2013.

Run, Taoyan. "Yisilan? Ta Tongzhi Buliao Zhongguo" (Islam? It Cannot Rule China). *wenxuecity.com*, November 15, 2015.

Runde, Daniel F., and Conor M. Savory. "Nation Building by Any Other Name." *Center for Strategic and International Studies*, January 23, 2017.

"Russia Asks China to Boost Moscow-Kazan Fast-Speed Rail Project Financing." *TASS*, May 18, 2017.

"Russia, China to Build High-Speed Rail Link." *Sputnik*, February 10, 2017.

Ryan, Fergus. "Islamic State Hostage Killing: China Vows Justice after Confirming Death." *The Guardian*, November 18, 2015.

Sachs, Jeffrey D. "Eurasia Is on the Rise, Will the US Be Left on the Sidelines?" *Boston Globe*, April 9, 2017.

Safi, Hiba. "Maximum Wage in Egypt: Who Pays the Bill?" *Center for International Private Enterprise*, May 6, 2015.

Sahi, Aoun and Shashank Bengali. "Panama Papers Expose Pakistan's Embattled Prime Minister to Allegations of Corruption." *Los Angeles Times*, April 4, 2017.

Salah-Ahmed, Amira and Isabel Esterman. "Crowdfunding the Canal?" *madamasr.com*, August 31, 2014.

Salaudeen, Leke. "Obasanjo's $8.3b Rail Deal Unsettles Yar'Adua." *Nigerian Muse*, March 19, 2008.

Salazar, Rafael. "Chinese Investment in Latin America: A Poisoned Chalice?" *Huffington Post*, June 19, 2015.

Saliba, George. *Islamic Science and the Making of the European Renaissance*. Cambridge, MA: The MIT Press, 2007.

Saliba, George. "China and Islamic Civilization: Exchange of Techniques and Scientific Ideas." *The Silk Road*, vol. 6, no. 1, Summer 2008, 9–16.

Salmon, Claudine and Roderich Ptak, eds. *Zheng He: Images and Perceptions*. Wiesbaden: Harrassowitz, 2005.

Salna, Karlis and Yudith Ho. "Jokowi Taps Ex-generals amid Terrorism Threat, China Tensions." *Bloomberg*, July 27, 2016.

Samir, Samar. "32 Chinese Firms Invest in 1st Phase of Suez Canal Area with $426 m: Xi." *The Cairo Post*, January 21, 2016.

Sampson, Ovetta. "Occupy Nigeria Victory: President to Cut Fuel Prices." *Christian Science Monitor*, January 16, 2012.

Sanchez, Dana. "Changing Economics of Canals: Large Ships Go Around Africa, Bypassing Suez and Panama." *AFK Insider*, June 28, 2016.

Sanger, David E. "Iran Sticks to Terms of Nuclear Deal, but Defies the U.S. in Other Ways." *New York Times*, July 13, 2016.

Sanusi, Lamido. "Africa Must Get Real about Chinese Ties." *Financial Times*, March 11, 2013.

Sarkar, Sudeshna. "Egypt Turning toward China for Investment." *African Business Magazine*, October 18, 2016.

Satoh, Masayoshi and Samir Aboulroos, eds. *Irrigated Agriculture in Egypt: Past, Present and Future*. Cham, Switzerland: Springer, 2017.

Sautman, Barry. "Peking Man and the Politics of Paleoanthropological Nationalism in China." *Journal of Asian Studies*, vol. 60, no. 1, 2001, 95–124.

Schechter, Danny. "#OccupyNigeria Shows the Movement's Global Face." *Al-Jazeera*, January 23, 2012.

Scheen, Lena. "Islam in China." *International Institute for Asian Studies Newsletter*, Autumn 2016 (http://iias.asia/the-newsletter/article/islam-china).

Schell, Orville. "China's Once and Future Democracy." *Wall Street Journal*, March 31, 2017.

Schiavenza, Matt. "Why Thailand Forced Uighurs to Return to China." *The Atlantic*, July 12, 2015.

Schneider, Laurence. *Ku Chieh-kang and China's New History: Nationalism and the Quest for Alternative Traditions*. Berkeley, University of California Press, 1971.

Schonhardt, Sara. "In Indonesia, Fears Rise among Ethnic Chinese amid Blasphemy Probe." *Wall Street Journal*, November 26, 2016.

Schonhardt, Sara and Anita Rachman. "Indonesian President Joko Widodo Shakes Up Cabinet." *Wall Street Journal*, July 27, 2016.

Schwarcz, Vera. *The Chinese Enlightenment: Intellectuals and the Legacy of the May Fourth Movement of 1919*. Berkeley: University of California Press, 1986.

Schwartzstein, Peter. "Forget ISIS, Egypt's Population Boom Is Its Biggest Threat." *Newsweek*, March 20, 2017.

Schweller, Randall L. and Xiaoyu Pu. "After Unipolarity: China's Visions of International Order in an Era of U.S. Decline." *International Security*, vol. 36, no. 1, Summer 2011, 41–72.

Scobell, Andrew and Andrew J. Nathan, "China's Overstretched Military." *The Washington Quarterly*, vol. 35, no. 4, Fall 2012, 135–148.

Scott, Brendan, Ting Shi, and Yinka Ibukun. "Nigeria Snubs Taiwan as China Pledges $40 Billion Investment." *Bloomberg*, January 12, 2017.

Scott, Emma. "Defying Expectations: China's Iran Trade and Investments." *Middle East Institute*, April 6, 2016.

Searcey, Dionne and Tony Iyare. "President Buhari Returns to Nigeria, Facing Serious Challenges." *New York Times*, August 21, 2017.

"Selections from the 'Silk Road and China Dream' Speech Contest." *Confucius Institute Magazine*, November 2016.

Selim, Sayed A. et al., "Groundwater Rising as Environmental Problem, Causes and Solutions: Case Study from Aswan City, Upper Egypt." *Open Journal of Geology*, vol. 4, no. 7, July 2014, 324–341.

Semerad, Tony. "Changing China: The Nation Places a Heavy Bet on One Belt, One Road." *Salt Lake Tribune*, April 17, 2017.

Shah, Idries. *The Pleasantries of the Incredible Mulla Nasrudin*. New York: Penguin, 1993.

Shah, Saeed and Jeremy Page. "China Readies $46 Billion for Pakistan Trade Route." *Wall Street Journal*, April 16, 2015.

Shah, Syed Ali. "Two Chinese Nationals Kidnapped from Quetta." *Dawn*, May 24, 2017.

Shahid, Kunwar Khuldune. "Trump's Warning to Islamabad Has Formalised the China-Pakistan-Russia Axis." *Huffington Post*, August 30, 2017.

Shahid, Usman. "Balochistan: The Troubled Heart of the CPEC." *The Diplomat*, August 23, 2016.

Shaikh, Ubaidullah and Javed Hussain. "Shahbaz to be PML-Ns Next Candidate for Prime Minister: Nawaz Sharif." *Dawn*, December 21, 2017.

Shambaugh, David. "China's Soft-Power Push: The Search for Respect." *Foreign Affairs*, vol. 94, no. 4, July/August 2015, 99–107.

Shams, Shamil. "China's Economic Corridor Creating New Conflicts in Pakistan." *Deutsche Welle*, August 28, 2016.

Shams, Shamil "Istanbul Attack: Why China's Uighurs Are Joining Global Jihadist Groups." *Deutsche Welle*, January 6, 2017.

Shan, Wei. "Explaining Ethnic Protests and Ethnic Policy Changes in China." *International Journal of China Studies*, vol. 1, no. 2, October 2010, 509–529.

Sharafedin, Bozorgmehr. "Iran Deploys Revolutionary Guards to Quell 'Sedition' in Protest Hotbeds." *Reuters*, January 3, 2018.

Shariati, Ali. *Hajj*. Bedford, OH: Free Islamic Literatures, 1977.

Shaughnessy, Edward L. *Rewriting Early Chinese Texts*. Albany: State University of New York Press, 2006.

Shekhar, Vibhanshu and Joseph Chinyong Liow. "Indonesia as a Maritime Power: Jokowi's Vision, Strategies, and Obstacles Ahead." *Brookings*, November 7, 2014.

Shen, Simon. "Why Nigeria Prefers China to the West." *Hong Kong Economic Journal*, May 4, 2016.

Shenker, Jack. "State Repression in Egypt Worst in Decades, Says Activist." *The Guardian*, January 24, 2016.

Shepard, Wade. "Investors from East and West Eager to Get a Piece of Russian High-Speed Rail Action." *Forbes*, November 15, 2016.

Shepard, Wade. "Japan Ups Its Game against China's Belt and Road." *Forbes*, December 1, 2016.

Shepard, Wade. *On the New Silk Road: Journeying through China's Artery of Power*. Chicago: University of Chicago Press, 2017.

Shepherd, Christian. "Chengdu Benefits from China's One Belt, One Road Strategy." *Financial Times*, August 18, 2016.

Sheriff, Abdul and Engseng Ho. *The Indian Ocean: Oceanic Connections and the Creation of New Societies*. London: Hurst, 2014.

Shi, Ting. "Qatar Standoff Tests China's Neutrality on Saudi-Iran Feud." *Bloomberg*, June 7, 2017.

Shi, Zhuying. "When Confucius Meets Rumi: Chinese, Turkish Scholars Discuss Academic Cooperation in Istanbul." Wordpress.com, May 23, 2012.

Shih, Gerry. "Islamophobia in China on the Rise Fuelled by Online Hate Speech." *The Independent*, April 10, 2017.

Shinn, David H. and Joshua Eisenman. *China and Africa: A Century of Engagement*. Philadelphia: University of Pennsylvania Press, 2012.

"Shipping News: Zheng He's Sexcentenary." *China Heritage Newsletter*, June 2005.

Shirky, Clay. "The Political Power of Social Media: Technology, the Public Sphere, and Political Change." *Foreign Affairs*, vol. 90, no. 1, January/February 2010, 28–41.

Shui, Zhai. "Li Xiguang Jiang 'Yidai, Yilu' Yu Daguo Boyi" (Li Xiguang Discusses "One Belt, One Road" and the Great Game). *Siyue Wang, tv.m4.cn*, March 29, 2016.

Siddiqa, Arhama. "The Sunni Allies of Tehran." *The Nation (Pakistan)*, May 20, 2017.

Sile, Aza Wee. "Why China Wants a Bite of the Booming Halal Food Market." *CNBC*, August 24, 2015.

Simmel, Georg. *Conflict; The Web of Group-Affiliations*, New York: Free Press, 1964.

Simmons, Ann M. "Meet the Pangolin, the Most Poached Mammal in the World." *Los Angeles Times*, September 1, 2016.

Siollun, Max. "How Goodluck Jonathan Lost the Nigerian Election." *The Guardian*, April 1, 2015.

"Sisi's Dream of New Egypt Capital in Tatters as China Pulls Out." *Middle East Eye*, February 9, 2017.

Siu, Phila. "What Indonesia Can Do to Be in China's Belt and Road Loop." *South China Morning Post*, April 29, 2017.

Skinner, G. William. "Presidential Address: The Structure of Chinese History." *Journal of Asian Studies*, vol. 44, no. 2, February 1985, 271–292.

Skinner, G. William. *Marketing and Social Structure in Rural China*. Ann Arbor, MI: Association for Asian Studies, 2001.

Skinner, G. William, ed. *The City in Late Imperial China*. Stanford, CA: Stanford University Press, 1977.

Sklar, Richard L. "An Elusive Target: Nigeria Fends Off Sanctions." In Kunle Amuwo, Daniel C. Bach and Yann Lebeau, eds., *Nigeria during the Abacha Years, 1993–1998*, Institut français de recherche en Afrique, 2001, 259–287.

Slawson, Nicola. "Saudi Execution of Shia Cleric Sparks Outrage in Middle East." *The Guardian*, January 2, 2016.

Sleeboom-Faulkner, Margaret. *The Chinese Academy of Social Sciences (CASS): Shaping the Reforms, Academia and China (1977–2003)*. Leiden and Boston: Brill, 2007.

Smith, Geoffrey. "Germany and China Position Themselves as World Climate Leaders." *Fortune*, June 1, 2017.

Smith, Helena. "Chinese Carrier Cosco Is Transforming Piraeus—And Has Eyes on Thessaloniki." *The Guardian*, June 29, 2014.

Solomon, Salem and Falastine Iman. "New African Railways Ride on Chinese Loans." *Voice of America*, January 24, 2017.

Solovieva, Daria. "Suez Canal: Egyptian Military Takes Charge of Economic Development." *International Business Times*, April 3, 2014.

"Some Died in the Hospital from Fake Chinese Anesthetics." *peykeiran.com*, August 22, 2011.

Song, Niu and Rawya Gamil Metwally. "The Hajj and Its Impact on International Relations." *Journal of Middle Eastern and Islamic Studies (in Asia)*, vol. 10, no. 3, 2016, 39–65.

Soniyi, Tobi and Zacheaus Somorin. "Nigeria Offered $6bn Chinese Loan, Agrees Currency Swap to Shore Up Naira." *This Day*, April 13, 2016.

Sonmez, Mustafa. "Canal Istanbul: Still Hyped, Still 'Crazy.'" *Al-Monitor*, February 22, 2017.

Sonwalkar, Prasun. "Baloch, Sindhi Leaders in London Protest China-Pak Corridor, Rights Violations." *Hindustan Times*, August 30, 2016.

Sowore, Omoyele. "Nigerians Still Waiting for Their 'African Spring'." cnn.com, January 14, 2013.

"Spotlight: Figures Show Growth in Egypt, China Cooperation on Belt and Road Initiative." *Xinhua*, May 3, 2017.

Spyer, Jonathan. "Is It Iran's Middle East Now?" *Fathom*, Autumn 2015.

Sridharan, Vasudevan. "Indonesian President Holds Cabinet Meeting on Board Warship in South China Sea." *International Business Times*, June 23, 2016.

Staalesen, Atle. "Norway, Finland Talk Arctic with China." *The Barents Observer*, April 10, 2017.

Stang, Gerald. "Global Commons: Between Cooperation and Competition." *European Union Institute for Security Studies*, April 2013.

Steimle, Joshua. "How China Can Lead the World, And Why Hong Kong Is the Key." *Forbes*, September 10, 2013.

Steinberg, David A. and Victor C. Shih. "Interest Group Influence in Authoritarian States: The Political Determinants of Chinese Exchange Rate Policy." *Comparative Political Studies*, vol. 45, no. 11, November 2012, 1405–1434.

Steinhardt, Nancy Shatzman. *China's Early Mosques*. Edinburgh: Edinburgh University Press, 2016.

"Street Protests Hit Iran for Third Straight Day as Pro-government Rallies Held." *Reuters*, December 30, 2017.

Su, Alice. "Harmony and Martyrdom among China's Hui Muslims." *The New Yorker*, June 6, 2016.

Su, Alice. "China's Separation between Mosque and State." *Pulitzer Center*, October 21, 2016.

Su, Alice. "Meet China's State-Approved Muslims." *Foreign Policy*, November 2, 2016.

Su, Alice. "China Doesn't Mind Islamic Extremists, As Long as They're Not Uighur." *Foreign Policy*, December 16, 2016.

Su, Shiqun, Ding Xieqin, and Qi Cheng. "Lun Zhongguo Yisilan Jiao de Shehui Gongneng" (On the Social Functions of Chinese Islam). *Chinese Muslim*, vol. 23, no. 3, 1999.

Sukma, Rizal. "A Post-ASEAN Foreign Policy for a Post-G8 World." *Jakarta Post*, October 5, 2009.

Sulaiman, Yohanes. "Global Maritime Nexus: Towards a Grand Strategy for Indonesia?" *RSIS Commentaries*, March 23, 2017.

Sun, Dazhang and Qiu Yulan. *Islamic Buildings: The Architecture of Islamic Mosques in China*. Beijing: CN Times Books, 2015.

Sun, Degang. *Duoyuan Pingheng Yu "Zhun Lianmeng" Lilun Yanjiu (Multipolarity and the Theory of "Quasi-alliances")*. Current Events Press, 2007.

Sun, Degang. "Six Decades of Chinese Middle East Studies: A Review." *Bustan: The Middle East Book Review*, vol. 2, no. 1, 2011, 15–32.

Sun, Degang. "China's Soft Military Presence in the Middle East." *Middle East Institute Blog*, March 11, 2015.

Sun, Degang and He Shaoxiong. "From a By-stander to a Constructor: China and the Middle East Security Governance." *Journal of Middle Eastern and Islamic Studies (in Asia)*, vol. 9, no. 3, 2015, 69–99.

Sun, Degang and Yahia H. Zoubir, eds. *Building a New Silk Road: China and the Middle East in the 21st Century*. Beijing: World Affairs Press, 2014.

Sun, Shuyun. "Chicken Broth for the Soul? No Thanks." *The Guardian*, May 16, 2009.

Sun, Xiaoling. "Shouyi, Guojian Yu Rentong: Shenzhen Musilin Yu Shenzhen Shi Da Guannian Rongru Du Diaocha Yanjiu" (Benefit, Build, and Identify: A Survey of the Degree of Shenzhen Muslims' Assimilation of Shenzhen's Ten Great Concepts). *Journal of Qinghai Nationalities Institute*, vol. 42, no. 4, 2016.

"Sun Bigan to Be Special Envoy on Middle East Issues." china.org.cn, March 30, 2006.

Sundaryani, Fedina S. "Indonesia Must Diversity China Trade." *Jakarta Post*, September 14, 2016.

Suryadinata, Leo, ed. *Southeast Asia's Chinese Businesses in an Era of Globalization: Coping with the Rise of China*. Singapore: Institute of Southeast Asian Studies, 2006.

Suryadinata, Leo, ed. *Ethnic Chinese in Contemporary Indonesia*. Singapore: Chinese Heritage Centre and Institute of Southeast Asian Studies, 2008.

Susanty, Farida. "China Strengthens Grip on Indonesia." *Jakarta Post*, November 24, 2016.

Susanty, Farida and Nurul Fitri Ramadhani. "Indonesia's Love of Mecca Boosts Lucrative 'Umrah' Business." *Jakarta Post*, January 21, 2017.

Sutherland, Heather. "Southeast Asian History and the Mediterranean Analogy." *Journal of Southeast Asian Studies*, vol. 34, no. 1, February 2003, 1–20.

Suzuki, Wataru and Erwida Maulia. "China Overtakes Japan in Indonesia Direct Investment." *Nikkei Asian Review*, January 25, 2017.

Swaine, Michael D. "Beijing's Tightrope Walk on Iran." *Carnegie Endowment China Leadership Monitor*, March 1, 2010.

Tagliacozzo, Eric and Wen-Chin Chang, eds. *Chinese Circulations: Capital, Commodities, and Networks in Southeast Asia*. Durham, NC: Duke University Press, 2011.

Takahashi, Tetsushi. "Belt and Road Conference Is Xi's Time to Shine." *Nikkei Asian Review*, May 16, 2017.

"Talking Points: Sikander Reaffirms QWP's Commitment to Developing K-P." *Express Tribune*, November 26, 2015.

Tan, Sor-Hoon. *Confucian Democracy: A Deweyan Reconstruction*. Albany: State University of New York Press, 2003.

Tan, Ta Sen. *Cheng Ho and Islam in Southeast Asia*. Singapore: Institute of Southeast Asian Studies, 2009.

Tan, Yifan. "Muslims' Spiritual Center in Shenzhen." *Shenzhen Daily*, August 15, 2013.

Tan, Ying. *Chinnovation: How Chinese Innovators Are Changing the World*. Hoboken, NJ, Wiley: 2011.

Tanchum, Michael. "China's One Belt, One Road Reshapes Mideast." *Jerusalem Post*, January 24, 2017.

Tasch, Barbara, "China's $10 Billion Railway across South America Is Either Bold or Insane." *Business Insider*, June 10, 2015.

Tayloe, Shane C. "Crossover Point: How China's Naval Modernization Could Reverse the United States' Strategic Advantage." *Journal of Asian Security and International Affairs*, vol. 4, no. 1, April 10, 2017, 1–25.

Taylor, Adam. "What Yemen's Crisis Reveals about China's Growing Global Power." *Washington Post*, March 31, 2015.

Teixeira, Lauren. "China's Middle Class Anger at Its Education System Is Growing." *Foreign Policy*, February 6, 2017.

Teriba, Ayo. "Nigeria's Economic Outlook in 2017." *SSRN*, March 23, 2017.

Tezkan, Yılmaz. *Uzak Ve Eski Komşumuz Çin (Our Distant and Ancient Neighbor China)*. Istanbul: Ülke Kitapları, 2002.

"The Chinese Community in Indonesia: A Force to Be Reckoned With." stirringtroubleinternationally.com, August 6, 2008.

"The Extraordinary Ways in Which China Humiliates Muslims," *The Economist*, May 4, 2017.

"The Future: A Mostly Muslim World." *The China Post*, April 9, 2015.

"The New Davos Man: Xi Jinping Portrays China as a Rock of Stability." *The Economist*, January 21, 2017.

"The Power of Fish: A Peculiar Distortion in Hong Kong's Political Structure." *The Economist*, March 5, 2015.

"The Rural-Urban Divide: Ending Apartheid." *The Economist*, April 19, 2014.

The State Council, The People's Republic of China. "The Belt and Road Initiative." August 8, 2018. *english.gov.cn*.

Thomas, Andrew R. "Suez and Panama: A Healthy Competition." *Industry Week*, May 10, 2015.

Thompson, John N. *The Geographic Mosaic of Coevolution*. Chicago: University of Chicago Press, 2005.

Thompson, John N. *Relentless Evolution*. Chicago: University of Chicago Press, 2013.

"Thousands of Members from Muslim Youth Organization Banser Ready to Guard Churches on Christmas." *Coconuts Jakarta*, December 21, 2016.

Tiefer, Charles. "As U.S. Resumes Military Aid to Egypt, Reports Show How Little We Know On How It's Being Used." *Forbes*, April 7, 2015.

Tiezzi, Shannon. "China Powers Up Pakistan: The Energy Component of the CPEC." *The Diplomat*, January 13, 2016.

Tiezzi, Shannon. "The Belt and Road and Suez Canal: China-Egypt Relations under Xi Jinping." *China Policy Institute*, February 2, 2016.

Tijani, Mayowa. "Buhari: I'm Committed to Jonathan's China Deal." *The Cable*, April 10, 2016.

Timm, Leo. "Indonesia to Bolster Defense at 'Front Door' after South China Sea Ruling." *Epoch Times*, July 14, 2016.

Timur, Şafak. "Local Uighurs Skeptical about Gül's Visit." *Hürriyet Daily News*, June 29, 2009.

Tjhin, Christine Susanna. "Indonesia's Relations with China: Productive and Pragmatic, But Not Yet a Strategic Partnership." *China Report* vol. 48, no. 3, 2012, 303–315.

"To Appease China, Egypt Arrests 500 Turkestani Student Studying in Al-Azhar." *Middle East Observer*, July 6, 2017.

"To De-politicize and Enculturalize Ethnicity? What's Wrong with China's Ethnic Relations." *Xinjiang Review*, November 1, 2011.

Tontini, Roberta. *Muslim Sanzijing: Shifts and Continuities in the Definition of Islam in China*. Leiden: Brill, 2016.

Toogood, Kimairis. "Understanding the Emerging Relationship between China and Africa: The Case of Nigeria." *Stimson Policy Papers*, December 2016.

Topsfield, Jewel. "Pluralism in Peril: Is Indonesia's Religious Tolerance under Threat?" *Sydney Morning Herald*, December 24, 2016.

Topsfield, Jewel. "Agus Yudhoyono Protests Explosive Allegations against His Father on Eve of Election." *Sydney Morning Herald*, February 15, 2017.

Torbakov, Igor and Matti Nojonen. "China, Turkey and Xinjiang: A Frayed Relationship." *Open Democracy*, August 5, 2009.

Totty, Michael. "The Rise of the Smart City." *Wall Street Journal*, April 16, 2017.

"Trade Union Rejects Chinese Unskilled Workers." *Jakarta Post*, February 9, 2016.

"Transformation in the South Atlantic." *Atlantic Future*, July 24, 2013.

Tremblay, Pinar. "Clash of the Anatolian Tigers." *Al-Monitor*, April 28, 2014.

Trevor-Roper, H.R. "Fernand Braudel, the Annales, and the Mediterranean." *The Journal of Modern History*, vol. 44, no. 4, December 1972, 468–479.

Trilling, David. "Arctic Melt Boosts Northern Trade Routes, Hurts Suez." *Journalist's Resource*, March 6, 2017.

Tschantret, Joshua. "How China's Repression in Xinjiang Can Backfire, Again." *Asia and the Pacific Policy Society Forum*, December 12, 2016.

Tunakan, Begüm. "Turkey Goes from a Transit Country to an Energy Hub." *Daily Sabah*, November 20, 2015.

Turgut, Pelin. "Turkey No Longer a Safe Have for Chinese Uighurs." *Time*, July 27, 2009.

"Turkey among Top 5 Violators of ILO Conventions: DİSK." *Hürriyet Daily News*, June 1, 2016.

"Turkey Builds Massive High-Speed Railway to Mark Centennial Anniversary." *Xinhua*, May 14, 2017.

"Turkey Opens Part of Real Estate Market to Chinese Nationals." *Xinhua*, August 24, 2012.

"Turkey Referendum Worries China over Pan-Turkism in Xinjiang." *Financial Express (India)*, April 18, 2017.

"Turkey to Chair 2017 Energy Club of Shanghai Cooperation Organization." *Daily Sabah*, November 23, 2016.

"Turkey's Diplomatic Steps Save Lives of Uyghur Refugees in Thailand." *Daily Sabah*, December 28, 2014.

"Turkey's Erdogan Urges Russia, China and Iran to Trade in Local Currencies." *RT News*, December 5, 2016.

"Turkish PM Erdogan Likens Xinjiang Violence to 'Genocide'." *Agence France-Presse*, July 10, 2009.
"Turkish President Wraps Up Visit in China." *Hürriyet Daily News*, June 28, 2009.
Tweed, David and Norman P. Aquino. "Duterte's Tilt toward China Upsets U.S. Strategy in Asia." *Chicago Tribune*, September 15, 2016.
"12 Energy Projects under CPEC to Be Completed by 2017–18." *Express Tribune*, January 18, 2017.
"2017 Lowy Institute Poll." *Lowy Institute for International Policy*, June 22, 2017.
Udo, Bassey. "As U.S. Gradually Closes Door, Nigeria Turns to China to Boost Economy." *Premium Times*, July 4, 2013.
Ukwu, Jerrywright. "China to Invest $750bn in Nigeria-Ambassador." *naij.com*, April 12, 2016.
Undu, Joseph. "Nigerian Allegedly Defrauds Chinese Firm of N165m." *Vanguard*, December 28, 2016.
Unger, Jonathan and Anita Chan. "State Corporatism and Business Associations in China: A Comparison with Earlier Emerging Economies of East Asia." *International Journal of Emerging Markets*, vol. 10, no. 2, April 2015, 178–193.
"Urban Legend: China's Tiered City System Explained." *South China Morning Post*, October 10, 2016, http://multimedia.scmp.com/2016/cities.
"U.S. Threatens Sanctions on China Banks over Iran." *Agence France-Presse*, September 28, 2011.
Uwaleke, Joe Uche, "Nigeria-China Currency Swap Deal at a Glance." *Punch*, April 19, 2016.
Van Kemenade, Willem. "Iran's Relations with China and the West: Cooperation and Confrontation in Asia." *Netherlands Institute of International Relations "Clingendael,"* November 2009.
Varagur, Krithika. "Amidst Protests, Tense Times for Chinese Indonesians." *Voice of America*, November 15, 2016.
Varagur, Krithika. "Evicted Jakarta Residents Join Hardline Rally against Governor." *Voice of America*, December 2, 2016.
Varagur, Krithika. "Majority of Religion School Teachers in Indonesia Support Sharia Law." *Voice of America*, December 27, 2016.
Varagur, Krithika. "As Jakarta Sinks, Government Pins Hopes on Bird-Shaped Sea Wall." *Voice of America*, January 10, 2017.
Varagur, Krithika. "Crackdowns Have Indonesia Gay Community on Edge." *Voice of America*, May 31, 2017.
"Varedat Gul Az Chin, Gusht Az Pakistan" (Importing Flowers from China, Meat from Pakistan). *icana.ir*, July 31, 2011.
Varrall, Merriden. "A Chinese Threat to Australian Openness." *New York Times*, July 31, 2017.
Wagner, Daniel and Giorgio Cafiero. "China and Nigeria: Neo-colonialism, South-South Solidarity, or Both?" *Huffington Post*, July 19, 2013.
Wainwright, Oliver. "The City Is Ours Review—Will Vertical Forests and Smart Street Lights Really Save the Planet?" *The Guardian*, July 13, 2017.
Walby, Sylvia. "Complexity Theory, Globalisation and Diversity." *www.leeds.ac.uk*, April 2003.

Walden, Max. "The Chinese Indonesians with Long Memories and Escape Plans in Case Racial Violence Flares Again—Despite Signs of Tensions Easing." *South China Morning Post*, October 18, 2017.

Waldron, Arthur. *The Great Wall of China: From History to Myth*. Cambridge: Cambridge University Press, 1992.

Wallace, Paul. "Nigeria Presidency Approves Borrowing from World Bank, China" *Bloomberg*, September 8, 2016.

Wallis, William. "Africa Told to View China as Competitor." *Financial Times*, March 12, 2013.

Walsh, Declan. "Pakistan's Secret Dirty War." *The Guardian*, March 29, 2011.

Walsh, Declan. "Egyptian Prosecutor Orders Release of Hosni Mubarak, President Toppled in 2011." *New York Times*, March 13, 2017.

Wan, Adrian. "Chinese Academy of Social Sciences Is 'Infiltrated by Foreign Forces': Anti-graft Official." *South China Morning Post*, 2014.

Wang, Brian. "China Moving Ahead with Trans-African Rail Line, New Silk Road Part of Global Land Bridge Vision." *Next Big Future*, October 17, 2014.

Wang, Brian. "Megacities and One Belt, One Road Are Core to China's 100 Year Economic Strategy." nextbigfuture.com, April 1, 2017.

Wang, Daiyu. "China Considering Nationwide Law on Halal Food." *Islam in China*, April 16, 2016.

Wang, Fan. *Daguo Waijiao: Cong "Taoguang Yanghui" Dao "Daguo Waijiao", Zhongguo Yao Gaosu Shijie Shenme? (Great Power Diplomacy: From "Concealing One's Strength" to "Great Power Diplomacy," What Will China Tell the World?)*. Beijing: Beijing United, 2016.

Wang, Gungwu. *The Chinese Overseas: From Earthbound China to the Quest for Autonomy*. Cambridge, MA: Harvard University Press, 2002.

Wang, Gungwu. "China's Cautious Pride in an Ancient Mariner." *Yale Global*, August 4, 2005.

Wang, Gungwu. "The China Seas: Becoming an Enlarged Mediterranean." In Angela Schottenhammer, ed. *The East Asian "Mediterranean": Maritime Crossroads of Culture, Commerce and Human Migration*. Wiesbaden: Harrassowitz Verlag, 2008.

Wang, Gungwu. *Renewal: The Chinese State and the New Global History*. Hong Kong: The Chinese University of Hong Kong, 2013.

Wang, Hongliang. "Gu Jiegang yu Minguo Shiqi de Bianzheng Yanjiu" (Gu Jiegang and Frontier Political Studies in the Republican Period). *Qilu Journal*, vol. 14, no. 1, 2013, 42–49.

Wang, Jessica Ching-Sze. *John Dewey in China: To Teach and to Learn*. Albany: State University of New York Press, 2007.

Wang, Jin. "Middle East Studies in China: Achievements and Problems." *Rubin Center Research in International Affairs*, September 5, 2016.

Wang, Jin. "U.S. Sanctions on Iran: Good or Bad News for China?" *The Diplomat*, February 7, 2017.

Wang, Jisi. "'Xi Jin': Zhongguo Diyuan Zhanlue de Zai Pingheng" ("Marching Westwards": Rebalancing China's Geostrategy). *Global Times Net*, October 17, 2012.

Wang, Jisi. "Da Qiju: Guanyu Zhongguo Diyuan Zhanlue de Ruogan Sikao," (The Great Chess Game: Thoughts on China's Geostrategy). *Strategic and International Studies Bulletin*, October 8, 2016.

Wang, Q. Edward. "World History vs. Global History? The Changing Worldview in Contemporary China." *Chinese Studies in History*, vol. 42, no. 3, 2009, 3–6.

Wang, Tao. "Establishing the Chinese Archaeological School: Su Bingqi and Contemporary Chinese Archaeology." *SOAS Antiquity*, vol. 71, no. 271, March 1997, 31–36.

Wang, Tian You and Wan Ming. *Zhenghe Yanjiu Bainian Lunwen Xuan (100 Years of Zheng He Studies: Selected Writings)*. Beijing: Beijing University Press, 2004.

Wang, Xinsong. "One Belt, One Road's Governance Deficit Problem: How China Can Ensure Transparency and Accountability." *Foreign Affairs*, vol. 96, no. 6, November 17, 2017.

Wang, Yongzhi, Song Jun, Han Xueshuang, and Xue Guifang. "Guanyu Nanhai Duan Xu Xian de Zonghe Tantao" (A Comprehensive Investigation of the Dotted Line in the South China Sea). *Journal of Ocean University of China, Social Sciences Edition*, vol. 8, no. 3, 2008, 1–5.

Wang, Yuan-Kang. *Harmony and War: Confucian Culture and Chinese Power Politics*. New York: Columbia University Press, 2010.

Wang, Zheng, Fangzhu Zhang, and Fulong Wu. "Social Trust between Rural Migrants and Urban Locals in China – Exploring the Effects of Residential Diversity and Neighborhood Deprivation." *Population, Space and Place*, vol. 23, December 11, 2015, 1–15.

Wang, Zhenping. *Tang China in Multi-Polar Asia: A History of Diplomacy and War*. Honolulu: University of Hawaii Press, 2013.

Wasim, Amri. "Kalabagh Dam Controversy Resurfaces in Senate." *Dawn*, June 7, 2016.

Watt, James C. Y., ed. *The World of Khubilai Khan: Chinese Art in the Yuan Dynasty*. New York: Metropolitan Museum of Art, 2010.

Watts, Jonathan. "Nicaragua Canal: In a Sleepy Pacific Port, Something Stirs." *The Guardian*, November 24, 2016.

Wedeman, Andrew. *Double Paradox: Rapid Growth and Rising Corruption in China*. Ithaca, NY: Cornell University Press, 2012.

Weitz, Richard. "China Balances between Iran and U.S." *World Politics Review*, August 13, 2013.

Wen, Philip. "Australia Receptive to China's Silk Road, But National Interest First." *Reuters*, May 14, 2017.

Wen, Philip. "Terror Threats Transform China's Uighur Heartland into Security State." *Reuters*, March 30, 2017.

Wen, Wang and Chen Xiaochen. "Who Supports China in the South China Sea and Why." *The Diplomat*, July 27, 2016.

Wen, Yi. "Interview with Former Chinese Ambassador Hua Liming," chinaculture. org, September 15, 2009.

Werr, Patrick. "Egypt Caught Up in a Vicious Circle with Its Finances." *The National*, April 27, 2016.

"We've Potentials to Replicate Commercial Success of Chinese Economy in Anambra-Ubah." *Vanguard*, February 7, 2017.

White, Hugh. *The China Choice: Why America Should Share Power*. Carlton, Australia: Black, 2013.

"Why Indonesia Is Chasing China's Billions." *Bloomberg*, October 31, 2016.

Wijaya, Callistasia Anggun. "Ahok Confused about Muhammadiyah Youth Wing Accusation." *Jakarta Post*, January 10, 2017.

Wijaya, Callistasia Anggun. "Ahok Guilty of Blasphemy, Sentenced to Two Years." *The Jakarta Post*, May 9, 2017.

"Will China Encircle the World with Rail?" *Global Construction Review*, October 17, 2014.

Williams, Peter. "Clear Air for China's Silk Road Project." *The West Australian*, May 19, 2017.

Williams, Sophie. "Chinese Muslims Are Banned from Having 'Abnormal' Beards or Wearing Veils as the Nation Calls for a 'People's War' against Islamic Extremism." *Daily Mail*, March 30, 2017.

Wilson, Jordan. "China's Alternative to GPS and Its Implications for the United States." *U.S.-China Economic and Security Review Commission*, January 5, 2017.

Wilson, Scott. "China's NGO Regulations and Uneven Civil Society Development." *China Policy Institute*, February 15, 2017.

Winsor, Morgan. "China Slowdown Worsens Nigeria's Economic Woes amid Buhari's War on Corruption, Boko Haram." *International Business Times*, August 27, 2015.

"With Buhari Away, Osinbajo Comes Out of the Shadows." *The Guardian*, February 25, 2017.

Witular, Rendi A. "Losing Jakarta: How Will It Impact Jokowi's 2019 Reelection Bid?" *Jakarta Post*, April 21, 2017.

Wolf, Jim. "China Mounts Air Exercise with Turkey, U.S. Says." *Reuters*, October 8, 2010.

Wolf, Siegfried O. "China-Pakistan Economic Corridor, Civil-Military Relations and Democracy in Pakistan." *South Asia Democratic Forum*, September 13, 2016.

Wong, Catherine. "Arab States' Rift with Qatar Clouds China's Plans for Gulf Free-Trade Deal." *South China Morning Post*, June 6, 2017.

Wong, Catherine. "China-Pakistan Military Ties Set to Get Even Closer as 'Iron Brothers' Eye New Alliance." *South China Morning Post*, January 7, 2018.

Wong, Edward. "Celebrating the Legacy of a Chinese Explorer." *New York Times*, December 18, 2014.

Wong, Edward. "Ethnic Tensions Complicate Turkey's Relationship with China." *New York Times*, July 29, 2015.

Wong, Edward. "Mongolian Warriors and Communist Soldiers: A Frontier Town in China." *New York Times*, June 18, 2017.

Wong, How Man. *Islamic Frontiers of China: Peoples of the Silk Road*. New York: I. B. Tauris, 2011.

Wong, R. Bin. "Between Nation and World: Braudelian Regions in Asia." *Review (Fernand Braudel Center)*, vol. 26, no. 1, 2003, 1–45.

Wong, Roy. "East Asia as a World Region in the 21st Century." *Nihon Kezai Shimbun*, August 13, 2004.

Wong, Roy Bin. "Reflections on Qing Institutions of Governance: Chinese Empire in Comparative Perspective." *Crossroads*, vol. 5, 2012, 103–114.

"World Bank, AIIB to Grant $380 Million to Andhra Pradesh Power Project." *The Economic Times*, June 23, 2017.

World Bank Group, Public Private Partnership in Infrastructure Resources. "Concessions, Build-Operate-Transfer (BOT) and Design-Build-Operate (DBO) Projects." *worldbank.org*, July 13, 2016.

World History Association. *China in World History, World History from the Center and the Periphery*. Beijing: Capital Normal University, July 2011.

Wright, Stephen. "New Indonesian Cabinet Includes Reformer, Rights Abuser." *Associated Press*, July 28, 2016.

Wu, Bing Bing. *Shiye Pai Xiandai Yisilan Zhuyi de Xingqi (The Rise of Modern Shi'i Islamism)*. Beijing: Chinese Academy of Social Science Press, 2004.

Wu, Bingbing. "Strategy and Politics in the Gulf as Seen from China." In Bryce Wakefield and Susan Levenstein, eds. *China and the Persian Gulf: Implications for the United States*. Washington, DC: Woodrow Wilson Center, 2011.

Wu, Bingbing and Li Weijian. "U.S. Focus Unchanged after Syria Attack." *Global Times*, April 16, 2017.

Wu, Lei. "Goujian 'xin sichou zhi lu': Zhongguo yu zhongdong guanxi fazhan de xin neihan" (Constructing "the New Silk Road": New Meanings of Developing Sino-Middle East Relations). *West Asia and Africa*, vol. 35, no. 3, 2014, 4–16.

Wu, Qinglong et al. "Outburst Flood at 1920 BCE Supports Historicity of China's Great Flood and the Xia Dynasty." *Science*, nol. 353, no. 6299, August 5, 2016, 579–582.

Wu, Wendy. "China, Pakistan and the Challenges of Silk Road Connectivity." *South China Morning Post*, June 20, 2017.

Wu, Yiye. "Zhongguo Yisilan Jiao de Tedian Ji Qi Yu Alabo Diqu Yisilan Jiao Zhi Bijiao" (The Special Characteristics of Chinese Islam Compared to the Islam of the Arab Region). *Researches on the Hui*, vol. 13, no. 2, 2003, 83–85.

Wu, Zhaoli. "Economic Corridor Will Be Lever for All of South Asia." *Global Times*, July 30, 2013.

Wulamu, Aikebair. *Jiangbuwan de Afanti Gushi: Fengci Gushi (Endless Tales of Afanti: Satirical Stories)*. Urumuqi: Xinjiang Youth Publishing House, 2012.

Wulamu, Aikebaier and Zhao Shijie. *Malu Shang de Zhizhe: Afanti de Da Zhihui (Sage on a Donkey: The Wisdom of Afanti)*. Urumuqi: Xinjiang Youth Publishing House, 2006.

Wuthnow, Joel. *Chinese Diplomacy and the U.N. Security Council: Beyond the Veto*. New York: Routledge, 2013.

Wuthnow, Joel. "China and the Iran Nuclear Issue: Beyond the Limited Partnership." *Testimony Before the U.S.-China Security and Economic Review Commission*, June 6, 2013.

Wuthnow, Joel. "Posing Problems without an Alliance: China-Iran Relations after the Nuclear Deal." *INSS Strategic Forum*, February 2016.

Wyatt, Don J. *Battlefronts Real and Imagined: War, Border, and Identity in the Chinese Middle Period*. New York: Palgrave Macmillan, 2008.

Xi Jinping. "Xieshou Tuijin 'Yi Dai Yi Lu' Jianshe" (Work Together to Build the Silk Road Economic Belt and the 21st Century Maritime Silk Road). *Xinhua*, May 16, 2017.

Xiang, Zhi. "Qian Yi Yisilan Jiao de Aiguo Zhuyi" (A Brief Discussion of Islamic Patriotism). *Journal of the Guangzhou Institute of Socialism*, vol. 5, no. 1, 2007, 64–66.

Xie, Chuanjiao. "'Blue Economy' Key to Qingdao's Future." *China Daily*, May 27, 2013.

Xie, Chuanjiao. "Qingdao Set for Leading Role in Global Economy." *The Telegraph*, July 27, 2016.

Xu, Beina and Eleanor Albert. "Media Censorship in China." *Council on Foreign Relations*, February 17, 2017.

Xu, Jiexun. *Xueqiu: Han Minzude Renleixue Fenxi* (*Snowball: An Anthropological Analysis of Han Nationality*). Shanghai: Shanghai People's Publishers, 1999.

Xu, Jiexun, "Understanding the Snowball Theory of the Han Nationality." In Thomas S. Mullaney, James Leibold, Stéphane Gros, and Eric Vanden Bussche, eds., *Critical Han Studies: The History, Representation, and Identity of China's Majority*. Berkeley: University of California Press, 2012.

Xu, Yihua. *Zongjiao yu Dangdai Guoji Guanxi* (*Religion and Contemporary International Relations*). Shanghai: Shanghai People's Publishing House, 2012.

Xu, Yihua. "Studies on Religion and China's National Security in the Globalization Era." *Journal of Middle Eastern and Islamic Studies, (in Asia)*, vol. 7, no. 3, 2013, 1–21.

Xu, Yihua and Zou Lei. "Geo-religion and China's Foreign Strategies." *China International Studies*, vol. 38, no. 1, January/February, 2013, 49–65.

Yalınkılıçlı, Eşref. "A Tale of Becoming an Energy Hub in Eurasia: Russian-Turkish Cooperation on the South Stream." *Daily Sabah*, December 7, 2014.

Yamada, Go. "Top Marks in 1st Term See Sharif Eyeing 2018 Re-election." *Nikkei Asian Review*, January 13, 2017.

Yan, Dongjie. "Chinese Government in Action: Protecting Citizens Overseas." *Xinhua*, January 19, 2016.

Yan, Xuetong. *Ancient Chinese Thought, Modern Chinese Power*. Princeton, NJ: Princeton University Press, 2011.

Yang, Mayfair Mei-hui, ed. *Chinese Religiosities: Afflictions of Modernity and State Formation*. Berkeley: University of California Press, 2008.

Yang, Yang. "Chinese, Foreign Experts Talk of Shared Values of Silk Road Program." *China Daily*, July 28, 2017.

Yang, Yi. "Zhoubian Anquan Xuyao Quan Fangwei Zhanlue" (Peripheral Security Requires a Comprehensive Strategy). *Global Times*, October 26, 2012.

Yang, Xingli. "Xin Zhongguo Yu Yilang Guanxi Liushi Nian" (Sixty Years of Relations between the New China and Iran). *Xiya Feizhou (Western Asia and Africa)*, vol. 31, no. 4, 2010, 63–67.

Yao, Chunjun. "Dui Xinjiang Weiwuer Zu Zongjiao Xinyangzhe Chaojin Wenti de Xinli Tanxi" (Psychological Analysis of Xinjiang Uyghur Muslims' Hajj). *Xinjiang Social Science*, April 2009.

Yates, Robert. "ASEAN as the 'Regional Conductor': Understanding ASEAN's Role in Asia-Pacific Order." *The Pacific Review*, vol. 30, no. 4, December 9, 2016, 1–19.

Ye, Hailin, Yang Rui, Du Ping, and Zhang Yiwu. "Cong Wu Du Dao Wu Du" (From Misreading to Poisoning). *Guoji Xianqui Daobao*, August 13, 2010.

Ye, Hailin, Wu Bingbing, and Christophe Bahuet. "'New Silk Road' Can Be Tailored for Each Side." *Global Times*, March 31, 2014.

Ying, Ding. "Egypt's Diplomatic Balancing Act." *Beijing Review*, September 6, 2012.

Yokkaichi, Yasuhiro. "The Eurasian Empire or Chinese Empire? The Mongol Impact and the Chinese Centripetal System." In Masaki Mukai and Shiro Momoki, eds., *Empires, Systems, and Maritime Networks*. Osaka: Japan Society for Promotion of Science, 2011, 23–34.

You, Tracy. "Muslim Protesters Clash with Armed SWAT Officers and Order Them to Kneel during a Riot at a Chinese Toll Station." *Daily Mail*, September 4, 2017.

Young, Elliott. *Alien Nation: Chinese Migration in the Americas From the Coolie Era through World War II*, Chapel Hill: University of North Carolina Press, 2014.

Younus, Uzair M. "CPEC Questions." *Dawn*, January 3, 2016.

Yousafzai, Fawad. "Experts Concerned over Lack of Transparency in CPEC Projects." *The Nation*, September 21, 2016.

Youssef, Nour. "Egyptian Police Detain Uighurs and Deport Them to China." *New York Times*, July 6, 2017.

Yun, Bao. "Publishing House Puts Chinese Books on Middle Eastern Shelves." *cgtn.com*, April 22, 2017.

Zafar, Mohammad. "APC Opposes Detours in Economic Corridor Route." *Express Tribune*, May 17, 2015.

Zaheer, Farhan. "Pakistan Imposes Anti-dumping Duty on China's Steel Products." *Express Tribune*, February 9, 2017.

Zahra-Malik, Mehreen. "In Pakistani Fray, Maryam Sharif Is on the Edge of Power, or Prison." *New York Times*, October 27, 2017.

Zaman, Qamar. "Pak-China Economic Corridor: Senators Issue Ominous Warning over Route Change." *Express Tribune*, February 4, 2015.

Zane, Damian. "Nigeria's Goodluck Jonathan: Five Reasons Why He Lost." *BBC News*, March 31, 2015.

Zang, Xiaowei and Chien-wen Kou, eds. *Elites and Governance in China*, Milton Park, Abingdon, Oxon: Routledge, 2013.

Zeine, Hatem. "The Problems with Smart Cities." *Forbes*, June 19, 2017.

Zeng, Xiangyu. "Bajisitan Guada'er Gang Dui Guoji Anquan Taishi de Yingxiang" (The Influence of Pakistan's Gwadar Port on the International Security Situation). *South Asian Studies Quarterly*, vol. 25, no. 2, September 29, 2009, 31–36.

Zhang, Baofeng. "Sheke Yuan: 'Yidai Yilu' Chonggou Diyuan Youshi Zhongguo Cheng Boyi Zhongxin" (Social Science Academy: "One Belt, One Road" Will Reshape the Geographic Advantage Making China the Center of the Game). *Dagong Wang*, May 5, 2017.

Zhang, Dainian. *Key Concepts in Chinese Philosophy*. Translated and edited by Edmund Ryden. New Haven, CT Yale University Press, 2002.

Zhang, Feng. "Confucian Foreign Policy Traditions in Chinese History." *Chinese Journal of International Politics*, vol. 8, no. 2, April 2015, 197–218.

Zhang, Jian. "China's New Foreign Policy under Xi Jinping: Towards 'Peaceful Rise 2.0?" *Global Change, Peace and Security*, vol. 27, no. 1, January 2015, 5–19.

Zhang, Jianxin. "Hou Xifang Guoji Tixi Yu Dongfang de Xingqi" (The Post-Western International System and the Rise of the East). *World Economics and Politics*, vol. 26, no. 5, July 9, 2012, 4–20.

Zhang, Joe. "The Disintegration of Rural China." *New York Times*, November 28, 2014.

Zhang, Lifan. "Zai Zhongguo Gaige Luntan de Fayin" (Pronouncement of the China Reform Forum). *cn.rfi.fr*, February 1, 2012.

Zhang, Yiqian. "Halal Hopes." *Global Times*, September 17, 2015.

Zhang, Yongjin and Barry Buzan. "The Triburary System as International Society in Theory and Practice." *The Chinese Journal of International Politics*, vol. 5, no. 1, 2012, 3–36.

Zhao, Hong. "China's Dilemma on Iran: Between Energy Security and a Responsible Rising Power." *Journal of Contemporary China*, vol. 23, no. 87, January 2014, 408–424.

Zhao, Suisheng, ed. "Historical Perspectives on the Rise of China: Chinese Order, Great Harmony, and *Tianxia*." *Journal of Contemporary China*, vol. 24, no. 96, 2015.

Zhao, Xinying. "Interest Growing in Study of Persian Language, History." *China Daily*, January 25, 2016.

Zhao, Zuoquan. "Zhongguo Juxing Qu Geju." *Chengshi Fazhan Yanjiu* (Megaregions in China. *Urban Development Studies*), vol. 20, no. 2, 2013, 62–70.

Zhen, Liu. "Pakistan Pulls Plug on Dam Deal over China's 'Too Strict' Conditions in Latest Blow to Belt and Road Plans." *South China Morning Post*, November 16, 2017.

Zheng, Bijian. "China's 'Peaceful Rise' to Great-Power Status." *Foreign Affairs*, vol. 84, no. 5, September/October 2005, 18–24.

Zheng, Hua. "Cong Daguo Boyi Kan 'Yidai Yilu' Zhanlue" (Viewing "The One Belt, One Road" Strategy in Terms of the Great Game). *Guangming Ribao*, November 29, 2015.

Zheng, Lifei and Yang Huiwen. "Qatar Seeks $5 Billion China QFII Quota." *Bloomberg*, June 24, 2012.

Zheng, Yongnian. *De Facto Federalism in China: Reforms and Dynamics of Central-Local Relations*. Singapore: World Scientific, 2007.

Zheng, Yongnian, Zhao Litao, and Sarah Y. Tong, eds. *China's Great Urbanization*. New York: Routledge, 2017.

"Zhongguo Yidai Yilu Wang" (China Belt and Road Portal). *yidaiyilu.gov.cn*.

Zhou, Bo. "Could Turkey Serve as a Bridge between NATO and SCO?" *China-U.S. Focus*, December 19, 2016.

Zhou, Chuanbin. "Ta Shan Zhi Shi: Xifang Xuejie Dui Zhongguo Huizu Yisilan Jiao de Yanjiu Shuping" (Stones from Other Hills [May Help to Polish the Jade of This One]: A Review of Western Academic Studies on the Islam of China's Hui Community). *Northwest Nationalities Studies*, vol. 22, no. 1, January 2005, 97–106.

Zhou, Chuanbin. "Yingxiang Xiandai Yisilan de San Zhong Sichao" (Three Trends of Influence on Modern Islam). *dxw.ifeng.com*, January 12, 2016.

Zhou, Pingjian Ambassador. "Made in Nigeria—With China." *This Day*, November 28, 2016.

Zhou, Viola. "'When Are You Going Back to Arabia?': How Chinese Muslims Became the Target of Online Hate." *South China Morning Post*, March 12, 2017.

Zhou, Yi Jun. *Zouchu Zhongdong: Quanqiu Minzhu Langchao de Jianzheng yu Xingsi (Out of the Middle East: Witnessing and Reflecting on the Global Tide of Democracy)*. Beijing: CITIC Publishing Group, 2017.

Zhu, Cuiping. *Yindu Yang Yu Zhongguo (The Indian Ocean and China)*. Beijing: Social Science, 2014.

Zhu, Liqun. "China's Foreign Policy Debates," *European Union Institute for Security Studies*. September 2010.

Zhu, Weilie. "Yisilan Wenming Yu Shijie" (Islamic Civilization and the World). *World Economy and Politics*, no. 7, July 2007, 57–61.

Zhu, Weilie. "Bawo Jiyu, Xuan Zhun Lujing, Shixian Ningxia Xin Tengfei" (Seize the Opportunity, Choose the Right Road, Achieve Ningxia's New Takeoff). *Hui Minority Studies*, vol. 20, no. 4, 2010, 44–48.

Zhu, Weilie. "Shilun Zhongguo Yu Zhongdong Yisilan Guojia de Zhanluexing Guanxi" (On the Strategic Relationship between China and Islamic Countries in the Middle East). *Journal of Sino-Western Communications*, vol. 3, no. 1, July 2011, 2–23.

Zhu, Xufeng. *The Rise of Think Tanks in China*. London and New York: Routledge, 2013.

Zi, Zhongyun. "Neng Fanxing Lishi de Minzu Cai You Guangming de Weilai" (Only a Nation That Can Reflect on Its History Will Have a Bright Future). *view.news.qq.com*, February 2, 2009.

Zi, Zhongyun. "Qimeng Yu Zhishi Fenzi de Chuantong" (Enlightenment and the Tradition of the Intellectuals). *aisixiang.com*, November 14, 2011.

Zou, Zhiqiang. "Zhongguo Canyu Zhongdong Diqu Jingji Zhili de Lilun Yu Shijian." *Guoji Zhanwang*. (The Theory and Practice of China's Participation in the Economic Governance of the Middle East. *International Outlook*), vol. 8, no. 5, October 2016, 113–153.

Zuo, Mandy. "China's Middle Class to Rise to More than Third of Population by 2030, Research Firm Says." *South China Morning Post*, November 3, 2016.

Zurndorfer, Harriet T. "Not Bound to China: Étienne Balazs, Fernand Braudel and the Politics of the Study of Chinese History in Post-War France." *Past and Present*, vol. 53, no. 185, November 2004, 189–221.

INDEX

Abacha, Sani, 102
Abbas, Mahmoud, 88–89
Abbot, Tony, 74
Abuja, 98, 102–3, 153
Aegean, 56
Afanti, 135
Afghanistan, 33–34, 41–43, 44
Africa, 5, 9–10, 12, 16, 18, 22–23, 27, 51, 55, 84, 87, 96, 97, 98, 99, 100–3, 111, 112, 115, 118, 134, 152, 156
Africans in China, 40, 100
Afro-Eurasia, 25, 26, 44, 47–48, 112, 127, 140, 152, 153–54
agency, 24
agrarian renovation, 120
Ahmadinejad, Mahmoud, 95
Ahok. *See* Purnama, Basuki Tjahaja
Ain Sukhna, 125
Aksai Chin, 43
Al-Ahram, 123–24
Al-Azhar University, 125
Al-Naggar, Ahmed el-Sayed, 123–24
Al-Qaeda, 154–55
Alexandria, 121, 125
Alibaba, 6
All-Party Conferences, 33
Angola, 101, 102–3, 111
Ankara, 9, 52, 53, 54, 55, 56, 60–61, 153
Annales School, 22
antipiracy, 6

anti-Silk Road campaign, 86
Arabian Sea, 30, 152
Arabization, 14
archeology, 129, 131, 132
Arctic Council, 16, 156
Arctic shipping lanes, 5, 16, 115
Artvin, 56
Arunachal Pradesh, 43
ASEAN-Plus, 74–75
Ashdod, 115
Asia-Pacific community, 74–75
Asian Development Bank, 6, 47
Asian Infrastructure Investment Bank, 6, 146
assimilation, 14, 130
Association of Southeast Asian Nations (ASEAN), 73, 74–75
Asyut, 121–22
Australia, 72, 74, 75, 87–88, 155–56, 157
Australian Labor Party, 157
Australian Liberal Party, 157
authoritarian regimes, 10, 84, 114, 141
Awolowo, Obafemi, 110
Azerbaijan, 53, 59–60, 89–90

balance of terror, 20
Balochis, 30, 35
Balochistan, 30, 33, 40, 152
Bandung, 76–77
Bank of China, 60–61

barbarians, 50–51, 137
Baswedan, Anies, 66–67
Beidou, 6
Beijing Consensus, 41
Beijing Olympics 2008, 18
Beni Suef, 121–22
Berlin, 61, 156
Beyazit, 51
Biafra, 102–3, 111–12
big history, 150
Bishop, Julie, 74
Black Sea, 27, 56, 60–62
Boko Haram, 102–3
bonds, 116, 156
Bosnia, 52
Braudel, Fernand, 22, 23, 24, 143–46
Brazil, 98, 101, 111
Bretton-Woods, 6
BRICS New Development Bank, 6
Brussels, 6, 61, 156
Buddhism, 133, 134
buffer zones, 20
Buhari, Muhammadu, 107–10

Cairo, 10, 113–14, 117–18, 120, 121–22, 125
Calabar, 98, 107
Camp David Accords, 113
Cape of Good Hope, 115
Caspian Sea, 53, 90–91
Caucasia, 53, 157–58
Central Anatolia, 56, 61
Central Asia, 15, 41, 49, 51, 52–53, 60–61, 131–32, 137–38
Central Bank of Nigeria, 99
Central Java, 73, 79
Chabahar, 44, 88
Charsadda, 33
chauvinism, 129, 133
Chechnya, 157–58
Chengdu, 16
China threat, introduction, 20–21, 156
China-Pakistan Economic Corridor (CPEC), 29, 33, 47
China's Islamic Silk Road, 7
Chinese diasporas, 97, 100–1
Chinese Indonesians, 65–67

Chinese Islam, 13–14, 51, 134
Chinese Mediterranean, 26–27, 146–47
Chinese Muslims, 63–64, 130–31, 134
Chinese Orientalism, 153
coevolution, 14, 24, 25, 26, 47–48, 112, 127, 147, 152
Columbia, 102, 111
Commonwealth, 157
concessions, 37–40
Confucianism, 130, 133–34, 149
connectivity, 7, 10, 25, 26, 27, 29, 30, 83, 90–91, 119, 121, 122, 146–47, 150, 151, 157–58
Constantinople, 51
continental drift, 20–21
corporatism, 141
Cultural Revolution, 15
Cyprus, 52

Dagestan, 157–58
dakwah (religious preaching), 67
Dams, 30, 45, 47
Daoism, 134, 135
Davos, 85
Davutoğlu, Ahmet, 53
debt, 10, 25, 37, 40, 97–99, 101–2
decentralization, 141
defective equipment, 100
deliberative democracy, 16
Demirel, Süleyman, 52
democracy, 8, 9–10, 16, 24, 29, 30, 41, 65, 69, 76, 95, 98, 112, 119, 129–30, 141–43, 148–49
Democratic Republic of the Congo, 101
Deng Xiaoping, 22
Dewey, John, 129–30
Diamer-Bhasha Dam, 47
Djibouti, 122
Doha, 87–88
doubting antiquity, 130
drug trafficking, 100
Dubai, 87–88

early harvest projects, 34–41
East Java, 65, 66
Eastern Europe, 90–91

Egypt, 10, 113–26, 151
  bypassed by Chinese investment, 123–26
  rethinking connectivity, 119–20
  Sisi's city in the desert, 117–18
  Suez Canal as a wasting asset, 114–17
  targeting the neediest sectors, 121–23
Eilat, 115
El-Sisi, Abdel Fattah, 113–14, 115–16, 117–18, 119, 122, 123, 125–26
emergence, 24
Erdoğan, Recep Tayyip, 53–54, 56, 59, 61, 62
Eskişehir, 56
Ethiopia, 103
ethnocentrism, 129
Eurasia, 5, 6, 9, 22, 25, 26, 44, 47–48, 49, 55, 59, 61, 85, 86, 111, 112, 127, 135, 140, 152, 153–54, 157
Eurasianists
  in Russia, 157
  in Turkey, 59, 61
European Union, 54, 59, 156

Far East, 88
Fayum, 121–22
federalism, 141, 147
Fei Xiao Tong, 131, 132, 133
Fertile Crescent, 83, 87, 95
Fletcher, Joseph, 2–3
folklore, 129–30
foreign investments
  Egypt, 10, 113, 117, 118, 122, 123–25, 126
  Indonesia, 76, 77–79
  Iran, 89
  Nigeria, 9–10, 98, 110–12
  Pakistan, 29, 30, 34, 35–36, 37, 40, 44–45
  Turkey, 59
foreign trade, 6, 16, 44, 137, 146
  Egypt, 115, 117–18, 123
  Indonesia, 65, 73, 77–79
  Iran, 85, 89
  Nigeria, 102, 103, 111
  Pakistan, 44
  Turkey, 53, 55, 59

Freedom and Justice Party, 120–22
functional representation, 143

G-20, 75
Gambir, 67–69
Gansu, 127
geoeconomics, 6, 136–37
geographic mosaic of coevolution, 26–27
geopolitics, 6, 25, 136–37, 157
geo-religion, 6, 136–37
Germany, 156
gerrymandering, 141–43
Gilgit-Baltistan, 47
global commons, 4, 152–53
global fracture, 20, 22
Gorbachev, Mikhail, 12
great game, 6, 20, 21, 22
Great Lakes, 101
Great Wall, 50
Greater Eurasia, 85
Greater Middle East, 81–82
Greece, 52, 115
Gu Jie Gang, 129–30, 133
Guangdong, 12, 18
Gül, Abdullah, 53
Gulf Cooperation Council, 87–88, 95–96
Gulf of Guinea, 101
Gwadar, 30–31, 40, 43, 44, 88

Hajj, 84, 87, 136–37
halal food, 13, 127
Hamburg, 16, 115
Hamedan, 92
Han, 11, 13, 14–15, 24–25, 27, 50–51, 127, 128–33, 134, 135, 137, 153–54
Han Kitab, 134
Harimurtri, Agus, 66
Himalayas, 157
Hodgson, Marshall, 153–54
Hong Kong, 8, 77, 88, 97, 141–43, 155–56
Hong Kong Legislative Council, 141–43
Hu Jintao, 20–21
Hu Shi, 129–30
Hua Liming, 81

Hua Tao, 136
Hui, 15, 51, 130–32, 134, 136, 137–38
human rights, 33–34, 40, 100, 102, 113–14, 156
Hussein, Saddam, 81–82
hydropolitics, 44–47

Ibadan, 107, 152
Ibn Khaldun, 130
Igbo, 27, 102–3
Igboland, 152
illegal logging, 100
Ilorin, 107–8, 152
Imam Ali, 95
India, 29, 34, 41–43, 44, 47, 49, 51, 54, 55, 56–57, 87–88, 89–90, 98, 100, 156–57
Indian Ocean, 5, 18, 25, 41, 44, 73, 89–90, 92–94, 101, 111, 115, 122, 134, 153–54, 157
Indonesia, 7, 9, 12, 15, 16, 19, 27, 41–43, 63–79, 80–81, 89, 113, 119–20, 122, 123, 151, 153–54
   anit-Chinese sentiment, 65–67
   politicized investments, 76–79
   reshaping the Pacific community, 69–75
Indonesia Ulama Council, 66
Indonesian Laborers Union Confederation, 76
Indus River, 33, 47
industrial zones, 79, 98, 111, 117, 122, 123, 147–48
industrialization, 9–10, 101–2, 111, 146
Inner Asia, 2–3, 51
International Monetary Agency, 37, 116
internet censorship, 10, 12
Iqbal, Ahsan, 33
Iran, 7, 10, 12, 15, 19, 27, 41, 43–44, 54, 80–96, 113, 119, 123, 136–38, 151, 153–54
   Chinese foreign policy debates concerning, 80–82
   electoral support for Rouhani and his rivals, 92–95

partnership with Russia and China, 85–86
regional divisions, 89–91
relations with China after the nuclear deal, 82–83
relations with neighboring countries, 86–88
Xi Jinping's 2016 visit, 84–85
Iraq, 55, 61, 81–82, 85
Isfahan, 92–94
Islamabad, 8–9, 29, 30–31, 33–34, 36–37, 41–43, 47, 52
Islamic civilization, 13, 27–28, 127, 128, 129, 146, 153–55
Islamic Defenders Front (Front Pembela Islam), 66
Islamic Revolutionary Guard Corps, 92–94
Islamic-Confucian literature, 128
Islamification of China, 14
Islamophobia, 129, 138
Israel, 54, 81–82, 88–89, 95–96, 113, 115, 136–37
Istanbul, 60–61

Jakarta, 9, 65–69, 74, 75, 76–77, 79, 153
Jakarta-Bandung high-speed rail, 76–77
Japan, 74, 75, 77, 155–57
Jaspers, Karl, 133
JD.com, 6
Jeddah, 87
Jhelum River, 47
Jokowi. *See* Widodo, Joko
Jonathan, Goodluck, 104–10
juju (witchcraft), 100–1
Justice and Development Party, 53
Justice and Prosperity Party (Partai Keadilan dan Sejahtera), 66–67

Kaduna, 98, 107
Kalabagh Dam, 33
Kalimantan, 72, 79
Kano, 98, 99, 107
Karachi, 30–31, 33–34, 43, 45
Kashgar, 8, 30, 52
Kashmir, 43, 47

Kazakhstan, 53
Kazan, 157–58
Kelapa Gading, 67–69
Kemalists, 59
Kenya, 12
Khamenei, Ayatollah Ali, 95
Khan, Imran, 37
Khorasan, 92
Khorshid, Dalia, 123–24
Khyber Paktunkhwa, 30, 33, 47
Kingdom of Heaven (Tian Xia), 26–27
Kissinger, Henry, 70–72
Kogi, 107–8
Konya, 54
Kublai Khan, 51
Kunming, 54–55
Kurds, 27, 61–62
Kuwait, 87–88
Kwara, 107–8

Lagos, 98, 100, 107, 110, 152
Lahore, 30–31, 36–37, 152
Lahore metro, 36–37
Laksamana Cheng Ho. *See* Zheng He
Lapidus, Ira, 2–3
Latin America, 9–10, 84, 101–2, 111
Lebanon, 81–82
Liberal Party of Australia, 157
life sciences, 155
Liu Zhentang, 81–82
logrolling, 34–35, 98
London, 156
Lunar New Year, 65

Maarif, Syafi'i, 66
Malacca Straits, 8–9, 83
Malaysia, 55, 72–73
Malinowski, Bronislaw, 131
Manchus, 137–38
Mandarin classes, 102–3
Mao Zedong, 80, 83, 99, 130–31, 133, 139
Marmara, 56, 60–61
Mecca, 87
Medina, 87
Mediterranean, 22, 41, 56, 61–62, 89–90, 115, 120, 121, 122, 137, 146–47, 152, 156

Mediterranean-like regions, 20, 22–23, 24, 26
megaregion, 5, 17, 18–19, 20, 22, 23–24, 25, 26, 27, 28, 47, 59, 74–75, 82–83, 85, 112, 127, 139, 140, 146, 152–53
melting pot, 131–32
metaphors in international relations, 18, 20
Middle East, 8–9, 15, 16, 27, 43, 44, 49, 51, 55, 61–62, 80, 81, 82, 83–84, 85, 87, 95–96, 113, 115, 118, 122, 131–32, 136–37, 140–41
Ming dynasty, 51, 134
Minya, 121–22
Modi, Narendra, 157
Moghul Empire, 153–54
money pits, 99
Mongols, 49, 50, 51, 55, 56–57, 130
Morsi, Mohamed, 113–14, 122
mosaics of coevolution, 25–26
Moscow, 61, 85, 86, 88–89, 157–58
Moscow-Kazan railway, 157–58
Mubarak, Husni, 122
Muhajir, 33–34, 35
Muhammadiya, 66
multipolar system, 7, 158
Muslim Brotherhood, 114, 121–22

Nahdlatul Ulama, 66
Nanguan Mosque, 128
Nanjing, 16, 136–37
Nasr, Seyyed Hossein, 136
Nasser, Gamal Abdel, 113
Natalegawa, Marty, 70–72
nationalities policy, 131
Natuna Islands, 72
naval power, 6, 44, 51, 72, 73–74, 122, 134, 157
neocolonialism, 2, 111, 146
Netanyahu, Benjamin, 88–89
New City (Egypt), 117–18, 125
New Culture Movement, 129–30
New Delhi, 44, 74, 88, 157
New Silk Road Summit (May 2017), 76
Nicaragua, 102, 111
Niger, 107–8
Niger Delta, 104–5, 107, 152

Index | 281

Nigeria, 97–112
   China's railroad diplomacy, 97–98
   indebtedness and anti-Chinese sentiments, 99–100
   intercontinental linkages, 101–2
   regional shifts in presidential elections, 107–10
   revisions in China's strategy, 101–2, 110–12
Nile Delta, 120, 121, 125
Nile River, 114, 117, 119–21
Ningxia, 15, 127, 128
Niu Song, 136–37
North Africa, 49, 130
North Atlantic Treaty Organization (NATO), 52, 54, 59–60
North Indus River Cascade, 47
Northwest Frontier Province. *See* Khyber Paktunkhwa
Nur Party, 121

Obama, Barack, 43, 102–3
Obasanjo, Olusegun, 98
oil prices, 84, 102–3, 115–16
Oman, 87
Ordos plateau, 50
Osinbajo, Yemi, 110
Ottoman Empire, 51, 153–54
Özal, Turgut, 52

Pacific Ocean, 5, 9, 12, 14, 41, 43, 49, 53, 69, 73, 74–75, 76, 79, 87–111, 137, 153, 156–57, 158
Pakhtuns, 27, 30, 33, 35
Pakistan, 7, 8, 12, 19, 29–47, 54, 56, 82–83, 88, 89, 113, 119–20, 122, 123, 151, 153–54, 157
   protests of regional and ethnic groups, 30–34
   renegotiations of projects and routes, 34–41
   significance for other Chinese partners, 47
   strategic interests in South Asia and the Middle East, 41–44
   water politics and India, 44–47

Pakistan Tehreek-e Insaf (PTI), 37
Pakistani Taliban, 33–34
Palestine, 88–89
Pan-African connections, 101
Pan-Asianism, 21
Pan-Turkism, 54
Panama Canal, 102, 115
Panama Papers, 36–37
Pancasila, 66–67
Pangestu, Mari Elka, 65
pangolin, 100–1
Penjaringan, 67–69
peresrtoika, 12
Persian Gulf, 27, 41, 51, 53, 83, 88–90, 92–94, 95–96, 122, 136–37, 152
Persian language, 81, 152
Peru, 111–12
Philippines, 73, 87
phony drugs, 100
pilgrimage, 65, 87, 136. *See also* Hajj, –37
pluralism, 64, 83, 129, 131, 133, 139, 147
political engineering, 148
pollution, 11, 120
Port Harcourt, 98, 107
Port Said, 117
power sharing, 7, 12, 24, 25, 41, 47–48, 139, 147, 151, 153, 155
Pretoria, 103
pribumi (native sons and daughters), 64
proxy wars, 4, 84
Punjab, 30–31, 33, 35, 36–37, 45–47
Purnama, Basuki Tjahaja (Ahok), 65–66, 67, 76
Putin, Vladimir, 54, 56, 86, 157

Qatar, 87–88
Qaumi Watan Party, 33
Qena, 121
Qian Xu Ming, 136–37
Qing dynasty, 134, 137–38
Qingdao, 16
Qinghai, 127
Quetta, 88
Qur'an, 65–66

race riots, 66
railroads, 16, 30, 60–61, 76–77, 87, 97–98, 99, 100, 101, 102, 104–5, 107–8, 111, 112, 150–51
Raisi, Ayatollah Ebrahim, 95
Red Sea, 115, 125, 134
Red Sea-Mediterranean link, 115
resource wars, 4
river gods, 143
Riyadh, 84, 87, 88
Romania, 98
Rotterdam, 16, 115
Rouhani, Hassan, 89, 91–95
Rudd, Kevin, 74
rural depopulation, 151
rural-urban divide, 149
Russia, 43–44, 53, 61, 75, 84–85, 86, 89–90, 156, 157

Sadat, Anwar, 113
Safavid Empire, 153–54
Sanusi, Lamido Sanusi, 99
Saraiki, 35
Saudi Arabia, 12, 65, 84, 86–87, 154–55
security dilemmas, 20
self-organization, 19, 24, 26
Seman, 92
Senegal, 87
Serbia, 52
Shaanxi, 127
Shanghai, 13, 100–1, 127, 128, 136–37
Shanghai Cooperation Organization, 6, 54, 59, 146
sharia, 66–67
Sharif, Nawaz, 29, 33, 35–37, 44
Sharif, Shehbaz, 35–37, 44
Shenzhen, 16
Sherpao, Aftab Khan, 33
Sherpao, Sikander Hayat Khan, 33
Shi'ites, 83
Silk Road Fund, 6, 146
Silk Road romanticism, 20, 21
Sindh, 45
Sindhis, 35
Singapore, 72, 73, 77, 156
smart cities, 150–51

snowball theory of evolution, 132–33
social inequality, 8
social sciences, 135
social warehousing, 147–48
soft power, 6, 20
Sohag, 121
Solo (Surakarta), 73
South Africa, 101, 103, 111
South Asia, 8–9, 15, 16, 32, 88, 157
South Atlantic, 101, 102, 111
South China Sea, 16, 72, 73–74, 103
South Korea, 100
South-South alliances, 9–10, 21, 27, 101
Southeast Asia, 64, 65, 75, 89–90
sovereignty, 24, 27, 72, 130
Soviet Union, 12, 52, 53, 153–54, 157
spoiled foods, 100
Sputnik moment, 158
statecraft, 6, 11, 17, 20, 21, 22, 23, 24–25, 28, 41, 140, 147, 158
Suez Canal, 10, 115–16
Suez Canal Industrial Zone, 114
Sufism, 134
Suharto, 65, 67, 76
Sukarno, 63
Sulawesi, 76, 79
Sumatra, 79
Sun Bigan, 81–82
Sun De Gang, 136–37
Supreme Court of Pakistan, 36–37
Syamsuddin, Din, 66
Syria, 55, 61, 81–82, 85, 154–55

Taiwan, 86, 97
Tamerlane. *See* Timur
Tang Jun Yi, 133
Tashkent, 52
Tatarstan, 157–58
Tehran, 80–81, 82–83, 84, 85, 86, 87, 88, 89–90, 92–95, 153
Thailand, 55
Tiananmen massacre, 102, 114
Tibet, 41
Timur, 51
Tokyo, 76–77, 156–57
tourism, 65, 74, 87, 115–16, 123, 128–29

Index | 283

Trans-Caspian energy corridor, 59–60
tribute system, 2, 50–51
Trump, Donald, 56, 74, 85–86, 88
Tu Wei Ming, 136
Turkey, 9, 12, 19, 27, 41–43, 49–62, 80–82, 87–88, 89–90, 119, 123, 125, 137–38, 151, 153–54
    Erdoğan's electoral support, 55–56
    Eurasian ambitions, 59–62
    historical ties to China, 50–51
    interests in Central Asia, 52–53
    obstacles to partnership with China, 56–59
    quarrels over Xinjiang, 53–55
Turkmenistan, 53

United Arab Emirates, 87
United Kingdom, 156
United Nations, 52, 53, 75, 103
United States, 6, 9, 18–19, 21, 27–28, 29, 33–34, 45, 54, 61, 73, 74, 75, 77, 80, 81, 88–89, 113–14, 138, 146, 154, 156, 157, 158
universalism, 133–34, 150
Upper Egypt, 120, 121
Ürümqi, 53–54
Uyghur, 14, 54, 55, 129, 134, 136

Vietnam, 73, 74
vigilantism, 76–77
Volga region, 157–58

Wang Shijie, 81–82
water shortages, 47, 120
Wen Jiabao, 20–21
White, Hugh, 74
Widodo, Joko, 66, 69–74, 76–77, 79

World Bank, 6, 47
World Economic Forum, 85
world history, 85, 155
World Muslim City, 128
Wu Bing Bing, 136–37

Xi Jinping, 16–17, 21, 23, 84, 85, 113–14, 140
Xie Xiaoyan, 81–82
Xinjiang, 8–9, 11, 12, 15, 30, 41, 52, 53, 54–55, 89–90, 125, 127, 128–29, 132, 134, 136, 152, 157–58

Yangshan Deep Water Port, 128
Yangtze River, 45
Yellow Emperor, 137
Yellow River, 50, 129–30, 132
Yeltsin, Boris, 12
Yinchuan, 128
Yiwu, 16
Yoruba, 27, 100–1, 104–10, 111–12
Yorubaland, 107
yuan, 6, 88, 103, 118
Yuan dynasty, 51, 135, 137–38
Yudhoyono, Susilo Bambang, 65, 66
Yunnan, 15, 54–55, 127

Zambia, 103
Zanjan, 92
Zarb-e-Azb campaign, 33
Zheng He, 18, 51, 65, 134
Zhu Wei Lie, 136
Zhuangzi, 135
Zimbabwe, 103
zombie industries, 16
Zonguldak, 56
Zuma, Jacob, 103